Constructing the World Polity

This volume of essays, with a new introduction and extensive connective sections, brings together John Ruggie's most influential theoretical ideas and their application to critical policy questions concerning the post-cold war international order. The book is divided into three parts:

International Organization. How the "new institutionalism" differs from the old. Introducing the concepts of regimes, epistemic communities, and multilateralism. Epistemological critiques of more conventional approaches.

The System of States. Explorations of political structure, social time, and territorial space in the world polity.

The Question of Agency. America in the post-cold war era. NATO and the future transatlantic security community. The United Nations and the collective use of force.

John Gerard Ruggie is currently serving on the executive staff of United Nations Secretary General Kofi Annan, at the rank of Assistant Secretary General, while on leave as Burgess Professor of Political Science and International Affairs at Columbia University.

The New International Relations

Edited by Barry Buzan,
University of Warwick, and

Gerald Segal,
International Institute for Strategic Studies, London

The field of International Relations has changed dramatically in recent years. This new series will cover the major issues that have emerged and reflect the latest academic thinking in this particular dynamic area.

Constructing the World Polity

Essays on international
institutionalization

John Gerard Ruggie

London and New York

First published 1998 by Routledge
2 Park Square, Milton Park, Abingdon, Oxon, OX14 4RN
Simultaneously published in the USA and Canada
by Routledge
270 Madison Ave, New York NY 10016

Reprinted 2000

Routledge is an imprint of the Taylor & Francis Group

Transferred to Digital Printing 2006

© 1998 John Gerard Ruggie

Typeset in Times by Routledge

British Library Cataloguing in Publication Data
A catalogue record for this book is available from the British Library

Library of Congress Cataloguing in Publication Data
A catalogue record has been requested for this title

ISBN 0–415–09990–0 (hbk)
ISBN 0–415–09991–9 (pbk)

For Mary Ruggie

and in loving memory of Franziska Macic

Contents

Foreword

In some ways this book parallels an earlier one in the series: the Neumann and Wæver volume *The Future of International Relations: Masters in the Making?* Like that book it takes individual authors and their opuses as a way of understanding the subject, rather than approaching it in terms of paradigms or schools of thought. The difference is that here only one author is under consideration, and he surveys, reviews and sums up his own work rather than having someone else do it. Ruggie is a subject of both books, and so we have an outside perspective with which to compare and contrast the inside one given in this volume. As Ole Wæver has already noted, Ruggie is not an easy figure to label. Some see him as a rather sophisticated neo-realist, some as a key figure in the liberal tradition, some even as a poststructuralist. His ideas have been most influential in liberal writing without Ruggie himself being clearly committed to that tradition. Wæver hesitates between labelling him a "postmodern liberalist" or an exponent of "post-sovereign realism," noting that his work has "proved prophetic a remarkable number of times."

That prophetic streak explains what a collection of past essays is doing in a collection titled "The New International Relations." John Ruggie has been an influential essayist in International Relations for twenty-five years: several of his articles have been milestones in the development of the discipline. But it has not been easy to see how his opus formed a coherent whole, and until recently he has denied us a book that attempted the task of integration. In this volume he remedies that defect by unfolding the story of his journey towards constructivism, and using that to tie his essays together. What follows is part autobiography, part intellectual history, and part reflection on the development of theory in thinking about international relations. It is also a powerful assault on what Ruggie labels the "neo-utilitarian" orthodoxies that have dominated IR theory over the last decades. Since constructivism is now making major strides against these rationalist and materialist theories, Ruggie's story is not only about what the new International Relations is, but also about how and why it came into being.

Barry Buzan

Preface and acknowledgements

The essays in this volume trace an intellectual journey over the course of a quarter century, toward an approach to international relations theorizing that is now known as social constructivism. Beginning in the early 1970s, I became increasingly concerned that the postwar aversion to idealism in the field of international relations, which resulted in the primacy of realism after the cold war broke out, had gone too far. I felt that it was responsible for the discipline's poor grasp on the role of ideational factors of all kinds in international life—be they collective identities, norms, aspirations, ideologies, or ideas about cause–effect relations.

Two subsequent trends have, if anything, reinforced this state of affairs. The first was the ascendancy of neorealism and neoliberal institutionalism in the 1980s, which render ideational factors, when they are examined at all, in strictly instrumental, neo-utilitarian terms. The second has been the widespread embrace by the field of a model of social science that is virtually Newtonian in character. As the physicist Gerald Feinberg puts it, "Newtonian mechanics . . . did not attempt to explain what forces might exist in nature, but rather described how motion occurred when the force was known" (1978: 9). One captures the essence of mainstream theorizing in international relations today merely by substituting the terms "interests" or "preferences" for "forces" in Feinberg's characterization.

Social constructivism, in contrast, rests on an irreducible specificity of human behavior. As Max Weber insisted at the turn of the century: "We are *cultural beings*, endowed with the capacity and the will to take a deliberate attitude towards the world and to lend it *significance*" (1949: 81, emphasis in original). Accordingly, constructivists hold not only that the interests and preferences of actors are socially constructed, but that they must share the stage with a whole host of other ideational factors comprising that human capacity and will of which Weber wrote. The fact that human behavior at all levels of social aggregation is constrained is not in dispute. Nor is the likelihood that some modal responses exist to certain types of structural constraints or situational exigencies. What constructivists reject, however, is the pretense or presumption that the study of such phenomena constitutes the totality of the social scientific enterprise.

Just as I was finishing work on this volume, Kofi Annan, the new Secretary-General of the United Nations, invited me to join his executive staff at the rank of Assistant Secretary-General. I would have no operational responsibilities, he promised, but provide strategic advice and help articulate his message regarding the major institutional challenges confronting the organization. I accepted as soon as I caught my breath, taking a leave of absence from Columbia University. The transition went surprisingly smoothly because it quickly became apparent that creative leadership in international organization is social constructivism in action. The looming presence of major member states, and the tenacity of some minor ones, make it abundantly clear that the interests and preferences of states circumscribe the range of the possible, in many instances quite severely. At the same time, it is also the case that these factors are neither fixed nor exogenously given, and that international organization does affect, even if only occasionally or at the margin, how they come to be defined and redefined. Indeed, the twentieth-century project of international organization is all about how to stretch states' interests and preferences, temporally as well as spatially, so as to produce in greater quantities the collective goods that the political marketplace of interstate behavior otherwise underproduces. Ideational factors are an absolutely critical means by which this stretching is achieved.

The very existence of this volume is due to Barry Buzan, co-editor of the series in which it appears. Buzan first suggested the idea of such a collection to me, and prodded me relentlessly until I got it done. He also commented extensively, almost in real-time via email exchanges as I was writing, on the introductory chapter, the briefer introductions to the three parts of the book, and the contextualizing capsules that precede each selection. I am immensely grateful to him for his faith, friendship, and help.

It has been a privilege to acknowledge the support over the years of my graduate school mentor, Ernst Haas. But it was not until I began to reflect on the intellectual journey documented in these essays that I came to realize fully how indebted I am to him. Not once, not even when I first walked into his classroom entirely unschooled in the field of international relations, did he attempt to force his own agenda on me. Perhaps because of that freedom, it has dawned on me only recently that in a certain sense I have worked on it all along, though we do it differently. Haas, too, read and commented on the introductory materials and, thereby, improved their contents.

Thanks are also owed to Robert Jervis, Robert Keohane, and Mark Zacher, who read the section introductions and helped me to clarify several key points I sought to make in them.

I dedicate this book to two women without whom the journey would have been, literally, unimaginable: my maternal grandmother, Franziska Macic, and my wife, Mary Ruggie. The first persuaded me that the structural constraints and situational exigencies into which I was born posed no obstacle or impediment that I could not overcome and turn to my advantage—though her vocabulary included none of these arcane terms, and she did not live to see her conviction vindicated. The latter, from the time we met in high school, has helped me to realize that dream and has been co-author of all the others. Both did so with determination, honesty, and unconditional love, which have made me who, and what, I am.

Essay 1 combines parts of two articles, as indicated in the text: "Collective Goods and Future International Collaboration," *American Political Science Review*, 66 (September 1972), and "International Responses to Technology: Concepts and Trends," *International Organization*, 29 (Summer 1975). Essay 2 first appeared as "International Regimes, Transactions, and Change: Embedded Liberalism in the Postwar Economic Order," *International Organization*, 36 (Spring 1982). Essay 3 combines parts of "International Organization: A State of the Art on an Art of the State," *International Organization*, 40 (Autumn 1986), co-authored with Friedrich Kratochwil, and "Peace in Our Time? Causality, Social Facts, and Narrative Knowing," *American Society of International Law, Proceedings, 89th Annual Meeting* (1995). Essay 4 was first published as "Multilateralism: The Anatomy of an Institution," *International Organization*, 46 (Summer 1992); Essay 5 as "Continuity and Transformation in the World Polity: Toward a Neorealist Synthesis," *World Politics*, 35 (January 1983); Essay 6 as "Social Time and International Policy: Conceptualizing Global Population and Resource Issues," in Margaret P. Karns (ed.), *Persistent Patterns and Emergent Structures in a Waning Century*, New York: Praeger, 1986; Essay 7 as "Territoriality and Beyond: Problematizing Modernity in International Relations," *International Organization*, 46 (Winter 1993); Essay 8 as "The Past as Prologue? Interests, Identity, and American Foreign Policy," *International Security*, 21 (Spring 1997); Essay 9 as "Consolidating the European Pillar: The Key to NATO's Future," *Washington Quarterly*, 20 (Winter 1997); and Essay 10 as "The United Nations and the Collective Use of Force—Whither or Whether?" *International Peacekeeping*, 3 (Winter 1996/97). All are reprinted with the appropriate permissions.

John Gerard Ruggie
Bronxville, New York
July 1997

Introduction
What makes the world hang together? Neo-utilitarianism and the social constructivist challenge

Edward Teller, the nuclear physicist, used to draw overflow crowds to his "physics for poets" course at Berkeley, despite his hawkish views on military matters and unwavering conservative politics. Through a thick Hungarian accent he would announce at the outset: "I will show you what makes the world hang together." And he did just that.

An analogous puzzle has defined my research interests from the start: what makes the world hang together in the international relations sense? Like every IR student of my generation I read, and greatly admired, Kenneth Waltz's classic, *Man, the State, and War*, and understood, as a result, the fundamental force of anarchy, the stag and hare parable, the central role of power and interests. In the stag hunt, as is well known, five individuals agree to cooperate in order to trap a stag but when a hare appears one of the five snags it, satisfies his own hunger, and leaves the other four with nothing but food for thought in return for their folly of trusting one another (Waltz 1959: 167ff.). What can break through this logic of anarchy? Only a superior force, Waltz stated then and elaborated later (1979): a hierarchy of formal authority, which he viewed virtually inconceivable at the international level, or power heavily concentrated in the hands of a few who were both able and willing to override the collective action problems that inhere in anarchy. Amid a delicately poised balance of nuclear terror that seemed, perversely, to deter major-power war, Waltz's argument had a certain, albeit dismal, attraction.

If Waltz was the leading realist theorist of his day, Ernst Haas was his counterpart on the liberal institutionalist side of the discipline. Haas once quipped about the stag hunt in a graduate seminar: "Those five guys weren't leaders of modern welfare states." His point was that the very fact of the welfare state propels its leaders to cooperate with one another to a greater extent than previous sociopolitical forms did if doing so is necessary to satisfy the everyday needs and demands of their domestic constituents. Haas went on to predict not only more extensive international cooperation than Waltz did but, in the case of Western Europe, economic and even political unification (E. Haas 1958). Whatever else has changed in the discipline since then, these core elements of realism and liberalism endure.

My point of entry into the debate was through a small analytical space these intellectual giants left vacant between them. The question—What makes the world hang together?—deserved a more general answer, I felt, than one that relied on the impact of the welfare state. Furthermore, economic and political unification struck me to be a limiting and perhaps even singular case, not fully representative of broader international processes. At the same time, key features of the stag hunt troubled me deeply: the five individuals just happened upon one another; they did not seem to belong to any organized social collectivity or have any ongoing social relations with each other or anyone else. They had only a rudimentary ability to speak. And they knew that they would go their separate ways again—where to?—once the project of trapping the stag was accomplished (or not, as it turned out). This, it seemed to me, was an unduly and unnecessarily undersocialized view of the world.

And so, the analytical space to which I laid claim was encompassed by the concept of institutionalization. International relations, like all social relations, exhibit *some* degree of institutionalization: at minimum, a mutual intelligibility of behavior together with the communicative mechanisms and organizational routines which make that possible. As a rule, international institutionalization is likely to fall far short of integrating the separate units even over the long term, but in real life it will rarely be as low as in the stag hunt. Moreover, institutionalization by definition transforms behavior by channeling it in one direction as opposed to all others that are theoretically possible, although how strong or weak a force it will be in any particular instance is an open, empirical question.

Institutionalization in the international polity takes place on at least two levels. The first is among states as we know them today and comprises the realm of international organization, broadly defined. What are the forms whereby relations among states are institutionalized? What are their determinants and consequences? The second level is the very system of states: that is, the system of states itself constitutes a form of institutionalizing political relations on the planet. How did it get here? What factors sustain it? In what manner and toward what new forms might it be transforming?

In a well-developed science, one would have proceeded from this point by postulating and testing alternative answers to these questions. But the field of international relations at the time—the late 1960s—lacked the conceptual vocabulary even to describe adequately the phenomena at issue. And what we cannot describe, we have little hope of being able to explain. The essays in the first two parts of this book, spanning the period from 1972 to 1995, reflect my endeavor to devise a set of appropriate concepts, to engage in what Geertz (1973) termed "thick description," and to move toward explanation.

Part I contains essays on various aspects of institutionalization within the system of states: the cognitive basis of institutionalization in epistemic communities; the formation of international regimes as a means to institute cooperative behavior; a "horizontal" rather than super-subordinate structure of international authority; intersubjective understandings as a major factor in sustaining international regimes; the role of multilateral organizing principles in facilitating peaceful change. The essays in Part II focus on the system of states itself: they seek to historicize this institutional form, to treat its structure as a living, not a sedimentary, thing; and they describe processes that may be transforming the system of states today.

If it is true, as Iver Neumann claims (1997: 365; also see Wæver 1997), that "Ruggie . . . excels in the art of nudging the course of the mainstream in some new direction," these essays have been the major tools of my nudging. Part III, containing more recent work, takes a more prescriptive turn and applies these earlier notions to the problem of international order in the post-cold war era. Each section is introduced by a snapshot of where the discipline stood vis-à-vis these issues when I began work on them, and each essay is preceded by a short sketch of its argument and of the proximate sources that animated its particular focus and formulation. Accordingly, they are not summarized any further here.

In the remainder of this introduction, I locate the theoretical posture developed in these essays within current disciplinary debates. Since 1980 or so, realism and liberalism have both produced "neo" variants: neorealism and neoliberal institutionalism (see Baldwin 1993 for an overview). Between them, they now occupy center stage. Over time, they have drawn increasingly close to one another. Indeed, Robert Keohane, a leading figure in neoliberal institutionalism, states that this approach "borrows as much from realism as from liberalism" (1993: 272). But the similarity goes beyond cross-fertilization. Most significantly, they share a view of the world of international relations in utilitarian terms: an atomistic universe of self-regarding units whose identity is assumed given and fixed, and who are responsive largely if not solely to material interests that are stipulated by assumption. The two bodies of theory do differ on the extent to which they believe institutions (and by extension institutionalization) to play a significant role in international relations, with neoliberalism being the more expansive in this regard. But they are alike in depicting institutions in strictly instrumental terms, useful (or not) in the pursuit of individual and typically material interests. Hence, I will refer to theorizing based on these premises as neo-utilitarianism. This approach has produced interesting analytical results, some of which have been subjected to empirical tests. But it also has blind spots and silences.

The essays in this volume work toward and exemplify a different theoretical approach. More sociological in orientation, it has come to be known as social constructivism. Though I was only dimly aware of it at the time, my constructivist turn precedes neorealism and neoliberalism (see 1975b, excerpted in Chapter 1). But since the 1980s my thinking has developed in continuous dialogue with their main premises. Arguments justifying specific aspects of social constructivism run throughout the entire volume and some of its key epistemological features constitute the explicit focus of Chapter 3.

At bottom, social constructivism seeks to account for what neo-utilitarianism assumes: the identity and/or interests of actors. It views international politics on the basis of a more "relational ontology," in Carol Gilligan's term (1993: 25–38), than the atomistic framing of neo-utilitarianism.[1] In addition, it attributes to ideational factors, including culture, norms, and ideas, social efficacy over and above any functional utility they may have, including a role in shaping the way in which actors define their identity and interests in the first place (Wendt 1994, 1995; Katzenstein 1996b). Finally, it allows for agency—actors doing things—to be not simply the enactment of pre-programmed scripts, as in neo-utilitarianism, but also reflective acts of social creation, within structured constraints to be sure.

In short, even as one disciplinary debate has narrowed in scope and diminished in intensity, another has begun. The latter is the focus of this chapter. The first section briefly summarizes the immediate antecedents to and the distinguishing features of neorealism and neoliberal institutionalism, and notes how they have converged on neo-utilitarian premises. The second section introduces social constructivism indirectly by discussing some of the key limitations of neo-utilitarianism that social constructivism seeks to avoid or overcome, and by summarizing constructivist efforts to do so. Section three presents a more synoptic sketch of the social constructivist project in international relations today. Finally, the fourth section takes up the issue of paradigmatic (ir)reconcilability, not only between neo-utilitarianism and social constructivism but also among the several subspecies of constructivism itself, the aim being not to vindicate one or another theoretical approach but to deepen our collective understanding of what each has to offer.

THE CONVERGENCE OF THE NEOS

This section summarizes briefly how postwar realism and liberalism in international relations theory evolved toward their respective "neo" variants and, despite the differences that remain, converged on a common neo-utilitarian analytical foundation.

Realism and liberalism

Among pundits, commentators, and academic specialists, the heavy guns in postwar America belonged to the realists: George Kennan, Walter Lippmann, Hans Morgenthau, Reinhold Niebuhr, and later, Arnold Wolfers, Kenneth Waltz, as well as Henry Kissinger—though the last never enjoyed the reputation as a scholar that he was accorded in policy circles. Morgenthau was the academic grandmaster, and *Politics Among Nations*, first published in 1948, the canon. In Morgenthau's pithy phrase, international politics was all about "interest defined as power" (1985: 5). That is to say, whatever the ends that leaders may seek to achieve, their doing so is mediated and constrained by all states deploying their power to pursue their own ends, so that power itself becomes the proximate interest of any state's foreign policy.

Notwithstanding Morgenthau's emphasis on power as the driving force, he saw the world of international politics in socially textured terms. For example, he differentiated between the classical European balance of power, which had existed "under the common roof of shared values and universal standards of action," and the "new," more "mechanical," balance of power which emerged between the United States and the Soviet Union after World War II (1985: 358–359, 388–391; also see Little 1989). And he felt that the latter posed a greater danger due to this difference. Moreover, although he rejected the idea that the international system could rest on law and organization, as pre-war idealists hoped, *Politics Among Nations* includes serious discussions of both. Similarly, Inis Claude, who wrote the definitive critique of the idea of collective security (1956), also ascribed to international organizations a non-trivial role in collectively (de)legitimating states' use of force (1966).

Initially, there were no comparable contenders on the liberal side. What the horrors of the Holocaust, World War II, and the outbreak of the cold war created on the ground, E. H. Carr's classic polemic, *The Twenty Years' Crisis* (1946), achieved in the realm of theory: pulverizing the utopian streak in liberal internationalism, which momentarily disoriented and discredited liberal international relations theory more generally. The first new serious social scientific form of liberalism took these new facts of life for granted and, indeed, looked to the rubble and ashes of postwar Western Europe as its point of departure. It went by the name of neofunctionalism, focused on regional and later global integration, and was associated with Ernst Haas and his colleagues (see, for example, Haas 1958, 1961, 1964).[2]

Haas expended little energy quarreling with realism as a description of the historical status quo; but he explored the question of whether it always had to be so. He drew on several strands of the liberal tradition in devising his analytical apparatus: republican liberalism, in the sense of stipulating that a pluralistic polity was a precondition for integration; the liberalism of the welfare state, which raised the salience of domestic economic and social issues in the calculus of decision makers; commercial liberalism, in that trade and other forms of cooperation were one vehicle for achieving domestic welfare aims; and what Joseph Nye (1988) calls sociological liberalism, or the growing and increasingly institutionalized transnational ties and coalitions among governments and actors in civil society, through which integrative politics is played out. Western Europe was the perfect laboratory for the new theory. Neofunctionalists were no more surprised than realists by the defeat of the Pleven plan, which would have established a European Defense Community. Their bets were on the Schuman plan, a more indirect, more gradual, and hence less threatening, step-by-step process toward integration, beginning with the declining coal and steel sectors—an approach associated philosophically with David Mitrany (1943) and in practice with Jean Monnet (Duchene 1994).

Neofunctionalism did not travel well beyond Western Europe, nor to the global level. Indeed, even within Europe, Haas (1976) came to feel, the theory failed to capture key elements of the integration process, which turned out to be more direct and more politically driven than the circuitous and largely technocratic mechanisms he had specified. As a result, he turned his attention to the study of international interdependence and regimes.

The transition essay between the integration and interdependence literatures was written by Robert Keohane and Joseph Nye (1975), who then went on to produce liberalism's core text for the next decade: *Power and Interdependence* (1977). In it, they ceded to realism primary explanatory efficacy for situations in which power is readily and at relatively low costs translated into pursuing desired outcomes. But they also stipulated several other situations—of power not being easily fungible across issue areas; being conferred or constrained by organizationally specific factors, as in international regimes; or having limited utility due to the high costs of disrupting a relationship—wherein realism, they argued, progressively loses its bite. Insofar as they believed international relations to be increasingly characterized by the condition they described as complex interdependence, they concluded that the future explanatory utility of realism was likely to be more circumscribed than in the past.

In short, the relationship between realism and liberalism had been specifically engaged, and the difference between the two hinged on judgments concerning the utility of force and institutionalized constraints on power.

Neorealism and neoliberal institutionalism

Rarely has a book so influenced a field of study as Kenneth Waltz's *Theory of International Politics* (1979)[3]—neorealism's foundational text. The model is summarized in Chapter 5. Briefly, it goes like this: the international system is characterized by the structural condition of anarchy, defined as the absence of central rule. As a result, states, the wielders of the ultimate arbiter of force, are its constitutive units. The desire of these units, at a minimum, to survive is assumed. And because no one can be counted on to protect anyone else, all are obliged to fend for themselves as best they can or must. Their doing so triggers corresponding efforts by similarly motivated others. Hence, the tendency to balance power is an inherent by-product of self-help. And the distribution of capabilities among states, therefore, is the most important determinant of outcomes—including the very interdependence that liberalism has viewed as an independent variable, with multipolar systems said to exhibit a higher level of interdependence among the major powers than bipolarity.

Waltz's model is almost entirely indeterminate; it directly predicts little more than that tendencies toward balancing will recur and that the system of states will reproduce itself. Numerous refinements have been made to the basic model by analysts sympathetic to its core premises, often supplementing its sparse formulations with additional factors that have yielded new insights: states do not balance power as raw capabilities so much as the powers that threaten them (Walt 1987); military doctrines reflect and, in turn, affect the degree to which potential adversaries view each other as threats (Jervis 1978; Van Evera 1984; Posen 1984; Snyder 1984); states not only balance but also bandwagon (Walt 1987; Schweller 1994) and "pass the buck" (Christensen and Snyder 1990) or "hide" by seeking neutrality (Schroeder 1994); and so on. Other analysts have extended the model to economic relations, arguing that the desire for relative gains that anarchy imposes limits cooperation even in non-military issue areas like international trade (Grieco 1988, 1990). Lastly, the only institutions that neorealists deem worthy of serious consideration are traditional alliances; otherwise, institutions are viewed as mere emanations of state power, such as the major international economic institutions (Gilpin 1975; Krasner 1978), or as window dressing (Mearsheimer 1995).

Waltz self-consciously distanced himself from classical realism in two critical respects; hence the prefix "neo." First, the earlier generation of realists in varying degrees had based their theory of international politics on some understanding of human nature, most dramatically in the case of Niebuhr's Christian realism,[4] but also Morgenthau's "will to power" (1946). In contrast, Waltz delivered on the premise and promise of his earlier theoretical inquiry (1959): neither man nor the state ultimately accounts for war or any other recurrent outcome in international politics; the structure of anarchy and its effects do. Similarly, Waltz shed all aspects of the "social texture" of international politics, as I termed it above, including "the common roof of shared values" under which Morgenthau contended traditional European power politics had been conducted. Waltz's model was strictly third image (that is, systemic) in orientation, and strictly physicalist in character.

Second, whereas classical realism tended to mix first principles with historical observation and prudential judgment, Waltz explicitly adopted a hypothetico-deductive approach to formulating theory and the "covering law" protocol of explanation that is characteristic of the natural sciences and economics (1979: chap. 1). Indeed, Waltz's model *is* the microeconomic model of the formation of markets transposed into the international political realm. The international system, he stipulated, is individualist in origin, more or less spontaneously generated as a by-product of the actions of its constituent units, "whose aims and efforts are directed not toward creating an order but rather toward fulfilling their own internally defined interests by whatever means they can muster" (1979: 90). Likewise, just as "market structure is defined by counting firms, international–political structure [is defined] by counting states. In the counting, distinctions are made only according to capabilities" (ibid.: 98–99). From that analytical base, Waltz derives some generic features of the international system, and he specifies the key differences between multipolar (oligopolistic) and bipolar (duopolistic) competition.

Finally, Waltz's turn to microeconomics provided a methodologically compatible depiction of the international system for game theoretic models of nuclear deterrence and other aspects of military strategy that dated back to the pioneering work of Thomas Schelling (1960, 1966).

The liberal institutionalist research program was moving in a similar direction. Interestingly, Robert Keohane, who had challenged realism's "state centrism" in the early 1970s (Keohane and Nye 1972) and sought to bracket the utility of force under conditions of complex interdependence in the late 1970s (Keohane and Nye 1977), was among the leading movers (1983, 1984). He now ceded to realism even more than he had before: states are the principal actors in international politics; they are driven by their conceptions of self-interests; a system of self-help prevails; and relative capabilities "remain important" (Keohane 1993: 271). But, he maintained, *"where common interests exist* realism is too pessimistic about the prospects for cooperation and the role of institutions" (ibid.: 277, italics in original). Here the continuity with liberal institutionalisms past is evident; the rest is "neo."

Where Waltz had looked to the microeconomic theory of markets, neoliberal institutionalists were drawn to corresponding theories of the firm, or industrial organization more generally. From Oliver Williamson (1975) came the core insight that "hierarchies" at the margin were often more efficient than "markets" by, for example, reducing transaction costs. Thus, in a pioneering work on international regimes, Keohane (1984) sought to specify the conditions under which and the manner whereby regimes may facilitate agreements among states by reducing transaction costs and producing reliable information about one another's intentions and behavior, relative to states "purchasing" those services in the political market place. And in an important paper written jointly with Robert Axelrod (Axelrod and Keohane 1985), game theory provided the analytical means of specifying when and how institutions may play roles in enhancing cooperation among states by reducing the incentives for defecting from agreements and compensating those who cooperate if others defect.

A mini-avalanche of analytical work followed on these and related issues: the problem of credible commitments, signaling, forms of contracting, shirking, monitoring, enforcement, and the like—in which institutions may be "functional" in the sense of enabling states to achieve benefits that would otherwise elude them. The substantive topics explored through this analytical perspective include international economic regimes (Keohane 1984), patterns of national economic adjustment to international changes (Simmons 1994), central bank cooperation (Simmons 1996), economic sanctions (Martin 1992), colonialism (Frieden 1994), European integration (Garrett 1993; Garrett and Weingast 1993), and environmental protection

(P. Haas, Keohane, and Levy 1993), among others. Incursions have also been made into the institutional dimension of military alliances (Duffield 1992, 1994/95; Wallander, Celeste, and Keohane 1995)—which had been a site of microeconomic modeling thirty years earlier (Russett 1968).

In the past, international relations theory was often criticized for being non-cumulative, consisting of one fad after another (see, for example, Strange 1982). Neither neorealism nor neoliberal institutionalism can be dismissed in those terms: they are serious research programs. Each is cumulative and, as we have seen, analytically the two have moved in ever-closer proximity to one another. I now turn to the basis of that proximity.

Neo-utilitarianism

Neorealism and neoliberal institutionalism have been able to converge to the extent that they have because they now share very similar analytical foundations. Both take the existence of international anarchy for granted, though they may differ as to its precise causal force. Both stipulate that states are the primary actors in international politics. Both stipulate further that the identities and interests of states are given, a priori and exogenously—that is to say, external to and unexplained within the terms of their theories. On that basis, both assume that states are rational actors maximizing their own expected utilities, defined in such material terms as power, security, and welfare.[5] And both *must* make assumptions of this sort for their hypothetico-deductive mode of theorizing to work; there is no other way to do that. From this starting point, both go on to explain patterns of interaction as the result of states, so conceived, using their capabilities to act on their preferences.

Analytical differences do remain between these two bodies of theory. Stephen Krasner describes the most significant (1997: 16): "for neorealism the basic issues are survival and distributional conflict while for neoliberalism they involve the resolution of market failures." What Krasner means is that neorealists and neoliberals are likely to stress two different effects of anarchy. Neorealists are likely to focus on the fact that the potential use of force is ever present in international relations and affects the calculus of states; for the same reason, states are obliged to worry about not only how much they gain from cooperation in absolute terms, but also how much they gain relative to others, who may become tomorrow's foe (see Grieco 1988 on this latter point). Neoliberals, on the other hand, are more likely to explore the impediments that anarchy poses to states' reaching and keeping agreements even where common interests to cooperate exist, which may reduce potential benefits all around unless means can be devised to overcome these institutional defects.

But there has been some ambiguity about whether these are differences in emphasis or kind. Grieco originally (1988, 1990) held to the latter position, arguing that in the neorealist world states do not seek to maximize absolute but relative gains, and that they are, therefore, positional, not atomistic in character.[6] Snidal (1991) provided interesting analytical results suggesting that the relative gains issue may be exaggerated, especially beyond dyadic relations. Powell (1991, 1994) pointed out that posing the relative gains issue in terms of preferences, as Grieco (and Waltz before him) had done, implies that different types of units are assumed to exist in the two bodies of theory—one driven by absolute gains, the other by relative—which limits the comparability of the theories' results. He suggested instead that the difference be recast in terms of the strategic contexts that like units face (Is the use of force plausible, and can the potential of its future use be plausibly attributed to relative gains?). In the end, Keohane (1993) conceded that he may have underestimated the problem of relative gains, Grieco (1993) that he may have overstated it, and both agreed that the units are, indeed, similar and that the impact of relative gains is conditional.[7]

A second difference concerns the role of institutions. Although he is sometimes characterized as a "hyper-realist," John Mearsheimer accurately reflects the neorealist position on this question: "The most powerful states in the system create and shape institutions so that they can maintain their share of world power, or even increase it." Internationally, outcomes are "mainly a function of the balance of power," and institutions at best are "intervening variables" (1994/95: 13). Other neorealists, notably Krasner (1983), have long allowed for "stickiness" of institutional arrangements, however, whereby they continue to function along their original paths even after power relations shift, or even take new departures, so long as they do not drift too far out of line of the underlying power-based structure.

Neoliberalism assigns greater scope to institutions, but their scope is similarly functionally determined—by political market failures, in this case, rather than power relations. As Blyth puts it (1997), "as a result of the 'discovery' that hierarchies at the margin were often more efficient than market exchange, it became possible to describe the existence of institutions in terms of their ability to either reduce or exacerbate transaction costs [or attenuate strategic dilemmas]. Consequently, information, enforcement and monitoring emerge as the central concerns of [neoliberal institutionalism] in the model of institutions they employ." This perspective leads to significantly different empirical expectations (see Keohane and Martin 1995, in response to Mearsheimer 1994/95), but the structure of the two arguments is very similar.

That, in brief, is the current state of the debate. Its tenor is barely a faint echo of the titanic intellectual and moral struggles between realism and liberalism down the centuries—Machiavelli or Hobbes versus Kant, for instance. This is so even if we take as our baseline the post-World War II academic literature, as I have done in this discussion. Convergence has been made possible, as noted, by the similar, neo-utilitarian analytical basis on which the two bodies of theory now rest. Neorealism and neoliberal institutionalism, in David Baldwin's words (1993: 3), "engage one another's arguments directly and [this] results in a more focused and productive debate." Baldwin is right up to a point: not only the debate, but also the empirical research programs based on the two theories, have been productive. But Baldwin is right *only* up to a point, because this productivity has been purchased at a price: by neglecting or misspecifying aspects of international relations that do not fit readily within the two theories' increasingly narrow analytical frame. If it can be shown that important elements of international reality are poorly understood, therefore, or misunderstood, or left unattended altogether, then the cost may be too high. The belief that this is so is the major animating source of social constructivism.

THE EMERGENCE OF SOCIAL CONSTRUCTIVISM

Unlike neorealism and neoliberal institutionalism, the constructivist approach has no direct antecedent in international relations theory. To that extent, it is *sui generis*. It is true that neofunctionalism embodied many of the methodological and philosophical precepts that we now recognize to be social constructivist, but it did so largely unconsciously. The so-called English school influenced many constructivists, myself included (Butterfield and Wight 1968; James 1973; Wight 1977; Bull 1977; Bull and Watson 1984; Watson 1992; for useful surveys, see Buzan 1993; Little 1995). It holds that the system of states is embedded in a society of states, which includes sets of values, rules, and institutions that are commonly accepted by states and which make it possible for the system of states to function—the balance of power, for example, being viewed as a deliberate institutional contrivance, valued by states because of its contribution to their liberty and to overall stability. But a major analytical objective of the English school has seemed to be to resist the influence of social scientific modes of analysis in international relations, and less to clarify and firm up its own theoretical basis. The actual label of social constructivism may not have been affixed to or by any international relations scholar prior to 1989, when it featured in an analytical study by Nicholas Onuf, *World of Our Making*—though Anthony Giddens' (1979) closely related term "structuration theory" was in use earlier (Ruggie 1983d (Chapter 5); Dessler 1989; Wendt 1987).[8]

By and large, scholarly interest in the social constructivist approach has grown as certain analytical and empirical limitations of conventional theories have become better understood, most emphatically after their neo-utilitarian turn. Ironically, this was true even in the context of my own work. My first publication (1972a, excerpted in Chapter 1) applied the microeconomic theory of collective goods to the problem of international cooperation. I was pleased with the analytical and empirical results, and even more so with having them published in the premier political science journal. But they left me with numerous puzzles that were not likely to be resolved by further work using similar analytical tools: How much, if anything, did the actors have to know about the acts the theory ascribed to them? To the extent that their knowledge was implicated, how much of it had to be mutual for things to work? Where did such mutual knowledge reside? Was it responsive to influence through discourse, or only through signaling based on material factors? Do actors ever accept the explanations of others for wrongful acts? Do social bonds form, and if so, when, where, how, and with what consequences? Come to think of it, how did the actors get here, anyway, and to acquire their current characteristics?

Questions of this sort are inescapable if one's research interests include the origins and possible transformation of the system of states, as mine do (see Chapters 5, 6, and 7). But they were also posed by far more prosaic empirical studies on international economic regimes, where I saw numerous instances of communicative and interpretive dynamics at work (Chapter 2, for example). States appeared to employ tacit means for assessing (in)appropriate behavior in monetary and trade relations, for example, understanding some deviations from rules in the dual sense of being able to comprehend them and willing to acquiesce in them. Though I claim no expertise in national security policy, as a lay observer I wondered if there were not important instances there as well. For example, the innovations in nuclear strategy developed by the Kennedy administration were far more complex, and at times counterintuitive, than the "massive retaliation" they replaced— "to blow hell out of them in a hurry if they start anything," as President Eisenhower had once described that (quoted in Gaddis 1982: 150). Was it necessary for the Soviets to understand the new strategies for them to work? If so, how did the Soviets learn to do so? If not, precisely how did the strategies work—and how do we know that they did? Or was nuclear war avoided because an "existential deterrence" came to take effect? But where would such an effect "exist"? And how could one test for it?

My brilliant and supportive colleague, Robert Jervis, has long studied cognitive factors in international security relations (1970, 1976). But his many insights could not be employed directly to resolve my puzzles because they concern individual actors (for which the international analogue is individual states): they take the form of, for example, A's unilateral assessment (accurate or not) of verbal and nonverbal cues from B, which includes A's estimation of B's expectations of A; and so on.

But, in some instances that I explored, more seemed to be at work than ideational attributes of individual states. Just as collectivities of individuals within states hold intersubjective understandings that affect their behavior, so too, it seemed, do collectivities of states. In both cases these understandings appear to differ from the mere aggregation of the individual parts. Following Durkheim (1938), I termed these "social facts" —which John Searle has recently (1995) defined simply as those facts that are produced by virtue of all the relevant actors agreeing that they exist. Social facts, so defined, include states and their collective institutional practices, my major research interest, and the likes of marriage, money, football, property, and Valentine's Day.[9] Social facts differ from two other kinds of socially relevant facts: "brute" facts, such as warheads, population size, market shares, or mountains, which are true (or not) apart from any shared beliefs that they are true; and (ontologically) "subjective" facts, so designated because their existence depends on being experienced by individual subjects, like an individual actor's perceptions of or preferences about the world—Jervis's studies of perception and misperception deal in facts of this sort.[10] The distinguishing feature of social constructivism is that it concerns itself with the nature, origins, and functioning of social facts, and what if any specific methodological requirements their study may entail.

In light of these interests, I left collective goods theory, initially for Berger and Luckman (1966) and the sociology of organizations; I took periodic forays into the classics of social science (above all, Durkheim and Weber, of whom more in Part III); I found Giddens' work helpful (particularly 1981); and, after exploring some of the extraordinarily creative intellectual outbursts in the humanities that took place in the 1980s, I have more recently found a relatively stable philosophical footing in the work of John Searle (1984, and especially 1995).[11]

Hence, because there is no received theory called social constructivism in international relations, I present the perspective here much as it evolved, by challenging the major limiting features of neo-utilitarianism. Below, I take up four such features, in logical order, not chronologically. Moreover, because the most common criticism of social constructivism by neo-utilitarians is that its arguments are largely metatheoretical, whereas the conventional theories are said to traffic in the empirical stuff of things, wherever possible I allow constructivism to speak through its empirical findings, insights, and concerns, becoming "philosophical" only when it is absolutely necessary for the immediate point at hand.

The core assumptions

It is widely accepted in the social sciences that the appropriate test of a model's efficacy is how fruitful its hypotheses are, not the accuracy of its assumptions. But, in the policy sciences, we also want to be right for the right reasons. For policy *is* the manipulation of initial conditions as well as causal factors all along causal paths in the pursuit of desired ends. Here, if a model misses or distorts significant aspects of the reality it purports to represent, there are grounds for caution or corrective measures.

Neorealism and neoliberal institutionalism, as we saw above, are obliged to treat the identity and interests of their constituent actors as being exogenous and given. Some neorealists claim to "derive" state interests from the condition of anarchy, but anarchy is so slippery a concept and the things one can "derive" from it are so indeterminate (Milner 1991) that interests are, in fact, handled by assumption, notwithstanding some claims to the contrary. The power and elegance of the neo-utilitarian model rests on this point of departure. But so, too, do some of its limitations.

First, neo-utilitarianism provides no answer to the foundational question: how the constituent actors—that is, territorial states—came to acquire their current identity and the interests that are assumed to go along with it. Similarly, any potential present or future change in this identity and in corresponding interests is beyond the scope of the theory. I take up the issue of foundational transformation separately below.

Second, while it is of course true that territorial states have generic identities and interests *qua* states, neo-utilitarianism has no analytical means for dealing with the fact that the specific identities of specific states shape their perceived interests and, thereby, patterns of international outcomes. In Chapter 4, I discuss briefly the obvious proposition that the world would look very different today if the Soviet Union or Nazi Germany had ended up as its hegemon after World War II. Indeed, important things would have differed even if Great Britain had done so. Accordingly, contra neorealism, I suggest that the fact of *American* hegemony was every bit as important as the fact of American *hegemony* in shaping the post-World War II international order. And, contra neoliberal institutionalism, I note in several of the essays that the origins of none of the major postwar international institutions—the United Nations, the Bretton Woods institutions, GATT, NATO, and what became the European Union—or of the League of Nations, for that matter, can be accurately rendered in marginal utility terms, though their functioning once in existence and patterns of compliance with the rules they generate may well exhibit elements of that logic.

Counterfactuals are impossible to prove, but there is evidence to suggest that the differences in hegemonic scenarios for the post-World War II international order are the product of not only the leading states' power and/or material interests, but also their identities, which affected their definition of interests. For example, I argue in Chapter 8 that internationally oriented leaders in the United States throughout this century have explicitly drawn on America's sense of exceptionalism in order to achieve and sustain US involvement in the maintenance of a stable international security order. More importantly, I seek to show that, after World War II, their doing so produced conceptions of US security interests which were both more inclusive and more extensively institutionalized—*even before the Soviet threat*—than they would have been had they merely followed the dictates of geostrategic logic. The creation of the United Nations and NATO's multilateralized security commitments, I contend, were among the effects of that conception of interests.

Likewise, the identity of the same state can change and pull its interests along. Thus, Thomas Berger (1996) argues that Germany and Japan today differ significantly from their pre-World War II predecessors. Antimilitarism, he maintains, has become integral to their sense of self as nations and is embodied in domestic norms and institutions. Peter Katzenstein (1996b) makes a similar case regarding the police and military in postwar Japan and Germany. Robert Herman (1996) describes the

Gorbachev revolution in the Soviet Union and its international aftermath in terms of identity shifts leading to a radical recalibration of interests. And Thomas Risse-Kappen (1996) suggests that a sense of collective identity within the transatlantic community of democracies specifies norms of appropriate behavior for its members. All remain aware of the possibility that these changes may not be irreversible. But Katzenstein in particular identifies the specific normative and institutional practices in Japan and Germany that any move toward reversal would have to contend with and overcome.

Third, there is growing empirical evidence that normative factors in addition to states' identities shape their interests, or their behavior directly, which neo-utilitarianism similarly does not encompass. Some of these factors are international in origin, others domestic.[12] More research needs to be done on this set of issues, but enough is available to merit serious reflection.

On the international side, the literature that Martha Finnemore (1996b) depicts as "sociological institutionalism," revolving around the work of John Meyer and his colleagues, has documented successive waves in the diffusion of cultural norms among states that differ radically in their circumstances, but which then express identical preferences for national policies and institutional arrangements. These include constitutional forms, educational institutions, welfare policies, human rights conventions, defense ministries in states that face no threat (including navies for landlocked states)—to which Finnemore, in her own work (1996a), adds science ministries in countries that have no scientific capability. The norms diffused are those of rationalized bureaucratic structures and, more generally, standards of what it means to be a modern state, which have spread far more rapidly than the technology or markets that neo-utilitarian explanations would utilize to explain the spread. It must be acknowledged, however, that these norms are diffused from core to periphery in the international system: diffusion results from the core as well as from international organizations "teaching" states in the periphery that to be modern states means to have these things.[13]

Finnemore has extended this research to include the emergence of norms among the core countries, such as the Geneva conventions on warfare (1996a) and the evolution of humanitarian intervention (1996c). Others have addressed normative taboos on the use of chemical weapons (Price 1995) and nuclear weapons (Price and Tannenwald 1996). In a completely different (and far more robust institutional context), Burley and Mattli (1993) show how the European Court of Justice shapes domestic legal practices within the member states of the European Union. All specify logics that depart significantly from neo-utilitarianism, even as they fully appreciate that power and interests are intimately involved in these processes.

On the domestic side, Elizabeth Keir (1995, 1996) and Alistair Johnston (1995, 1996) raise serious questions about neo-utilitarian renderings of the origins of strategic cultures and military doctrines, contending that—at least in the cases of France and China, respectively—they are not simply functionally determined either by external or internal factors, but reflect broader cultural and political considerations.

In an oft-cited remark, Waltz has said that his theory does not pretend to explain everything, but what it does explain is important (1986: 329). He is right on both counts. But the subjects addressed in the studies noted above (and others like them) are hardly unimportant either. Indeed, all are important for precisely those dependent variables that Waltz's theory claims to explain. The same point also holds, correspondingly, for neoliberal institutionalism. More empirical work in the social constructivist vein is necessary, and the origins of identities and other normative factors need to be better theorized. But it is not an undue stretch to conclude even at this point that neo-utilitarianism's assumptions that the identities and interests of states are exogenous and given—in contrast to being treated as endogenous and socially constructed—pose potentially serious distortions and omissions— even as they provide the basis on which neo-utilitarianism's theoretical pay-off rests.

Ideational causation

Neo-utilitarianism has a narrowly circumscribed view of the role of ideas in social life. But because neorealism and neoliberal institutionalism differ somewhat in this respect, I discuss them separately.

Waltz's model, as noted above, is physicalist in character. Accordingly, ideational factors make only cameo appearances in it. Take, as an example, his reference to the recurrent normative element in US foreign policy: "England claimed to bear the white man's burden; France spoke of her *mission civilisatrice*. In like spirit, we [the United States] say that we act to make and maintain world order ... For countries at the top, this is predictable behavior" (1979: 200). And that is Waltz's *sole* reference to the role of norms. Ideational factors enter the picture again briefly in the form of socialization, one of the mechanisms by which states, according to Waltz, learn to conform to the dictates of the system (1979: 127). Numerous critics have been puzzled by the presence of socialization in a physicalist model that disclaims any sociality on the part of its actors and their interactions. But even more disturbing is the fact that Waltz, in this instance as elsewhere in *Theory* (see Chapter 5), turns what is supposed to be a methodological principle into an ontological one: Waltz has *actual states* become socialized to *his model* of the international system, not to the more variegated world of actual international relations.

Other neorealists have modestly modified Waltz's model. For example, Krasner (1978) has explored the role of ideology in North–South economic negotiations, and more recently he refers to states' "ideational interests" (1997: 3). But neither factor has been fully squared with his enduring neorealist commitments (Ruggie 1980b; also Chapter 3). In addition, following the collapse of the Soviet system several neorealists discovered nationalism, which was previously black-boxed into domestic factors, said to have no role in systemic theory (Mearsheimer 1990; Posen 1993a, 1993b). However, as Lapid and Kratochwil suggest (1997: 113), their interest in nationalism is largely limited to its role as a source of conflict or in affecting the capability of existing or would-be states to wage conflicts, thus "making it difficult to conceive of a nontautological relationship between 'nation' and 'state'."

Finally, Katzenstein has pointed out (1996c: 26–27) that neorealists who seek to add greater determinative content to the predictions of Waltz's sparse model often do so by importing into it unacknowledged ideational factors, particularly the role of culture as an instrument of social mobilization or in generating threat perceptions.

Generally speaking, neoliberal institutionalism also assigns a limited causal role to ideational factors. In strictly rationalist explanations, Goldstein and Keohane note (1993: 4), "ideas are unimportant or epiphenomenal either because agents correctly anticipate the results of their actions or because some selective process ensures that only agents who behave as if they were rational succeed." Goldstein and Keohane believe otherwise, and present a framework for analyzing the impact of ideas on policy outcomes. It serves as a useful point of reference for our discussion because, even though the framework is posed as a challenge to both neo-utilitarianism and social constructivism, Goldstein and Keohane are quickly drawn back into the neo-utilitarian fold.

One part of the framework consists of three causal pathways through which ideas may influence policy outcomes. The first is by serving as "road maps," a role that "derives from the need of individuals to determine their own preferences or to understand the causal relationship between their goals and alternative political strategies by which to reach those goals" (ibid.: 12). The second is as "focal points" in strategic situations of multiple equilibria, that is, several equally "efficient" outcomes. Here, ideas can help individuals select one from among the set of viable outcomes (ibid.: 17). The third causal pathway is through "institutionalization," whereby ideas, once they have become encrusted in institutions, continue to "specify policy in the absence of innovation" (ibid.: 13).

Goldstein and Keohane also define three types of ideas that may do these things. One they call "world views," which are "entwined with people's conceptions of their identities, evoking deep emotions and loyalties" (ibid.: 8). Another is "principled beliefs," which "specify criteria for distinguishing right from wrong and just from unjust" (ibid.: 9). The last is "causal beliefs," that is, beliefs about cause–effect relations (ibid.: 10), which derive from the shared consensus of recognized authorities.

The framework holds promise, but the pull of neo-utilitarian precepts is stronger. Most significantly, what Goldstein and Keohane call world views are disposed of summarily: "Since all the subjects discussed in this volume [of which theirs is the introductory essay] have been profoundly affected by modern Western world views, and our authors all share this modernist outlook, we can say relatively little about the impact of broad world views on politics" (ibid.: 9). Set aside, thereby, are ideas related to state identities and corresponding interests—the heart of the social constructivist project. Left unexplored, thereby, are ideas of the sort that John F. Kennedy had in mind when he honored Jean Monnet by saying: "you are transforming Europe by a constructive idea" (Duchene 1994: 6). Similarly, Samuel Huntington's "clash of civilizations" (1996) finds no place here. Lastly, it is unclear where ideologies fit, not only those for which an instrumental rationalization can be readily claimed, like the resurgence of neo-laissez faire today, but others, such as the Nazi concept of Aryan superiority or Mao's Great Leap Forward and Cultural Revolution. None of these ideational factors are principled or causal beliefs as we normally understand those terms. So they must be parts of world views, which Goldstein and Keohane treat as though they were transcendent and/or invariant and therefore decline to specify.

But what of principled and causal beliefs? Do they not fare better? From a social constructivist vantage, not much. For the individuals featured in the Goldstein–Keohane story are not born into any system of social relationships that helps shape who they become. They are already fully constituted and we find them poised in a policy-making/problem-solving mode. As a result, neither principled beliefs nor ideas as road maps are intended to tell us much about those individuals, only about how they go about their business. By a process of elimination, then, the heavy lifting in the Goldstein–Keohane scheme ends up being done by principled and causal beliefs functioning as focal points in multiple equilibria situations, and as sunk costs embedded in institutions—both fully consistent with neo-utilitarian precepts.[14]

What is the social constructivist contribution to the ideational research program? According to Goldstein and Keohane (1993: 6), "without either a well-defined set of propositions about behavior or a rich empirical analysis, the [constructivist] critique remains more an expression of understandable frustration than a working research program." Let us be more precise—and, as a result, also more generous. Social constructivists have sought to understand the full array of systematic roles that ideas play in world politics, rather than specifying a priori roles based on theoretical presuppositions and then testing for those specified roles, as neo-utilitarians do. Because there is no received theory of the social construction of international reality, constructivists have gone about their work partly in somewhat of a barefoot empiricist manner and partly by means of conceptual analysis and thick description—in addition to expressing "understandable frustration." So Goldstein and Keohane may be right about the shortage of well-defined propositions, and this state of affairs should be improved in due course. But empirical and conceptual work is rich and accumulating. Indeed, it has become so large that we cannot summarize it all here. To briefly flag constructivist research on ideational factors, I begin by using Goldstein and

Keohane's own typology and then push beyond it.

A core constructivist research concern is what happens *before* the neo-utilitarian model purportedly kicks in. Accordingly, what Goldstein and Keohane call "world views" are of great interest: civilizational constructs, cultural factors, state identities, and the like, together with how they shape states' interests and patterns of outcomes. I identified some of the empirical constructivist work on these subjects in the previous section. In addition, such world views presumably would include changing forms of nationalism in its constitutive and transformative roles, as Ernst Haas has studied it extensively (1986, 1997), and not simply as adjunctive to states and state power. They presumably include the globalization of market rationality and its effects, which has been of particular interest to constructivists who work in the tradition of Gramsci (Gill 1995), Polanyi (Ruggie 1995a), and the so-called sociological institutionalists (Finnemore 1996b). And they include emerging bonds of "we-feeling" among nations, such as appear to have taken effect within the transatlantic security community—much as Karl Deutsch predicted forty years ago (1957) and explored more recently by Adler and Barnett (1996; also see Chapter 9)—and, of course, in the European Union.

Constructivist empirical studies documenting the impact of principled beliefs on patterns of international outcomes include, among other subjects, the evolution of the human rights regime (Forsythe 1991; Sikkink 1993), the institutionalization of foreign aid (Lumsdaine 1993), decolonization (Jackson 1993), and international support for the termination of apartheid (Klotz 1995); as well as the already mentioned studies on increasingly nondiscriminatory humanitarian interventions (Finnemore 1996c), the emergence of weapons taboos (Price 1995; Price and Tannenwald 1996), and the role of multilateral norms in stabilizing the consequences of rapid international change (Chapter 4). The single most important feature differentiating constructivist from other readings of these and similar phenomena is that they make the case that principled beliefs are not simply "theoretical fillers," to use Blyth's term (1997), invoked to round out or shore up instrumentalist accounts, but that in certain circumstances they lead states to redefine their interests or even their sense of self.

The major venue for constructivist explorations of the impact of causal beliefs has been via "epistemic communities," or transnational networks of knowledge-based experts (P. Haas 1992a). Here the empirical research seeks to relate the roles that such communities play in policy-making processes to the impact of their ideas on resolving particular policy problems, such as ozone depletion (P. Haas 1992b; Litfin 1994); providing operational content to general and sometimes ambivalent state interests, as in the Bretton Woods negotiations (Ikenberry 1992); and redefining states' interests, as in the antiballistic missile treaty (Adler 1992) and the pollution control regime for the Mediterranean Sea (P. Haas 1990). Disentangling strictly ideational from institutional impacts is difficult in practice, but that problem is not unique to the epistemic community literature (see Yee 1996; Blyth 1997).

Moreover, the further up one climbs on this impact ladder, the more is "learning" said to come into play (for the most extensive discussion, see E. Haas 1990). On the higher rungs, learning progressively means more than merely adapting to constraints, imitating the successful, or undertaking bounded search processes until a viable solution is identified—its typical meaning in conventional theories. Instead, it becomes second-order learning or, as Haas and some of his associates have termed it, "evolutionary episte-mology" (E. Haas 1983a, 1990; Adler 1991, 1992; Adler and P. Haas 1992).[15] This refers to the process whereby actors change not only how they deal with particular policy problems but also their very concept of problem solving—resulting from the recognition that they and other actors face similar conditions, have mutual interests, and share aspirations—by moving toward adopting what neo-utilitarians would describe as interdependent utility functions. That possibility takes us well beyond the Goldstein–Keohane typology.

But when all is said and done, the critical difference between the social constructivist and neo-utilitarian ideational research programs does not lie in empirical issues of the sort we have been looking at, as important as they are. They have to do with the neo-utilitarian misspecification of certain kinds of ideas. Let me explain. Goldstein and Keohane define ideas as "beliefs held by individuals" (1993: 3). It is of course true that, physiologi-cally speaking, only individuals can have ideas or beliefs. But the reverse proposition, that all beliefs are individual beliefs or are reducible to indi-vidual beliefs, does not follow. It is the product of the methodological individualism on which neo-utilitarianism rests. Social constructivism, in contrast, also deals in the realm of "intersubjective beliefs," which cannot be reduced to the form "I believe that you believe that I believe," and so on. They are "social facts," and rest on what Searle calls "collective intention-ality" (1995: 24–25). The concept of collective intentionality, Searle stresses, does not require "the idea that there exists some Hegelian world spirit, a collective consciousness, or something equally implausible" (ibid.: 25). Why not? Because the intentionality remains in individual heads. But within those individual heads it exists in the form "we intend," and "I intend only as part of our intending" (ibid.: 26).

Constructivists have explored the impact of collective intentionality, so understood, at several levels in the international polity. At the deepest is the question of who counts as a constitutive unit of the international system. The mutual recognition of sovereignty, I argue in Chapter 7, is a precondi-tion for the normal functioning of a system of sovereign states. Sovereignty, like private property or money, can only exist within a social framework that recognizes it to be valid—that is, by virtue of collective intentionality. But its impact is not limited to the one-time designation, "you are in this game, and you are out." Over time, sovereignty has affected patterns of conflict between sovereign states and other types of political formations (Strang 1991). And it continues to empower and provide resources to some states, irrespective of how dysfunctional they may be, that might not otherwise survive (Jackson 1990). Though this is not the place to pursue the issue, constructivists also tend to believe, as a working hypothesis, that insofar as sovereignty is a matter of collective intentionality, in the final analysis, so, too, is its future.

In addition to this constitutive role, collective intentionality also has a deontic function within the system of states—that is, it creates new rights and responsibilities. The process that Claude (1966) called collective legitimation includes an entire class of such functions which, if anything, has expanded since he wrote his classic article (see Barnett 1996). For example, Finnemore (1996c) observes that humanitarian intervention not only is becoming more nondiscriminatory, but that states increasingly tend to seek the endorsement of international organizations before undertaking such interventions. Searle, viewing the subject through a philosopher's eyes, finds that human rights are "perhaps the most amazing" instance of creating rights through collective intentionality—amazing because it ascribes rights "solely by virtue of being a human being" (1996: 93). Constructivists are equally amazed by the fact it ascribes rights to individuals vis-à-vis their own states.

At the most routine level, collective intentionality creates meaning. In Chapter 2, for example, I suggest that the Bretton Woods monetary negotiations and the corresponding negotiations to establish an international trade regime produced more than standards of behavior and rules of conduct. They also established intersubjective frameworks of meaning that included a shared narrative about the conditions that had made these regimes necessary and what they were intended to accomplish, which in turn generated a grammar, as it were, on the basis of which states agreed to interpret the appropriateness of future acts that they could not possibly foresee (for an empirical update, see Ruggie 1996a: chap. 5).

Theoretical analysis along these lines is most advanced among German international relations scholars, who are more directly influenced by the work of Juergen Habermas than their American counterparts. One of the key questions is the extent to which Habermas's theory of communicative action (1979, 1984, 1987) can or cannot be reconciled with rational-choice theory and neo-utilitarianism more generally (Mueller 1994; Keck 1995; Risse-Kappen 1995; Schmalz-Bruns 1995; Mueller 1995; also see Kratochwil 1989 and Alker 1990, 1996). The consensus appears to be that accommodating communicative action, including acts of deliberation and persuasion, requires devising a conception of actors who are not only strategically but also discursively competent, a feat that is unlikely to be achieved at least within currently available neo-utilitarian formulations.[16]

There is yet another major difference between social constructivism and neo-utilitarianism on the issue of ideational causation: it concerns how "causation" is understood. Some ideational factors simply do not function causally in the same way as either brute facts or the agentive role that neo-utilitarianism attributes to interests. As a result, the efficacy of such ideational factors is easily underestimated. This is too complex a problem to be resolved here, so I merely acknowledge its existence (see Chapter 3 for a fuller discussion). Aspirations are one instance, legitimacy is another, and rights a third. They fall into the category of *reasons for actions*, which are not the same as *causes of actions*—so that, for example, the aspiration for a united Europe has not caused European integration but it is the reason the direct causal factors have had their causal capacity (on causal capacity, see Yee 1996).

In sum, by now the constructivist ideational research program adds up to considerably more than "an expression of understandable frustration"—and it includes entire domains of ideational causation that even an expanded neo-utilitarian agenda does not and cannot comprise.

Constitutive and regulative rules

Thus far, we have focused largely on the independent variable side of things; we now shift our concern to some critical limits and omissions of neo-utilitarianism in regard to dependent variables, the types of things it does and does not seek to explain. The first has to do with the distinction between constitutive and regulative rules, which goes back at least to a seminal article by John Rawls (1955; see Chapter 3). But Searle (1995: 27–29) offers an easier point of entry.

Let us begin with a simple illustration. We can readily imagine the act of driving cars existing prior to the rule that specified "drive on the right (left)-hand side of the road." In an account that is perfectly consistent with neo-utilitarianism, the rule would have been instituted as a function of increased traffic and growing numbers of fender-benders. Specifying which side of the road to drive on is an example of a regulative rule; as the term implies, it regulates an antecedently existing activity. To this rule were soon added others, requiring licenses, imposing speed limits, forbidding driving under the influence of alcohol, yielding at intersections, and so on.

Now imagine a quite different situation: playing the game of chess. "It is not the case," Searle notes sardonically (ibid.: 28), "that there were a lot of people pushing bits of wood around on boards, and in order to prevent them from bumping into each other all the time and creating traffic jams, we had to regulate the activity. Rather, the rules of chess create the very possibility of playing chess. The rules are constitutive of chess in the sense that playing chess is constituted in part by acting in accord with the rules." Regulative rules are intended to have causal effects—getting people to approximate the speed limit, for example. Constitutive rules define the set of practices that make up any particular consciously organized social activity—that is to say, they specify *what counts as* that activity.

This basic distinction permits us to describe a profound limitation of neo-utilitarianism: it lacks any concept of constitutive rules. Its universe of discourse consists entirely of antecedently existing actors and their behavior, and its project is to explain the character and efficacy of regulative rules in coordinating them. This feature accounts for the fact that within the terms of their theories, neorealism and neoliberal institutionalism explain the origins of virtually nothing that is constitutive of the very possibility of conducting international relations: not territorial states, not systems of states, not any concrete international order, nor the whole host of institutional forms that states use, ranging from promises or treaties to multilateral organizing principles. All are assumed to exist already or they are misspecified—as, for example, when the post-World War II international order is attributed to American hegemony, taking the specificity of American identity for granted.

Why is this the case, and is it inherent to the enterprise? The reason is not difficult to decipher: neo-utilitarian models of international relations are imported from economics. The economy, we well know, is embedded in broader social, political, and legal institutional frameworks that make it possible to conduct economic relations—that are *constitutive of* economic relations. Economic actors and economists, appropriately, take their existence for granted. The problem arises because when neo-utilitarian models are imported into other fields they leave those constitutive frameworks behind. This seems not to matter for some (as yet unspecified) range of political phenomena, domestic and international, which has been explored by means of microeconomic models and the microfoundations of which are now better understood than before. But there are certain things that these models are incapable of doing. Accounting for constitutive rules—which they were not responsible for in economics—is among the most important.

Furthermore, this defect cannot be remedied within the neo-utilitarian framework. The terms of a theory cannot explain the conditions that are necessary for that theory to function, because no theory can explain anything until its necessary preconditions hold. Thus, Alexander James Field (1979, 1981, 1984) has demonstrated from within the neoclassical tradition, and Robert Brenner (1977) the neo-Marxist, that market rationality cannot account for the constitutive rules that are required to make market rationality work, as specified by modern economic theory[17]—an insight that Max Weber (1958) had already established at the turn of the century.

Social constructivists in international relations have not yet managed to devise a theory of constitutive rules, but the phenomenon itself is of central concern to them (for general theoretical treatments, see Kratochwil 1989; Onuf 1989; Wendt forthcoming). Take first the very system of states. In Chapter 5, I contend that the concept of the modern state was made possible only when a new rule for differentiating the constituent units within medieval Christendom replaced the rule of heteronomy (interwoven and overlapping jurisdictions, moral and political). And in Chapter 7, I describe the various material and ideational factors that interacted to produce the institutional form of exclusive territoriality, by which the new principle of differentiation was instantiated, and which then served as the constitutive rule defining the spatial organization of modern international politics.

Moreover, Hedley Bull (1977) of the English school argued that norms regarding contracting and promise-keeping are constitutive of order in the international realm no less than domestic—in the sense that the institution of contracts or the concept of promises must be recognized and enjoy legitimacy before there can be any talk of regulative rules designed to deal with problems of incomplete contracting or cheating on agreements. Kratochwil (1989) elaborates on these issues fruitfully in an explicitly constructivist vein.

In addition, even as they acknowledge that the specific (as opposed to generic) identities of states are defined primarily internally, constructivists have shown that to some extent such identities are also mutually constituted. Wendt (forthcoming) draws on G. H. Mead's theory of symbolic interactionism to elucidate the process. On the premise that every identity implies a difference, constructivist scholars have also explored the role of "the other"—whether denigrated, feared, or emulated—in the mutual constitution of identities: Neumann and Welsh (1991) on the role of the Ottoman Empire, "the Turk," in consolidating the civilizational construct of Europe; Campbell (1992) on the "old world," the communist menace, as well as various internal "others" in forging America's sense of self; and Der Derian (1987) on the mediating role of diplomacy in sustaining relations among culturally estranged entities.

Lastly, it is necessary to take note of a philosophical point: in some cases, constitutive rules themselves provide the desired explanation. If we are asked to "explain" the game of chess, the appropriate response consists of its constitutive rules. In Searle's simple formulation (1995: 28), constitutive rules are of the type "X [a move] counts as Y [checkmate] in context C [chess]." Because X does not temporally precede and is not independent of Y, it follows that these are noncausal explanations. (A causal explanation is called for in response to questions such as, "Why do I keep losing at chess?") Precisely the same holds for "explaining" modern international politics in contrast to the medieval or classical Greek systems: the relevant answer is provided by their respective constitutive rules. Indeed, it also holds for social constructions that are closer to the surface level of the international system, such as the cold war or the embedded liberalism compromise. The point to note is this: lacking a conception of constitutive rules makes it impossible to provide endogenously the noncausal explanations that constitutive rules embody and which are logically prior to the domain in which causal explanations take effect.[18]

Constitutive rules are the institutional foundation of all social life. No consciously organized realm of human activity is imaginable without them, including international politics—though they may be relatively more "thin" in this than in many other forms of social order. Some constitutive rules, like exclusive territoriality, are so deeply sedimented or reified that actors no longer think of them as rules at all. But their durability remains based in collective intentionality, even if they started with a brute physical act such as seizing a piece of land. The sudden and universally surprising collapse of the Soviet Union's East European empire illuminates vividly what can happen, Searle observes (1995: 92), "when the system of status-functions [assigned by constitutive rules] is no longer accepted"—despite the fact that, in that instance, brute force remained *entirely* on the side of the status quo (see also Koslowski and Kratochwil 1995). A similar erosion of collective intentionality, only partly related to shifts in brute force or material interests, was evidenced in the termination of colonialism and of the slave trade before it. Under certain circumstances, it seems, collective intentionality can "will" the rules of the game to change.

Constructivists do not claim to understand the extraordinarily complex processes regarding constitutive rules fully (or even mostly). But neorealists and neoliberal institutionalists lack even a space for them in their ontology. The scope of their theories, as a result, is confined to regulative rules that coordinate behavior in a pre-constituted world.

Transformation

In light of the foregoing discussion, it follows almost axiomatically that neo-utilitarian models of international relations theory would have little to offer on the subject of systemic transformation: doing so would require them to problematize states' identities and interests and to have some concept of constitutive rules. Neoliberal institutionalism did not yet exist when I first noted of Waltz's model that it contained only a reproductive logic, but no transformative logic (Chapter 5). While neorealists have made some effort to respond by claiming, in essence, that no theory of transformation is necessary, neoliberal institutionalism has remained relatively silent on the subject.[19]

The neorealist claim that no theory of transformation is necessary takes one of two forms. The first argues that there is no decisive difference between medieval Europe and the modern system of states because conflict groups, striving for advantage, forming alliances, and using force to settle disputes, existed in both and were not visibly affected by whatever common norms that medieval Christendom may have embodied (Fischer 1992). Mearsheimer (1994/95: 45) infers from this claim that "realism . . . appears best to explain international politics in the five centuries of the feudal era"—a claim that will surprise medievalists[20]—and, of course, ever since. Fischer's historiography and selection bias of cases have been challenged by Hall and Kratochwil (1993). But even if Fischer were correct, the point he makes is irrelevant to the issue at hand: the personalized and parcelized structure of political authority relations in feudal society collapsed and was replaced by the completely different institutional system of modern states.[21]

The second neorealist argument is that not enough is happening in the world today to warrant a theory of transformation. This was implied by Waltz (1979), and has been explored extensively by Krasner (1993, 1995/96, 1997). Krasner maintains that the "Westphalian baseline"—the Peace of Westphalia (1648) symbolizing the beginning of the modern state system— was never as clear-cut as some analysts have made it out to be, has been compromised throughout by recurrent forces, and with some exceptions (most notably the European Union) it remains the rough approximation of the international polity that it has always been. Nevertheless, as Krasner acknowledges when he grapples with the elusive concept of sovereignty, even the markers of international transformation are badly underspecified and ill-understood. A deeper theoretical understanding of possible processes of transformation, of course, would go some way toward clarifying its indicators.

Here again, constructivists have not yet managed to devise a fully fledged formulation of their own. They have come at the problem from three sides. The first is a purely theoretical "solution," and rests on Giddens' notion (1978) of the "duality of structure"—that structure both constrains action but is also the medium through which actors act and, in doing so, potentially transform the structure. David Dessler (1989) goes so far as to posit what he calls a "transformational ontology" to subsume neorealism's "positional" one (for a similarly inspired "dialectical" rendering of "agent-structure" relations, see Wendt 1987). These endeavors are thought-provoking, and they help avoid the reification of structures. But as they stand they rely too heavily on the linguistic analogy: any given language precedes its individual speakers and thereby constrains how they communicate; at the same time, their use of that language can change it over time—and so the practice alters the structure. This is all well and good in the realm of language, but linguistic structures, as sociologist William Sewell (1992: 23–24) observes, "are much less implicated in power relations" than most other social structures, and altering a linguistic practice "has minor power consequences" compared to changes in other social structures. It follows that "particularly poor candidates for the linguistic analogy would be state or political structures, which commonly generate and utilize large concentrations of power."

A second constructivist tack is more empirical, albeit in a "jumbo" sense. It consists of attempts to specify the macro-structural dimension of international politics in a manner that shows it to be space–time contingent: that is to say, to make transparent the fact that "structure" is the aggregation of specific social practices that are situated in time and space; to specify what the characteristic forms of those social practices are; and to discern how they may become susceptible to change. The introduction to Part II of this volume ("Problematizing Westphalia") describes this approach in somewhat greater detail, and Chapters 5 to 7 reflect my efforts to pursue it. In Chapter 7, for example, I speculate that the characteristically modern form of organizing political space may be undergoing slow but fundamental change as a result of the sectoral unbundling of territoriality in various functional regimes, together with the emergence of multiperspectival state identities in contrast to identities based strictly on single-point perspective. Both of these processes are most advanced in the European Union, I argue, but are not limited to it.

The third constructivist line of transformational research is to identify, inventory, and specify the consequences of innovative micro-practices in international relations today. Examples include Saskia Sassen's work (1996) on the institutional mechanisms that are reconfiguring global economic geography today, ranging from legal practices and financial instruments to accounting rules and telecommunication standards. Kathryn Sikkink's work on the subject of "advocacy networks" (1993, forthcoming) exemplifies this genre. So too does a host of studies on the growing role of nongovernmental actors and the emergence of transnational civil society (see, for example, Wapner 1995). This approach is most productive when it is linked up with work on macro-structures, to determine which micro-practices are potentially transformative agents.

Finally, I point out in Chapter 7 that the emergence of the modern state was shaped repeatedly and fundamentally by the unanticipated consequences triggered by the behavior of various social actors. That fact makes it difficult to devise any comprehensive theory of transformation, but especially one based on the rationalistic assumptions of neo-utilitarianism.

Let us draw this discussion to a close. Social constructivism in international relations has come into its own during the past decade or so, not only as metatheoretical critique but increasingly in the form of empirical evidence and insights. Constructivism addresses many of the same issues that neo-utilitarianism has addressed, though typically from a different angle, but also some that neo-utilitarianism treats by assumption, discounts, ignores, or simply cannot apprehend within its ontology and/or epistemology. Constructivists seek to push the empirical and explanatory domains of international relations theory beyond the analytical confines of neorealism and neoliberal institutionalism in all directions: by problematizing states' identities and interests; by broadening the array of ideational factors that affect international outcomes; by introducing the logically prior constitutive rules alongside regulative rules; and by including transformation as a normal feature of international politics that systemic theory should encompass even if its empirical occurrence is episodic and moves on a different time line from everyday life.

There can be little doubt but that subsequent research will show some constructivist claims to be in error, others even misguided. What is more, constructivism is still unable to specify a fully articulated set of propositions and rigorous renderings of the contexts within which they are expected to hold. Indeed, for reasons explored below, it may never be able to do so entirely to the satisfaction of neo-utilitarianism and the epistemological preferences it embodies. But having now described the emergence of social constructivism in international relations, stressing its dialogue and tension with the ascendancy of neo-utilitarianism, we can turn next to developing a more synoptic overview of the main constructivist precepts and practices.

THE SOCIAL CONSTRUCTIVIST PROJECT

Because of the inductive manner in which constructivism emerged in the field of international relations, both empirically and theoretically, there may be almost as many variants of it—or at least emphases—as there are practitioners. To gain a more synoptic understanding of what constructivism is "all about," I undertake three tasks in this section. First, I briefly summarize the analytical means whereby Durkheim and Weber resisted the ascending tide of utilitarianism, and methodological individualism generally, striving to put the emerging discipline of sociology on a more "social" footing. For if neorealism and neoliberal institutionalism are contemporary theoretical branches that continue to draw sustenance from utilitarianism's nineteenth-century roots, social constructivism in international relations today remains indebted to Durkheim and even more so to Weber. With that foundation in place, I enumerate the main common features of the constructivist project. Finally, I differentiate briefly among three subspecies of this approach.

The classical precursors

Emile Durkheim is perhaps best known to students of international relations as a result of being invoked by Waltz (1979: 104, 115n, 121, 197) to buttress his claim that the international system shapes and constrains the relations among its units.[22] Durkheim did propound such a perspective. But one would not know from Waltz's references that Durkheim's primary research interest was moral phenomena in society. In his major empirical studies he sought to demonstrate how a variety of social outcomes, ranging from patterns of social cooperation to individual feelings of anomie and differential suicide rates, were influenced by the different bonds of social order that are embodied in the reference groups to which individuals belong, from the family on up to society as a whole. Thus, in *Suicide* (1951) Durkheim attributed its lower incidence among Catholics to the fact that the practice of their faith makes more extensive use of integrative rituals within a stronger and more hierarchical moral community than does Protestantism.

Durkheim's concern with moral phenomena is as interesting for our purposes as his attributing causality to forms of sociality. For it meant that he had to come to grips with two issues: the role of ideational factors in social life, and how ideas, which can exist only in individuals' heads, become socially causative. On both issues, Durkheim differentiated himself from the utilitarians, on the one hand, and from transcendentalists, on the other.

With regard to ideational factors, Durkheim wrote (1953b: 32): "A third school is being born which is trying to explain [mental phenomena] without destroying their specificity." For the Kantians and idealists, he stated, "mental life certainly had a nature of its own, but it was one that lifted the mental out of the world and above the ordinary methods of science" (ibid.). For the utilitarians, in contrast, mental life "was nothing in itself, and the role of the scientist was to pierce the superficial stratum in order to arrive at the underlying realities" (ibid.). The third school, to which he adhered, aimed to bring "the faculty of ideation ... in its various forms, into the sphere of nature, with its distinctive attributes unimpaired" (1953c: 96). In short, Durkheim held that ideational factors have their own specificity, their own integrity, as a result of which they cannot be reduced to other factors. But at the same time ideational factors are no less "natural" than material reality and, therefore, are susceptible to normal scientific modes of inquiry.

Durkheim's position on how ideas, of which individuals are carriers, come to express a social force, is derived from his understanding of the nature of social order generally. Here, too, he differentiated himself vigorously from utilitarianism. If societies were based on its atomistic premises, he rebutted Herbert Spencer, "we could with justice doubt their stability" (1933: 203). And to the instrumental, contractarian view of social relations that Spencer advocated he retorted: "Wherever a contract exists," it rests on "regulation which is the work of society and not that of individuals" (1933: 211). But Durkheim also rejected organic conceptions of society and other forms of "substantial social realism," to use Ernest Wallwork's term (1972: 16–26), such as Auguste Comte's. Instead, Durkheim held what Wallwork describes as a "relational social realism," in which social facts are constituted by the combination of individual facts via social interactions. As a result of their combination, these individual facts become transformed: "Whenever certain elements combine and thereby produce, by the fact of their combination, new phenomena, it is plain that these new phenomena reside not in the original elements but in the totality formed by their union" (Durkheim 1938: lxvii). Among the "elements" so transformed to become "social facts" are linguistic practices, religious beliefs, moral norms, and similar ideational factors. And once constituted as social facts, these ideational factors in turn influence subsequent social behavior.

Contemporary social constructivists in international relations remain indebted to Durkheim for his concept of social facts, the centrality of ideas and beliefs ("*la conscience collective*") in them, and for an ontology that steered clear of both individualism and transcendentalism. But Durkheim did not actually study concrete processes whereby individual elements, including ideas, are transformed to become social facts. Instead, he inferred them from the forms of social expression ("*représentations collective*") that he believed to be their products, ranging from liturgical practices to legal codes and similar representations of civic morals. In other words, Durkheim "solved" the methodological problem of social constructivism by means that are roughly analogous to the stipulation of "revealed preferences" in economics—a problematic methodological maneuver. Doing so permitted him, however, to use "objective" indicators and thereby to adhere to positivist practices, which he believed necessary to establish the scientific legitimacy of sociology. Weber's influence on social constructivism remains the greater for having tried to work this problem through.

Like Durkheim, Weber found himself amid disciplinary conflicts (see Schluchter 1989: chap. 1). And like Durkheim, Weber sought to avoid the pitfalls of prevailing alternatives. The major methodological opposition he confronted was between the historicism of the German Historical School and the positivism of the Austrian Theoretical School (marginal utility theory) and Marxism. While the latter two differed in many respects, both sought to reduce problems of social action and social order to material interests, and both embraced naturalistic monism, that is, the idea that the natural sciences embody the only valid model of science to which the social sciences should, therefore, aspire.

Weber believed strongly in the possibility of a social science. But to be valid it had to give expression to the distinctive attributes of social action and social order. "We are *cultural beings*," he wrote in his classic methodological essay on "Objectivity" (1949: 81, emphasis in original), "endowed with the capacity and the will to take a deliberate attitude towards the world and to lend it *significance*. Whatever this significance may be, it will lead us to judge certain phenomena of human existence in its light and to respond to them as being (positively or negatively) meaningful. Whatever may be the content of this attitude—these phenomena have cultural significance for us and on this significance alone rests its scientific interest." In short, the task of interpreting the meaning and significance that social actors ascribe to social action differentiates the social and natural sciences. Weber's major methodological innovations followed directly from this premise.

The natural and social sciences both use concepts and both seek causal knowledge, according to Weber. But they use different kinds of concepts and the way concepts are ordered to provide explanations differ. Natural science aims at the general, seeks to establish universally valid laws, and identifies individual events as types to be subsumed under those laws. Its concepts are constructed accordingly, to facilitate generalizability. But in the study of social behavior, concepts in the first instance must aid in uncovering the meaning of specific actions and in demonstrating their social significance. That is to say, they must be capable of grasping the distinctiveness of the particular. As Weber put it (ibid.: 72, emphasis in original): "We wish to understand on the one hand the relationships and the cultural significance of individual events in their contemporary manifestations and on the other the causes of their being historically *so* and not *otherwise*."

Meaning and significance are, of course, ideational phenomena, so the role of ideas is central to Weber's social science. And he included not only the instrumental but also the normative role of ideas. "One thing is certain," he wrote (ibid.: 56), namely, "the broader [the] cultural significance [of a social phenomenon], the greater the role played [in it] by value-ideas." Accordingly, when social scientists seek to attribute meaning to actions they must include the normative self-understanding of the ends that govern the behavior of a population. This premise meant, according to Schluchter (1989: 9), that Weber "had to go beyond the concept of utility."

Weber proposed to uncover social meanings and significance by means of an analytic method he termed *Verstehen*, or, loosely, "understanding" (for a summary with international relations examples, see Hollis and Smith 1990: 78–82). Somewhat simplified for our purposes here, Weber took this method to include three steps. The first is to discern a "direct" or an "empathetic" understanding of whatever act is being performed, from the vantage point of the actor. The second is to devise an "explanatory understanding" of that act by locating it in some set of social practices recognized as such by the relevant social collectivity—in the language of the previous section, to identify what the act "counts as." And the third is to unify such individualized experiences into a historical phenomenon of broad social significance—of "objectivating" *Verstehen* (ibid.: 19).[23] Weber accomplished this last task primarily through the use of "ideal types." He described these as:

> a conceptual construct which is neither historical reality nor even the "true" [i.e., some underlying] reality. It is even less fitted to serve as a schema under which a real situation or action is to be subsumed as one *instance*. It [is] a purely ideal *limiting* concept [or analytical benchmark] with which the real situation or action is *compared* and surveyed for the explication of certain of its significant components.
>
> (1949: 93, emphasis in original)

Among the best-known ideal types employed by Weber are traditional, charismatic, and rational-legal forms of authority; the "modern Occidental type" of persons; and their distinctive institutions, including bureaucracy, capitalism, and the state.

In constructing his own causal explanations—whether of the impact of the distinctive spirit of Protestant asceticism on the rise of capitalism, or the growing pervasiveness in the West of a certain form of rationality and its positive as well as negative consequences for social order—Weber linked together multiple ideal types. Moreover, for analytical purposes, Weber had no objection to sequencing ideal types (for example, his concepts of authority). Lastly, he even accepted marginal utility theory as an ideal type, defending it on that basis against claims that it needed a more robust psychological foundation (Weber 1975). But Weber warned that ideal types must not be confused either with social reality, or (even in developmental sequences or axiomatic formulations) with causal explanation. They are selective and deliberately one-sided abstractions from social reality, and their methodological role is to serve as "heuristic" devices in the "imputation" of causality (Weber 1949: 90, 103)—for example, by pinpointing differences between the logic of the ideal type and patterns of outcomes on the ground. Actual causal knowledge of social action and social order, Weber insisted, remains concrete and anchored in meaning, showing why things are historically *so* and not *otherwise*. Though Weber gave it no name, today we call this a "narrative explanatory protocol," in contrast to the deductive-nomological model that is favored in all forms of naturalistic monism (including neo-utilitarianism).[24]

It has not been my aim to vindicate Durkheim or Weber, nor to suggest that social constructivists in international relations today directly apply or copy their insights and methods. It is their theoretical objectives that are of interest, and what they thought they had to do to achieve them, because these efforts illuminate the contemporary constructivist project. Both Durkheim and Weber held that the critical ties that connect, bond, and bind individuals within social collectivities are ideational, and they sought to establish the roles of ideational factors by rigorous social scientific means. In doing so, both rejected utilitarianism on the grounds of its methodological individualism and because it failed to encompass normative self-understandings of the ends, in addition to merely the means, of social action. And both believed that material and ideational factors stand in mutually conditioning relationships. For our purposes, the major difference between them is that Durkheim inferred ideational social facts from "objective" indicators represented by their institutionalized forms of expression, and thereby was able to remain within a conventional positivist epistemological framework. In contrast, Weber explored actual processes whereby individual meanings become social forces, as a result of which he felt the need to depart from several positivist precepts, in particular the influence of its naturalistic monism on concept formation, the study of meaning, and the character of causal explanation.

John Searle is surely correct when he states (1995: xii) that "we are much in debt to the great philosopher-sociologists of the nineteenth and early twentieth centuries—one thinks especially of Weber, Simmel, and Durkheim." Nevertheless, he adds, "they were not in a position to answer the questions that puzzle [us] because they did not have the necessary tools. That is, through no fault of their own, they lacked an adequate theory of speech acts, of performatives, of intentionality, of collective intentionality, or rule-governed behavior, etc." Based on these classical foundations, and with these additional tools in hand, what, then, are the main features of constructivism in international relations today?

Constructivism's core features

In light of our discussion thus far, we can readily dismiss a stereotype one sometimes encounters in the literature, especially among hyper-realists: that constructivists discount the potential for conflict in international politics, and that they believe in the Dorothy principle—that extant reality, as in the Land of Oz, can be changed by closing one's eyes and wishing hard. Emanuel Adler, a constructivist, responds thusly (1997): "If international reality is socially constructed, then World War II, the Holocaust, and the Bosnian conflict must also have been socially constructed." At bottom, constructivism concerns the issue of human consciousness: the role it plays in international relations, and the implications for the logic and methods of social inquiry of taking it seriously. Constructivists hold the view that the building blocks of international reality are ideational as well as material; that ideational factors have normative as well as instrumental dimensions; that they express not only individual but also collective intentionality; and that the meaning and significance of ideational factors are not independent of time and place.

The most distinctive features of constructivism, then, are in the realm of ontology, the real-world phenomena that are posited by any theory and are invoked by its explanations (for a good discussion of ontology in the context of international relations theory, see Dessler 1989). As summarized in section two of this essay, at the level of individual actors constructivism seeks, first of all, to problematize the identities and interests of states, to show that and how they are socially constructed. Neorealists come close to believing that states' identities and interests are, in fact, given and fixed. For neoliberal institutionalists, this posture is more likely to reflect merely a convenient assumption, designed to permit their analytical apparatus to function. When neoliberal institutionalists are pressed about the origins of either, however, they turn immediately to domestic politics (see, for example, Keohane 1993: 294). Social constructivists, in contrast, argue and have shown that even identities are generated in part by international interaction—both the generic identities of states *qua* states, as well as their specific identities, as in America's sense of difference from the old world or from godless communism. Still at the level of individual actors, constructivism also seeks to map the full array of additional ideational factors that shape actors' outlooks and behavior, ranging from culture and ideology, to aspirations and principled beliefs, on to cause/effect knowledge of specific policy problems.

At the level of the international polity, the concept of structure in social constructivism is suffused with ideational factors. There can be no mutually comprehensible conduct of international relations, constructivists hold, without mutually recognized constitutive rules, resting on collective intentionality. These rules may be more or less "thick" or "thin," depending on the issue area or the international grouping at hand. Similarly, they may be constitutive of conflict or cooperation. But in any event, these constitutive rules prestructure the domains of action within which regulative rules take effect. In some circumstances, collective intentionality includes an interpretive function—as in the case of international regimes, which limit strictly interest-based self-interpretation of appropriate behavior by their members.

And in others collective intentionality also includes a deontic function—creating rights and responsibilities in a manner that is not simply determined by the material interests of the dominant powers. In short, constructivists view international structure to be a social structure—the concept of "relational social realism" that Wallwork uses to describe Durkheim's ontology is apt—made up of socially knowledgeable and competent actors who are subject to constraints that are in part material, in part institutional.

These ontological characteristics have implications for the logic and methods of constructivist inquiry. First, constructivism is not itself a theory of international relations, the way balance-of-power theory is, for example, but a theoretically informed approach to the study of international relations. Moreover, constructivism does not aspire to the hypothetico-deductive mode of theory construction. It is by necessity more "realistic," to use Weber's term, or inductive in orientation. Additionally, its concepts in the first instance are intended to tap into and help interpret the meaning and significance that actors ascribe to the collective situation in which they find themselves. It is unlikely that this function could be performed by concepts that represent a priori types derived from some universalizing theory sketch or from purely nominal definitions.[25]

Finally, constructivism differs in its explanatory forms. As discussed previously, for some purposes constitutive rules in themselves provide an appropriate and adequate, albeit non-causal, explanatory account. And in its causal explanations, constructivism, again by necessity, adheres to narrative explanatory protocols, not the nomological–deductive (N–D) model prized by naturalistic monism. The N–D model establishes causality by subsuming the explanandum under a covering law or law-like generalizations. Causality in the narrative explanatory form, as described in greater detail in Chapter 3, is established through a process of successive interrogative reasoning between explanans and explanandum, anticipated by Weber with his heuristic use of ideal types, and called "abduction" by the American pragmatist philosopher Charles Peirce (1955: 151–152). At least in these respects, then, constructivism is non- or post-positivist in its epistemology.

These epistemological practices of constructivism have not been well received in the mainstream of the discipline. Part of the problem is that the mainstream has become increasingly narrow in its understanding of what constitutes social science, so that on the dominant conception today Weber might no longer qualify. The other part of the problem is that there are very different strands of constructivism in international relations and they differ precisely on epistemological grounds, not surprisingly creating confusion as a result. I briefly summarize the main differences.

Variants of constructivism

Any distinction ultimately is arbitrary, and so it is with constructivism. There are sociological variants, feminist variants, jurisprudential approaches, genealogical approaches, an emancipatory constructivism and a more strictly interpretive kind. What matters most for the purposes of this essay is their underlying philosophical bases, and how those relate to the possibility of a social science. Accordingly, I differentiate among three variants.

I propose to call the first *neo-classical* constructivism—not to strive for parity with the two mainstream "neos" but to indicate that it remains rooted in the classical tradition of Durkheim and Weber. The analytical means by which this foundation is updated differs among scholars who work in this genre. But typically they include an epistemological affinity with pragmatism; a set of analytical tools necessary to make sense of inter-subjective meanings, be it speech act theory, the theory of communicative action, their generalization as in the work of Searle, or evolutionary episte-mology; and a commitment to the idea of social science—albeit one more plural and more social than that espoused in the mainstream theories, while recognizing fully that its insights will be temporary and unstable. I put myself in this category—and I believe that the work of E. Haas, Kratochwil, Onuf, Adler, Finnemore, and recently Katzenstein, as well as of some feminist scholars, such as Jean Elshtain (1987, 1996), also exhibits this neo-classical orientation.

A second variant may be termed *post-modernist* constructivism. Here the intellectual roots are more likely to go back to Friedrich Nietzsche, and any updating to the writings of Michel Foucault and Jacques Derrida, marking a decisive epistemic break with the precepts and practices of modernism. Richard Ashley (1984, 1987, 1988) first drew the attention of the field to this constructivist genre. Other contributors include David Campbell (1992), James Der Derian (1987), R. B. J. Walker (1989, 1993), and feminist scholars such as Spike Peterson (Peterson and Runyan 1993). Here the linguistic construction of subjects is stressed, as a result of which discursive practices constitute the ontological primitives, or the foundational units of reality and analysis. Little hope is held out for a legitimate social science. In its place, a "hegemonic discourse" is seen to impose a "regime of truth" (Keeley 1990: 91), instituted through disciplinary powers in both senses of that term. Lastly, causality is considered chimerical: "I embrace a logic of interpreta-tion that acknowledges the improbability of cataloging, calculating, and specifying the 'real causes'," writes Campbell (1992: 4), "and concerns itself instead with considering the manifest political consequences of adopting one mode of representation over another."

A third constructivist variant is located on the continuum between these two. It combines aspects of both; like the neo-classical variant, it also shares certain features with mainstream theorizing; but it is grounded in the philosophical doctrine of scientific realism, particularly the work of Roy Bhaskar (1979). The writings of Alexander Wendt (1987, 1991, forthcoming) and David Dessler (1989) exemplify this genre. Scientific realism, according to Wendt, offers the possibility of a wholly new "naturalistic" social science (1991: 391). On its basis, it is no longer necessary to choose between "insider" and "outsider" accounts of social action and social order, not because social science is made to emulate the natural sciences, as it was under the old naturalistic monism, but because there is little difference in their respective ontologies to begin with. Scientific inquiry of both material and social worlds deals largely in non-observables, be they quarks or international structures, and much of the time even the intersubjective aspects of social life exist independently of the mental states of most individuals that constitute it. I call this *naturalistic* constructivism. As of yet, little empirical research has been informed by this perspective, so we do not know what difference it makes in practice. On theoretical grounds, however, the dilemma identified by Hollis and Smith (1991: 407) poses a serious and as of yet unmet challenge: "To preserve naturalism, the scientific realist must either subordinate the interpreted social world to [the] external mechanisms and forces [that govern the physical world] or inject similarly hermeneutic elements into 'outsider' accounts of nature." Bhaskar struggles heroically with this problem but, as Hollis and Smith conclude, "we do not believe that he has settled the matter, nor even that he would claim that honour."[26]

In sum, there are distinctive attributes that differentiate constructivism from mainstream theorizing, especially the neo-utilitarian kind. But there are also significant differences among the various strands of constructivism. As a result of the latter, Mark Neufield observes shrewdly (1993: 40), "the debate within the camp of [constructivists] may prove to be as vigorous as that between [them] and their positivist critics."[27] We turn, in conclusion, to the question of how to relate (or not) these various modes of theorizing in international relations.

PARADIGMATIC (IR)RECONCILABILITY

The "great debates" that have swept through the field of international relations over the decades typically have been posed in terms of the alleged superiority of one approach over another. But the fact that these debates recur so regularly offers proof positive that no approach can rightfully claim a monopoly on truth—or even on useful insights. The current encounter between neo-utilitarianism and constructivism exhibits the additional feature that the strength of each approach is also the source of its major weakness. As a result, the issue of any possible relationship between them must be joined.

The strength of neo-utilitarianism lies in its axiomatic structure, which permits a degree of analytical rigor, and in neoliberal institutionalism's case also of theoretical specification, that other approaches cannot match. This is not an aesthetic but a practical judgment. Rigor and specificity are desirable on intellectual grounds because they make cumulative findings more likely, and on policy grounds because they raise the probability that predicted effects will actually materialize. At the same time, neo-utilitarianism's major weakness lies in the foundations of its axiomatic structure, its ontology, which for some purposes is seriously flawed and leads to an incomplete or distorted view of international reality. That problem is particularly pronounced at a time such as today, when states are struggling to redefine stable sets of interests and preferences regarding key aspects of the international order—a set of issues addressed in Part III of this volume.

The obverse is true of constructivism. It rests on a deeper and broader ontology, thereby providing a richer understanding of some phenomena and shedding light on other aspects of international life that, quite literally, do not exist within the neo-utilitarian rendering of the world polity. At the same time, it lacks rigor and specification—in fact, it is still relatively poor at specifying its own scope conditions, the contexts within which its explanatory features can be expected to make how much difference. Improvements are inevitable as work in the constructivist vein continues to expand, but given the nature of the beast there are inherent limits to the endeavor.

Where do we go from here? Can a systematic relationship between the two approaches be articulated, and if so how? A substantial number of adherents to each is unlikely to be interested in any such effort. Hard-core rational choice theorists, post-modernist constructivists, and most neorealists will reject any need to do so. But even coalitions of the willing may find the going difficult as they discover the analytical boundaries beyond which their respective approaches cannot be pushed.

The first instinct of willing neo-utilitarians is to expand their analytical foundation in the direction of greater sociality. For example, Keohane (1993: 289) states that his version of institutionalist theory "embeds it selectively in a larger framework of neoliberal thought," which also includes commercial, republican, and sociological liberalism. Doing so, Keohane believes, provides a richer and more robust social context for neoliberal institutionalism. Keohane is right up to a point: that point is defined by the boundaries of methodological individualism and instrumental rationality. Commercial liberalism poses few problems in this regard, nor does the transnational bureaucratic politics that comprises one aspect of what he calls sociological liberalism. But republican liberalism? It would be enormously surprising if the ties among democratic societies, especially those in "the West," did not reflect an intersubjective cultural affinity, a sense of "we-feeling," a shared belief of belonging to a common historical project, which fall well beyond the "selectively" expanded foundation of neoliberalism that Keohane proposes.

Indeed, Keohane acknowledges that not even the most fundamental attribute of liberalism, that which distinguishes it from all other views on the nature of humanity, justice, and good government, can be accommodated within his version of neoliberalism. He writes (1990a: 174): "the emphasis of liberalism on liberty and rights only suggests a general orientation toward the moral evaluation of world politics," but it does not lend itself to the analysis of choice under constraints that he wishes to employ. As a result, he finds it "more useful" to put that "emphasis" aside for his analytical purposes. All deontic features of social life go with it.

In short, a selective expansion of neo-utilitarianism's core is possible, and it may even be desirable. But we should not expect it to carry us far toward a "social"—ideational and relational—ontology.

The first instinct of the willing constructivist is to incorporate the study of norms, identities, and meaning in the study of international relations with minimum disruption to the field's prevailing epistemological stance, on which hopes for analytical rigor and cumulative knowledge are believed to rest. Typically, this takes the form of maintaining that constructivist concerns are a useful tool in the context of discovery, but that at the end of the day they do not affect the logic of inquiry (see Neufield 1993 for an extended criticism of this practice). For example, I read the methodological discussions in Katzenstein's edited volume, *The Culture of National Security* (1996b), in this light. The essays in that book, Jepperson, Wendt, and Katzenstein insist (1996: 65), neither advance nor depend on "any special methodology or epistemology . . . When they attempt explanation, they engage in 'normal science,' with its usual desiderata in mind."

Everything hinges, of course, on what is meant by "normal science." On my reading, "normal science" in international relations has a hard time grasping truly intersubjective meanings at the international level, as opposed to aggregations of meanings held by individual units; it lacks the possibility that ideational factors relate to social action in the form of constitutive rules; it is exceedingly uncomfortable with the notion of noncausal explanation, which constitutive rules entail; and even though it is almost never achieved in practice—and in most instances perhaps cannot be achieved—the "normal science" of international relations nevertheless aspires to the deductive-nomological model of causal explanation, while dismissing even rigorous forms of the narrative mode as mere story-telling.

The sanguine view of normal science expressed by Katzenstein and his colleagues may have something to do with the fact that, as the self-criticism they include in their volume notes, "the essays that make up the body of this book tend to treat their own core concepts as exogenously given" (Kowert and Legro 1996: 469). To underscore the importance of this point, let me relate it back to our discussion of Durkheim and Weber. In a manner reminiscent of Durkheim, Katzenstein and his colleagues tend to cut into the problem at the level of "collective representations" of ideational social facts, and then trace their impact on behavior. They do not, like Weber, begin with the actual social construction of meanings and significance from the ground up, showing how they came to be "historically *so* and not *otherwise*." It will be recalled that Durkheim, too, felt no need to move beyond the normal science of his day as a result, whereas Weber did.

Having said all that, I nevertheless conclude with the conviction that both of these moves are fruitful. In the hope of gaining at once a deeper and clearer understanding of the structure and functioning of the world polity, neo-utilitarians should strive to expand their analytical foundations, and constructivists should strive for greater analytical rigor and specification. The two approaches are not additive, and they are unlikely to meet and merge on some happy middle ground. But by pushing their respective limits in the direction of the other, we are more likely to discover precisely when one approach subsumes the other, when they represent competing explanations of the same phenomenon, and when one complements or supplements the other (for an excellent beginning, see Jepperson, Wendt, and Katzenstein 1996: 68–72). The stakes are high enough, and the limits of the two approaches inherent and apparent enough, for any claims of universal priority at this point to be entirely unwarranted.

Part I

International organization
"I wouldn't start from here if I were you"

Folklore has handed down numerous versions of the apocryphal story in which a laconic country dweller responds to the lost urbanite's request for directions to the big city with the quip, "I wouldn't start from here if I were you." That advice would also have served well to alert the young scholar who entered the field of international organization in graduate school in the late 1960s, as I did, that the trajectory from its intellectual locale was problematic.

Robert Keohane and Joseph Nye, who were already young Turks in the profession when I came along, challenged the "Everest syndrome" they found in the literature—as they put it, studying international organizations "because they are there" (1972: vii). Indeed, for two decades or so after World War II the presumption was widespread that the field of international organization *is* what international organizations *do*, and that the formal attributes of international organizations, such as charters, voting procedures, committee structures, and the like, account for or at least are the appropriate referents of what they do. When the so-called behavioral revolution first hit this field, it accomplished little more than to render the marginal more rigorously—for example, through exhaustive factor analyses of roll-call voting in the United Nations General Assembly, which at best had limited theoretical or practical significance. Realists discounted the field as not being worthy of serious attention even as they warned of the dangers that its idealist inclinations posed. Neither neorealism nor neoliberal institutionalism had yet been invented. The field of international organization was woefully undertheorized.

There was one major exception to these generalizations: so-called neofunctionalist theory, of which Ernst B. Haas, with whom I studied at Berkeley, was the leading exponent. The analytical scope of neofunctionalism comprised the manner whereby relations among states might come to be organized differently from the dictates of traditional balance of power politics; what roles international organizations and organizational leadership play in that process; and which functional issue areas were most conducive to such a transformation. Haas had worked on decolonization, conflict resolution, the creation of regional common markets, and the internationalization of labor standards. Moreover, he and his followers drew on a wide array of social science literatures, including pluralism, corporatism, and studies of the welfare state, coupled with systems theory and organization theory, and by the then standards of the field they adopted quite rigorous research designs. However, neofunctionalism was framed primarily to detect the possible emergence of state-like political community above the level of the nation state (see Haas 1961 for a reprise). It was, in short, a theory of supranational integration, not of international organization more generally conceived.

A theoretical anchor for the study of international organization needed to be devised. Keohane and Nye approached the problem by taking aim at the "state-centrism" of international relations theory: the assumptions that states are the only significant actors and that they act as coherent units. Within the broader "world politics" paradigm Keohane and Nye proposed, international organizations were depicted as one of the actors in, and one of the venues for, the conduct of "transnational" relations (involving nongovernmental entities) and "transgovernmental" relations (involving sub-units of states). Their conceptual scheme stimulated lively debates and generated interesting empirical work (though Keohane himself later (1983, 1984) abandoned this perspective for a unitary rational actor model within which institutions serve to facilitate cooperation by reducing transaction and information costs).

In some respects my project was less sweeping than the transnationalist challenge, confined to what the British school calls "the society of states" (Bull 1968). Like Haas, I conceived of international organization as the principles, processes, and mechanisms whereby relations among states are organized. I also shared his interest in the nature and possible evolution of international political community. But I jettisoned the neofunctionalist expectation that political community among states necessarily implied organization *above* states, as well as the assumption that functional contexts possess inherent logics which affect that outcome. Thus, I defined the object of my concern not as international integration, but institutionalization. The essays in Part I define and explore the processes of institutionalization and its transformative effects *within* the system of states, while those in Part II address the possible institutional transformation *of* the system of states.

As a starting point for the analysis of institutionalization within the system of states, I stipulated that the international polity circa 1970 constituted a modified Westphalian system: decentralized and largely self-regarding, but within those constraints capable of organizing cooperative activities. And as a first cut at the question of what gets institutionalized and how, I constructed a simple microeconomic model of state choices under resource constraints, in which international organization functioned as a means to compensate for instances of political market failure (excerpted in Chapter 1). This struck me as a plausible metaphorical first approximation of core features of a Westphalian-like system. Thus, my professional

debut took the form of what later became known as neoliberal institutionalism. The assumptions of the model were highly restrictive, but it generated
several cogent hypotheses: most notably, that no snowballing momentum
was built into the process of international institutionalization leading to a
"higher" form of sociopolitical organization.

The puzzles that interested me soon took me away from this microeconomic beginning, however, in a more sociological direction, toward what is
now called social constructivism. The chain of reasoning in the first instance
went something like this: Institutionalization embodies elements of
authority. Authority typically is understood as the conjunction of power and
legitimate social purpose. But social purpose is neither fixed nor exogenously given; and in some measure it is subject to communicative dynamics
among knowledgeable actors. Nor is social purpose a brute or palpable
observational fact; it is an intersubjective state of mind among relevant
social actors, for some issues including society as a whole. Therefore, it
seemed reasonable to require that the analysis of institutionalization reflect
these specific ontological qualities of its component parts.

That inference entailed two further implications, one concerning the definition of core concepts, the other being epistemological. Core concepts, it
followed, had to be defined in such a way as to tap into these intersubjective
elements. Accordingly, I proposed two forms by which international relations are institutionalized in ways not captured by the conventional
understanding of international organizations: epistemic communities, of
which, I suggested, the modified Westphalian system itself is a deep expression, and regimes, or convergent norms and expectations that coordinate
collaborative behavior (also excerpted in Chapter 1). In addition, core
concepts had to reflect not only the nominal but also the normative meanings of institutional forms. Thus, I defined multilateralism, for example, not
merely by virtue of encompassing three or more states but also as
embodying certain normative principles for organizing the relations among
those states, above all generalizable and non-discriminatory norms (see
Chapter 4).

The epistemological implication had to do with the problem that the
intersubjective dimension of institutionalization as I conceived of it—and
ideational factors more generally—fit poorly into the mechanical notions of
causality and explanatory protocols that came to occupy a central place in
international relations theorizing, because they were formulated for a world
of brute facts. So I made a plea for, and endeavored to apply empirically,
more interpretive epistemological strains that ultimately were rooted in, as
was my understanding of institutionalization itself, the work of Max Weber.

Part I consists of four chapters. Two are purely theoretical. Chapter 1
defines my analytical points of departure, indicating why and how international institutionalization takes place among, not above, states, as well as
why and how institutionalization inescapably involves elements of intersubjectivity. Chapter 3 explores the epistemological implications of this stance,

and describes the main features of interpretive techniques and explanatory protocols.

The other two chapters are more empirical, illustrating my constructivist conceptions at work. The essay in Chapter 2 devised a formulation of the post-World War II international economic order that predicted far greater stability than was held likely by the prevailing wisdom when it was published in 1982, as a result of examining its basis not only in the domain of international power but also authority. On the same grounds, the essay anticipated that the most serious challenge to future stability would come not from producer-initiated protectionism, as was widely believed, but from a resurgence of neo-laissez faire attitudes toward the role of the state in the domestic economy. Thus, this early constructivist venture produced a relatively novel interpretation at the time and one that still resonates today, when the relationship between economic globalization and the shredding of domestic safety nets has become a serious social concern throughout the capitalist world.

The essay in Chapter 4, published more recently, explores the relationship between international organization and international political community, centered on the institution of multilateralism. It is, in a sense, a summing up on the "big" question with which the international organization part of my project began in the first place. It took as its point of reference the durability and adaptability of the international order in the face of the fundamental changes triggered by the collapse of the Soviet system. By now, my main protagonists had become neorealists and neoliberal institutionalists, the one believing that institutions matter little, the other paying little attention to their normative meanings. In contrast to the former, the essay contends that the efficacy of international community has, indeed, become enhanced in the second half of the twentieth century, albeit modestly and unevenly, and that international organization is implicated in that fact. In contrast to the latter, the essay seeks to show that the mechanism whereby this transformation has occurred is the institutionalization of a growing sphere of international relations based not merely on some generic demand for institutional routines, but on the specific normative features of multilateral organizing principles.

1 The new institutionalism in international relations

This first section of this chapter is based on 1972a, the rest on 1975b, supplemented by brief excerpts from 1972b and 1978a. Though the two core articles were written at different times and for different purposes, they were part of a systematic effort to reconceptualize the fundamental features of international organization.

Devising a simple microeconomic formulation of choice under constraints, extended by the analytics of collective goods, 1972a sought to show how unlikely it was that the process of international organization would approximate the expectation that it was part of some evolutionary trend whereby authority was transferred to ever higher and more encompassing political entities.

The 1975b article challenged another assumption of the traditional literature, that international organization is what international organizations do. Drawing on sociological and organization theory, it suggested that international institutionalization could take the form of "epistemic communities" and "regimes" as well as formal organizations. In addition, the article developed a conception of international authority that was consistent with a "modified Westphalian" view of the international polity.

Finally, the discussion of structure throughout, and most explicitly in 1972b, reflected thinking in a variety of fields on the inadequacy of prevailing "pyramidal" models of social structure, ranging from organization theory to urban planning and the beginnings of post-modernist literary theory.

Each article drew on illustrative cases from international cooperation in science, technology and the human environment in the 1960s and early 1970s; 1975b was the introductory essay to an edited volume on that subject. I have omitted most of these empirical references because they are dated, leaving mainly the exposition of key concepts. In addition, the microeconomic model in 1972a is presented here in narrative form only; a more elaborate technical exposition seemed necessary in the original because the approach was relatively novel at the time. None of the sections reproduced have been substantively altered however.

Waltz (1979: 197) used the word "deft" to describe 1972a, which is still cited as a Model-T on the road to neoliberal institutionalism, though my own interests subsequently led me to take a different theoretical direction. Keohane generously wrote about 1975b that it "foreshadowed much of the conceptual work of the next decade" (1990b: 755).

As a field of study, international organization has always concerned itself with the same phenomenon: in the words of a classic text (Mower 1931), it is an attempt to describe and explain "how the modern Society of Nations governs itself." In that text, the essence of "government" was assumed to comprise the coordination of group activities so as to conduct the public business, and the particular feature distinguishing international government was taken to lie in the necessity that it be consistent with national sovereignty. Few contemporary treatments of international organization differ significantly from this definition.

At the same time, the literature suffers the debilitating effects of two sets of assumptions. The strong version of the first is that international organization *is* whatever international organizations *do* (Claude 1956, 1971 is a rare text that casts its analytical net more broadly). The weak version is that international organizations are closely involved in the process of international governance. The strong version is debilitating because it rules out too much, above all the many informal and tacit ways by which states conduct their "public business" collectively. And the weak version offers no formulation of the broader process of governance in which international organizations may—or may not—be involved, thus providing no basis for assessing their actual roles and importance.

In recent years, and to some extent all along, thinking about international organization has also been strongly shaped by "functionalist" premises, the belief that specialized international structures evolve in a quasi-automatic manner to perform new tasks or fulfill new needs as they arise (see Sewell 1966 for a good review). This is especially the case in considerations of the impact of science and technology on international relations, where technocratic and ecological "imperatives" loom large. The boldest variant of functionalism actually posits the existence of evolutionary trends: that in reacting and adapting to its environment, humanity will build for itself ever-higher forms of sociopolitical organization, from tribes to baronies, from national states to global authorities:

> The long-run trend toward integration seems to be for functions, authority and loyalties to be transferred from smaller units to larger ones; from states to federations; from federations to supranational unions; and from these to super-systems.
>
> (Etzioni 1966: 147)

Neofunctionalism is the least presumptuous and most social-scientific variant of functionalism in international relations theory (see Haas 1966 for an overview). Nevertheless, even though shorn of teleology, neofunctionalism still attributes significant existential autonomy to the integrative potential of "functional contexts." But functional contexts do not exist apart from particular configurations of actor attributes in relation to any given issue: different actors' differing objectives, pursued with unequally distributed resources, define "functional" contexts. In addition, neofunctionalism still retains the implausible working hypothesis that state-like forms of organization will emerge at the level "beyond the nation state" (Haas 1964).

As models of the process of international organization, all versions of functionalism ultimately rest on an apolitical understanding of "how the modern Society of Nations governs itself." And as models of the structure of international organization, they hold the expectation that international governance ultimately will conform to hierarchically ordered relations between superordinate and subordinate units, characteristic of Weber's rational–legal notion of domestic authority. The problem with both premises is that, at bottom, they are inconsistent with national sovereignty and the structure of the modern world polity.[1] As a result, the enterprise is doomed to theoretical and practical failure by its very nature.

I, too, am interested in the possibility of new international policies and arrangements, in new aims and expectations that national actors may come to hold, and in new forms of global sociopolitical organization. But I do not equate international organization with the activities of international organizations, and I make no assumptions about policies or institutions evolving in quasi-automatic fashion from new functional contexts or springing from new and inherently international needs. My starting point is the international political system as it is. Given that perspective, the relevant questions about international organization become: When and how do states choose to organize activities internationally? What particular modes of organization—coordination, collaboration, integration—are selected under what conditions? And what are their consequences for the manner in which political life is organized, both nationally and internationally?

This chapter is organized as follows. The first section sketches out a model of the core logic of choice under different kinds of constraints that characterizes national decisions about international organization in a system governed by national sovereignty. The second section proposes a conceptual framework for analyzing the forms in which states' decisions to organize internationally become institutionalized collectively. And the third section develops an understanding of authority relations that remains consistent with the structure of the international polity and yet allows for the possibility that international authority will emerge from the processes of institutionalization.

CHOICE

The contemporary interstate system is here viewed as a modified Westphalia system (Gross 1968; Falk 1969). Since the Peace of Westphalia, the interstate system, in principle, has been a decentralized one: states are subject to no external earthly authority, and there exists no organization above states, only between them. The Westphalia system consists of a multiplicity of independent states, each sovereign within its territory, and each legally equal to every other. This system recognizes only one organizing principle, the will of states, thereby giving the collective decision-making system its decentralized character. In practice, the Westphalia system has become partially but progressively modified: spheres of influence modify the principle of equality; supranational actors modestly modify the principle of no external earthly superior authority; an ever more complex pattern of interconnectedness of decisions, events, and developments modifies the principle of independence. And to the extent that states subsequently "will" collective principles and forms of decision-making, the decentralized character of the system is itself modified—much as a market economy is modified by governmental intervention and regulation. In fact, one can sensibly speak of an interstate system only insofar as the systematic collective organization of activities exists, however informal or minimal it may be.

The general model

Our analysis of the process of international organization will begin with the least complex case: one state producing one good (performing one task); and the least complex issue: what combination of international and national efforts that state will choose in doing so. In the modified Westphalian world described above, a state can be expected to tend toward international production to the extent it lacks sufficient capabilities to produce the good itself. The state's resources may be inadequate because it does not have enough of them, or because the extant definition of property rights places the source of the problem within the jurisdiction of another. International, for the time being, will refer to any non-national form.

At the same time, however, cooperating with and thereby becoming dependent on others for the production of a good itself poses a problem for the state by giving rise to "interdependence costs" (Buchanan and Tullock 1962), reckoned in such terms as circumscribed options or general loss of autonomy. These costs are incurred over and above the more direct payments, to whatever institutional arrangement the state has selected, for the actual production costs. Given our assumptions, even though interdependence costs may not appear significant or may not be calculable for any one particular instance, over the long run a state is expected to keep these costs to the least necessary level. Hence, in calculating whether to organize activities internationally, a state will include not only the direct gains and the direct costs of producing a good with others, but also the overall interdependence costs of international organization.

Thus we arrive at our basic proposition: the propensity for international organization will be determined by the interplay between the need to become dependent on others for the production of a specific good (or performance of a specific task), and the general desire to keep that dependence to the minimum level necessary. And the equilibrium point for the state under consideration is defined where the marginal benefit gained by one extra unit of international production, less the extra cost of producing it internationally (direct and interdependence costs), equals zero (Bator 1957).

A number of important corollaries follow from this basic proposition. First, and comparing states with different levels of capabilities, there will be an inverse relationship between the ratio of international over national production (i/n) and the total level of national capabilities: smaller (less capable) states will exhibit a higher ratio of i/n; larger (more capable) states, a lower ratio. Second, it follows that as the capabilities of states change over time so, too, will the ratio of i/n: as national capabilities increase, the ratio will decrease.

Hence—and most critically—built into the international performance of any given task is a process of encapsulation, ending in a situation where no further commitments are made, and in which no further increase in the scope of the collective arrangement nor in its institutional capacity occurs. The processes of "task-expansion" and "spillover" that neofunctionalists expect cannot take place, therefore, unless the factors held constant in our model are also shown to change. Thus, to predict the growth of collective arrangements internationally, it will not do simply to point to new problems that states will face (such as those generated by science, technology, or the human environment), and then to posit new tasks for international arrangements. For unless the constants also change, such growth will be truncated.*

Collective goods

This general model describes only an exceedingly restrictive case: no direct interaction between states; completely undifferentiated tasks or activities; and in which the international organizational arrangement is simply any non-national form. Yet we know that the activities of one state are affected by others and, in turn, have consequences for others—that there is a collective dimension to the behavior of states. And we know that different kinds of activities lead to different forms of organizational arrangements internationally. Here I will seek to demonstrate, in a manner consistent with the general model, that different kinds of activities will lead to different organizational forms—not because of a priori substantive differences, however, but because of the impact the collective dimension of states' behavior may exhibit.

According to the classical definitions, goods and services are of two polar types: purely private or purely collective, or public (Samuelson 1945; Head 1962; Buchanan 1968). Purely private goods and services can be parceled out among different individuals in such a way that the total quantity available to the group equals the sum of the quantities available to the

---

* In the original (1972a: Tables 1 and 2), these propositions were illustrated statistically by correlations between the ratio of international over national governmental research and development expenditures, and national capabilities (percentage of GNP devoted to R and D), globally and for a European sub-sample; as well as by changes in the ratio of international over national distribution of development assistance over time as national capabilities (GNP) increased (no comparative time series of R & D expenditures were available). The correlation coefficients ranged from modest to strong and were statistically significant.

individuals within the group. Purely collective goods are common to the group in that their benefits are perfectly indivisible among the separate individuals, so that the total quantity available to the group is precisely the same as that available to any member of the group, and no one individual's consumption of the good in any way subtracts from the consumption of it by any other.

Thus, were A's production of a good to exhibit the attributes of pure publicness, the benefits of A's activity would be extended to each and every member of the entire system. If those benefiting from A's production fail to pay for those benefits, and if state A acts in accordance with our assumptions, then A would cease the activity that provides the collective benefits, or seek to have their production organized collectively. In its pure form, public goods would appear to be limited to very special cases indeed. A closer examination of the concept reveals two major dimensions, however, yielding a more discrete and more broadly applicable fourfold classification.

The first dimension of a collective good is that it may be "indivisible" or in "joint supply." By joint supply is meant that once the good or service is produced or performed, for and by one producer, its extension to others is facilitated: once produced, any given unit of the good can be made equally available to all. And, up to a point, its extension to any additional individual does not imply a corresponding reduction in the quantity of the good available to others (Head 1962: 201–207). Simply because such an indivisibility exists, however, does not necessarily imply that the good *must* be made equally available to all; it may be perfectly possible to exclude outsiders. It means only that the opportunity cost of extending the good or service to any additional individual may be negligible.

There is a second basic dimension of a collective good. It may, in fact, be impossible to exclude others from sharing, or to charge them the full cost of sharing, the benefits of the good. (Or it may be impossible to exclude oneself from the suffering caused by the production of a good by others, or to obtain compensation for such suffering.) Here, a state would confront an "impossibility of exclusion," or a "nonappropriability of costs" (ibid.). But impossibility of exclusion or nonappropriability of costs do not necessarily mean that the good in question is in joint supply; in the technical sense the good may be perfectly divisible. What is implied is that there exist "imperfections in property titles," making it impossible to contain benefits or exclude suffering.

These two dimensions of a collective good yield a fourfold classification.

(1) *Divisibility and appropriability*

In the strict sense employed here, A's production of a good or service that is perfectly divisible and from which others can be kept from benefiting (or be charged for benefiting) exhibits no collective dimension whatever. Yet, it is the production of just these goods and services that accounts for most of the activities of international organizations. This is the case in part for the kinds of reasons explicated in the general model: deficiency of national capabilities. In addition, states may bring to bear various efficiency considerations, such as economies of scale, and therefore seek the collaborative production of a particular good or service. Simply in order to be able to do what they cannot now do, or to do more—or more efficiently—what they are already doing, states may enter into international arrangements that facilitate these objectives.

What kinds of organizational arrangements would these be? Their purpose, clearly, would be to facilitate or enhance particular national capacities—to enlarge the range of what is technically possible for their members. But their role would likely be limited to the simple pooling or coordination of national activities. For given the grounds for entering into such arrangements in the first place, the interdependence costs of more demanding organizational forms would quickly exceed the benefits obtained from them.

(2) *Joint supply and appropriability*

The second case arises when the product of A's activities is in joint supply, in the sense that extension of the good to others is facilitated, even though others can be excluded or charged for it. If other states were of the impression that A would supply the good or service in any case, they would have no incentive to contribute to its production. But even if others were willing to contribute, the opportunity cost of supplying the good or service to the last user might well be negligible. In all probability, A would try to charge average costs, but so long as any state were willing to pay marginal costs a socially suboptimal outcome would exist by excluding any such state. Finding itself in a dilemma of this kind, A has a number of available options: exclude others and ignore the social pressure that may result; extend the good to others and absorb the cost; cease the production and deny itself the benefit of the good; or seek to organize production internationally in the first place, with all contributing from the beginning. Any of these are possible, depending on circumstances.

What kinds of international arrangements would these be? Their purpose would no longer be merely to enhance or facilitate national capabilities or actions. They would also be designed to compensate for the decentralized structure of the interstate decision-making system that created the inefficiencies. Modest forms would include joint observation, surveillance and monitoring, thereby enhancing the transparency of the condition of jointness, and facilitating movement toward greater social efficiency. Where symmetry in jointness among states is approximated (that is, where a number of states are in roughly the same situation), the arrangement may be designed to collect "taxes" to help pay for the production of the good.

(3) *Divisibility and nonappropriability*

The third case that may affect a state's basic propensity toward international organization is that in which the good or service in question is strictly divisible, but because of "imperfections in property titles"—i.e., the nature of political jurisdictions—others cannot be excluded from benefiting from it, or cannot protect themselves from any disservice it might be causing them. If other states are enjoying the benefits of A's production of a good or service and A can in no way exclude them or charge them the cost of partaking, it would be unrealistic—given our assumptions—to expect them to contribute voluntarily. Or, if other states are suffering from A's production of a good or service and cannot exclude themselves from that suffering, it would be unrealistic to expect A voluntarily to offer compensation. In both cases, a divergence between private and social costs results, as A would tend to underproduce the first kind of good, and to overproduce the second.

Organizational arrangements constructed in this context would have still different characteristics. They would be required to compensate for the "imperfections in property titles" that generated the divergence between private and collective costs in the first place. Depending on task-specific contexts, this might range from providing shared information about the difference in private and social costs, to devising off-set formulas, or reconfiguring property rights.

(4) *Joint supply and nonappropriability*

The fourth and final set of characteristics approximates a pure collective good: equal potential availability to all exists once the good or service is provided for one state; and it is impossible to exclude other states from sharing in the benefits (or for other states to protect themselves from the suffering) provided by the good or service. In other words, state A may be providing a good which must be extended to all, or others must suffer from A's production of a good (or "bad," as it would be). To the extent that such situations become relatively symmetrical and costly among states, it would become more likely that the goods in question would be produced internationally, or the common resources at stake subject to some form of collective regulation, or the non-national territory involved put under common ownership.

In sum, the general model explored only the most restrictive set of behavioral and organizational forms. These indicated the general conditions under which joint production and/or regulation would or would not be sought. Here, on the basis of more specific collective effects exhibited by the actions of states, more specific organizational forms were explored. The fourfold classification by no means exhausts the range of possibilities. But, together with the general model, it does facilitate the explication of the fundamental dynamics of international organization, which has been our objective. These formulations suggest that the process of international organization in a world of sovereign states is unlikely to exhibit the logic of functionalism, in any form; and that the task environments of international organizations are defined by the strategic attributes of the goods states have chosen to produce, not any intrinsic feature.

Structural implications

We turn, finally, to some overall structural implications of the process of international organization, so depicted.[†] By structure we mean, following Bronowski (1965: 59), "both a logical and an architectural conception: the recognition of an order among individual pieces in which the pieces are illuminated by their total arrangement." In the language of graph theory, the functionalist image of emerging global "super-systems" conforms to a *tree* (Alexander 1965): a partially ordered collection of sets (previously mutually exclusive social groupings), with every two sets having a least upper bound (arranged hierarchically), and for any two upper bounds one being an upper bound of the other (in the form a pyramid). As powerful a cognitive image as this may be, we await its materialization with the success of Vladimir and Estragon in *Godot*. Far more likely, from the vantage of the process as we have depicted it, is the vanishing of such singular forms into clusters of *lattice-like* arrangements (ibid.; also see Hassan 1971).

Our analysis suggests that the structural dimension of international organization consists of the differentiation and disaggregation of existing forms across states (see Keohane and Nye 1971 for a compatible characterization at the global level, and Caporaso and Pelowski 1971 for the European Community). This devolution is issue-specific and actor-specific. It is asymmetrical, reflecting differences in national capacities to perform different tasks, the differential impact of interdependence costs for different states in different issue areas, and the need for collective arrangements to compensate for different imperfections in the interstate system. Finally, it generates discontinuous clusters of collective arrangements that exist at different levels in the interstate system, In sum, this analysis suggests that the process of international organization is likely to yield complex rearticulations of functional spaces and authority relations, not above, but across states.

INSTITUTIONALIZATION[‡]

Our model of the process of international organization is premised on the principle that in the international arena "objective rights and duties are non-existent, so that no one is entitled to anything, and nothing can be expected

---

[†] This paragraph is taken from 1972b (pp 79, 88), part of the original draft of 1972a, which was too long for a single article
[‡] Except where indicated, the rest of the essay is taken from 1975b.

of anyone" (James 1973: 65). At the same time, however, the area of unpredictability of state behavior clearly is limited, complex relations are pursued within sets of stable expectations, and jurisdictional competencies are allocated to a variety of actors other than states. In other words, despite the nature of the international political system, international behavior is institutionalized. Institutionalization, as sociologists define the term, is said to coordinate and pattern behavior, to channel it in one direction rather than all others that are theoretically and empirically possible. In this section, we develop a richer understanding of the forms of international institutionalization.

We begin with what gets institutionalized. Taking any two actors, A and B, the general answer is those activities that are "relevant to both A and B in their common situation" (Berger and Luckman 1966: 65)—what we shall call the collective situation of groups of states. The collective situation is a social milieu. It does not emerge out of nature but out of patterns of international exchange and domination. The logic of choice outlined in the previous section takes effect only if states act on it. Hence, there is nothing inevitable about any particular collective situation. Each is negotiated by the parties concerned. Each represents an agreement that one particular configuration of attributes and not some other will constitute their collective situation.**

It follows that any given expression of the collective situation will not capture the individual situations of all participants equally well, and it will not conform to the individual situation of any single participant perfectly. Thus, any given collective situation is inherently unstable. It may change as knowledge of cause/effect relations changes, as prevailing configurations of interdependence alter and, of course, as capabilities or objectives change. Each collective situation is, therefore, subject to continued renegotiation, which becomes ever more likely and pressing if and as new individual situations move further away from it.

The concept of collective situation depicts the *problematique* to which states choose to respond: we developed a simple fourfold typology in the previous section. Let us now turn to the institutional forms that states' collective responses will take. We noted at the outset of this essay a common tendency to equate institutionalization with the behavior of formal organizations.[2] This has three adverse analytical consequences.

First, it leads students of international organization to ignore collective behavior not performed by or through international organizations. Second, lacking a conception of the broader institutionalized contexts within which international organizations operate, it is impossible to determine precisely what role they do play. There are cases in which a collectivity is coterminous

** I should have made it clear in the original that I was using the terms "negotiate" and "agreement" in the tacit, sociological sense of Erving Goffman (1973) more than in their formal political or legal meanings, though, of course, I did not rule out the latter

with a particular organization, and there are instances of collectivities that exist without formal organizations altogether. In some cases international organizations play an operational role, in others their task is purely facilitative. But, whatever their role may be, it cannot be determined or its significance assessed without prior knowledge of a broader context. Third, this orientation has led to the misleading "sovereignty at bay" syndrome in the literature, the assumption that what new units gain old units must somehow lose[3]—so that if, for example, international organizations or multinational corporations are becoming more important, other actors, including states, must be becoming less important. The possibility that international organizations, multinational corporations, states, and sub-state actors all may be becoming stronger in an expanding domain of international authority, coexisting as allies as well as competitors, is ruled out.

In defining the collective responses of states, I differentiate three levels of institutionalization: (1) a purely cognitive level, or what I term epistemic communities; (2) sets of mutual expectations, agreed-upon rules, regulations and plans in accordance with which organizational energies and financial commitments are allocated—what I call international regimes; and (3) formal international organizations.[††]

Epistemic communities

Institutionalization involves not only the organizational grids through which behavior is acted out, but also the *epistemes* through which political relationships are visualized. I have borrowed this term from Michel Foucault (1970) to refer to a dominant way of looking at social reality, a set of shared symbols and references, mutual expectations and a mutual predictability of intention. Epistemic communities, then, may be said to consist of interrelated roles that grow up around an *episteme*: they delimit, for their members, the "proper" construction of social reality (cf. Holzner 1972).

What we have called the modified Westphalian system is itself mapped into an epistemic community that derives from the role of representing national public authority internationally. This mapping produces behavior rules that we modeled in the previous section, and which may be summarized roughly as follows. No state goes out of its way to construct international collective arrangements. Where possible, unilateral or bilateral arrangements are preferred. Collective arrangements are turned to only when national objectives cannot be achieved in their absence. Thus, collective arrangements are derivative and their purpose is to compensate for "imperfections" in the state system. Since they are derivative and compen-

---

[††] I subsequently paid little attention to epistemic communities, focusing on regimes and to a lesser extent organizations. Peter Haas (1992b) fleshed out the concept and with a group of colleagues used it productively as an independent variable to help explain patterns of cooperation.

satory, it follows that collective arrangements must not impose a greater cost on states than does the situation to which states are responding. If they do, the continuation of a problem, or the forgoing of an opportunity, is preferable to the collective arrangements designed to respond to the problem or exploit the opportunity. Lastly, future interests are discounted in favor of more immediate ones, and the viability of the collectivity of states is simply an instrument for the viability of individual states.

Posing the issue in this manner permits us to ask whether behavior rules from other epistemic communities—more specialized or more encompassing—are becoming institutionalized among states, and with what effects. These could derive from shared disciplinary paradigms (neoclassical economics, for example), similarities in scientific and technocratic outlooks (such as a cognitive and/or normative commitment to ecological holism), or corresponding bureaucratic positions (networks of finance ministers or central bankers come to mind).

International regimes

The term "regime," as indicated, refers to a set of mutual expectations, rules and regulations, organizational plans, energies, and financial commitments that have been accepted by a group of states.[‡‡] One example of a regime is the international arrangement for safeguarding civilian nuclear materials, involving obligations to submit specified aspects of national behavior to the regime's purview, prescribed rules and practices for national materials accounting, and regulations governing international inspection. Another is the set of mutual expectations, rules, and regulations concerning currency exchange rates, reserves, and the international provision of balance-of-payments financing.

International organizations

International organizations are the most concrete of the three forms of institutionalization. Their general environment includes the principal actors and characteristics of world politics (Cox and Jacobson 1973). Their immediate task–environment consists of the regimes they serve. Thus, international organizations may be visualized as operating within a policy space whose axes are defined by the purposes and instrumentalities of the regimes they serve. Only once we have located an organization in this policy space does it make sense to attempt to assess the significance of its task, for only then do

---

[‡‡] I had employed the concept of regimes in my doctoral dissertation (1974a) and formulated this particular definition in outlining the core concepts that contributors to 1975a were asked to use The concept originated in the field of international law; I blended its narrow and technical legal meaning with broader insights into rules and plans derived from organization theory.

we know what the task contributes to. Apart from this broader policy space, international organizational tasks are indeterminate parts in an undefined whole.[4]

To conclude, the process of institutionalization channels behavior in one direction rather than all others that are theoretically or empirically possible. Instances of institutionalization are situation-specific. That is, they are specific to given sets of actors who stand in specific relation to one another in the context of particular issues. Like the collective situation, the collective response is negotiated. It represents agreement that certain aspects of national behavior, and not others, will be institutionalized internationally. And, also like the collective situation, any given manifestation of collective responses is inherently unstable. Beyond a certain threshold of inertia and sunk costs, it will change as the collective situation is redefined.

Some patterns of association[***]

It is not possible to predict the specific collective responses to any given collective situation. Nevertheless, broad patterns of association may be described that exhibit the trade-offs between interdependencies and interdependence costs described in the first section. The human environment and nuclear non-proliferation serve as illustrations.

One dimension by which the collective situation of states may be described is the locus of any given policy interdependence that exists among them. By this we mean the functional distance of that interdependence from core domestic policy domains. In the case of the environment, for example, the locus of interdependence traditionally has been "external"—we concern ourselves with ours, others with theirs, and no one with the commons. Increasingly, a second type has grown in salience: the externalities of domestic behavior (typically, divisibility and non-appropriability in the language of the previous section). Transborder pollution is a case in point, and was a major issue of contention at the 1972 Stockholm UN Conference on the Human Environment. Yet a third type concerns the delimitation of property rights as between external and internal domains, and the domestic consequences of different formulas for doing so (commons become a case of indivisibility and nonappropriability by virtue of being created). It is illustrated by Canadian initiatives at the UN Law of the Sea Conference to extend functional and non-acquisitive jurisdiction by coastal states based on environmental grounds (Gottlieb and Dalfen 1973), on the belief that a commons-based regime would be less robust. At the other end of the spectrum, what a society can and should do domestically is the issue at stake. At the Bucharest UN Population Conference reproductive habits in the Third

---

[***] This section is drawn from 1978a, pp. 391–392, 397–398, 400–403. The original exposition in 1975b was entirely in terms of the specific case study chapters in 1975a, making it difficult to use here

World were added to the international policy agenda, and at the Rome UN Food Conference the feeding of livestock in the industrial countries joined the list, too. (These were transparency-enhancing strategies designed to encourage states to internalize the social costs of their actions.)

In the future, particularly if projections of the "outer limits" of global ecosystems have any validity, patterns of domestic behavior, consumption, and even life-styles, increasingly will become the focal points of foreign and international policy. Under those circumstances, little can be accomplished directly at the international level as traditionally conceived; the solution increasingly involves facilitating appropriate internal change. The first step toward that end is to strengthen the domestic constituencies that have an interest in as well as the ability to help bring about such internal changes— as the preparatory and follow-up processes of the Stockholm conference did by occasioning the proliferation of national environmental ministries, whereas only a handful had previously existed.

Shifts in collective situations along this axis from "external" to "domestic" policy domains ultimately should be reflected in the character of collective responses. So long as the locus of policy interdependence remains external, we would expect states to institutionalize relatively undemanding purposes into their collective response: for example, conducting additional research in various environmental issues. Movement along the axis implies steps toward more demanding purposes, including coordination, regulation, or prohibition. These changes are unlikely to be unidirectional, however, because, in keeping with our general model, we would also expect states to compensate for more demanding *purposes* by reducing interdependence costs elsewhere: by circumscribing the *instrumentality* of the collective response, for example. Thus, a move toward a regulatory purpose in the first instance may be coupled with limiting the collective instrumentality to monitoring national behavior and counting on self-enforcement. Furthermore, whereas a formal organization might have performed an operational or managerial role at the external end of the axis, at the domestic end it is likely to be limited to a forum role. And so on. Should the intensity of any particular problem increase, this cycle starts all over again. Ultimately, this process may end with fairly demanding collective responses, but always in a fragmentary, and never in a unidirectional, manner.

Such compensatory moves are broadly illustrated by the nuclear safeguarding regime. The pre-Nonproliferation Treaty (NPT) arrangement was applicable to specific installations in countries that received international assistance of nuclear materials or technology. For those, the regime included unprecedented authority of inspection by the International Atomic Energy Agency (IAEA). The post-NPT arrangement is applicable to entire domestic nuclear industries in signatory nonweapon states, thereby being broader in scope. But the role of the IAEA under the NPT is reduced to verifying that national self-inspection systems are operating properly and in accordance with standards that are collectively formulated. Neither arrangement, we should note, was designed to prevent the diversion of nuclear materials—that is to say, to regulate directly what states do domestically. They are purely transparency-enhancing in that they are charged with reporting instances of diversion to the UN Security Council—where, however, no protocol is in place on how to respond.

These and similar patterns of association in other instances indicate that considerable fluidity exists in the mixing and matching of collective responses to collective situations; that the underlying logic, nevertheless, exhibits strong signs of the type of dynamic we modeled in the previous section; that the cumulative effects of constructing and modifying international arrangements may well lead to more demanding forms over time; but that it is virtually inconceivable that these would reflect any linear evolutionary pattern toward some overarching international whole.

INTERNATIONAL AUTHORITY†††

One final step is required in our reconceptualization of the process and structure of international organization. It concerns the issue of authority, the essence of governance internationally no less than domestically. Over time, stable patterns of institutionalized behavior within any collectivity come to embody elements of authority. International collectivities are no exception in this regard. But if, as we have implied, international authority is not likely to move along a decentralization–centralization axis, or from states to some higher entity, how can there be international authority?

Some would argue that international authority exists only in restrictive contexts. Harry Eckstein (1973), in a conceptual effort to define political science as the study of authority patterns, would inadvertently *exclude* from the domain of political science the most common of all international political relationships: those among formal equals. Supranational integration is one of the few areas of international relations that would qualify for inclusion on Eckstein's criteria. Why? Because Eckstein adopts the usual conception of authority, as existing only within formal superordinate and subordinate relations: denoting the power of one to command and the duty of another to obey. Supranational integration is one of the few instances of such formal hierarchies of authority in the international realm, hence only it qualifies. But must the very *concept* of authority necessarily be synonymous with any particular *manifestation* of it? If not, how ought we to conceive of international authority?

What we are confronted with in the literature is a fusion of the idea of authority with the particular form in which it has been historically expressed within the highly bureaucratized and legalistic Western societies. The context for which the rational–legal Weberian notion of authority was developed

---

††† This section returns to 1975b.

was, of course, one of the unequal distribution of formal authority among layers of superordinates and subordinates in bureaucratic settings. It is usually expressed by the ideal-type of a pyramid (Weber 1946). If we are to portray international authority adequately, however, a separation of concept and manifestation must first be effected.

The seminal works of Chester Barnard (1938) and Peter Blau (1963) suggest an alternative path. In his more recent reformulation of the Weberian concept, Blau argues that Weber's exposition includes three fundamental criteria for the existence of authority. First, authority is distinguished from other forms of *power* by, quoting Weber, a "certain minimum of voluntary submission, by an obedience which is voluntary rather than stimulated by coercion" (Blau 1963: 306). Second, authority is distinguished from other means of *persuasion* by the a priori suspension of judgment on the part of subordinates, without having to be convinced that the superordinate is correct. Lastly, authority is distinguished from other means of *control* by the presence of a belief system that socially legitimates the exercise of control by the superior and makes it illegitimate to refuse his or her commands.

Weber tended to assume the presence of *some* form of authority as a given, and therefore did not elaborate at length the processes whereby legitimate authority develops from other forms of power, persuasion, and control. Blau's analysis, and the work of Barnard before him, go a long way toward supplying the missing links. Despite the existence of many and varied instruments of power, persuasion, and control available to superordinates, Blau argues, *legitimate* authority will develop only to the extent that a superordinate is perceived to further the common interests of subordinates to remain under his or her control. This common interest will be expressed in shared loyalty to the superior, Blau continues, "and in group norms making compliance with his directives an obligation enforced by the subordinates themselves." Thus:

> structural constraints rooted in the collectivity of subordinates rather than instruments of power or influence wielded by the superior himself enforce compliance with his directives. To discharge its joint obligations to the superior, the group of subordinates is under pressure to make compliance with his directives part of the common norms, which are internalized by its members, and which are socially enforced by them against potential deviants.
>
> (Blau 1963: 312)

Barnard had carried this line of reasoning toward a still more radical— and for us, even more useful—conclusion, by separating the idea of authority from superordinate and subordinate relations altogether. First, he maintained, the concept of authority has no meaning apart from a specific order of relations that was voluntarily created or entered into: "authority is always concerned with something *within* a definitely organized system" (Barnard 1938: 172). Moreover, within such an order of relations the ultimate basis of authority is subjective; that is, it resides in the individual actor to whom "an order" is addressed. Is the "order" compatible with that actor's understanding of the purpose of the collectivity? Is it consistent with his or her individual interests as a member of that collectivity? If so, an inducement to the actor exists to accept the order (ibid.: 166). Lastly, and for us most critically, Barnard contends that authority does not become externalized and transferred as a result of routinization or other means of institutionalization. Ultimately, its basis remains with the individual actor: "no absolute or external authority can compel the necessary effort beyond a minimum insufficient to maintain efficient or effective organizational performance . . . Authority lies always with him to whom it applies" (ibid.: 182–183). In other words, "Authority is another name for the willingness and capacity of individuals to submit to the necessities of cooperative systems" (ibid.: 184).

Adopting the Barnard/Blau perspective allows us to propose a very different conception of international authority than one requiring formal super/subordinate relations. To the extent that an international regime furthers the interests of state actors, a sense of joint obligation within it may emerge. To the extent that joint obligations emerge, norms of compliance may follow. And to the extent that norms of compliance follow and are incorporated into the determinants of national decisions, the institutionalization of authority within that particular regime has taken place. But it would be incorrect to argue that the regime, therefore, acts as a superordinate vis-à-vis its members. Why? Because the institutionalization of authority takes place at the level of the state, and because jurisdiction is not transferred to some other entity but is exercised collectively by states. Thus, international authority may be conceived as a *transordinate* structure, in contradistinction to superordinate and subordinate structures.[5]

In conclusion, a possible "end point" of international institutionalization is, indeed, the emergence of authority relations, as prior literature in international organization has led us to expect. But only in special and limited cases will the structure of those authority relations conform to traditional expectations. International authority is far more likely to take the form of specific clusters of obligations and norms of compliance that are incorporated within states and instituted in relations of mutual accountability among states. But it is authority nonetheless: the willingness and capacity of states to submit to the necessities of cooperative systems.

2 Embedded liberalism and the postwar economic regimes

The concept of international regimes became a major focal point of institutionalist analysis from the late 1970s on. This was due initially to the first sustained use of it in an important book by Keohane and Nye (1977), and to the efforts of Krasner (1983), who convened a group of scholars to hammer out common definitions and produce a set of analytical and empirical studies based on them. The present chapter is a shortened version of my contribution to that collaborative project (1982a).

This essay differed in two related respects from the prevailing understanding in the literature of the issues it addressed. First, the liberal character of the postwar regimes for money and trade was almost uniformly attributed to American hegemony. US hegemony, in turn, was widely believed to be in decline. Hence, a move away from liberalism toward neomercantilist practices was frequently predicted. Second, the theoretical warrant for this argument was informed by a comparison with the rise and decline of nineteenth-century British hegemony and the corresponding fate of that liberal international economic order.

In contrast, I noted that the two international economic orders were quite different: laissez-faire liberalism in the nineteenth century and embedded liberalism in the postwar era—adapting this term from Karl Polanyi's profound analysis of the collapse of laissez-faire. Moreover, I argued that interstate hegemony, in any case, does not account for such substantive features of international economic orders. They are the product of state–society relations in the economic powers that matter. State–society relations express shared social purposes regarding the appropriate role of authority vis-à-vis the market: the nineteenth-century laissez-faire state and the postwar interventionist state, in the two instances under discussion. Thus, to the extent that economic regimes continue to express shared social purposes they have an authoritative basis that functions apart from the configuration of interstate power—an inference that followed directly from the analysis of authority in the previous essay. The instruments of the regimes may change as power shifts, I concluded, but their underlying objectives and normative structure should remain relatively stable unless their authoritative basis in domestic state–society relations also erodes—which, I suggested, had not yet happened.

After some initial skepticism, the embedded liberalism concept gained broad currency and even found its way into non-academic writings (Mead 1987; Kuttner 1991) It has recently been (re)discovered by economists and policy analysts concerned with the possibility that adverse domestic effects attributed to economic globalization may undermine public support for the international trade regime even as producer-based protectionist demands have receded due to globalization (Bhagwati 1997; Kapstein 1996; Rodrik 1997; also see Ruggie 1996a: chaps. 5–6)

International regimes have been defined as social institutions around which actor expectations converge in a given area of international relations (Young 1980; Krasner 1983). Accordingly, as is true of any social institution, international regimes limit the discretion of their constituent units to decide and act on issues that fall within the regime's domain. And, as is also true of any social institution, ultimate expression in converging expectations and delimited discretion gives international regimes an intersubjective quality. To this extent, international regimes are akin to language; and language is inherently "dialogical," in that it must be shared to be effective. The constituent units of a regime, like speakers of a common language, generally have little difficulty in determining what even an entirely new usage signifies. Should it be technically inappropriate or incorrect, they nevertheless may still "understand" it—in the dual sense of being able to comprehend it and willing to acquiesce in it (cf. Chomsky 1964: chap. 1).

Thus, it follows that we know international regimes not simply by some descriptive inventory of their concrete elements, but also by their generative grammar, the underlying principles of order and meaning that shape the manner of their formation and transformation. Likewise, we know deviations from regimes not simply by a categorical description of acts that are undertaken, but also by the intentionality and acceptability others attribute to those acts in the context of an intersubjective framework of meaning.

The analytical components of international regimes, following Krasner (1983), we take to consist of principles, norms, rules, and procedures. As the content for each of these terms is specified, regimes diverge from social institutions like language, for we do not normally attribute to language any "consummatory" as opposed to "instrumental" values (Weber 1978: 24–26). Insofar as regimes, on Kranser's definition, embody principles about fact, causation, and rectitude, as well as rights and obligations that participants regard as legitimate, they fall toward the consummatory end of the spectrum, into the realm of political authority. Thus, the formation and transformation of international regimes may be said to represent a concrete manifestation of the internationalization of authority, as discussed in the previous essay.

What is the "generative grammar" that shapes the internationalization of authority? The most common interpretation has been stated succinctly by Kenneth Waltz (1979: 88): the elements of international authority, he maintains, "are barely once removed from the capability that provides [their] foundation." On this interpretation others, in turn, have built what now amounts to the prevailing theory of international economic regimes, known as "hegemonic stability" (the relevant literature is reviewed in Keohane 1980). In its simplest form, the theory makes this prediction: if economic capabilities are so concentrated that a hegemon exists, as in the case of Great Britain in the mid-to-late nineteenth century and the United States after World War II, an "open" or "liberal" international economic order will come into being. In the organization of a liberal order, pride of place is given to market rationality. This is not to say that authority is absent from such an order. It is to say that authority relations are constructed in such a way as to give maximum scope to market forces rather than to constrain them. Specific regimes that serve such an order, in the areas of money and trade, for example, limit the discretion of self-seeking states to intervene in the functioning of self-regulating currency and commodity markets. Accordingly, they may be termed "strong" regimes. And their strength, of course, is backed by the capabilities of the hegemon. If, and as, such a concentration of economic capabilities erodes, the liberal order is expected to unravel and its regimes to weaken, ultimately being replaced by mercantilist arrangements, that is, by arrangements under which the constituent units yield to domestic pressures and reassert national political direction over transnational economic forces. If the international economic order established by British supremacy in the nineteenth century and that reflecting American supremacy after World War II illustrate liberal orders with strong regimes, the interwar period illustrates the darker corollary of the axiom.

I do not claim that this theory is fundamentally wrong. But it does not take us very far in understanding international economic regimes, and, by extension, the formation and transformation of international regimes in general. This is so precisely because it does not encompass the intersubjective dimensions of international regimes.

In contrast, I develop two theoretical arguments, each of which yields an interpretation of central features of the postwar international economic order that differs from the prevailing view.

The first concerns the "generative grammar" of international authority. Whatever its institutional manifestations, political authority represents a fusion of power with legitimate social purpose. The prevailing interpretation of international authority focuses on power only; it ignores the dimension of social purpose—more specifically, it either assumes social purpose (Waltz 1979) or seeks to deduce it from state power (Krasner 1976). The problem with this formulation is that power may predict the *form* of the international order, but not its *content*.

For example, in the era of the third hegemon in the complex of modern state-system and capitalist-world-economy, the Dutch in the seventeenth century, the condition of hegemony coexisted with mercantilist behavior (Wallerstein 1980: chap. 2). It would strain credulity to attribute this difference solely or even mainly to differences in the relative economic supremacy of the three hegemons without discussing differences in social purpose. Moreover, had the Germans succeeded in their quest to establish a "New International Order" after World War II, the designs Hjalmar Schacht would have instituted were the very mirror image of Bretton Woods (Hirschman 1945). Obviously, differences in social purpose again provide the key. Lastly, the common tendency to equate the nineteenth-century liberal international economic order and its post-World War II counterpart itself obscures exceedingly important differences in their domestic and international organization, differences that stem from the fact that the one represented laissez-faire liberalism and the other did not.

In sum, to say anything sensible about the *content* of international economic orders and about the regimes that serve them, it is necessary to look at how power and legitimate social purpose become fused to project political authority into the international system. Applied to the post-World War II context, this argument leads me to characterize the international economic order by the term "embedded liberalism," which I show to differ from both its classical ancestor and its ignominious predecessor even as it has systematically combined central features of both.

My second theoretical argument concerns the occurrence of change in and of regimes. The prevailing model postulates one source of regime change, the ascendancy or decline of economic hegemons, and two directions of regime change, greater openness or closure. If, however, we allow for the possibility that power and purpose do not necessarily covary, then we have two potential sources of change and no longer any simple one-to-one correspondence between source and direction of change. For example, we could have a situation in which a predominant economic power exists whose economic program differs fundamentally from that of its leading rivals— e.g., Dutch supremacy in the seventeenth century. Or, we could have a situation in which power and purpose covary negatively, that is, in which neither a hegemon nor a congruence of social purpose exists among the leading economic powers (the interwar period approximates this case). We could have a situation in which power and purpose covary positively—e.g., Bretton Woods. There remains the situation of no hegemon but a congruence of social purpose among the leading economic powers—albeit imperfectly, the post-1971 international economic order illustrates this possibility.

It is the last possibility that interests me most. It suggests the need for a more nuanced formulation of regime change than is currently available. If and as the concentration of economic power erodes, and the "strength" of international regimes is sapped thereby, we may be sure that the instruments of regimes also will have to change. However, as long as purpose is held constant, there is no reason to suppose that the normative structure of regimes must change as well. In other words, referring back to our analytical components of international regimes, rules and procedures (instruments) would change but principles and norms (normative structure) would not. Presumably, the new instruments that would emerge would be better adapted to the new power situation in the international economic order. But insofar as they continued to reflect the same sense of purpose, they would represent a case of norm-governed as opposed to norm-transforming change.

Applying this argument to the post-1971 period leads me to suggest that many of the changes that have occurred in the regimes for money and trade have been norm-governed changes rather than, as is usually maintained, reflecting the collapse of Bretton Woods and a headlong rush into neo-mercantilism. Indeed, in certain cases earlier acts by the hegemon had violated the normative frameworks of these regimes, so that some post-1971 changes may be viewed as adaptive restorations of prior sets of norms in the context of a new and different international economic environment. Both occurrences may be taken to demonstrate what we might call "the relative autonomy" of international regimes (with due apologies to the appropriate quarters).

The two parts of my argument stand or fall together. Ultimately, they rest on my depiction of international authority as reflecting a fusion of power and legitimate social purpose. A historical illustration of this interpretation of international authority, therefore, serves as my point of departure.

POWER AND SOCIAL PURPOSES

In his magisterial work, *The Great Transformation*, Karl Polanyi drew a distinction between "embedded" and "disembedded" economic orders: "normally, the economic order is merely a function of the social, in which it is contained. Under neither tribal, nor feudal, nor mercantile conditions was there . . . a separate economic system in society. Nineteenth century society, in which economic activity was isolated and imputed to a distinctive economic motive, was, indeed, a singular departure" (1944: 71). The best known international forms taken by this "singular departure" were, of course, the regimes of free trade and the gold standard. What were their bases?

The internationalization of domestic state–society relations

Charles Kindleberger, who is justly accorded a leading role in having established the "hegemonic stability" theory in his book on the Great Depression (1973), subsequently managed to write an account of the rise of free trade in western Europe without so much as mentioning British economic supremacy as a possible explanation (Kindleberger 1975). He focused instead on a fundamental reordering of the relationships between domestic political authority and economic processes. Free trade, he reminds us, was due first of all to the general breakdown of the manor and guild system and the so-called policy of supply, through which a complex structure of social regulations rather than market exchange had determined the organization of economic activity at home and abroad. Indeed, the earliest measures undertaken in order to free trade were to dismantle prohibitions on *exports*, prohibitions that had restricted the outward movement of materials, machinery, and artisans. The bulk of these prohibitions was not removed until well into the 1820s and 1830s, and in some instances even later. A second part of the stimulus "came from the direct self-interest of particular dominant groups" (ibid.: 50). In the Netherlands, these were merchants, shipowners, and bankers; in Great Britain, the manufacturing sectors backed by the intellectual hegemony established by the Manchester School; in France, largely industrial interests employing imported materials and equipment in production, though they would not have succeeded against the weight of countervailing interests had not Louis Napoleon imposed free trade for unrelated reasons of international diplomacy; in Prussia, grain and timber exporters, though Bismarck was not averse to using trade treaties in the pursuit of broader objectives, and free trade treaties seemed to be *au courant*; in Italy, the efforts of Cavour, which prevailed over disorganized opposition. Equally particularistic factors were at work in Belgium, Denmark, Norway, Sweden, Spain, and Portugal.

But how did such diverse forces come to converge on the single policy response of free trade? In a certain sense, Kindleberger contends, Europe in this period should be viewed not as a collection of separate economies, but "as *a single entity* which moved to free trade for ideological or perhaps better doctrinal reasons" (ibid.: 51, emphasis added). The image of the market became an increasingly captivating social metaphor and served to focus diverse responses on the outcome of free trade. And unless one holds that ideology and doctrine exist in a social vacuum, this ascendancy of market rationality in turn must be related to the political and cultural ascendance of the middle classes. In Polanyi's inimitable phrase, therefore, "Laissez-faire was planned" (1944: 141).

In sum, this shift in what we might call the balance between "authority" and "market" fundamentally transformed state–society relations, by redefining the legitimate social purposes in pursuit of which state power was expected to be employed in the domestic economy. The role of the state became to institute and safeguard the self-regulating market. To be sure, this shift occurred unequally throughout western Europe, and at uneven tempos. And of course nowhere did it take hold so deeply and for so long a period as in Great Britain. Britain's supremacy in the world economy had much to do with the global expansion of this new economic order, and even more with its stability and longevity. But the authority relations that were instituted in the international regimes for money and trade reflected a new balance of state–society relations that expressed a collective reality.

These expectations about the proper scope of political authority in economic relations did not survive World War I. Despite attempts at restoration, by the end of the interwar period there remained little doubt about how thoroughly they had eroded. Polanyi looked back over the period of the "twenty years' crisis" from the vantage point of the World War II —at the emergence of mass movements from the Left and the Right throughout Europe, the revolutionary and counter-revolutionary upheavals in central and eastern Europe in the 1917–20 period, the British General Strike of 1926, and, above all, the rapid succession of the abandonment of the gold standard by Britain, the instituting of the Five Year Plans in the Soviet

Union, the launching of the New Deal in the United States, unorthodox budgetary policies in Sweden, *corporativismo* in Fascist Italy, and *Wirkschaftslenkung* followed by the creation of both domestic and international variants of the "new economic order" by the Nazis in Germany. Running throughout these otherwise diverse events and developments, he saw the common thread of social reaction against market rationality. State–society relations again had undergone a profound—the *great*—transformation, as land, labor, and capital had all seized upon the state in the attempt to reimpose broader and more direct social control over market forces.

Once this domestic transformation began, late in the nineteenth century, international liberalism of the orthodox kind was doomed. Thus, it was the singular tragedy of the interwar period, Polanyi felt, to have attempted to restore internationally, in the form of the gold-exchange standard in particular, that which no longer had a corresponding social base domestically. The new international economic order that would emerge from World War II, Polanyi concluded, on the one hand would mark the end of "capitalist internationalism," as governments learned the lesson that international automaticity stands in fundamental and potentially explosive contradiction to an active state domestically, and, on the other hand, the emergence of deliberate management of international economic transactions by means of collaboration among governments.

Some of Polanyi's thoughts about the future had already been entertained by the individuals who would come to be directly responsible for negotiating the monetary component of the postwar international economic order. In the depth of the Depression, Harry Dexter White had pondered the problem of how to buffer national economies from external disturbances without, at the same time, sacrificing the benefits of international economic multilateralism. "The path, I suspect, may lie in the direction of centralized control over foreign exchanges and trade" (quoted in Van Dormael 1978: 41). Indeed, in 1934 White had applied for a fellowship to study planning techniques at the Institute of Economic Investigations of Gosplan in Moscow. Instead, he accepted an offer to go to Washington and work in the New Deal. For his part, one of the first assignments that Keynes undertook after he joined the British Treasury in 1940 was to draft the text of a radio broadcast designed to discredit recent propaganda proclamations by Walther Funk, minister for economic affairs and president of the Reichsbank in Berlin, on the economic and social benefits that the "New Order" would bring to Europe and the world. Keynes was instructed to stress the traditional virtues of free trade and the gold standard. But this message, he felt, "will not have much propaganda value." Britain would have to offer "the same as what Dr. Funk offers, except that we shall do it better and more honestly" (quoted in ibid.: 7). He had reached the conclusion that only a refinement and improvement of the Schachtian device would restore equilibrium after the war. "To suppose that there exists some smoothly functioning automatic mechanism of adjustment which preserves equilibrium if only we trust to methods of laissez-faire is a doctrinaire delusion which disregards the lessons of historical experience without having behind it the support of sound theory" (quoted in ibid.: 32).

Polanyi's prediction of the end of capitalist internationalism does not stand up well against the subsequent internationalization of production and finance; White's views were altered considerably over the years as a result of negotiations within the bureaucracy as well as by the adversarial process with Congress, before he was driven from Washington altogether in an anti-communist witch-hunt; and American resistance scaled down even the multilateral variants of Keynes's ambitious vision. Yet, each had been correct in the essential fact that a new threshold had been crossed in the balance between "market" and "authority," with governments assuming much more direct responsibility for domestic social security and economic stability. The extension of the suffrage and the emergence of working-class political constituencies, parties, and even governments was responsible in part; but demands for social protection were very nearly universal, coming from all segments of the political spectrum and from all ranks of the social hierarchy (with the possible exception of orthodox financial circles). Polanyi, White, and Keynes were also correct in their premise that, somehow, the postwar international economic order would have to reflect this change in state–society relations if the calamities of the interwar period were not to recur.

Transformations in power versus purpose

Changes in the distribution of power and in the structure of social purpose covaried from the pre-World War I era through to the interwar period, so that we cannot say with any degree of certainty what might have happened had only one changed. However, by looking at the relationship between the two in greater detail in a single, circumscribed domain, we may get closer to a firm answer. I focus on the monetary regime under the gold standard before World War I, and its attempted approximation in the gold-exchange standard of the interwar period.

I begin with the domestic side of things—though this distinction itself would barely apply to currencies under a "gold specie" standard, where both domestic circulation and international means of settlement took the form largely of gold, and the domestic money supply therefore was determined directly and immediately by the balance of payments (this discussion draws on Nurkse (1944)). Under the more familiar "gold bullion" standard prior to World War I, where the bulk of domestic money took the form of bank notes and deposits, backed by and fixed in value in terms of gold, there still existed a strong relationship between domestic money supply and the balance of payments, but it was more indirect. In theory, it worked via the effects of gold movements on the domestic credit supply: an expansion of credit in the gold-receiving country, and a contraction in the gold-losing country, affecting prices and incomes so as to close the balance-of-payments discrepancy that had triggered the gold movement in the first place. This was reinforced by an attending change in money rates, which would set off equilibrating movements in short-term private funds. In practice, gold movements among the major economies were relatively infrequent and small. Temporary gaps were filled largely by short-term capital movements, responding to interest differentials or slight variations within the gold points, though these flows did not function as smoothly as subsequent economic folklore has claimed (Bloomfield 1963). More fundamental adjustments were produced by the impact of the balance of payments not only on domestic money stock and the volume of credit, but also through the effects of export earnings on domestic income and demand.

In sum, even in its less than pristine form, the pre-World War I gold standard was predicated upon particular assumptions concerning the fundamental purpose of domestic monetary policy and the role of the state in the process of adjusting imbalances in the level of external and internal economic activity. With respect to the first, in Bloomfield's words, the "dominant and overriding" objective of monetary policy was the maintenance of gold parity: "The view, so widely recognized and accepted in recent decades, of central banking policy as a means of facilitating the achievement and maintenance of reasonable stability in the level of economic activity and prices was scarcely thought about before 1914, and certainly not accepted, as a formal objective of policy" (1959: 23). Second, insofar as the adjustment process ultimately was geared to securing external stability, non-intervention by states was prescribed so as not to undermine the equilibrating linkages between the balance of payments, changes in gold reserves and in domestic credit supply, income, and demand. This was not incompatible with partial efforts by governments to "neutralize" such effects; "all that was required . . . was that countries should not attempt to control their national income and outlay by deliberate measures—a requirement which in the age of laissez-faire was generally fulfilled" (Nurkse 1944: 213).

It is impossible to say precisely when these assumptions ceased to be operative and their contraries took hold. But after World War I there was a growing tendency, in Nurkse's words (ibid.: 230), "to make international monetary policy conform to domestic social and economic policy and not the other way round." The proportion of currency reserves held in the form of foreign exchange more than doubled between 1913 and 1925, to 27 percent; by 1928, it stood at 42 percent. And currency reserves increasingly came to function as a buffer against external economic forces rather than as their transmitter: Nurkse found that during the interwar years the international and domestic assets of central banks moved in opposite directions far more often than in the same direction (ibid.: 68–88). After the collapse of the gold-exchange standard in 1931, exchange stabilization funds were established in the attempt to provide more of a cushion than "neutralization" had afforded; stabilization in many instances was followed by direct exchange controls, with the gold bloc countries attempting to achieve analogous insulation through import quotas (Briggs 1968). Governments everywhere had developed increasingly active forms of intervention in the domestic economy in order to affect the level of prices and employment, and in the attempt to protect themselves against external sources of dislocation. As a result, the previously integrated international monetary order fragmented into five more or less distinct blocs, each with its own prevailing currency arrangements.

On the international side, there is little doubt that the pre-World War I gold standard functioned as it did in large measure because of the central part Great Britain played in it. In general terms, "if keeping a free market for imports, maintaining a flow of investment capital, and acting as lender of last resort are the marks of an 'underwriter' of an international system, then Britain certainly fulfilled this role in the nineteenth-century international economy" (Skidelsky 1976: 163). More specifically, in the domain of monetary policy it was the role of sterling as the major international currency, held by foreign business, banks, and even central banks, that gave the Bank of England the influence to shape international monetary conditions consistent with the fundamental commitments and dynamics of the regime. And yet, the critical issue in the stability of this regime was not simply some measure of material "supremacy" on the part of Britain, but that "national monetary authorities were inclined to follow the market—and indirectly the Bank of England—rather than to assert independent national objectives of their own" (Cleveland 1976: 57).[1] Thus, the international gold standard rested on both the special position of Great Britain and prevailing attitudes concerning the role of the state in the conduct of national monetary policy. It reflected a true "hegemony" as Gramsci used the term (Cox 1977).

What of the interwar period? Counterfactual history is slippery when an outcome is as overdetermined as institutional failure in the international economy between the wars. It seems reasonable to assume, though, that with the end of monetary laissez-faire, "the monetary leader would need to dispose of more monetary influence and political authority than Britain ever possessed, except within its own imperial system" (Cleveland 1976: 57). Indeed, where British hegemony lingered on, as in the League of Nations' Financial Committee, the outcome was not salutary. The eastern European countries that had their currencies stabilized by the League and were put under the gold-exchange standard before the major countries had fixed their currency rates did so at considerable domestic social cost (Polanyi 1944: 233). And virtually every effort to construct a viable international monetary regime in the interwar period, in all of which Britain took a leading role, did little more than to decry the newly prevailing social objectives of state policy while pleading for a speedy return to the principles of "sound finance" (Traynor 1949). The consequences, of course, were counterproductive: just as the rhetoric of the League concerning collective security and disarmament sought and in some measure served morally to undermine the balance of power system without providing a viable alternative (Carr 1946), so, too, did the League and successive international gatherings in the monetary sphere seek to undermine the legitimacy of domestic stabilization policies while offering only the unacceptable gold-exchange standard in their place.

It is hardly surprising, therefore, that apart from Britain, seized by its own ideology and institutional past and willing to pay the domestic social cost, there were few takers among the major countries.[2] In sum, efforts to construct international economic regimes in the interwar period failed not because of the lack of a hegemon. They failed because, even had there been a hegemon, they stood in contradiction to the transformation in the mediating role of the state between market and society, which altered fundamentally the social purpose of domestic and international authority. As Nurkse observed (1944: 230):

> There was a growing tendency during the inter-war period to make international monetary policy conform to domestic social and economic policy and not the other way round. Yet the world was still economically interdependent; and an international currency mechanism for the multilateral exchange of goods and services, instead of primitive bilateral barter, was still a fundamental necessity for the great majority of countries. The problem was to find a system of international currency relations compatible with the requirements of domestic stability. Had the period been more than a truce between two world wars, the solution that would have evolved would no doubt have been in the nature of a compromise.[3]

Ultimately, it was. The liberalism that was restored after World War II differed in kind from that which had been known previously. My term for it is "embedded liberalism."

THE EMBEDDED LIBERALISM COMPROMISE

Laissez-faire orthodoxy, most prominent in New York financial circles, proposed to reconstruct the postwar economic order simply by shifting its locus from the pound to the dollar and by ending discriminatory trade and exchange practices.[4] Opposition to orthodoxy, nearly universal outside the United States, differed in substance and intensity depending upon whether it came from the Left, Right, or Center, but was united in its rejection of unimpeded laissez-faire.[5] The task of postwar institutional reconstruction, as Nurkse sensed, was to maneuver between these two extremes and to devise a framework which would safeguard and even aid the quest for domestic stability without, at the same time, triggering the mutually destructive external consequences that had plagued the interwar period. This was the essence of the embedded liberalism compromise: unlike the economic nationalism of the thirties, it would be multilateral in character; unlike the liberalism of the gold standard and free trade, its multilateralism would be predicated upon domestic interventionism.

If this was the shared objective of postwar institutional reconstruction for the international economy, there remained enormous differences among countries over precisely what it meant and what sorts of policies and institutional arrangements, domestic and international, the objective necessitated or was compatible with. This was the stuff of the negotiations on the postwar international economic order. The story of these negotiations has been told by others, in detail and very ably (Gardner 1980; Van Dormael 1978). I make no attempt to repeat it here. I simply summarize the conjunction of the two themes that constitutes the story's plot.

The first theme, which we tend to remember more vividly today, concerned multilateralism versus discrimination. It was an achievement of historic proportions for the United States to win adherence to the principle of multilateralism, particularly in trade. It required the expenditure of enormous resources. Still, it would not have succeeded but for an acceptable resolution of the dilemma between internal and external stability, the story's second theme. Here, history seemed not to require any special agent. True, the United States from the start of the negotiations was far less "Keynesian" in its positions than Great Britain. Within the United States, the social and economic reforms of the New Deal had lacked ideological consistency and programmatic coherence, and opposition had remained more firmly entrenched. The transformation of the full-employment bill into the Employment Act of 1946 demonstrated the country's continuing ambivalence toward state intervention. This, of course, affected the outcome of the negotiations. Indeed, the United States would come to use its influence abroad in the immediate postwar years, through the Marshall Plan, the Occupation Authorities in Germany and Japan, and its access to transnational labor organizations, for example, to shape outcomes much more directly, by seeking to moderate the structure and political direction of labor movements, to encourage the exclusion of communist parties from participation in government, and generally to discourage collectivist arrangements where possible or at least contain them within acceptable Center–Left bounds (Cox 1977, Maier 1977). But these differences among the industrialized countries concerned the forms and depth of state intervention to secure domestic stability, not the legitimacy of the objective.

In the event, on the list of Anglo-American postwar economic objectives, multilateralism was joined by collaboration to assure domestic economic growth and social security as early as the Atlantic Charter, issued in August 1941. Indeed, progress on multilateralism seemed to be made contingent upon progress in expanding domestic production, employment, and the exchange and consumption of goods in Article VII of the Mutual Aid Agreement (Lend Lease), which was signed in February 1942.

On the monetary side, however different White's Stabilization Fund may have been from Keynes's Clearing Union (and there were substantial differences), they shared a common aim: intergovernmental collaboration to facilitate balance-of-payments equilibrium, in an international environment of multilateralism and a domestic context of full employment. Early in 1943, Adolf Berle foresaw that the compromise on the means to achieve these ends would have to "free the British people from their fear that they might have to subordinate their internal social policy to external financial policy, and to assure the United States that a share of its production was not claimable by tender of a new, 'trick' currency, and that the economic power represented by the US gold reserves would not be substantially diminished" (paraphrased by Van Dormael 1978: 103).

By the time of the Anglo-American "Joint Statement of Principles," issued not long before the Bretton Woods Conference, the consensus that had emerged provided for free and stable exchanges, on the one hand, and, on the other, the erection of a "double screen," in the words of Richard Cooper (1975: 85), to cushion the domestic economy against balance-of-payments strictures. Free exchanges would be assured by the abolition of all forms of exchange controls and restrictions on current transactions. Stable exchanges would be secured by setting and maintaining official par values, expressed in terms of gold. The "double screen" would consist of short-term assistance to finance payments deficits on current account, provided by an International Monetary Fund, and, so as to correct "fundamental disequilibrium," the ability to change exchange rates with Fund concurrence. Governments would be permitted—indeed, were expected—to maintain capital controls.

In devising the instruments of the monetary regime, the most intense negotiations were occasioned by the functioning of the "double screen." On the question of the Fund, Keynes had argued for an international overdraft facility. This would have created some $25 billion to $30 billion in new liquidity, with the overall balance of credits and debits in the Fund being expressed in an international unit of account, which was to be monetized. The arrangement would have been self-clearing unless a country were out of balance with the system as a whole, in which case corrective measures were called for on the part of creditors and debtors alike. The White plan originally called for a $5 billion Fund, though the US ultimately agreed to $8.8 billion. However, these funds would have to be paid in by subscription. Access to the Fund as well as total liability were strictly limited by quotas, which in turn reflected paid-in subscriptions—the initial US contribution was $3.175 billion. In addition, any country that sought to draw on the Fund had to make "representations" that the particular currency was needed for making payments on current account. Thus, with the United States, the sole major creditor country, seeking to limit its liabilities, the first part of the "double screen" was both more modest and more rigid than the United Kingdom and other potential debtor countries would have liked. But there was no question about its being provided.

On the second part of the screen, exchange rate changes, the UK was more successful in ensuring automaticity and limiting intrusions into the domain of domestic policy. The Fund was required to concur in any change necessary to correct a "fundamental disequilibrium," and if the change was less than 10 percent the Fund was given no power even to raise objections. Most important, the Fund could not oppose any exchange rate change on the grounds that the domestic social or political policies of the country requesting the change had led to the disequilibrium that made the change necessary. Lastly, the final agreement did include a provision to shift at least some of the burden of adjustment onto creditor countries. This was by means of the "scarce currency" clause, which Keynes, in the end, thought to be quite important. It empowered the Fund, by decision of the Executive Directors, to ration its supply of any currency that had become scarce in the Fund and authorized members to impose exchange restrictions on that currency.

Once negotiations on postwar commercial arrangements got under way seriously, in the context of preparations for an International Conference on Trade *and* Employment, the principles of multilateralism and tariff reductions were affirmed, but so were safeguards, exemptions, exceptions, and restrictions—all designed to protect the balance of payments and a variety of domestic social policies (Curzon and Curzon 1976; Gardner 1980). The US found some of these abhorrent and sought to limit them, but even on so extraordinary an issue as making full employment an international obligation of governments it could do no better than to gain a compromise. The US Senate subsequently refused to ratify the Charter of the International Trade Organization (ITO); its provisions had become internally so inconsistent that it is difficult to say just what sort of a regime it would have given rise to (Diebold 1952). As a result, a far smaller domain of commercial relations became subject to the authority of the international trade regime than would have been the case otherwise. The regulation of commodity markets, restrictive business practices, and international investments were the most important areas excluded. But within this smaller domain, consisting largely of point-of-entry barriers to trade as well as such practices as dumping and providing export subsidies, the conjunction of international openness and safeguarding domestic stability that had evolved over the course of the ITO negotiations remained intact.

Jacob Viner summarized the prevailing consensus at the time of the negotiations for a General Agreement on Tariffs and Trade (GATT): "There are few free traders in the present-day world, no one pays any attention to their views, and no person in authority anywhere advocates free trade" (Viner 1947: 613). The United States, particularly the State Department, was the prime mover behind multilateralism in trade. But this meant nondiscrimination above all. The reduction of barriers to trade, of course, also played a role in American thinking, but here, too, the concern was more with barriers that were difficult to apply in a nondiscriminatory manner. Tariff reduction was subject to much greater domestic constraint. For their part, the British

made it clear from the beginning that they would countenance no disman-
tling of imperial preferences unless the US agreed to deep and linear tariff
cuts. The proposed Commercial Union, put forward by James Meade on
behalf of Britain, contained such a formula, together with an intergovernmental code of conduct for trade and machinery to safeguard the balance of
payments. But the US Congress would not accept linear tariff cuts.

The General Agreement on Tariffs and Trade made obligatory the most-
favored-nation rule, but a blanket exception was allowed for all existing
preferential arrangements, and countries were permitted to form customs
unions and free trade areas. Moreover, quantitative restrictions were prohib-
ited, but were deemed suitable measures for safeguarding the balance of
payments—*explicitly* including payments difficulties that resulted from
domestic policies designed to secure full employment. They could also be
invoked in agricultural trade if they were used in conjunction with a
domestic price support program. The substantial reduction of tariffs and
other barriers to trade was called for; but it was not made obligatory and it
was coupled with appropriate emergency actions, which were allowed if a
domestic producer was threatened with injury from import competition that
was due to past tariff concessions. The Agreement also offered a blanket
escape from any of its obligations, provided that two-thirds of the
contracting parties approved. Lastly, procedures were provided to settle
disputes arising under the Agreement and for the multilateral surveillance of
the invocation of most (though not all) of its escape clauses. The principle of
reciprocity was enshrined as a code of conduct, to guide both tariff reductions and the determination of compensation for injuries suffered.

To repeat my central point: that a multilateral order gained acceptance,
especially in the area of trade, reflected the power and perseverance of the
United States. But that multilateralism and the quest for domestic stability
were coupled and even conditioned by one another reflected the shared legitimacy of a set of social objectives to which the industrial world had moved,
unevenly but, borrowing Kindleberger's phrase, "as a single entity."
Therefore, the common tendency to view the postwar regimes as straight
liberal regimes, with lots of cheating taking place on the domestic side, fails
to capture the complexity of the embedded liberalism compromise.[6]

NORM-GOVERNED CHANGE

The postwar regimes for trade and money got off to a slow start. The early
GATT rounds of tariff negotiations were modest in their effects. As a lending
institution, the IMF remained dormant well into the 1950s. Bilateral currency
arrangements in the late 1940s and early 1950s became far more extensive
than they had ever been in the 1930s, doubling to some four hundred between
1947 and 1954, of which 235 existed in Europe (De Vries and Horsefield 1969:
vol. 2, chap. 14). But by the late 1950s, the Europeans had "the worst of their
post-war problems behind them—and new ones had not yet come to take

their place"; and Europe and the United States were poised "on the brink of a decade of phenomenal expansion which imperiously demanded wider markets through freer trade" (Curzon and Curzon 1976: 149–150). This in turn also demanded the elimination of exchange restrictions on current account. Liberalization in trade and money soon followed.*

But the "golden age" was brief. By the 1970s, gloomy predictions about imminent "erosion" and even "collapse" of the monetary and trade regimes began to appear and build momentum. Robert Triffin (1976) depicted the Jamaica Accords adopting floating exchange rates as "slapstick comedy" rather than monetary reform, while according to an ex-US trade official the GATT's Tokyo Round "performed the coup de grâce" on liberal trade (Graham 1979: 49). Some analysts even feared "the first real international trade war since the 1930s" (Bergsten 1972). The decline of US hegemony was the most frequently adduced cause, beginning with the Nixon administration's severing the link between gold and the dollar and imposing a temporary import surcharge, followed by general malaise produced by twin oil crises and rapidly escalating inflation. A sense of unraveling is pervasive. But is it justified?

I take momentary refuge in hypothesis. If we allow that international regimes are not simply expressions of the underlying distribution of inter-state power, but represent a fusion of power and legitimate social purpose, our cause-and-effect reasoning becomes more complex. For then the decline of hegemony—assuming that it has occurred—would not necessarily lead to the collapse of regimes, provided that shared purposes are held constant. Instead, one ought to find changes in the instruments of regimes, which, under hegemony, are likely to have relied on disproportionate contributions by and therefore reflected the preferences of the hegemon. At the same time, one ought to find continuity in the normative structure of regimes, which would still reflect shared purposes. Moreover, the new instruments ought to be more appropriate to the new power distribution while remaining

---

* A section has been omitted from the original here. It documented that the subsequent liberalization among the industrialized countries predominantly took a very specific form: trade in products originating in the same sector, or intra-industry trade, where specialization occurs by firms narrowing their product range but nations as a whole strive to maintain a diverse portfolio of industrial sectors. It contrasts with inter-sectoral trade wherein greater specialization takes place at the level of the national economy, which was more pronounced in the nineteenth century. Converging production structures and economies of scale are among the factors responsible for this pattern. But I argued that embedded liberalism, too, was responsible. For governments pursuing domestic stabilization it is safer to liberalize intra-industry trade, because it does not threaten entire sectors of national production and employment and thus poses fewer domestic adjustment costs and lower vulnerabilities. Indeed, governments in successive GATT rounds encouraged precisely this kind of liberalization. The point remains of interest because it offers a simple explanation of the most serious international trade disputes of the 1980s and early 1990s: why Japan's trading partners have had more trouble with Japan than with one another. Japan's level of intra-industry trade is far lower than the OECD norm, posing vulnerabilities that other intra-OECD trade does not pose (Lincoln 1990; Ruggie 1993c)—a practice which, at the extreme, has been described as "adversarial trade" (Drucker 1986).

compatible with the existing normative structure. In short, the result would be "norm-governed" change.

Let us turn back to the post-1971 changes in the regimes for money and trade. On the monetary side, the major changes at issue are the end of the dollar's convertibility into gold and the adoption of floating rates of exchange, both in violation of the original IMF Articles of Agreement. On the trade side, no discrete event fully symbolizes the perceived discontinuities, though they are characterized generally as "the new protectionism" and include the proliferation of nontariff barriers to trade, and violations of the principle of nondiscrimination in the form of internationally negotiated export restraints. In both cases a weakening of the central institutions, the IMF and the GATT, is taken to reflect the same syndrome.

It is my contention that, on balance, the hypothesis of norm-governed change accounts for more of the variance than claims of fundamental discontinuity.

Baseline

The baseline against which change must be assessed consists of two parts. The first is the institutional nexus of embedded liberalism. If we compare changes in the monetary and trade regimes against the ideal of orthodox liberalism, then we are bound to be disappointed if not shocked by recent trends. But we are also bound to be misled. For orthodox liberalism has not governed international economic relations at any time in the postwar period. Within the embedded liberalism framework, it will be recalled, multilateralism and domestic stability are linked to and conditioned by one another. Thus, movement toward greater international openness is likely to be coupled with measures designed to cushion the domestic economy from external disruptions. At the same time, the measures adopted to effect such domestic cushioning should be commensurate with the degree of external disturbance and compatible with the long-term expansion of international transactions. Moreover, what constitutes a deviation from this baseline cannot be determined simply by an "objective" examination of individual acts in reference to specific texts. Rather, deviations will be determined by the intersubjective evaluation of the intentionality and consequences of acts within the broader normative framework and prevailing circumstances.

The second component of the baseline is the peculiar relation of the United States to the institutionalization of embedded liberalism immediately after the war. The United States was, at one and the same time, the paramount economic power *and* the country in which the prevailing domestic state–society shift remained the most ambivalent. This had several complex consequences, with differential effects on the two regimes. The United States would have to provide the bulk of the material resources required to translate the negotiated compromises into institutional reality. This would give the US influence that it could be expected to exercise in keeping with its preferred interpretations of both the compromises and how they were to be realized. US influence on the institutionalization of the trade agreement, once the ITO was abandoned, on the whole supported the basic design and need not detain us. But the institutionalization of the monetary regime was profoundly skewed by the asymmetrical position of the United States.[7]

At Bretton Woods, through a combination of stealth and inevitability, the dollar became equated with gold and was recognized officially as the key currency—apparently without the knowledge of Keynes as well as some members of the American delegation, including Dean Acheson (Van Dormael 1978: 200–203). Once the IMF came into existence, the United States insisted on terms of reference, and a series of "interpretations" of the Articles as well as on decisions by the Executive Directors, all of which had the effect of launching what became known as "IMF orthodoxy" (requiring exchange depreciation, domestic austerity measures, and reduced public spending in return for access to stabilization loans); and, inadvertently or otherwise, guaranteeing that there would be no intergovernmental alternative to US payments deficits as the major instrument of international liquidity creation (De Vries and Horsefield 1969: vol. 3, 227–228; Strange 1976: 93–96; Block 1977: chap. 5). Thus, the monetary regime that emerged in the 1950s already differed in several key respects from the original intent of Bretton Woods.

It is against this baseline that subsequent developments are assessed.

The evolving monetary regime

The post-1971 inconvertibility of the dollar into gold may be usefully framed within the broader rubric of liquidity problems, and floating rates of exchange within adjustment problems. I take up each in turn, and conclude with a comment on the IMF.

As noted, the liquidity provisions of Bretton Woods were inadequate from the start, even though, as Cohen (1983) points out, an adequate supply of international liquidity was one of its cardinal principles. The growing volume of international trade increased liquidity requirements, as did the growing magnitude of speculative pressure on exchange rates. The dollar exchange standard, which had "solved" this problem in the short run, was already in trouble when the monetary regime first began to function without the protective shield of the postwar transitional arrangements. In 1958, just as the Europeans were resuming full convertibility of their currencies, US gold reserves fell permanently below US overseas liabilities. And before the next year was out, Triffin (1960) articulated the dilemma that bore his name: If the United States corrected its balance of payments deficit, the result would be world deflation because gold production at $35 an ounce could not adequately supply world monetary reserves. But if the United States continued running a deficit, the result would be the collapse of the monetary standard because US foreign liabilities would far exceed its ability to convert dollars into gold on demand.

Throughout the 1960s, a seemingly endless series of stop-gap measures was tried in an effort to devise what Robert Roosa, former US under-secretary of the treasury, later called "outer perimeter defenses" for the dollar. Roughly speaking, these measures were designed to make gold conversion financially unattractive, to increase modestly the capacity of the IMF to supply liquidity, and to increase the capacity of central banks to neutralize the flow of speculative capital. The US also undertook limited domestic measures to reduce its payments deficits and pressured surplus countries to revalue their currencies. By 1968, however, the dollar had become in effect inconvertible into gold; it was declared formally so in 1971.

The rise and fall of the gold-convertible dollar has placed the monetary regime in a paradoxical predicament from beginning to end. It has altered profoundly central instruments of the regime having to do with the creation of international liquidity, the system of currency reserves, and the means of ultimate settlement. It has also violated procedural norms, as unilateral action usurped collective decision. But, at the same time, it seems to have been understood and acknowledged all around that, under the material and political conditions prevailing, neither the substantive norms of Bretton Woods nor the compromise of embedded liberalism itself could have been realized through any other available means. So the regime became stuck with the undesired consequences of means that helped bring about a desired end.

With respect to the problem of adjustment, as we saw, few provisions for international measures to affect the economic policies of deficit or surplus countries survived the Bretton Woods negotiations. And once the new creditor–debtor relationships became established in the late 1950s, the mechanism of exchange rate changes also failed to operate effectively. There was no means to compel surplus countries to appreciate, and among the largest deficit countries, Great Britain resisted depreciation fiercely in a vain attempt to preserve an international role for sterling while the United States, as the "Nth country," necessarily remained passive. Thus, the only real international leverage for adjustment was the conditionality provision developed by the Fund—on which the industrialized countries depended less and less. The adjustable peg system became intolerable when imbalances in the external trade account came to be overshadowed, both as a source of problems and as a response to them, by massive movements of short-term speculative funds. This made it increasingly difficult for governments to conduct domestic macroeconomic policy, and to support exchange rates under pressure. When, in the late 1960s, the full attention of these funds came to be focused on the dollar as a result of dramatic deficits in the US trade balance and current account, the system of fixed rates of exchange was doomed.

Shifting to floating rates required formal amendment of the IMF's Articles of Agreement, the "slapstick comedy" of which Triffin spoke. This is prima facie evidence of discontinuity. However, living within the Articles provided the international monetary system with an adjustment mechanism that neither functioned effectively nor fulfilled the expectations of Bretton Woods. What of the present arrangement? Three aspects bear on the argument. First, it is important to keep distinct the instrument of fixed rates from the norm of outlawing competitive currency depreciation and thus providing a framework for relatively stable exchanges. There is a good case to be made that the norm had become sufficiently well institutionalized and recourse to competitive depreciation sufficiently unnecessary given other means of influencing domestic macroeconomic factors that reliance on an increasingly burdensome instrument, which itself had begun to contribute to currency instability, could no longer be justified. Moreover, experience since then has shown the managed float to be capable of avoiding serious disorderliness—the early months of the Carter and Reagan administrations alike being major exceptions—and to have few if any deleterious consequences for international trade. Second, floating exchange rates were widely perceived to provide a greater cushion for domestic macroeconomic policy, which was increasingly subjected to dislocation from speculative capital flows that were often quite out of proportion to underlying economic reality. It is clear now that the degree of insulation is less than was advertised, but in the absence of uniform and fairly comprehensive capital controls it is probably as much as can be secured. Third, as an adjustment mechanism, the managed float appears to function more symmetrically than fixed rates did. Not only have surplus countries been forced to take notice, but the precipitous depreciation of the US dollar caught the attention of American policymakers in the autumn of 1978 more effectively than any past balance-of-payments deficit had done.

On the evolution of the IMF we can be brief; the tendency seems to be for it to come full circle. One does not want to exaggerate recent changes in the Fund. Nevertheless, its financing facilities have been considerably expanded, repayment periods lengthened, and conditionality provisions relaxed somewhat, as well as requiring the Fund "to pay due regard to the domestic social and political objectives" of borrowing countries (*New York Times*, 5 February 1980). Moreover, decision-making power within the IMF has been reapportioned at least to the extent of distributing veto power more equitably. These changes began in the late 1950s, to make the Fund more acceptable to the Europeans once they accepted the full obligations of IMF membership; they continued in the 1960s to reflect the economic status of the European Community and Japan; and they were accelerated and aimed increasingly at the developing countries in the 1970s, as a result of the massive payments imbalances produced by new energy terms of trade and subsequent fears about the stability of the international financial system.

The evolution of the trade regime

The sense of discontinuity concerning the international trade regime is illustrated in the following excerpt from a *Wall Street Journal* article (14 April 1978), entitled "Surge in Protectionism Worries and Perplexes Leaders of Many Lands":

> After three decades of immense increase in world trade and living standards, exports and imports are causing tense pressures in nearly every nation and among the best of allies. The US sets price floors against Japanese steel, Europe accuses the US of undercutting its papermakers, the Japanese decry cheap textiles from South Korea, French farmers have smashed truckloads of Italian wine, and AFL-CIO President George Meany rattles exporters world-wide by calling free trade—'a joke.'

By now, even its most severe critics realize that "the new protectionism" is not simply the latest manifestation of "old-style" protectionism. "The emergence of the new protectionism in the Western world reflects the victory of the interventionist, or welfare, economy over the market economy" (Krauss 1978: 36). However, they continue to have difficulty appreciating that this new protectionism is not a deviation from the norm of postwar liberalization, but an integral feature of it.

Today, tariffs on products traded among the industrialized countries are an insignificant barrier to trade. The Tokyo Round instituted further tariff cuts, and began to cope with nontariff barriers for the first time. It produced codes to liberalize such barriers resulting from domestic subsidies and countervailing duties, government procurement, product standards, customs valuation, and import licensing. All formal barriers to trade in civil aircraft and aircraft parts were removed. And preparations for a new GATT round, addressing investment and services, have commenced. What is more, the volume of world trade continues to increase and its rate of growth, though declining, still exceeds economic growth rates in most OECD countries. In sum, liberalization and growth have continued apace despite the erosion of postwar prosperity, and despite the erosion of American willingness to absorb disproportionate shares of liberalized trade (Krasner 1979).

Restraints on trade have also grown. Much of the time they take one of two forms: domestic safeguards, and "voluntary" or negotiated export restraints. Under the GATT, domestic safeguards may be invoked for balance-of-payments reasons (Article XII), or to prevent injury to domestic producers caused by a sudden surge of imports that can be attributed to past tariff concessions (Article XIX). The first of these provisions has caused little difficulty, notwithstanding several deviations from prescribed procedure.[8] Article XIX lends itself to greater abuse. It permits alteration or suspension of past tariff concessions in a nondiscriminatory manner, provided that interested parties are consulted. It has been invoked with growing frequency, particularly by the US and Australia. It is quite clumsy, however, because by-standers are likely to be affected and because it may involve renegotiation or even retaliatory suspension of concessions. As a result, "most governments, on most occasions, have simply short-circuited Article XIX altogether, going straight to the heart of the problem by negotiating a minimum price agreement, or a 'voluntary' export restraint with the presumably reluctant exporter who has previously been 'softened' by threats of emergency action under GATT" (Curzon and Curzon 1976: 225).

Many of these agreements do not involve governments at all, but are reached directly between the importing and exporting industries concerned. They take place beyond the purview of the GATT and therefore are not subject to official multilateral surveillance. An attempt, made during the Tokyo Round, to conclude a safeguards code that would have provided detailed rules and procedures was unsuccessful, though negotiations are continuing. However, these problems do not afflict the entire trading order, but are sectorally specific, and a close sectoral analysis will show that there is not "any decisive movement toward protectionism" (Krasner 1979: 507). Lastly, so-called orderly marketing arrangements, of which the Longterm Textile Agreement of 1962 was the first multilateral variant, have also proliferated. However, most have provided for a regular expansion of exports, though of course more limited than would have been obtained under conditions of "free" trade.

In sum, the impact of these restraints on international trade, even by the GATT's own reckoning, has been relatively modest. Their purpose, moreover, has not been to freeze the international division of labor but to minimize the social costs of domestic adjustment to structural changes in the international division of labor.

With respect to the institutional role of the GATT, legal scholars in particular have lamented the passing of "effective and impartial" dispute settlement mechanisms. However, these mechanisms had begun to fall into disuse by the late 1950s—that is, just as production and trade began to soar and serious tariff reductions commenced. They were replaced by consultations and negotiations among instructed representatives of the disputants.

Assessment

This chapter has not argued that the world it describes is the best of all possible worlds. I have argued only that the world has to be looked at as it is. When the regimes for money and trade are viewed in the light not of orthodox liberalism but of the embedded liberalism compromise, the hypothesis of norm-governed change accounts for more of the variance than claims of fundamental discontinuity. Much of the observed change has been at the level of instrument rather than norm. Moreover, in most cases the new instruments are not inimical to the norms of the regimes but represent adaptations to new circumstances. And, in some cases, the collective response by governments to changing circumstances reflects an even greater affinity with the expectations of original regime designs than did the arrangements that held in the interval. Suboptimal outcomes may prevail, to be sure. "But the relevant question is whether a liberal international economy could have been purchased at any more acceptable price" (Hirsch 1978: 279).

Our analysis also suggests that considerably more continuity can attend hegemonic decline than would be predicted by the hegemonic stability thesis, provided that social purposes are held constant.[9] Finally, because social purposes reflect configurations of state–society relations, it suggests that the foremost force for discontinuity at present is not "the new protectionism" in money and trade, which is most feared by observers today. Rather, it is the threat posed to embeddedness by the resurgent ethos of neo-*laissez-faire*.

Finally, the discussion illustrates the efficacy of the concept of authority in international regimes—as distinct from power. Legitimate authority rests on shared social purposes, in the case under consideration, shared purposes prescribing the domestic social and economic role of state under embedded, as opposed to *laissez-faire*, liberalism.

3 Epistemology, ontology, and the study of international regimes

This chapter combines the main sections of 1986b with 1995c. 1986b was co-authored with Friedrich Kratochwil, to whom I remain indebted for having deepened my own philosophical understanding of some of the issues involved. These issues are highly complex and hotly contested; in 1995c I sought to clarify one key aspect that we had not conveyed effectively. The original article triggered an avalanche of correspondence from and with leading figures in the field. Almost all took exception to what they viewed as our criticism of the scientific method. Almost all made reference to the danger of sending the wrong signals to graduate students; indeed, one feared that we were encouraging them to "write anything they feel like writing in their dissertations." But nothing was further from our intent. We sought to rectify confusion, not create it.

The fuss was mostly about our observation that the prevailing epistemological posture in regime analysis contradicts the ontological basis of regimes. Regimes, according to the standard definition, are constituted by convergent expectations, shared principles, and norms—that is, they are inherently intersubjective in nature. But the epistemology reflected in much of regime analysis conforms, roughly speaking, to a soft version of logical positivism. Adjustments had to be made on one or the other side, we argued. Our own preference was for the adoption of more interpretive epistemological procedures. In fact, over time the issue seems to have been resolved in the opposite direction: in the mainstream regimes have been gradually and without much discussion reconceived largely as "injunctions"—that is, external constraints on state behavior that function either as independent or intervening variables.

To know how regimes function as injunctions is, obviously, both interesting and important. But it also lops off a big chunk of the original research program which I am not yet willing to abandon. With the benefit of hindsight, therefore, I want to be more explicit here about our argument and also more circumspect about its scope.

First of all, by "intersubjective" we did not mean a state of affairs that exists among analysts, as some of our interlocutors thought; we meant a state of affairs existing among the actors that comprise any given regime. What is *their* understanding of the nature of the regime and of what constitutes unacceptable deviations from it?

Second, our critique was not of the scientific method in any overall sense—we are hardly epistemological anarchists. But it was a criticism of certain epistemological practices as they pertain to certain aspects of regime analysis.

To begin with, regimes, like principles and norms more generally, function not only in the causal sense of injunctions but also in a broader communicative and even constitutive sense. That is to say, regimes encompass the dimension of reasons and meaning as well as efficient causes. Part of the efficacy of regimes in practice has to do with the mutual intelligibility and acceptability of actions within the intersubjective framework of understanding that is embodied in the regime's principles and norms. This dimension gets lost by focusing on the regulative role of regimes only. Yet it may tell us more about how robust a regime is than its more "objective" *aspects*, such as formal compliance with its specific injunctions. Thus, interpretive epistemologies remain central to appreciating how regimes function.

In addition, regime analysis suffers from severe small-numbers problems. Relatively few regimes have been identified and studied in any comparable fashion, so that inferences about regimes tend to rest neither on firm statistical nor experimental grounds. What is more, many of the law-like generalizations that are invoked to explain whatever empirical patterns are discovered are on even shakier grounds. How many cases of nuclear bipolarity have there been, on the basis of which one could say with some assurance that it caused this or that pattern in international regimes? Indeed, how many cases of bipolarity, period? How many cases of hegemony are there "like" Britain in the nineteenth century or "like" the United States in the postwar era? These problems suggest that narrative forms of explanation—in contrast to the deductive–nomological ideal—retain a significant role in regime analysis.

Finally, we cannot, as one interlocutor proposed, simply "begin with objectivist explanations, see how far they take us, and add complexity to gain more accuracy." Why not? Because the different approaches construe the social world differently—just as Newtonian mechanics and quantum mechanics do in the physical universe. What we can do is to become more self-conscious about which epistemological approaches are appropriate for the analysis of what aspects of regimes, which had been our aim in the first place.

Students of international organization have progressively shifted their focus beyond formal organizations, toward broader forms of international institutionalized behavior. This shift does not reflect a haphazard sequence of theoretical or topical fads (Strange 1982), but is rooted in a core concern or "set of puzzles" (Kuhn 1962) that gives coherence and identity to this field of study. The substantive core around which various theoretical approaches have clustered is the problem of international governance. And the shifts in analytical foci can be understood as "progressive problem shifts," in the sense of Imre Lakatos's criterion for the heuristic fruitfulness of a research program (Lakatos 1970). This evolution brought the field to its focus on the concept of international regimes.

Formulating and agreeing to a new unifying concept for the field is no small accomplishment. And that accomplishment is not diminished by the fact that serious problems remain to be resolved. One of the major criticisms made of the regimes concept is its "wooliness" and "imprecision" (Strange 1982). The point is well taken. There is no agreement in the literature even on such basic issues as boundary conditions: Where does one regime end and another begin? What is the threshold between regime and nonregime? Embedding regimes in "meta-regimes," or "nesting" one within another, as suggested by Aggarwal (1985), displaces the problem; it does not resolve it. The same is true of the suggestion that any set of patterned or conventionalized behavior be considered as prima facie evidence for the existence of a regime (Young 1983).

The only cure for wooliness and imprecision is, of course, to make the concept of regimes less so. Definitions can still be refined, but only up to a point. Two fundamental impediments stand in the way. One is absolute: ultimately, there exists no external Archimedean point from which regimes can be viewed as they "truly" are. This is so because regimes are conceptual creations not concrete entities. As with any analytical construction in the human sciences, the concept of regimes will reflect commonsense understandings, actor preferences, and the particular purposes for which analyses are undertaken. Ultimately, therefore, the concept of regimes, like the concepts of "power," "state," or "revolution," will remain a "contestable concept" (Connolly 1983).

Well short of this absolute impediment stands another. It is not insuperable, but a great deal of work must be done in order to overcome it. The problem is this: the practice of regime analysis reflects epistemological anomalies that derive from the largely unreflective logical positivist premises in international relations theory, irrespective of whether or not this orientation is appropriate to the particular epistemological situation at hand. These anomalies debilitate efforts to achieve clarity and precision in the concept of regimes and to enhance its productive capacity as an analytical tool. Without pretending that we can resolve these epistemological problems here, we do hope to achieve their serious consideration by the discipline.

Our discussion is organized as follows. The first section summarizes the immediate antecedents to the focus on international regimes, demonstrating their evolutionary pattern. Section two explores several core epistemological problems exhibited by the dominant theoretical approaches in international relations, from which the regimes literature is not exempt. The third section shows how these general problems affect regimes analysis specifically, and it makes some modest suggestions for how they might be dealt with.

REGIMES ANTECEDENTS

By the 1960s, a key assumption of the formal institutionalist approach had been abandoned: namely, that international governance is whatever international organizations do. Instead, the focus shifted to the actual and potential roles of international organizations in a more broadly conceived process of international governance. This, of course, had been the concern of regional integration studies for some time, particularly the neofunctionalist variety (Schmitter 1969). There it was fueled by the belief that the jurisdictional scope of the state and international organizations alike was increasingly exceeded by the functional scope of international problems. And integration studies sought to discern the extent to which institutional adaptations to this disjuncture might be conducive to the emergence of governance structures "beyond the nation state" (Haas 1964). Neofunctionalists assigned a significant role in this process of transformation to international organizations, not simply as passive recipients of new tasks but as active agents of "task expansion" and "spillover."

The next cluster of theorizing began with a critique of the superstate end-state expectations of integration theory and shifted attention to the more general question of how international organizations "reflect and to some extent magnify or modify" the characteristic features of the international system (Hoffmann 1970). The possible roles of international organizations that were explored from this vantage included their potential for being forums facilitating the formation of transgovernmental coalitions as well as instruments of transgovernmental policy coordination (Keohane and Nye 1971, 1974), vehicles in the international politics of agenda formation (Kay and Skolnikoff 1972; Russell 1973; Weiss and Jordan 1976; Ruggie 1980a), dispensers of collective legitimacy (Claude 1966), and mechanisms through which the global structure of dominance is enhanced or can possibly come to be undermined (Cox 1977, 1983). The theme that unified all works of this genre is that the process of global governance is not coterminous with the activities of international organizations but that these organizations do play some role in that broader process (also see Chapter 1).

The focus on regimes was a direct response both to this intellectual odyssey as well as to certain developments in the real world of international relations in the 1970s. Regimes are broadly defined as governing arrangements constructed by states to coordinate their expectations and organize aspects of their behavior in various issue-areas (Krasner 1983). When the presumed identity between international governance and international organizations was explicitly rejected, however, beyond integration theory no overarching conception remained of international governance itself. And integrationists themselves soon abandoned their early notions, ending up with a formulation of integration that did little more than recapitulate the condition of interdependence which was assumed to trigger integration in the first place (Keohane and Nye 1975 made this point; also see Haas 1976). Thus, for a time the field of international organization lacked any systematic conception of its traditional analytical core: international governance. The introduction of the concept of regimes reflected an attempt to fill this void. International regimes were taken to express both the parameters and the perimeters of international governance.[*]

The impact of international affairs during the 1970s came in the form of an anomaly for which no ready-made explanation was at hand. Important changes occurred in the international system, typically associated with the

---

[*]   The generic study of international cooperation—rather than governance specifically—took off at roughly the same point in time, based largely on models adapted from microeconomics—initially collective goods theory (for example, Sandler, Loehr, and Cauley 1978), and from the mid-1980s on, game theory (see Axelrod and Keohane 1985). This branch of the literature now goes by the name of neoliberal institutionalism (Baldwin 1993).

relative decline of US postwar hegemony: the achievement of nuclear parity by the Soviet Union, the economic resurgence of Europe and Japan, and the success of OPEC together with the severe international economic dislocations that followed it. Specific agreements that had been negotiated after World War II increasingly were violated, and institutional arrangements, especially in money and trade, came under enormous strain.

Yet—and here is the anomaly—governments on the whole did not respond to these difficulties in beggar-thy-neighbor terms. Neither systemic factors nor formal institutions alone apparently could account for this outcome. One way to resolve the anomaly was to question the extent to which US hegemony in fact had eroded (Strange 1982; Russett 1985). Another and by no means incompatible route was via the concept of international regimes. The argument was advanced that regimes continued in some measure to condition and constrain the behavior of states toward one another, despite systemic change and institutional erosion. International regimes were seen to enjoy a degree of relative autonomy, though of unknown strength and duration (Krasner 1983; Keohane 1984).

In sum, in order to help resolve both disciplinary and real-world puzzles the process of international governance has come to be associated with the concept of international regimes, occupying an ontological space somewhere between the level of formal organizations, on the one hand, and systemic factors, on the other.

THE LIMITS OF POSITIVISM

International regimes are commonly defined as social institutions around which states' expectations converge in different issue-areas. The emphasis on convergent expectations as the constitutive basis of regimes gives regimes an inescapable intersubjective quality. It follows that we know regimes by their shared understandings of desirable and acceptable forms of social behavior. Moreover, the universe of international regimes—though never precisely delineated—is relatively small; what we know about regimes comes from the study of a still smaller number of cases; and empirical findings are based largely on qualitative data. These ontological, epistemological, and methodological features of the object of study stand in contrast to the positivist precepts and prescriptions that prevail in the field of study. This section outlines some general problems posed by this discrepancy; the next relates them specifically to the study of regimes.[†]

---

† This section is drawn from 1995c. That article was originally written as a methodological rejoinder to Mearsheimer's realist critique of institutionalist theories (1994/95), to go with my substantive rejoinder (Ruggie 1995b). I have deleted some of the references to realism as well as illustrations intended specifically to counter Mearsheimer's anti-institutionalist posture, and have added one illustration to clarify my own argument, as indicated in the text. The rest is unaltered.

Social facts

The linguistic philosopher John Searle has expressed well a central and recurrent philosophical problem of the social sciences: "We have a certain common-sense picture of ourselves as human beings which is very hard to square with our overall 'scientific' conception" (1984: 13). That is, we view ourselves as intentionalistic human beings capable of representing the world meaningfully to one another; yet our scientific ideal is drawn from a physical world made up of unconscious particles in mechanical interaction. Can these two views be reconciled in the social sciences, Searle asks? In the desire to emulate the physical sciences, he notes, many fashionable conceptions of social science—he cites behaviorism, functionalism, and physicalism—often deny or misconstrue the efficacy of subjective and intersubjective "mental phenomena" (ibid.: 15).

Neorealism is an archetype of physicalist social science, and institutions, along with ideas and norms, are factors it does not fully grasp and whose roles, therefore, it downgrades or distorts. But the atomistic premises of neoliberal institutionalism are not much better suited for the analysis of intersubjective phenomena.

Elaborating on Searle's basic distinction between physical and mental states, Kratochwil (1989: 22–28) differentiates three worlds of social facticity in international politics: the worlds, respectively, of brute or palpable observational facts, of intentionality and meaning, and of institutional facts. The world of "brute" facts is the familiar world of material capabilities and similar palpable properties, of pre-given and fixed preferences, of increases in trade restraints and depreciations of currencies, and so on. It is often described as "objective" reality, though by now everyone readily acknowledges that observation of it is mediated by concepts and theories.

The second world of social facticity comprises intentionality and meaning. This gets more complicated. " 'Intentionality'," Searle indicates, "doesn't just refer to intentions, but also to beliefs, desires, hopes, fears, love, hate, lust, disgust, shame, pride, irritation, amusement, and all of those mental states (whether conscious or unconscious) that refer to, or are about, the [external] world" (1984: 16). These "mental states" cannot be reduced to structural (physicalist) factors. But once they are granted a degree of autonomy from structure, a non-physicalist epistemological framework is required because the mind, unlike physical objects, can bring about, in Searle's words, "the very state of affairs that it has been thinking about" (ibid.: 61). Simply put, physical objects cannot *will* things to happen; within limits, human agency can. Accordingly, social facts in the world of "intentionality" both influence actions and make intelligible to others the grounded reasoning behind actions.

The world of institutional facts is perhaps the most complex of the three. This world consists in the first instance of constitutive or enabling rules, and secondarily of specialized regulative and enforcement rules (the distinction derives from Rawls 1955). Regulative rules are more easily understood; they are the "injunctions" that some analysts now associate with the very phenomenon of regimes. Constitutive or enabling rules are of a different nature; a lengthy excerpt from Rawls's classic essay on this point may help illustrate it (ibid.: 25).‡

> Many of the actions one performs in a game of baseball one can do by oneself or with others whether there is the game or not. For example, one can throw a ball, run, or swing a peculiarly shaped piece of wood. But one cannot steal a base, or strike out, or draw a walk, or make an error, or balk; although one can do certain things which appear to resemble these actions such as sliding into a bag, missing a grounder, and so on. Striking out, stealing a base, balking, etc., are all actions which can only happen in a game. No matter what a person did, what he did would not be described as stealing a base or striking out or drawing a walk unless he could also be described as playing baseball, and for him to be doing this presupposes the rule-like practice which constitutes the game. The practice is logically prior to particular cases: unless there is the practice the terms referring to actions specified by it lack a sense.

Thus, social institutions, before they do anything else—for example, act as injunctions—express rule-like practices that constitute different social "games," or more generally, classes of social actions defined by a practice. These practices include marriage, kinship, contracts, political office, and the many other institutionalized relationships that make routine social interaction possible by making it mutually comprehensible. In other words, institutional facts—such as he is getting *married*, I am a *father*, we signed a *lease*, she is *president*—make sense only "within an intersubjectively understood context" (Kratochwil 1989: 24). The same holds true of the statement, this is a *regime*. These practices communicate meaning and constitute practices as much as they "cause" things to happen.

Causality

In the previous section, we tried to show that the further one moves away from the world of "brute" or observational facts, into the domains of intentionality and practices, the more do social facts have functions other than to "cause," as we normally understand that term. Searle lists beliefs, desires, hopes, and fears among his examples of intentionality. A hope does not work like the law of gravity; it functions differently. So, too, does a marriage and, by extension, a regime. In other words, the language of causality needs to be supplemented by languages that capture these additional social functions.

‡   Rawls's distinction was used in both articles but this example was cited in neither.

But there are problems even within the traditional language of causality as it pertains to the study of international regimes: a Newtonian notion of causality continues to occupy a central place in the field. This is so despite the tumultuous history of the concept of causality in this century—being declared a "fetish" by Karl Pearson, the "relic of a bygone age" by Bertrand Russell, a "superstition" by Ludwig Wittgenstein, and a "myth" by Stephen Toulmin (see the summary in Bernert 1983). Cook and Campbell have observed that "the epistemology of causation . . . is at present in a productive state of near chaos" (1979: 10).

The fundamental problem, first explicated by Hume, is that causality per se is unobservable and must be inferred (this discussion draws on Berk 1988). Building on the work of Hume, John Stuart Mill provided a set of procedures by which, through a process of successive elimination, a cause could be identified as the necessary and sufficient condition for an effect. But Mill, like Hume and virtually all other pre-twentieth-century philosophers of science, assumed that relations among empirical phenomena were fully determined.

This deterministic view started to come under increasing pressure at the turn of this century, and by the 1930s it had been replaced in physics by the understanding that subatomic relationships were inherently stochastic. For example, an electron has only a probability of being at a specific location. "It cannot be overemphasized that the stochastic subatomic world was *not* a product of measurement error or incomplete knowledge. Indeterminacy was an essential feature of the subatomic physical world" (Berk 1988: 157, italics in original).

In recent decades, an entirely new view of uncertainty or chance has emerged under the rubric of chaos theory. Berk explains, using a metaphor dear to the realist enterprise:

> Consider the opening break in a game of eightball. All of the billiard balls obey the usual deterministic laws of Newtonian mechanics. However, because of the curvature of each ball, small differences in where the balls make contact with one another translate into big differences in trajectory. With each collision, the importance of earlier small differences in points of collision are amplified so that after several collisions, the trajectories are effectively unpredictable. In other words, relationships that begin as effectively deterministic become effectively random.
>
> (ibid.: 158)

By now, it is generally accepted that the social world is inherently indeterminate. Two types of techniques are widely employed, therefore, in the attempt to enhance the credibility of causal inferences: (1) various statistical operations that reduce selection or estimation biases as well as spurious or confounding relationships, and (2) randomized experiments or quasi-experimental designs. The first of these requires reasonably large and robust sets of observational data; and the second requires that causal variables be subject to manipulation, at least in principle. In the field of international relations, neither condition holds for the international system *as a whole*. And neither condition holds well for international regimes. Hence, we should be modest in making causal claims about international regimes. Causal inferences about regime outcomes based on such commonly employed systemic factors as polarity, for example, are of a particularly questionable epistemological status.

Explanations

Yet a third epistemological problem is pervasive in the field. Even though the dominant concept of explanation fails to meet the formal criteria of the deductive-nomological or covering-law model, nevertheless most types of international relations theorizing embrace—often unconsciously—this Hempelian ideal. In this schema, an event is explained when it can be formally deduced from a general law and a set of initial conditions (Hempel 1965: chap. 5). Mearsheimer, for example, states that his scenarios of future instability in Europe rest "chiefly on deduction"—the law-like generalization being that multipolar systems are more unstable than bipolar systems, and the initial condition that the European security context is becoming multipolar (1990: 18). We have already commented on the dubious epistemological status of this covering law; our concern here is with the concept of explanation in which it is embedded. What is more, even many scholars who understand fully that the Hempelian ideal is not now met, and perhaps never will be met, nonetheless continue to adhere to it as an aspiration on the assumption that there are no "scientific" alternatives. But it is far from clear what science is being practiced by doing so. And alternative concepts of explanation have existed for the better part of the past century—though, in Jerome Bruner's words, social scientists today pay "precious little" attention to how they function (1986: 11). A brief sketch follows.

According to Hempel (1965: 243), the "methodological unity of empirical science" demands that the deductive-nomological construction is the only acceptable logical protocol for scientific explanations. Fields of inquiry that may fall short, such as history, are not fundamentally different, he contends, merely less well developed. And yet, even a philosopher of science so firmly committed to the "unity of science" premise as Ernest Nagel conceded long ago (1942, reprinted in 1961) that the covering-law model is inappropriate in explaining "aggregative events"—he mentions revolutions as an example: there are too few of them, they are highly complex, and there are bound to be important differences between them, all of which render problematical the necessary condition that they be instances of recurring "types" (1961: 568–575). Nagel suggests that aggregative events and large-scale social structures be "analyzed"—that is, broken down—into their component parts or aspects (ibid.: 571)—a practice that Waltz and his followers, interestingly enough, reject on the grounds that it is "reductionist" (Waltz 1979: chaps. 2 and 4). These parts, Nagel believes, may still be susceptible to covering-law explanations even when the larger whole is not. So that would be one route to go, entirely consistent with the dictates of the established "scientific" tradition. But how, then, do we "explain" the larger whole as a whole?

The major alternative may be described as "narrative" explanation.** Polkinghorne's discussion is by far the fullest (1988). In the narrative mode, causality is not defined in terms of a "constant antecedent" (gravity, for instance), but conforms to its ordinary language meaning of whatever antecedent conditions, events, or actions are "significant" in producing or influencing an effect, result, or consequence. Significance, in turn, is attributed to antecedent factors by virtue of their role in some "human project" as a whole—such as a revolution, in Nagel's example.

The narrative explanatory protocol comprises two "orders" of information: the descriptive and the configurative. The first simply links "events" along a temporal dimension and seeks to identify the effect one has on another. These events may be more or less "thickly" (i.e., analytically) described (Geertz 1973). The second organizes these descriptive statements into an interpretive "gestalt" or "coherence structure" (Polkinghorne 1988). These operations rest not on deduction, but on a method of interrogative reasoning that Charles Peirce called "abduction": the successive adjusting of a conjectured ordering scheme to the available facts (involving "a certain element of guess-work," Peirce pointed out), until the conjecture provides as full an account of the facts as possible (1955: 151–152). Polkinghorne uses the literary term "emplotment" to describe the same practice: "[it] is not the imposition of a ready-made plot structure on an independent set of events; instead, it is a dialectic process that takes place between the events themselves and a theme which discloses their significance and allows them to be grasped together as parts of one story" (1988: 19–20). The aim is to produce results that are verisimilar and believable to others looking over the same events.

But is not this explanatory mode arbitrary, subjective, and soft? Perhaps. Yet is it preferable to employ an explanatory mode that is not designed for the epistemological situation at hand? Besides, analytical tools exist that can render the narrative mode more rigorous. Noteworthy examples include the use of ideal-types and historical counterfactuals associated with Max Weber (1949). In recent years, Arthur Danto (1985) and Paul Ricoeur (1984) have made more firm the philosophical foundations of narrative historiography. Ronald Dworkin's work illustrates a complementary mode of legal reasoning (1986, for example). Furthermore, the narrative explanatory mode

---

** Some reactions I received to this formulation suggest that I may have made it sound too much like the "one damn fact after another" practice of standard historical narratives, which I did not intend. For one thing, sophisticated historiography is inherently analytical. But I also had in mind Weber's account of the rise of capitalism (1958), for example.

is not limited to "events" as traditionally understood, but can encompass human projects on a Braudelean scale.[1] In international relations, as Richard Ashley has noted (1984), classical realism, in contrast to neo-realism, was more likely to have utilized a narrative as opposed to a deductive-nomological explanatory scheme, though on the whole it was relatively unselfconscious about epistemological issues. Alexander George's method of structured, focused comparison (1979) illustrates another attempt to provide a degree of rigor in the analysis of cases characterized by small numbers and qualitative data.

In short, the issue cannot be posed in terms of logical positivism (even when inappropriate), on the one hand, or epistemological chaos, on the other. Alternatives exist.

REGIME ANALYSIS

These general epistemological issues, as indicated in passing, affect the study of regimes as well. We now take up three sets of issues in greater detail.

Ontology versus epistemology

The ontology of international regimes, we noted above, rests upon a core element of intersubjectivity. But the prevailing epistemological position in regime analysis typically is positivistic in orientation. Before it does anything else, positivism posits a separation of subject and object. It then focuses on the "objective" forces that move actors in their social interactions: regimes become external constraints on actors, not intersubjective frameworks of meaning. Intersubjective meaning, where it is considered at all, is inferred from behavior.

Here, then, we have the most debilitating problem in regime analysis: epistemology contradicts ontology. Small wonder that deep disagreement exists on what should be fairly straightforward empirical questions: Did Bretton Woods "collapse" in 1971–73 or was the change "norm governed"? Was the upsurge of trade restraints in the early 1980s indicative of renewed protectionism or not? How was the Non-Proliferation Treaty in 1985 successfully extended for yet another five-year term when so many states that voluntarily adhere to it protest its inequitable terms? And on and on.

In many such puzzling instances, actor *behavior* has failed adequately to convey intersubjective *meaning*. But intersubjective meaning seems to have had considerable influence on actor behavior. It is precisely this factor that limits the practical utility of, for example, the fascinating insights into the collaborative potential of rational egoists that are derived from laboratory or game-theoretic situations (most notably, Axelrod 1984; Axelrod and Keohane 1985). To put the problem in its simplest terms: in the simulated world, actors cannot communicate *and* engage in behavior; they are condemned to communicate *through* behavior. In the real world, the situation of course differs fundamentally. Here, the very essence of international regimes is expressed in cases such as that of France in 1968, asking for "sympathy and understanding" from its trading partners, as France invoked emergency measures against imports after the May disturbances of that year—and getting both from GATT (General Agreement on Tariffs and Trade) even though no objective basis existed in fact or in GATT law for doing so (see Chapter 2). A positivist epistemology cannot accommodate itself easily to so intersubjective an ontology. Hence, the case is treated in the literature as illustrating cynicism, complicity, and the erosion of respect for the GATT regime.

The contradiction between ontology and epistemology has occasioned surprisingly little concern in the regimes literature. Once it is realized that it exists what options are available to deal with it? One possibility would be to try to deny it. Theodore Abel's (1948) classic neopositivist response to the challenge posed by Weber's concept of *Verstehen* illustrates this tack: the concept aids in "the context discovery," Abel contended, but ultimately it is not relevant to "the context of validation." Hence it poses no challenge. Interpretive epistemologies, in contrast, stress the intimate relationship between validation and the uncovering of intersubjective meanings.[2]

A second possibility would be to try to formulate a rendition of the intersubjective ontology that is compatible with positivist epistemology. One plausible means of executing this maneuver would be to follow the economists down the road of "revealed preferences"—that consumption behavior, for example, reveals true consumer preferences. If our epistemology does not enable us to uncover meaning, the analogous reasoning would hold, then let us look for "revealed meaning," that is, for "objective" surrogates. It should suffice to point out that this is a solution by displacement only: it displaces the problem into the realm of assumption, that "objective" surrogates can capture "intersubjective" reality. Where intersubjectivity is the essence of the phenomenon under study, however, this is a dubious practice.

A third option would be to render a conception of regimes that is compatible with prevailing epistemological preferences, that is, regimes are regulative rules. The problem with that is that it omits a great many things that regimes are and do in addition to embodying regulative rules.

That leaves us with the option of turning to interpretive epistemological strains, more closely attuned to the reality of regimes. Experimentation along these lines has begun in the field of international relations. Ernst Haas has been moving toward his own brand of an "evolutionary epistemology" (see 1983a), wherein consensual knowledge about various aspects of the human condition becomes one of the forces behind the rise and decline of international regimes. Robert Cox (1986) has developed an unconventional historical materialist epistemology, which gives pride of place to shifting intersubjective frameworks of human discourse and practice. An epistemological position derived from the "universal pragmatics" of Juergen Habermas has been found fruitful (Kratochwil 1989), and other possibilities have been probed as well (for examples, see Alker 1981; Ashley 1984). The burden of our discussion is not to advocate any one such alternative but to urge that their consideration be delayed no longer.

Norms in explanation

In deductive-nomological explanation, even a single counterfactual occurrence, in principle, may be taken to refute the covering law (Popper 1968: chaps. 3–4). A probabilistic formulation would, of course, appropriately modify the criteria for refutation, but without, thereby, altering the basic structure of the explanation. What distinguishes international regimes from similar phenomena—from strategic interaction, let us say—is a specifically normative element.[3] Indeed, norms are specified to be one of the four analytical components of the concept of regimes: "standards of behavior defined in terms of rights and obligations" (Krasner 1983). But the covering-law model of explanation is not easily applied to cases in which norms are a significant element, in the phenomena to be explained. Two problems need to be addressed (Kratochwil 1984).

First, unlike the initial conditions in positivist explanations, norms can be thought in limited instances as "causing" occurrences. Norms may "guide" behavior, they may "inspire" behavior, they may "rationalize" or "justify" behavior, they may express "mutual expectations" about behavior, or they may be ignored. But they do not effect *cause* in the sense that a bullet through the heart causes death or an uncontrolled surge in the money supply causes price inflation. Hence, where norms are involved, the first component of the standard model of explanation is problematic.

The second is even more so. For norms are counterfactually valid. No single counterfactual occurrence refutes a norm. Not even many such occurrences *necessarily* do. Does driving while under the influence of alcohol refute the law (norm) against drunk driving? To be sure, the law (norm) is violated thereby. But whether or not violations also invalidate or refute a law (norm) will depend upon a host of other factors, not the least of which is how the community assesses the violation and responds to it (compare the very different community attitudes toward drunk driving with exceeding the 55 mile-an-hour speed limit). This is equally true of the norms of nondiscrimination in trade, free and stable currency exchanges, and adequate compensation for expropriated foreign property.

Indeed, it is possible to turn this around and argue that norms need not "exist" in a formal sense in order to be valid. It is often said, for example, that the Bretton Woods monetary regime did not "exist" prior to 1958, because only then did Europe assume the obligation of full currency convertibility for transactions on current account. But surely the norms of the regime guided the behavior of European states *toward* that event for some years before it actually took place. Thus, neither the violation of norms, nor, in some special circumstances, even their "nonexistence," necessarily refutes their validity.

Let it be understood that we are not advocating a coup whereby the reign of positivist explanation is replaced by explanatory anarchy. But we would insist that, just as epistemology has to match ontology, so too does the explanatory model have to be compatible with the basic nature of the particular scientific enterprise at hand. The impact of norms within international regimes is not a passive process, which can be ascertained analogously to that of Newtonian laws governing the collision of two bodies. Precisely because state behavior within regimes is interpreted by other states, the rationales and justifications for behavior that are proffered, together with pleas for understanding or admissions of guilt, as well as the responsiveness to such reasoning on the part of other states, all are absolutely critical component parts of any explanation involving the efficacy of norms. Indeed, such communicative dynamics may tell us far more about how robust a regime is than overt behavior alone. And only where noncompliance is widespread, persistent, and unexcused—that is, presumably, in limiting cases of regime-ness—will an explanatory model that rests on overt behavior alone suffice.[4]

To be sure, communicative dynamics may be influenced by such extra-contextual factors as state power, but that is no warrant for ignoring them. On the contrary, it suggests a potentially important relationship to be explored.[5] Similarly, the fact that verbal behavior may lend itself to manipulation suggests only that it be treated as judiciously as any other piece of scientific evidence.

The hierarchy of regime components

The concept of international regimes is defined as a composite of four analytical components (Krasner 1983): principles ("beliefs of fact, causation, and rectitude"), norms ("standards of behavior defined in terms of rights and obligations"), rules ("specific prescriptions and proscriptions for action"), and decision-making procedures ("prevailing practices for making and implementing collective choice"). At first blush, the four fit together neatly in the specific case that was uppermost in everyone's mind when this conception was formulated: the GATT-based trade regime. There, the story goes like this: The principle that liberalized trade is good for global welfare and international peace was readily translated by states into such norms as nondiscrimination, which in turn suggested the most-favored-nation rule, all of which led to negotiated tariff reductions based on reciprocal concessions.

But matters were more complicated right from the start due to the fact that GATT contained not one but at least two such scripts, and the second was very different from the first. The second ran from the responsibility of governments to stabilize their domestic economies on through the norm of safeguarding the balance of payments and, under certain circumstances, domestic producers, to rules defining specific GATT safeguarding provisions, and finally to establishing mechanisms of multilateral surveillance over their operations (see Chapter 2). Different governments weighted these two scripts differently, but over time they seem not to have been unduly perturbed by the need to live with the ambiguity of their juxtaposition. Ambiguity, however, appears to be more troublesome for analysts, even when it is a deliberate creation of policymakers. And therein lies another epistemological tale.

The notion prevails in the regimes literature that the four analytical components are related instrumentally and that the greater the coherence among them is, the stronger the regime will be (Haas 1983a). There is an a priori attractiveness to this notion, in that it is esthetically pleasing and our collective research program would be eased considerably were it to obtain. But reality is not so obliging. Let us take up first the instrumentalist idea.

A basic epistemological problem with instrumentalism is its presumption that it is always possible to separate goals (presumably expressed in principles and norms) from means (presumably expressed in rules and procedures), and to order them in a superordinate–subordinate relationship. But this relationship need not hold. As R. S. Summers has aptly remarked (1977): "However true this might be of constructing houses or other artifacts, it is not always so in law. In law when available means limit and in part define the goal, the means and the goal thus defined are to that extent inseparable." What is true of law may also be true of regimes, for, as Kenneth Waltz has argued (1979: 109), international collaboration is shaped primarily by the availability and acceptability of means not by the desirability of ends. Thus, notions such as reciprocity in the trade regime are *neither* its ends *nor* its means: in a quintessential way, they *are* the regime—they *are* the principled and shared understandings the regime comprises.

The idea that the four regime components should also be coherent, and that coherence indicates regime strength, is even more profoundly problematic. The fallacy in this notion is its presumption that, once the machinery is in place, actors merely remain programmed by it. But this is clearly not so. Actors not only reproduce normative structures, they also change them by their very practice, as underlying conditions change, as new constraints or possibilities emerge, or as new claimants make their presence felt. Sociologists call this "structuration" (Giddens 1981), and lawyers, "interstitial lawmaking." Only under extremely unusual circumstances could we imagine parallel and simultaneous changes having taken place in each of the four component parts of regimes such that they remained coherent—assuming that they were so at the outset. In any case the robustness of international regimes has little to do with how coherent they remain—how coherent is the very robust US Constitution?—but depends on the extent to which evolving and even diverging practices of actors express principled reasoning and shared understandings.

We have now reached the same conclusion through three different routes: the conventional epistemological approaches in regime studies do not and cannot suffice. Allow us, before ending this section, to resist the claim that we have opened up a proverbial Pandora's box. The box was opened when the discipline gravitated, appropriately, toward an intersubjective ontology in the study of international regimes. We have merely pointed out that this first, critical choice has consequences and implications that have not yet been adequately addressed. No discipline can resolve anomalies or reduce the wooliness of concepts when its ontological posture is contradicted by its epistemological orientation, models of explanation, and the presumed relationships among its analytical constructs. The problems we have pointed out are not insuperable, but their resolution will require the incorporation into prevailing approaches of insights and methods derived from more interpretive modes of social science.

CONCLUSION

In this chapter, we set out to provide a methodological assessment of the study of international regimes. In the first section, we tried to dispel the notion that the field of international organization has floundered from one "dependent variable" to another, as dictated by academic fashions. On the contrary, the analytical shifts leading up to the regimes focus were both progressive and cumulative, and were guided by an overriding concern with what has always preoccupied students of international organization: how the modern society of nations governs itself.

We also noted, however, that the study of regimes is afflicted by serious epistemological problems, stemming from a disjuncture between the nature of its object of study, on the one hand, and the prevailing epistemological precepts and prescriptions for its study, on the other. In the second section, we suggested how and why positivism is a problematic basis for explaining social phenomena characterized by such attributes as small numbers of cases, especially if they are aggregative events, and in which a significant role is played by ideas, norms, and social institutions. We also pointed to some alternative explanatory protocols, which have a history going back at least as far as Dilthey and Weber.

In the third section, we addressed the core epistemological problem in regime analysis: the tension between its ontological posture and epistemological practices. In contrast to the epistemological ideal of positivism, which insists on a separation of "object" and "subject," we proposed a more interpretive approach that would open up regime analysis to the communicative rather than merely the referential functions of norms in social interactions. Thus, what constitutes a breach of an obligation undertaken within a regime is not simply an "objective description" of a fact but also an intersubjective appraisal. Likewise, what constitutes reciprocity or reasonableness of behavior within regime contexts is not an issue that can be resolved simply by a monological treatment of "objective information," as is characteristic of a propositional language. For regimes are inherently dialogical in character.

To be sure, in circumstances that require little interpretation on the part of the relevant actors—because the environment is placid, because shared knowledge prevails, or because coercion determines outcomes—interpretive epistemologies will not be required. But we do not take such occurrences to be broadly representative of contemporary international regimes. For the more general universe of cases, once it was decided that the ontology of regimes consists of an intersubjective basis—and the consensus definition of regimes suggests as much—then what Frank Lentricchia (1983: 3) has called "spectator epistemology" ipso facto became insufficient.

4 Multilateralism at century's end

The discipline of international relations failed to predict the collapse of the Soviet empire. A rupture of that kind was not part of the analytical domain of any major body of theory, though in many instances a scramble took place after the fact to retrofit theories to events. But scholars soon began to theorize about the longer-term consequences of that rupture, producing scenarios that ranged from the imminence of collective security in Europe, if not the world, to why we would soon wish the cold war were back This chapter originated as 1992a and was the concept paper for a study group that eventually produced 1993a.

I wrote the article with two sets of protagonists in mind. The first was that group of theorists for whom institutions matter little, above all neorealists Institutions seemed far more important in the post-1989 transformation than neorealists allowed; the project sought to test that hypothesis.

The second set of protagonists were my fellow institutionalists for whom the principled or normative bases of institutions had increasingly been left unexplored, above all neoliberal institutionalists. As a result of their focus on the functional determinants of cooperation they have significantly deepened our understanding of that phenomenon But what was striking about the role of institutions in helping to stabilize the post-1989 transformation was their specific form: multilateralism. When defined in principled rather than purely nominal terms, this is a highly unusual and demanding institutional form, and one which does not self-evidently flow from neoliberal premises.

In writing the article, I also tried to be more self-conscious about the epistemological issues raised in the previous essay than I had been, for example, in the essay that forms the basis of Chapter 2, which, though of the same genre, remained largely implicit on these matters.

Finally, in some sense, 1992a closed the circle back to 1972a: the questions asked concerned similar macro-issues of international organization, though now the task was not to establish a new mode of analysis but to devise answers to real-world questions drawing on the vibrant and vital literature on the new institutionalism that had emerged in the two-decade interval.

In 1989, peaceful change, which a leading realist theorist had declared a low-probability means of adjusting to major power shifts in international politics less than a decade before,[1] accommodated the most fundamental such shift of the postwar era and perhaps of the entire twentieth century: the collapse of the Soviet East European empire and the attendant end of the cold war. Many factors were responsible for that shift. But there seems little doubt that multilateral norms and institutions helped stabilize their international consequences. Indeed, these norms and institutions appear to be playing a significant role in the management of a broad array of regional and global changes in the world system today.

In Europe, by one count, at least fifteen multilateral groupings are involved in shaping the continent's collective destiny (Clarke 1990; Stokes 1990). The European Community (EC) is the undisputed anchor of economic relations and increasingly of a common political vision in the West. And the former East European countries want nothing so much as to tie their economic fate to the EC, a goal that EC members have facilitated through the creation of the European Bank for Reconstruction and Development and, in some cases, through the prospect of association agreements. Yet the author of another influential realist treatise published a decade ago gave the EC only a few fleeting references—and then only to argue that it would never amount to much in the international "structure" unless it took on the form of a unified state (Waltz 1979: 201–202), which it shows no signs of doing even now.

In the realm of European security relations, the central policy issue of the day concerns the adaptation of the North Atlantic Treaty Organization (NATO) to the new European geopolitical realities and the question of whether supplementary indigenous West European or all European multilateral security mechanisms should be fashioned. The Soviet Union, contrary to most predictions, posed no obstacles to German reunification, betting that a united Germany firmly embedded in a broader Western institutional matrix would pose far less of a security threat than a neutral Germany tugged in different directions in the center of Europe. But perhaps the most telling indicator of institutional bite in Europe today is the proverbial dog that has not barked: no one in any position of authority anywhere is advocating, or quietly preparing for, a return to a system of competitive bilateral alliances—which surely is the first time that this has happened at any comparable historical juncture since the Congress of Vienna in 1815.[2]

Security relations in the Asia–Pacific region make the same points in the negative. In the immediate postwar period, it was not possible to construct multilateral institutional frameworks in this region. Today, the absence of such arrangements inhibits progressive adaptation to fundamental global shifts. The United States and Japan are loath to raise serious questions about their anachronistic bilateral defense treaty, for example, out of fear of unraveling a fragile stability and thereby triggering arms races throughout the region. In Asia–Pacific, there is no EC and no NATO to have transformed the multitude of regional security dilemmas, as has been done in Europe with Franco-German relations. Indeed processes through which to begin the minimal task of mutual confidence building barely exist in the region. Thus, whereas today the potential to move beyond balance-of-power politics in its traditional form exists in Europe, a stable balance is the best that one can hope to achieve in the Asia–Pacific region.[3]

At the level of the global economy, despite sometimes near-hysterical predictions for twenty years now of imminent monetary breakup and trade wars that could become real wars, "just like in the 1930s,"[4] the rate of growth in world trade continues to exceed the rate of growth in world output; international capital flows dwarf both; and the eighth periodic round of trade negotiations, which had been prematurely pronounced dead, is moving toward completion—this time involving difficult domestic and new transnational issues that the originators of the regime never dreamed would become subject to international rules. And despite considerable tension between them, the United States and Japan continue, in Churchill's phrase, to "jaw-jaw" rather than "war-war" over their fundamental trade differences.

Limited multilateral successes can be found even in the global security realm. One is in the area of nuclear nonproliferation. Many responsible officials and policy analysts in the 1960s predicted that by the 1980s there would exist some two dozen nuclear weapons states (Reiss 1988: chap. 1). As it has turned out, however, the total set of actual *and potential* problem states today consists of only half that number. According to a former official of the US Arms Control and Disarmament Agency and an analyst at the Lawrence Livermore National Laboratory, this is at least in part due to the nonproliferation treaty (NPT) regime: "Virtually every nonproliferation initiative has turned out to be much more effective than expected when it was proposed or designed, and nonproliferation success has been cheaper than expected. The fact that the nuclear proliferation problem has been 'bounded' by the NPT regime means that policy initiatives can be focused on a handful of states" (Graham and Mullins 1991: 3; also see Pilat and Pendley 1990).

Moreover, after years of being riveted by the cold war, the United Nations (UN) has been rediscovered to have utility in international conflict management: its figleaf role proved useful in Afghanistan, and its decolonization function aided Namibia. It serves as one means by which to try to disentangle regional morasses from Cambodia to the Western Sahara. And perhaps of greatest importance for the new, post-cold-war era, the decisions adopted by the UN Security Council to sanction Iraq for its invasion and annexation of Kuwait were the organization's most comprehensive, firm, and united response ever to an act of international aggression.*

Seen through the lenses of conventional theories of international relations, which attribute outcomes to the underlying distribution of political or economic power, the roles played by norms and institutions in the current international transformation must seem paradoxical. Norms and institu-

---

* The subsequent experiences of UN intervention in Somalia and Bosnia were less salutary largely because neither governments nor the UN itself strictly speaking knew what they were doing, politically or doctrinally. Indeed, I wrote even before those setbacks (1992c: 5): "it is a miracle of no small magnitude that disaster has not yet befallen one of these [new] peacekeeping missions" (also see Chapter 10).

tions do not matter much in that literature to begin with; they are viewed as by-products of, if not epiphenomenal adjuncts to, the relations of force or the relations of production. What is more, insofar as the conventional literature has any explanation of extensive institutionalization in the international system, the so-called theory of hegemonic stability is it. But in addition to all the other historical and logical problems from which that theory suffers (Keohane 1980; Stein 1984; Snidal 1985; Conybeare 1987), merely finding the hegemony to which the current array of regional and global institutional roles could be ascribed is a daunting challenge.

The fact that norms and institutions matter comes as no surprise to the "new institutionalists" in international relations; after all, that has long been their message (Keohane 1988). But, curiously, they have paid little explicit and detailed analytic attention to a core feature of current international institutional arrangements: their multilateral form. A literature search keyed on the concept of multilateralism turns up relatively few entries, and only a tiny number of these are of any interest to the international relations theorist. The focus of most new institutionalists has been on "cooperation" and "institutions" in a generic sense, with international regimes and formal organizations sometimes conceived as specific institutional subsets (Krasner 1983; Keohane 1984; Oye 1986). For example, no scholar has contributed more to the new institutionalism in international relations than Robert Keohane. Yet the concept of multilateralism is used sparingly in his work, even in a literature survey on that subject. And the definition of multilateralism that he employs is purely nominal: "the practice of coordinating national policies in groups of three or more states" (1990b: 731).

The nominal definition of multilateralism may be useful for some purposes. But it poses the problem of subsuming institutional forms that traditionally have been viewed as being expressions of bilateralism, not multilateralism—instances of the Bismarckian alliance system, for example, such as the League of the *Three* Emperors. In short, the nominal definition of multilateralism misses the *qualitative* dimension of the phenomenon that makes it distinct—it misses, in short, that feature of multilateralism which, in the language of the previous essay, distinguishes it as institutional fact.

In a superb discussion of this issue, attempting to sort out the enormous variety of trade relations in the world today, William Diebold insists for starters on the need to distinguish between "formal" and "substantive" multilateralism, by which he means roughly what I mean by nominal versus qualitative. "But that is far from the end of the matter. The bilateral agreements of Cordell Hull were basically different from those of Hjalmar Schacht" (Diebold 1988: 1). That is to say, the issue is not the number of parties so much, Diebold suggests, as it is the kind of relations that are instituted among them. It is this substantive or qualitative characteristic of multilateralism that concerns me in the present essay, not only for trade but also for the institutional dimension of international relations in general.

Nor is the missing qualitative dimension captured entirely by the concepts of international regimes or intergovernmental organizations. There are instances of international regimes that were not multilateral in form, such as the Nazi trade and monetary regimes, to which we will return momentarily. As for multilateral formal organizations, although they entail no analytic mystery, all theorists of the new institionalism agree that these organizations constitute only one small part of a broader universe of international institutional forms that interest them.

The missing qualitative dimension of multilateralism immediately comes into focus, however, if we return to an older institutionalist discourse, one informed by the postwar aims of the United States to restructure the international order. When we speak here of multilateralism in international trade, we know immediately that it refers to trade organized on the basis of certain principles of state conduct—above all, nondiscrimination [see Chapter 2]. Similarly, when we speak here of multilateralism in security relations, we know that it refers to some expression or other of collective security or collective self-defense (Dallek 1979; Pollard 1985). And when President Bush today proclaims a "new world order"—universal aspirations, cooperative deterrence, and joint action against aggression—whether vision or rhetoric, the notion evokes and is consistent with the American postwar multilateralist agenda, as I argue below. In sum, what is distinctive about multilateralism is not merely that it coordinates national policies in groups of three or more states, which is something that other organizational forms also do, but that it does so on the basis of certain principles of ordering relations among those states.

Thus, there exists a compound anomaly in the world of international relations theory today. An institutional phenomenon of which conventional theories barely take note is both widespread and significant; but at the same time, the particular features that make it so are glossed over by most students of international institutions themselves. This essay is intended to help resolve both parts of the anomaly.

My premise is that we can better understand the role of multilateral norms and institutions in the current international transformation by recovering the principled meanings of multilateralism from actual historical practice; by showing how and why those principled meanings have come to be institutionalized throughout the history of the modern interstate system; and by exploring how and why they may perpetuate themselves today, even as the conditions that initially gave rise to them have changed.

This "grounded" analysis of the concept suggests a series of working hypotheses, which require more extensive testing before strong validity claims can be made for them. Nevertheless, the hypotheses are sufficiently interesting and plausible to warrant such further study, and I present them here in that spirit. The argument, in brief, goes something like this: Multilateralism is a generic institutional form of modern international life, and as such it has been present from the start. The generic institutional form of multilateralism must not be confused with formal multilateral organizations, a relatively recent arrival and still of only relatively modest importance. Historically, the generic form of multilateralism can be found in institutional arrangements to define and stabilize the international property rights of states, to manage coordination problems, and to resolve collaboration problems. The last of these uses of the multilateral form is historically the least frequent. In the literature, this fact traditionally has been explained by the rise and fall of hegemonies and, more recently, by various functional considerations. Our analysis suggests that permissive domestic environments in the leading powers of the day are at least as important and, in some cases, more important. When we look more closely at the post-World War II situation, then, this implies that it was less the fact of American *hegemony* that accounts for the explosion of multilateral arrangements than it was the fact of *American* hegemony. Finally, we suggest that institutional arrangements of the multilateral form have adaptive and even reproductive capacities which other institutional forms lack and which, therefore, may help explain the roles that multilateral arrangements play in stabilizing the current international transformation.

THE MEANINGS OF MULTILATERALISM

At its core, multilateralism refers to coordinating relations among three or more states in accordance with certain principles. But what, precisely, are those principles? And to what, precisely, do those principles pertain? To facilitate the construction of a more formal definition, let us begin by examining a historical instance of something that everyone agrees multilateralism is not: bilateralism.

Earlier in this century, Nazi Germany succeeded in finely honing a pure form of bilateralism into a systemic organizing principle. Now, as Diebold (1988) notes, the everyday term "bilateral" is entirely neutral with regard to the qualitative relationship that is instituted among countries. So as to give expression to its qualitative nature, the Nazi system therefore typically has been referred to as bilateral*ist* in character or as embodying bilateral*ism* as its organizing principle. In any case, once the New Plan of the Nazi government took effect in 1934, Hjalmar Schacht devised a scheme of bilateralist trade agreements and clearing arrangements (Hirschman 1945; Yaeger 1976). The essence of the German international trade regime was that the state negotiated "reciprocal" agreements with its foreign trading partners. These negotiations determined which goods and services were to be exchanged, their quantities, and their price. Often, Germany deliberately imported more from its partners than it exported to them. But it required that its trading partners liquidate their claims on Germany by reinvesting there or by purchasing deliberately overpriced German goods. Thus, its trading partners were doubly dependent on Germany.

This trade regime in turn was linked to bilateralist monetary clearing arrangements. Under these arrangements, a German importer would, for example, pay marks to the German Reichsbank for its imports rather than to the foreign source of the goods or services, while the foreign counterpart of the transaction would receive payment in home country currency from its central bank—and vice versa for German exports. No foreign exchange changed hands; the foreign exchange markets were bypassed; and artificial exchange rates prevailed. The permissible total amounts to be cleared in this manner were negotiated by the two states.

German bilateralism typically, but not exclusively, focused on smaller and weaker states in East Central Europe, the Balkans, and Latin America, exchanging primary commodity imports for manufactured exports. But several major states, including Britain and the United States, had limited agreements with Germany involving *Sondermarks*—marks which foreigners could earn through the sale of specified products to Germany but which Germany in turn restricted to particular purchases from Germany. In any case, the scheme had no inherent geographical limit; it could have been universalized to cover the entire globe, with an enormous spiderweb of bilateralist agreements radiating out from Germany.

The nominal definition of multilateralism would not exclude the Schachtian bilateralist device: it coordinated economic relations among three or more states. Nor is the fact decisive that negotiations took place bilaterally: after all, many tariff reductions in the General Agreement on Tariffs and Trade (GATT) are also negotiated bilaterally. The difference is, of course, that within GATT bilaterally negotiated tariff reductions are extended to all other parties on the basis of most-favored-nation (MFN) treatment, whereas the Schachtian scheme was inherently and fundamentally discriminatory, so that bilateral deals held only on a case-by-case and product-by-product basis, even if they had covered the entire globe in doing so.

Let us examine next an institutional arrangement that is generally acknowledged to embody multilateralist principles: a collective security system. None has ever existed in pure form, but in concept the scheme is quite simple. It rests on the premise that peace is indivisible, so that a war against one state is, ipso facto, considered a war against all. The community of states therefore is obliged to respond to threatened or actual aggression, first by diplomatic means, then through economic sanctions, and finally by the collective use of force if necessary. Facing the prospect of such a community-wide response, any rational potential aggressor would be deterred and would desist. Thus, the incidence of war gradually would decline.

A collective security scheme certainly coordinates security relations among three or more states. But so, too, as noted above, did the League of the Three Emperors, which was nothing more than a set of traditional alliances (Taylor 1971: chap. 12). What is distinct about a collective security scheme is that it comprises, as Sir Arthur Salter put it a half-century ago, a permanent potential alliance "against the *unknown* enemy" (1939: 155, emphasis in original)—and, he should have added, on behalf of the *unknown* victim. The institutional difference between an alliance and a collective security scheme can be simply put: in both instances, state A is pledged to come to the aid of B if B is attacked by C. In a collective security scheme, however, A is also pledged to come to the aid of C if C is attacked by B. Consequently, as G. F. Hudson (1968: 176–177) points out, "A cannot regard itself as the ally of B more than of C, because theoretically it is an open question whether, if an act of war should occur, B or C would be the aggressor. In the same way B has indeterminate obligations towards A and C, and C towards A and B, and so on with a vast number of variants as the system is extended to more and more states."

It was precisely this difference between a collective security system and alliances that ultimately doomed the fate of the League of Nations in the US Senate.[5] NATO reflects a truncated version of the model, in which a subset of states organized a collective self-defense arrangement of indefinite duration, de jure against any potential aggressor though de facto against one. Nevertheless, internally the scheme was predicated on two multilateralist principles. The first was the indivisibility of threats to the collectivity—that is, it did not matter whether it was Germany, Great Britain, the Netherlands, or Norway that was attacked, nor in theory by whom. And the second was its requirement of, and organization for, a collective response.

We are now in a position to be more precise about the core meaning of multilateralism. Keohane has defined institutions, generically, as "persistent and connected sets of rules, formal and informal, that prescribe behavioural roles, constrain activity, and shape expectations" (1990a: 732). Very simply, the term "multilateral" is an adjective that modifies the noun "institution." How does multilateral modify institution? Our illustrations suggest that multilateralism is an institutional form which coordinates relations among three or more states on the basis of "generalized" principles of conduct—that is, principles which specify appropriate conduct for classes of actions, without regard to the particularistic interests of the parties or the strategic exigencies that may exist in any specific occurrence. MFN treatment is a classic example in the economic realm: it forbids discrimination among countries producing the same product—period. Its counterpart in security relations is the requirement that states respond to aggression whenever and wherever it occurs—whether or not any specific instance suits their individual likes and dislikes. In contrast, the bilateralist form, such as the Schachtian device and traditional alliances, differentiates relations case-by-case based precisely on a priori particularistic grounds or situational exigencies.

Bilateralism and multilateralism do not exhaust the institutional repertoire of states. Imperialism can be considered a third institutional form. Imperialism also is an institution that coordinates relations among three or more states though, unlike bilateralism and multilateralism, it does so by denying the sovereignty of the subject states.[6]

Two corollaries follow from our definition of multilateralism. First, generalized organizing principles logically entail an indivisibility among the members of a collectivity with respect to the range of behavior in question. Depending on circumstances, that indivisibility can take markedly different forms, ranging from the physical ties of railway lines that the collectivity chooses to standardize across frontiers, all the way to the adoption by states of the premise that peace is indivisible. But note that indivisibility here is a *social construction*, not a technical condition: in a collective security scheme, states behave *as if* peace were indivisible and thereby make it so. Similarly, in the case of trade, it is the GATT members' adherence to the MFN norm which makes the system of trade an indivisible whole, not some inherent attribute of trade itself.[7] Bilateralism, in contrast, segments relations into multiples of dyads and compartmentalizes them. Second, as discussed in further detail below, successful cases of multilateralism appear to generate among their members what Keohane (1986) has called expectations of "diffuse reciprocity." That is to say, the arrangement is expected by its members to yield a rough equivalence of benefits in the aggregate and over time. Bilateralism, in contrast, is premised on specific reciprocity, the simultaneous balancing of specific quid pro quos by each party with every other at all times.[8]

It follows from this definition and its corollaries that multilateralism is a highly demanding institutional form. Its historical incidence, therefore, will be less frequent than that of its alternatives; and if its relative incidence at any time were to increase, that would pose an interesting puzzle to be explained.

The obvious next issue to address is the fact that the generic concept of international institution, as Keohane (1988) points out, applies in practice to many different types of institutionalized relations among states. So too, therefore, does the adjective multilateral: the attribute of multilateralism that it coordinates relations among three or more states in accordance with generalized principles of conduct will have different specific expressions, depending on the type of institutionalized relations to which it pertains. Let us examine some instances. Common usage in the literature distinguishes among three institutional domains of interstate relations: international orders, international regimes, and international organizations. Each type can be, but need not be, multilateral in form.

The literature frequently refers to international economic orders, international security orders, international maritime orders, and so on. An "open" or "liberal" international economic order is multilateral in form, as is a maritime order based on the principle of *mare liberum*. The New Economic Order of the Nazis was not multilateral in form, for reasons we have already suggested, and neither was the European security order crafted by Bismarck. The concept of multilateralism here refers to the constitutive rules that order relations in given domains of international life—they define what Rawls calls "practices" (designating a bag a base in baseball, for example, as we saw in the previous essay). Thus, the quality of "openness" in an international economic order refers to such characteristics as the prohibition of exclusive blocs, spheres, or similar barriers to the free flow of international economic transactions. The corresponding quality in an international security order—the quality that would cause it to be described as "collective"—is the condition of equal access to a common security umbrella. To the extent that the characteristic conditions are met, the order in question may be said to be multilateral in form. In short, multilateralism here depicts the character of an overall order of relations among states; definitionally it says nothing about how that order is achieved.

A regime is more concrete than an order. Typically, the term "regime" refers to a functional or sectoral component of an order. Moreover, the concept of regime encompasses more of the "how" question than does the concept of order in that, broadly speaking, the term "regime" is used to refer to common, deliberative, though often highly asymmetrical means of conducting interstate relations. That much is clear from common usage. But while there is a widespread assumption in the literature that all regimes are, ipso facto, multilateral in character, this assumption is egregiously erroneous. For example, there is no reason not to call the Schachtian schemes for organizing monetary and trade relations international regimes; they fully meet the standard criteria specified by Krasner and his colleagues (1983). Moreover, it is entirely possible to imagine the emergence of regimes between two states—superpower security regimes, for example, have been a topic of some discussion (Weber 1990; also see Jervis 1983, 1985)—but such regimes by definition would not be multilateral either. In sum, what makes a regime a *regime* is that it satisfies the definitional criteria of encompassing principles, norms, rules, and decision-making procedures around which actor expectations converge. But what makes a regime *multilateral* in form, beyond involving three or more states, is that the substantive meanings of those terms roughly reflect the appropriate generalized principles of conduct. By way of illustration, in the case of a multilateral trade regime, these would include the norm of MFN treatment, corresponding rules about reciprocal tariff reductions and the application of safeguards, and collectively sanctioned procedures for implementing the rules. In the case of a collective security regime, they would include the norm of nonaggression, uniform rules for use of sanctions to deter or punish aggression, and, again, collectively sanctioned procedures for implementing them.

Finally, formal international organizations are palpable entities with headquarters and letterheads, voting procedures, and generous pension plans. They require no conceptual elaboration. But, again, their relationship to the concept of multilateralism is less self-evident than is sometimes assumed. Two issues deserve brief mention. The first issue, though it may be moot at the moment, is that there have been international organizations that were not multilateral in form. The Comintern and the Cominform come to mind; they were based explicitly on Leninist principles of organization, which were hierarchical, not multilateral, in character (Borkenau 1962).

Along the same lines, the recently collapsed Soviet–East European system of organizations differed from multilateral forms by having been based on a series of dyadic ties to Moscow (Holden 1990).

The second issue is more problematic even today. There is a common tendency in the world of actual international organizations, and sometimes in the academic community, to equate the phenomenon of multilateralism with the universe of multilateral organizations or diplomacy. The preceding discussion makes it clear why that view is in error. It may be the case empirically that decisions concerning aspects of international orders or, more likely, international regimes are made in or by multilateral forums. The EC exhibits this pattern most extensively; the failed quest by developing countries for a New International Economic Order in the 1970s exhibits the desire to achieve it; decisions on most international trade and monetary matters fall in between. But definitionally, multilateral organization is a separate and distinct type of institutionalized behavior, defined by such generalized decision-making rules as voting or consensus procedures.

In sum, the term "multilateral" is an adjective that modifies the noun institution. What distinguishes the multilateral form from other forms is that it coordinates behavior among three or more states on the basis of generalized principles of conduct. Accordingly, any theory of international institutions that does not include this qualitative dimension of multilateralism is bound to be a fairly abstract theory and one that is silent about a crucial distinction within the repertoire of international institutional forms. Moreover, for analytic purposes, it is important not to (con)fuse the very meaning of multilateralism with any one particular institutional expression of it, be it an international order, regime, or organization. Each can be, but need not be, multilateral in form. In addition, the multilateral form should not be equated with universal geographical scope; the attributes of multilateralism characterize relations within specific collectivities that may and often do fall short of the whole universe of nations. Finally, it should be kept in mind that these are formal definitions, not empirical descriptions of actual cases, and we would not expect actual cases to conform fully to the formal definitions. But let us turn now to some actual historical cases exhibiting the multilateral form.

MULTILATERALISM IN HISTORY

The institutional form of multilateralism has now been defined. What can we say about its specific instances over time, their frequency distribution, and some possible correlates? A brief historical survey will situate the phenomenon of multilateralism better and help us begin to answer these questions. To organize the discussion, I adapt a typology of institutional roles from the literature: defining and stabilizing international property rights, solving coordination problems, and resolving collaboration problems.[9]

Property rights

Not surprisingly, the earliest multilateral arrangements instituted in the modern era were designed to cope with the international consequences of the novel principle of state sovereignty. The newly emerged territorial states conceived their essence, their very being, by the possession of territory and the exclusion of others from it. But how does one possess something one does not own? And, still more problematic, how does one exclude others from it?

The world's oceans posed this problem. Contiguous waterways could be shared, administered jointly, or, more than likely, split down the middle; the international property rights of states thereby were established bilaterally. The oceans were another matter. States attempted to project exclusive unilateral jurisdiction, but they failed. Spain and Portugal tried a bilateral solution, whereby Spain claimed a monopoly of the western trade routes to the Far East and Portugal claimed the eastern routes. But they, too, failed. All such efforts failed for the simple reason that it is exceedingly difficult if not impossible in the long run to vindicate a property right that is not recognized as being valid by the relevant others in a given community, especially when exclusion is as difficult as it was in the oceans. Attempts to do so lead to permanent challenge and recurrent conflict. A multilateral solution to the governance of the oceans, therefore, was inescapable. The principle which was first enunciated by Hugo Grotius at the beginning of the seventeenth century and which states slowly came to adopt was one that defined an international maritime order in two parts: a territorial sea under exclusive state control, which custom set at three miles because that was the range of land-based cannons at the time; and the high seas beyond, available for common use but owned by none (Aster Institute 1985). Under this arrangement, all states were free to utilize the high seas, provided only that they did not thereby damage the legitimate interests of others (for the case of piracy and its abolition, see Ritchie 1986). And each state had the same rules for all states, not one rule for some and other rules for others.

An even more profound instance of delimiting the property rights of states—more profound because it concerned internal, as opposed to external, space—was the invention of the principle of extraterritoriality as the basis for organizing permanent diplomatic representation. As Garrett Mattingly put it in his magisterial study of the subject (1964: 244): "By arrogating to themselves supreme power over men's consciences, the new states had achieved absolute sovereignty. Having done so, they found they could only communicate with one another by tolerating within themselves little islands of alien sovereignty." Instituting those alien islands in the end required a multilateral solution, though differential arrangements based on the religious preferences and social status of rulers were tried first. And their maintenance came to be seen as being necessary to the very existence of a viable political order among states (ibid.; also see Bozeman 1960). As a result, grave breaches of the principle of extraterritoriality are, ipso facto, deemed to be a violation against the entire community of states.

Until quite recently, neither regimes nor formal organizations played significant roles in the definition and stabilization of international property rights. Conventional practice and episodic treaty negotiations sufficed to establish multilateral orders of relations.

Coordination problems

States have strong and conflicting preferences about international property rights. In the case of the oceans, for example, coastal states were favored over landlocked states by the allocation of any territorial sea; different coastal states ended up with differentially sized territorial seas by virtue of the length of their coastlines; coastal states nevertheless would have preferred no limit at all to the territorial sea; and so on. There is also a class of problems in international relations wherein states are more or less indifferent in principle to the actual outcome, provided only that all accept the same outcome. These are typically referred to as coordination problems.

A paradigmatic case of a coordination problem was posed by the growing use of electronic telegraphy in the mid-nineteenth century and concerned what would happen to a message as it came, for instance, to the border between France and the Grand Duchy of Baden. The following procedure was followed: "A common station was established at Strasbourg with two employees, one from the French Telegraph Administration, the other from Baden. The French employee received, for example, a telegram from Paris, which the electric wires had transmitted to him with the speed of light. This message he wrote out by hand onto a special form and handed it across the table to his German colleague. He translated it into German, and then sent it again on its way" (ITU 1965: 45). With the intensification of trade, the desire for the latest stock market information from London, Paris, and Berlin, and important diplomatic messages that governments wished to send to one another, this arrangement became untenable. Its costs in profits lost, opportunities forgone, and administrative resources expended mounted rapidly. The initial response was to negotiate a series of bilateral treaties. But in the dense communications complex of the European continent, bilateral solutions soon also proved inadequate. Several multilateral arrangements were therefore constructed and were subsequently combined in 1865, when the International Telegraph Union was established.

The multilateral arrangement for telegraphy consisted of three parts. First, the parties devised rules governing the network of telegraph lines that were to connect countries within Europe (and, later, in other parts of the world), the codes to be used, the priorities of transmission, the languages that were permissible, the schedule of tariffs to be levied, the manner in which proceeds would be divided, and so on. Second, they established a permanent secretariat to administer the day-to-day implementation of these rules and to coordinate the technical operations of the system. And, third, they convened periodic conferences to make any such revisions in the basic system as became necessary over time.

Much the same kind of arrangement had already been anticipated in the domain of European river transport, as on the Rhine and the Danube, typically consisting of commissions, secretariats, and judicial bodies—and, in some instances, even uniforms for officials (Chamberlain 1923). Later in the nineteenth century, similar multilateral arrangements were instituted in the field of public health (Haas 1964: 14–17).

In situations exhibiting coordination problems, the incentives are high for states to organize their relations on the basis of generalized principles of conduct. At least in the long run, therefore, the desire to reduce transaction costs tends to be a driving factor. Not surprisingly, historically the highest incidence of multilateral regimes and organizations is found in this domain.

Collaboration problems

Where the definition and stabilization of at least some international property rights is concerned, there appears to exist an ultimate inevitability to multilateral solutions, though "ultimate" may mean after all other options, including war, have been exhausted. In cases of coordination problems, there appears to exist an ultimate indifference as to which one of several outcomes is selected, though "ultimate" here may mask such concrete problems as sunk costs that individual states may have invested in the "equally acceptable" outcome that did not get adopted.

Between the two extremes of inevitability and indifference lies the domain of mixed-motive, conflict of interest situations. Even in this domain, however, cooperation occurs. And sometimes it occurs on a multilateral basis. Before 1945, however, it did not do so very often.

In the security realm, the most celebrated case is the Concert of Europe. But students of international relations have paid far more attention to the issue of whether or not it constituted a security regime than to the fact that it exhibited elements of the multilateral form. Charles and Clifford Kupchan (1991: 120) have provided us with a useful continuum of collective security arrangements, with the "ideal" form at one end and concerts at the other. We have already examined the formal attributes of the "ideal" model. According to the Kupchans, the concert version is characterized by the dominance of the great powers, decisions taken by informal negotiations and consensus, and no explicit specification of the mechanisms for implementing collective action. But—and this is what puts it in the class of collective security mechanisms—a concert nevertheless is "predicated on the notion of all against one." That is, a concert is predicated on the indivisibility of peace among its members and on their obligation to respond to acts of aggression.[10]

Between the Napoleonic and the Crimean wars, from 1815 to 1854, peace in Europe was maintained, in Henry Kissinger's words (1964: 5), by an institutional "framework" that was regarded by participants as being "legitimate," so that "they sought adjustment within [it] rather than in its overthrow." In doing so, according to Robert Jervis, they "behaved in ways that sharply diverged from normal 'power politics' " (1983: 178; also see Jervis 1985 and Elrod 1976).

As Jervis describes it, the five leading powers—Austria, Great Britain, Prussia, Russia, and a French monarchy restored with the aid of the other four—refrained from seeking to maximize their relative power positions vis-à-vis one another, instead moderating their demands and behavior; they refrained from exploiting one another's temporary weaknesses and vulnerabilities; and they threatened force sparingly and used it rarely as a means to resolve differences among them—except, Kalevi Holsti adds (1991), that they "were clearly of the opinion that force could be used individually or collectively for enforcing certain decisions and for coercing those who threatened the foundations of the order or the system of governance."

How were these feats achieved? The five constituted themselves as "an executive body" of the European international system (Craig and George 1983: 31), convening extensive multilateral consultations through which they acted on matters that could have undermined the peace. For example, they collectively created and guaranteed the neutrality of Belgium and Greece, thereby removing those territories from the temptations of bilateral partition or competition. As Rene Albrecht-Carrié has argued (1968: 22), the "Eastern question" in general—that is, the problem of how to secure orderly change and national independence in the wake of the irreversible decay of the Ottoman Empire—"provides many illustrations of an authentic common preference for orderly and peaceful procedure, more than once successfully implemented."

What could account for this unusual institutional development? It seems that the threat posed by Napoleon's imperial ambitions to the very principle of the balance of power proved weightier than the usual risks and uncertainties that plague cooperation in the security realm. Moreover, the threat posed by the French revolutionary wars to the very principle of dynastic rule seems to have proved weightier than the differences in domestic social formations, such as those existing between liberal and Protestant England on the one hand and the more conservative and Catholic Austria and orthodox Russia on the other. These two threats helped crystallize the norm of systemic stability—the "repose" of Europe was the term the five preferred—that the concert was geared to sustain. They emboldened rulers to place a *collective* bet on their future. And the multilateral consultations instituted via the concert limited the extent of cheating on that bet by providing a forum within which intelligence could be shared, states' intentions questioned, and justifications for actions proffered and assessed.

The Concert of Europe gradually eroded not only because the memory of the initial threats faded but also because over time the parameters of the situation were transformed. Above all else, the revolutions of 1848 seriously shook the prevailing concept of legitimate political order from within, and the sense of international cohesion diverged sharply thereafter. "I do not see Europe anymore," the French foreign minister lamented (quoted by Hinsley 1963: 243). In the second half of the nineteenth century, multilateral consultation and self-restraint yielded to the striving for unilateral advantage checked only by external constraints, while bilateral alliance formation was raised to a new level of sophistication by Bismarck (Taylor 1971).

In the economic realm, the nineteenth century witnessed what economists consider to be paradigms, if not paragons, of multilateralism: the regimes of free trade and the gold standard [see Chapter 2]. By free trade is meant two things: a minimum of barriers to trade, including tariff and nontariff barriers; and nondiscriminatory treatment in trade. An international gold standard exists when two sets of conditions are approximated. First, the major countries must maintain a link between their domestic money supply and gold at substantially fixed ratios. Second, in principle they must allow the outflow of gold to liquidate an adverse balance of current obligations and must accept a corresponding inflow in case of a favorable balance. These conditions also establish the convertibility of currencies at relatively fixed rates, and they facilitate international adjustment insofar as the initial imbalance in the current account in principle will be rectified automatically in both surplus and deficit countries by the appropriate domestic measures that follow from the inflow and outflow of gold.

By the mid-nineteenth century, Great Britain—the front-runner in the Industrial Revolution, the foremost importer of raw materials and exporter of manufactured products, and the enthusiastic occupant of the doctrinal house built by Adam Smith and David Ricardo—was prepared to move toward free trade on a unilateral basis. Prime Minister Robert Peel declared in Parliament that "if other countries choose to buy in the dearest market, such an option on their part constitutes no reason why we should not be permitted to buy in the cheapest" (quoted by Bhagwati and Irwin 1987: 114). Indeed, Britain did liberalize trade unilaterally, culminating in the abolition of the Corn Laws in 1846. Others, however, did not follow the British example as Britain had expected. Reluctantly, therefore, and in part also inspired by broader diplomatic considerations, Britain commenced a series of bilateral tariff negotiations with other countries, and those other countries did the same with third parties, which had the effect of significantly lowering tariff barriers. The model was the 1860 Cobden–Chevalier Treaty between Britain and France. Although this was a bilateral treaty, it had multilateral *consequences* because it contained an unconditional MFN provision: it committed Britain and France to extend to each other any subsequent concessions obtained from agreements with any third party. Bismarck, Louis Napoleon, and Cavour all viewed such trade treaties primarily as instruments of traditional bilateral diplomacy and less as means to multilateralize trade. But they negotiated them, and they included the MFN provision. The inclusion of this provision in a series of trade treaties had the effect of multilateralizing the trading order (Viner 1951).

As it did in international trade, Britain followed the rules of the gold standard more closely than anyone else. It thereby provided the world economy with a pillar of financial stability in the pound sterling, making multilateral convertibility and adjustment that much easier to achieve (Eichengreen 1987). Britain's policies were conducive to multilateralism in two other ways as well. As the world's largest creditor country, Britain did not exploit its position to accumulate large gold stocks but instead made those surpluses available for additional overseas investments and loans. The international economy as a result functioned more smoothly and grew more steadily than would otherwise have been the case. In addition, Britain always allowed debts to Britain incurred by its trading partners to be canceled by credits they earned elsewhere, from countries with which Britain was in negative balance. That practice in turn facilitated the multilateral clearing of payments balances (Briggs 1968).

The multilateralism of free trade and the international gold standard appears to have been created and sustained by two sets of factors. Although it may appear paradoxical, these paragon cases of multilateralism were not achieved by multilateral means. The decisive factor was Britain's unilateral move toward free trade and the gold standard and its bilateral dealings to achieve both goals. Britain thereby signaled its willingness to bear the costs of an open trading order and a stable monetary order and thus reduced the distributive and strategic uncertainties of these arrangements for others (Stein 1983). In that sense, free trade and the gold standard can be said to have been less "regime-ish" than the Concert of Europe. Another critical factor was a permissive domestic political environment. As Bloomfield has pointed out with regard to the monetary realm (1959: 23), "The view, so widely recognized and accepted in recent decades, of central banking policy as a means of facilitating the achievement and maintenance of reasonable stability in the level of [domestic] economic activity and prices was scarcely thought about before 1914, and certainly not accepted, as a formal objective of monetary policy." Indeed, many countries lacked the institutional capacity to pursue such a monetary policy, in some cases including even a central bank itself. That permissive domestic environment collapsed well before the leading role of Britain did (Gourevitch 1986: chap. 3).

This brief overview of multilateralism prior to the twentieth century suggests several broad generalizations that shed further light on the character of the multilateral institutional form. First, the strategic task environment has an impact on the form that agreements take [as was suggested formally in Chapter 1]. Defining and delimiting the international property rights of states is as fundamental a collective task as any in the international system. The performance of this task on a multilateral basis seems inevitable in the long run, although in fact states appear to try every conceivable alternative first. Moreover, in the past the multilateral arrangements that did emerge in this domain were monopolized by states and essentially codified state practice into prevailing orders of relations. At the other extreme, limiting transaction costs by solving coordination problems is institutionally neither complex nor particularly demanding, and it was the domain in which multilateralism in all three institutional expressions—orders, regimes, and organizations—flourished in the nineteenth century. Between these two lies the problematic terrain of significant conflict of interest situations, in which states *sometimes*, but prior to the twentieth century not often, construct multilateral arrangements even though alternatives are available and viable. The major powers could have selected bilateral alliances in the early nineteenth century and discriminatory economic arrangements in the mid-nineteenth century, as they had done before and as they would do again subsequently. But at those particular points in time, they did not. Why not? Presumably, multilateralism was in their interest. But what, concretely, does that mean? How and why did states come to define their interests in a manner that yielded such an unusual institutional outcome? As noted above, it seems that the Concert of Europe was due in part to exogenous shocks to both the international system and the system of domestic rule. Free trade and the gold standard in part seem to have been due to the willingness and the capability of Great Britain to take the lead. Both cases also were made possible by the existence of compatible or at least permissive domestic settings.

Second, as was alluded to earlier, it seems that successful instances of multilateralism come to exhibit "diffuse reciprocity." For example, what was crucial to the success of the Concert of Europe, according to Jervis (1983: 180), "is that 'self-interest' was broader than usual [and] also longer-run than usual . . . For this system to work, each state had to believe that its current sacrifices would in fact yield a long-run return, that others would not renege on their implicit commitments when they found themselves in tempting positions."

Third, the record shows that prior to the twentieth century, very few instances of multilateralism generated formal organizations. The Concert of Europe never went beyond great power consultations, while free trade and the international gold standard were instituted and sustained by even more ad hoc bilateral and unilateral means. The multilateral organizations that did exist functioned exclusively in the domain of coordination problems, where the task at hand was to devise mutually acceptable rules of the road and to change them as technology and other such factors changed. And the role of these organizations was strictly circumscribed by the overall normative structure within which they existed.

The twentieth-century discontinuity

An important break in this third pattern occurred with the twentieth-century "move to institutions," as the critical legal theorist David

Kennedy has described it (1987)—by which he means the move to formal organizations.

Above all, a completely novel form was added to the institutional repertoire of states in 1919: the multipurpose, universal membership organization, instantiated first by the League of Nations and then by the UN. Prior international organizations had but limited membership, and they were assigned specific and highly circumscribed tasks. In contrast, here were organizations based on little more than shared aspirations, with broad agendas, in which large and small had a constitutionally mandated voice. Moreover, decision-making within international organizations increasingly became subject to the mechanism of voting, as opposed to treaty drafting or customary accretion; and voting itself subsequently shifted away in most instances from the early unanimity requirement that was consistent with the traditional mode of conducting international proceedings. Finally, the move amplified a trend that had begun in the nineteenth century, a trend toward multilateral as opposed to merely bilateral diplomacy, especially in the form of "conference diplomacy" (Rittberger 1983).

This move to institutions had several important consequences for the status of multilateralism. First, it complicated, and in some instances actually reversed, the straightforward ends–means relation that previously prevailed between the goals embodied in multilateral arrangements and whatever formal organizational mechanism may have existed to serve them. Or, to put it differently, it created principal–agent problems that had not existed before. Any form of organizational mediation is capable of affecting outcomes, of introducing elements into the substance or process of decision making that previously were not present. A multipurpose, universal membership organization complicates that situation by involving itself even in areas where no normative consensus exists; aspects of both the League of Nations and the UN illustrate that problem in spades. Second, multilateral forums increasingly have come to share in agenda-setting and convening powers previously held solely by states. For example, such forums increasingly drive international conference diplomacy. Third, and perhaps most important, multilateral diplomacy has come to embody a procedural norm *in its own right*—though often a hotly contested one—in some instances carrying with it an international legitimacy not enjoyed by other means.

In short, as a result of the twentieth-century move to institutions, a multilateral political order has emerged that is "capable of handling at least some collective tasks in an *ex ante* coordinated manner" (ibid.: 167–168). I might add in conclusion that while numerous descriptions of this "move to institutions" exist, I know of no good explanation in the literature—whether neorealist or neoliberal in orientation—of why states should have wanted to complicate their lives in this manner. And I would think it particularly difficult to formulate any straightforward explanation within their respective logics of instrumental rationality.

THE UNITED STATES AND POSTWAR MULTILATERALISM

The preceding discussion makes it clear that multilateralism was not invented in 1945. It is intrinsic to the modem state system, and incipient expressions of it have been present from the start. However, the breadth and diversity of multilateral arrangements across a broad array of issue-areas increased substantially after 1945. Quite naturally, therefore, one associates this change with the postwar posture of the United States.

According to the theory of hegemonic stability, hegemonic powers are alike in their quest to organize the international system. Hegemonic stability theory is right up to a point. However, to the extent that it is possible to "know" these things, historical counterfactuals suggest that the likeness among hegemons stops short of the *institutional form* by which they would choose to organize the system. For instance, had Nazi Germany or the Soviet Union ended up as the world's leading power after World War II, there is no indication whatsoever that the intentions of either country included creating anything remotely like the international institutional order that came to prevail.[11] Politically, Germany pursued an imperial design in the European core, complete with tributary states on the periphery. Economically, the Nazi scheme of bilateral, discriminatory, and state-controlled trade pacts and monetary clearing arrangements undoubtedly would have been extended geographically to complement Germany's political objectives. The Soviet Union presumably would have sought political control through a restored Comintern while causing the modes of production in its subject economies to be socialized and the relations among those economies to be administered on a planned and discriminatory basis.

In point of fact, and this we can say with greater certainty, things would have differed in some respects even if Britain had become the hegemon. Colonialism as a political institution would have continued longer. And while monetary relations probably would have been organized similarly, merely based on sterling rather than the dollar, British imperial preferences would have remained a central feature of international trade, possibly forcing others to carve out regional trading blocs for themselves.

Finally, Europe certainly would have been "integrated" by a German or a Soviet hegemony—but in a markedly different fashion than exists via the EC today. And in a British-run system, Europe most probably would have returned to pre-war multipolarity and the continued existence of separate national economies.

Thus, all hegemonies are not alike. The most that can be said about a hegemonic power is that it will seek to construct an international order in *some* form, presumably along lines that are compatible with its own international objectives and domestic structures. But, in the end, that really isn't saying very much.

For American postwar planners, multilateralism served as a foundational architectural principle on the basis of which to reconstruct the postwar world. Take first the economic realm. During the war, the Nazi economic order was the focal point of American antipathy, as the provisions of the 1941 Anglo-American Atlantic Charter make quite clear. It had effectively excluded nonparticipants, which not only limited American trade opportunities but, according to US officials, also triggered economic conflicts that readily spilled over into the security realm. "Nations which act as enemies in the market-place cannot long be friends at the council table," warned the assistant secretary of state for economic affairs, William Clayton, echoing a favorite refrain of his boss, Cordell Hull (quoted in Pollard 1985: 2).

The defeat of Germany and the allied occupation of its Western sector afforded the United States an opportunity to help implant the domestic social bases for a markedly different form of foreign economic policy by the new West German state. Much of the negotiating energy expended by the United States on the creation of the postwar economic order, therefore, was directed toward undoing the more benign but still vexing British position. It consisted of a commitment to imperial preferences on the part of the Tories and to extensive controls on international economic transactions by the Labour party as part of its objective to institute systematic national economic planning. Both were inherently discriminatory. The United States sought to substitute in their place a global version of the "open door." As we saw in Chapter 2, discriminatory trade barriers and currency arrangements were to be dismantled and tariffs reduced. Decolonization was actively supported. But nowhere would domestic politics allow a mere return to the nineteenth-century laissez-faire of unrestricted trade and the gold standard, wherein the level of domestic economic activity was governed by the balance of payments. Even for the relatively more liberal United States, the international edifice of the "open door" had to accommodate the domestic interventionism of the New Deal.

There is little debate in the literature about the role of multilateralism in organizing the postwar economic order; the consensus is that its role was substantial. There has been little debate about its role in the security domain either—but here for the very different reason that students of international relations have assumed that there was none. That interpretation is not supported by the historical record, however, if we think of multilateralism in its broad sense rather than merely as multilateral organizations.

As World War II drew to a close, President Roosevelt faced an institutional problem. The United States must not retreat back into a "fortress America," Roosevelt insisted, or else it would once again have won the war only to lose the subsequent peace. Winning the peace, Roosevelt felt, would require active US international involvement (Dallek 1979). But at the same time, the American public would not accept international involvement via "entangling alliances." Hence, some other form would have to be found. To complicate matters further, as John Gaddis puts it (1982: 9), Roosevelt favored a policy of "containment by cooptation" toward the Soviet Union and felt that a stable postwar security order required "offering Moscow a prominent place in it; by making it, so to speak, a member of the club." That in turn required a club to which both belonged.

Given that combination of objectives, Roosevelt had little alternative but to move toward some form of collective security organization.[†] But it was to be a modified form in that it stripped away the Wilsonian aspiration that collective security somehow be *substituted for* balance-of-power politics. That was too wild and woolly a notion for depression- and war-hardened US officials in 1945. Instead, they sought to make the two compatible, so that the collective security mechanism would have a basis in the balance of power but also mute the more deleterious effects of balance-of-power politics. Thus was the UN born: at its core, an enforcement mechanism "with teeth," but subject to great power veto.

Once the iron curtain went down and Europe was split, containing Moscow by exclusion became the dominant US objective, and the UN became marginalized to core US security concerns.[12] But the American problem of simultaneously avoiding both a retreat into fortress America and an entrance into entangling alliances still had to be resolved vis-à-vis a threatened Europe. As Steve Weber (1993) reminds us, the United States repeatedly turned back requests from its European friends to form bilateral alliances with them. Instead, the United States initially pursued a strategy of "economic security" (Pollard 1985), of providing the Europeans with the economic wherewithal to take care of their own security needs. By 1947, bilateral economic assistance to Europe gave way to the more comprehensive Marshall Plan, which required the Europeans to develop a multilateral framework for their own postwar reconstruction in return for receiving aid. Moreover, the United States was an early advocate and strong supporter of European efforts to achieve economic and political integration.[13]

But European security demanded more. Driven by *"la grande peur"* of 1948, the Europeans came to feel that "it was [also] necessary to have some measure of military 'reassurance'," as Michael Howard has put it (1985: 14). Still, the United States continued to resist bilateral deals and avoid military commitments of any kind. Eventually, the State Department relented, but not until succeeding in its insistence that the United States would only aid a European-initiated collective self-defense effort. The Belgians under Paul-Henri Spaak took the lead. In March 1948, the Benelux countries, France, and Britain signed a mutual assistance treaty. But how could they tie the United States to this framework? The British played a critical role in defining an indivisible security perimeter from Scandinavia to the Mediterranean and, with Canadian help, getting it to reach across to the Western hemisphere (Folly 1988). The concept of the "North Atlantic" emerged as the spatial image that helped tie the knot. Its formulation and acceptance perhaps were facilitated by the recent revolution in military

---

† This issue is taken up in greater detail in Chapter 8.

cartography, whereby the "airman's view," and thus the polar proximity of the Soviet Union to the United States, came to shape US strategic thinking (Henrikson 1975). The North Atlantic Treaty was concluded in 1949. "The signing of the NATO Alliance," Howard has said (1985: 16), "provided a sense that now at last all were for one and one was for all." This, of course, is what the notion of collective security has always meant.

Indeed, NATO was conceived and justified as an expression of the collective self-defense provision of the UN Charter. There is a direct path from the negotiations over Article 51 of the UN Charter, endorsing an inherent right of individual and collective self-defense, to the drafting of the North Atlantic Treaty (Hudson 1977; Tillapaugh 1978). The same cast of characters who negotiated the UN provision at San Francisco, Gladwyn Jebb on the British side and Senator Arthur Vandenberg on the American side, also sought to ensure that the North Atlantic Treaty would be compatible with it. That accomplishment allowed the United States to operate "within the Charter, but outside the [Soviet] veto," as Vandenberg liked to say (quoted by Hudson 1977: 63). Nor was Article 51 drafted with a future NATO in mind; it was instigated by the Latin Americans to allow for a Latin American regional security organization that was beyond the reach of the US veto in the UN Security Council.

To underscore the obvious, the United States did not seek to endow formal international organizations with extensive independent powers; that was not its multilateralist agenda. The Americans insisted on a veto in the UN Security Council every bit as much as the Soviets did. Voting in the international financial institutions was and remains weighted, the United States still having the largest single share. GATT barely exists as a formal organization (it was supposed to have been folded into the International Trade Organization), and State Department funding for it came out of an account for ad hoc international conferences. And the "O" in NATO never has and does not now independently determine the security of its members.

The American postwar multilateralist agenda consisted above all of a desire to restructure the international order along broadly multilateral lines, at the global level, and within Western Europe and across the North Atlantic. In East Asia, on the other hand, the potential was lacking to construct anything but the bilateral security ties on which the United States turned its back in Europe (Gallicchio 1988; Pollard 1985: chap. 8). Secondarily, the United States occasioned the creation of several major multilateral regimes, as in the fields of money and trade, and also helped establish numerous formal international organizations to provide technically competent or politically convenient services in support of those objectives.

To be sure, the United States hardly acted against its self-interests. But the fact that US behavior was consistent with its interests does not explain the behavior. Nor was multilateralism what some neoliberal institutionalists would call "a consumption good" for the United States, an end in itself. So how do we explain US actions? One possible source of explanation for the

American multilateralist agenda is the international system itself. System-level theories of international relations, much favored in the discipline at the moment, essentially are of two sorts. One is structural, the other functional. Both offer parsimonious and often powerful first-cut explanations. Structural accounts of the postwar multilateralist posture of the United States would focus either on US hegemony or on strategic bipolarity as the independent variable. The problem with using hegemony—*tout court*—as an explanation has already been addressed: other hegemons would have done things differently, and so subsequent history would have been different. Hence, we still require insight into why this particular hegemon did things in this particular way.

Invoking bipolarity as an explanation is more promising (Gowa 1989)—once bipolarity exists. But it is not without problems for the earliest postwar years, when bipolarity was just in the process of becoming, even as some of the multilateral developments described above were taking place. Indeed, it took policy makers and analysts quite some time to grasp the fact of bipolarity. Serious postwar planning by the United States began in 1942. William Fox's 1944 book, *The Super-Powers*, which introduced that term into the political lexicon, still assumed that there would be three of them. The Bretton Woods conference was held that year, with the Soviets in attendance. Moreover, the option of dividing the world into three spheres of influence for the purposes of conflict management had not yet been entirely discarded in 1944. By 1945, it had been, but in favor of the universal UN. In his 1946 "long telegram" and again in his 1947 "Mr. X" article, George Kennan warned about the emerging Soviet sphere of influence, but he explicitly expected multipolarity to reemerge from the devastation of the war before long, and he designed his proposed containment strategy in order to achieve that goal (Gaddis 1982: 25–53). Moreover, as late as 1947, trade negotiators were trying to square circles to devise a multilateral trade regime that could accommodate socialist state trading countries (Viner 1947; Feis 1947). Also in 1947, Lucius Clay, the US military governor in Germany, initially blamed the French, not the Soviets, for impeding quadripartite government there when he thought it was still doable; the failure to achieve it resulted ultimately in the bizonal division of Germany that became emblematic of the cold war (Smith 1990: 423–449).

Admittedly, actor perceptions do not matter much in structural theories. Nevertheless, it does seem more than a little awkward to retroject as incentives for actor behavior structural conditions which had not yet emerged, were not yet fully understood, and which in some measure only the subsequent behavior of actors helped to produce.[14]

Functional theories of international institutions, as we noted at the outset, thus far have focused largely on undifferentiated "cooperation" and "institutions," not the specific form of multilateralism. The limits of their utility on this count has already been commented on. Moreover, functional theories have been concerned largely with such factors as the desire to minimize transaction costs, information costs, and similar institutional inefficiencies. This rationale, too, has limits. First, although our historical cases are too few to make a strong case, they do suggest that the drive to limit institutional inefficiencies of this kind is most decisive in the realm of coordination problems. When it comes to shedding blood or hopes for lasting peace, the calculus of countries appears to draw on a different realm of human experience. Second, it also seems that what constitutes institutional inefficiencies or costs is not entirely independent of the attributes of the states making the calculation. For example, it is difficult to imagine an institutional arrangement that imposed higher transaction costs on all concerned than the Nazi trade and monetary regimes. But given the overall strategic objectives of the German state at the time, the price of administering those arrangements was viewed as an investment, not an expenditure to be minimized. The domestic mechanisms that shape Japan's foreign trade posture today, with all their reputed "inefficiencies," reflect a similar calculus.

In short, to determine why *this* particular institutional agenda was pursued, it is inescapable at some point to look more closely at *this* particular hegemon. That in turn requires not only examining the hegemon's international situation but also delving into its domestic realm.

It seems clear that across a broad array of social and economic sectors, the United States after World War II sought to project the experience of the New Deal regulatory state into the international arena (Hogan 1984; Burley 1993). According to Burley, this endeavor entailed two distinct dimensions. The first was a belief that the long-term maintenance and success of domestic reform programs required a compatible international order. The second was a commitment at the international level to institutional means which had already been tried domestically and which grew out of the legal and administrative revolution that accompanied the New Deal. The combination of the two translated into an active US effort to institutionalize a multilateral international economic and social order.

In the security realm, a count of domestic political noses led President Roosevelt to the belief that isolationist tendencies could not be neutralized by having the United States form bilateral alliances with or against the very European states that kept dragging it into war—which is how the isolationists viewed the world. Accordingly, the notion was foremost in Roosevelt's mind that only by "binding" the United States to a more permanent multilateral institutional framework, which promised to *transform* the traditional conduct of international politics, could a relapse into isolationism be avoided (Dallek 1979). By 1947, the Truman administration discovered anticommunist rhetoric to be a useful tool toward that same end.

More generally, Peter Cowhey (1993) has advanced the provocative thesis that the very structure of the US polity enhanced the credibility of America's postwar commitment to multilateralism. The problem of "defection" that is explored at length in the literature focuses not on the hegemon but, rather, on the other states, potential free riders one and all. But multilateralism is an extremely demanding institutional form, and the fact is that the hegemon has far more unilateral and bilateral options available to it than any other state. So how does the hegemon make its own commitment to multilateralism credible? How can other states be assured that the hegemon will not defect if it should change its mind or recalculate its short-term interests, and leave them in the lurch? Ironically, Cowhey attributes the credibility of the American commitment to multilateralism to the very features of the US polity that are often said to hamper its effective conduct of foreign policy. These include the institutional consequences of an electoral system geared to the median voter; a division of powers making reversals of fundamental policy postures difficult; and greater transparency of and access to the domestic political arena even on the part of foreign interests.

In sum, in one crucial sense the origins of multilateralism in the postwar era reiterate the record of prior periods. Between the deep level of defining and stabilizing the international property rights of states and the relatively superficial level of solving coordination problems, a pronounced shift toward multilateralism in economic and security affairs requires a combination of fairly strong international forces and compatible domestic environments. If that is so, then it was the fact of an *American* hegemony that was decisive after World War II, not merely American *hegemony*. And this, in turn, makes the role of multilateralism in the current international transformation of even greater interest.

MULTILATERALISM AND TRANSFORMATION

The issue of whether the United States is in relative decline and, if so, whether it is taking the international order along with it has been debated in the literature for nearly two decades. More recently, the end of bipolarity has been adduced as a cause for similar alarm (Mearsheimer 1990). The new institutionalists were the first to question any direct relationship between international power shifts and institutional unraveling. They suggested several reasons why states would, under certain circumstances, remain committed to existing institutions even "beyond hegemony," focusing on such factors as institutional inertia, sunk costs, the services that institutions continue to provide, and the common objectives that they may continue to pursue (Krasner 1983; Keohane 1986b).

But as we saw at the outset of our discussion, the situation today, especially but not exclusively in Europe, is not simply one of past multilateral arrangements hanging on for dear life. There are numerous instances of active institutional adaptation and even creation. Again, there is not much in the theoretical literature that provides ready explanations. The definitional and historical analysis of multilateralism presented here, however, does suggest several factors that may be at work.

Ironically, the very features that make it strategically difficult to establish multilateral arrangements may enhance the durability and adaptability of these arrangements once they are in place. Three factors appear to be particularly salient.

First, all other things being equal, an arrangement based on generalized organizing principles should be more elastic than one based on particularistic interests and situational exigencies. It should, therefore, also exhibit greater continuity in the face of changing circumstances, including international power shifts. A trade regime based on MFN treatment more readily absorbs such shifts, and so, too, presumably would a collective security arrangement. It is hard to imagine the discriminatory order of the Nazis surviving the hegemony of the Third Reich, however. And even in the case of traditional alliances, the major means of adjustment is simply to abandon prevailing dyadic ties and to start again from scratch. Although the cases may be overdetermined, the ready adaptation of NATO versus the total collapse of the Warsaw Pact nevertheless may help illustrate this point.

Similarly, we noted that successful multilateral arrangements in the past have come to exhibit expectations of diffuse reciprocity. It seems plausible to hypothesize that as long as that expectation continues to hold, as long as each party does not insist on being equally rewarded on every round, the sustainability of the arrangement should be enhanced because it makes both cross-sectoral and intertemporal trade-offs and bargains feasible. Cooperation within the EC seems most clearly to exhibit this pattern. It may have benefited from or perhaps even required active US encouragement at the start, but obviously it has long since taken off on a self-sustaining institutional path.

Third, and closely related, multilateralism by definition offers greater third-party opportunities than bilateralism, and so should elicit a broader sense of ownership in the system. Moreover, where ex ante uncertainty is high, multilateral principles offer a degree of risk insurance against losses[‡]— which, presumably, is why smaller countries are more uniformly in favor of such principles. Both features should have positive consequences for the adaptability of and voluntary compliance with multilateral principles.

The durability of multilateral arrangements, the analysis presented here suggests, is also a function of domestic environments. For example, there was no shift in multipolarity around the mid-nineteenth century that could have accounted for the final collapse of the Concert of Europe and the reemergence of competitive alliances, but domestic environments did diverge sharply after the revolutions of 1848. The erosion of the gold standard and free trade to some extent may be overdetermined in that both sets of factors changed; but even before Britain declined appreciably as a world power, governments felt politically compelled to intervene in their domestic economies in ways that were incompatible with the two multilateral regimes.

In fact, even Charles Kindleberger's "climacteric" case of the 1933

---

‡   This last point was suggested to me by Hein Goemans, in a comment on 1992a (personal communication, 5 September 1992).

London Economic Conference—when "the British couldn't and the United States wouldn't"—does not lend itself to a straightforward systemic account. What the United States "wouldn't" was to support the *prevailing form* of economic multilateralism: the laissez-faire kind, the London and New York bankers' kind, Herbert Hoover's kind. But no one, including President Roosevelt, had yet figured out a viable and mutually acceptable alternative (Feis 1966). As Arthur Schlesinger notes in his classic account (1958: vol. 2, 229): "This difference [between the United States and Britain] was too great to be bridged by any form of economic or diplomatic legerdemain. The London Conference did not create the difference. It simply came along too late or too early—to do anything about it" (for a game-theoretic rendering, see Oye 1985). No domestic divergence that stark exists among the major powers today. The collapse of the Soviet Union and the domestic changes in Eastern Europe have eliminated the socialist economic model. The domestic economic structure of Japan may pose a remotely comparable problem, but it is hardly of the same magnitude.

Fifth, multilateral arrangements with well-defined tasks simply have not lived up to the bad billing they get in some of the literature as unwieldy expressions of the law of large numbers. This is so for several reasons. First of all, most major multilateral arrangements in practice are governed by subsets of states—the "k-groups" that Snidal (1985), following Hardin (1982), suggests attenuate many international collective action problems. Kahler (1993) shows empirically what Snidal postulates theoretically: the major postwar global regimes have been governed by what he terms "minilateralist" groupings within them. Thus, the regimes were not mere expressions of hegemony, and they thereby avoided obvious legitimacy problems. Nor did they operate purely on the basis of egalitarian decision-making rules, however. Decolonization began to strain this "minilateralist" solution in the 1960s and 1970s. Nevertheless, whether in the subsequent Law of the Sea negotiations, GATT rounds, or drafting of global environmental conventions, Kahler finds little evidence that states encountered insuperable difficulties in devising institutional mechanisms which, simultaneously, accommodated larger numbers of participants and retained their capacity to reach decisions. Even in the extraordinarily complex and "democratic" context of the UN Conference on the Law of the Sea, as Buzan has shown in great detail (1981), the institutional inventiveness of states to accommodate large numbers was impressive, and the failure to obtain a universally ratified treaty resulted from fundamental conflicts of interest, not from any mechanical problem of size.

A final factor to be considered in explanations for the adaptability of multilateral arrangements is that in some instances the twentieth-century "move to institutions" clearly has also kicked in. Indeed, much of the institutional inventiveness within multilateral arrangements today comes from the institutions themselves, from platforms that arguably represent or at least speak for the collectivities at hand. Again, the EC offers the most dramatic illustration, whether it concerns plans for orchestrating EC relations with the European Free Trade Area, the East European states, or the future of the Community itself. Patrick Morgan (1993) goes so far as to argue that West European actors today are explicitly applying to Eastern Europe some of the institutional lessons that they derived from their own earlier postwar experience with the United States, not only in the economic realm but also in the security realm. Beyond Europe, the convening- and agenda-setting power of multilateral organizations is perhaps best illustrated in the area of the commons. There would be no plan to try to salvage the Mediterranean from pollution were it not for multilateral players, as Peter Haas has shown (1990). Similarly, multilateral players kept first the ozone issue and now global warming on the negotiating table even when major powers, including the United States, were reluctant participants at best (Benedick 1991; P. Haas 1992a; Zacher 1993).

In sum, parts of the international institutional order today appear quite robust and adaptive. This conclusion challenges neorealist premises to the contrary. But our discussion also suggests that the reason is not merely that these are institutions, and that institutions are "in demand," as neoliberals are prone to argue. The reason is that these institutions are multilateral in form and that this form has characteristics which enhance its durability and ability to adapt to change, and which helps stabilize the consequences of change—such as those the international system has seen since 1989.

Part II

The system of states
Problematizing Westphalia

Institutionalization takes place within the system of states, as we saw in Part I, and different patterns of institutionalization have different effects on the conduct of international relations. But the system of states is itself a form of institutionalization, the embodiment of deeper and more profound shared practices and expectations about the organization of political life on the planet. It was the aim of various types of integration theory to explore the possible transformation of this form of international institutionalization. For example, Karl Deutsch and his associates examined the possible emergence of international security communities, "in which there is real assurance that the members . . . will not fight each other physically" but resolve their disputes by peaceful means, "normally by institutionalized procedures" (1957: 5). They could be pluralistic in character (maintaining the separate identity of the constituent units), or amalgamated (forming larger units). Neofunctionalism focused on a specific subset of the latter: the processes whereby political expectations, activities, and loyalties may shift to new and larger centers that exercise jurisdiction over the pre-existing nation states (Haas 1958, 1961).

But integration theory was it; no other mainstream literature addressed transformative questions on that scale. Consequently, when integration theory fell out of favor or was abandoned by its own practitioners (Haas 1976), the discipline also lost its only systematic means by which to speak about the very possibility of institutional transformation *of* the system of states, not merely *within* it. Nor did subsequent theoretical developments provide an alternative. On the contrary. Neorealism, fashioned in the 1970s (Waltz 1975, 1979), entailed what appeared to be compelling grounds for believing that such a transformation was highly unlikely to occur (due to the very dynamics of balance-of-power politics), or if it did, that it would be inconsequential (simply reducing the number of units in international politics). Neoliberal institutionalism, which followed a few years later (Keohane 1984; Oye 1986), was silent on the subject altogether. In short, as conceived by the major bodies of international relations theory the overall system of states simply *was*: endowed with an ontological state of being, but not becoming, to borrow a phrase from Nobel laureate Ilya Prigogine (1980). As a result, the student who retained a substantive interest in the "becoming" of the state system, as I did, was either left in a theoretical void or was obliged to turn to historical materialism and its derivatives (Wallerstein (1974a, 1974b) was a popular "soft" Marxist source), in which political transformation was, however, considered largely a by-product of changes in modes or relations of production.

In 1972a (Chapter 1), I had stipulated a starting point that held for this project as well: the international polity as a modified Westphalian system. And from it I derived a theoretical sense of the trajectory that any potential transformation would take: along a "horizontal" axis, continuing to involve states though perhaps not in the same capacity, not along a "vertical" axis toward their withering away under some "higher" institutional form. But beyond that I was adrift. I made the colossal mistake of trying to tackle an issue of this magnitude in my dissertation (1974a). The jump was exhilarating but the parachute failed to open; luckily I already had my first job. Thereafter, I put this project on inactive status and, while continuing the work illustrated by the essays in Part I, went on an intellectual scavenger hunt.

The first real breakthrough was prompted by an unlikely source: Kenneth Waltz. He and I joined the Berkeley faculty in the same year and we often discussed theoretical issues, as I continued to do with Ernst Haas. In due course, Waltz asked me to read a long paper on his reformulation of realism (Waltz 1975), and then, in several iterations, the manuscript that became *Theory of International Politics* (Waltz 1979). After I moved to Columbia University, I was asked to write a review essay of the book.

Waltz's *Theory* was central to my project in two respects. First, in a discipline starved for parsimonious theories it was intellectually so powerful and elegant that it was destined to have a fundamental impact—while, at the same time, it left no room for doubt that projects like mine were futile because it rendered implausible international transformation of the kind that interested me. Therefore, the only viable way for me to advance my cause, I realized, was through Waltz, not around him: any circumvention could be too easily dismissed for not having passed the toughest test available. Second, I was encouraged to find what I believed to be a major flaw in Waltz's model that was directly linked to his regarding system transformation highly unlikely. Waltz knowingly exogenized from his model all sources of systemic change by pushing them down into the units, with which his theory was not intended to deal. That seemed like an odd move, but fair enough. However, inadvertently Waltz also dropped out of his definition of international structure a key dimension that would record one type of transformation if it were to occur: the basis on which the constitutive units of the system are differentiated from one another and on the basis of which they assume their identity *as* constitutive units. The gates swung open.

Without challenging Waltz from a theoretical perch external to his own enterprise, I was able to argue that *Theory* is incapable not only of explaining so profound a shift in international politics as from the medieval to the modern, Westphalian system, but even of describing it. For that shift involved precisely a change in the principles of differentiating the constituent units in international politics: they established the modern territorial state as the prevailing, and ultimately sole, form of universal political organization. Furthermore, according to Durkheim, on whom Waltz draws explicitly in determining what is system and what is unit, the principles on the basis of which units are differentiated in society are subject to a system-level source of change. Durkheim calls it "dynamic density"—the volume and intensity of social interactions—and regards it to be an emergent property of the system of relations among units, much as Waltz's concept of polarity is. But dynamic density also dropped out of the model when Waltz abandoned differentiation as a component of structure. Therefore, I concluded, the theoretical warrant for Waltz's prediction that the system of states merely reproduces itself over time but does not undergo fundamental change is weak: continuity is overdetermined as an artifact of Waltz's premises. Moreover, by reinserting the omitted dimension—the principles of differentiation among units—it becomes possible to identify a source of potential structural change in the Westphalian system. My critique and reformulation is included in Chapter 5.

Waltz's *Theory* also shared a questionable analytical practice with a number of other theories of large-scale social formations: the tendency to treat structure as sedimentation, the residue left behind by long-ceased historical processes, which leads ultimately to the complete reification of structure. But to understand the possibility of system transformation structure has to be historicized, that is, itself shown to be a living thing. Anthony Giddens (1981) addressed this issue productively. He urged adopting a perspective that expressed the "duality" of structure: at once constraining human action but also being (re)created by it. Accordingly, Giddens went on to propose a theory, not of structure, but of structuration. The first step in a theory of structuration is to render social structure in a way that it becomes explicitly time–space contingent. "Structural principles," Giddens acknowledged, "are principles of organization implicated in those practices most 'deeply' (in time) and 'pervasively' (in space) sedimented into society" (ibid.: 55). But the key to understanding system transformation, he stated, is to make transparent the contingent nature of structure defined as social practices situated in time and space. Giddens' formulation of structure pointed me toward the dimensions of time and space. By the very nature of the exercise, this took me well beyond a Waltzian understanding of how the world works, in a social constructivist direction.

Temporality plays little role in international relations theorizing, and when it does it denotes little more than "elapsed time." Pushing beyond that everyday meaning without giving way to Heideggerian flights of mysticism is not easy. I first took up time in 1986a, included in Chapter 6 (also see 1989a). The *Annales* school of historiography proved suggestive, especially the work of Fernard Braudel (see 1980 for an overview) and Jacques Le Goff (1980). The key, as they make clear in concrete terms, is to understand time not merely as duration but as comprising different temporal forms. Thus, for example, the history of *la longue durée* differs from *l'histoire événementielle* not so much in its longer duration as in its deeper and wider framing of the factors related to the formation and transformation of social structures. The implication for the study of international transformation is this: one is unlikely to fully grasp its potential if time is conceived merely as a succession of increments, which is how most international relations theory views it, rather than as different temporal forms that bring wider "presents" into view. Structure as constraining residue becomes structure as contingent practice only when it is located within its own "present," even though the sources of its contingency may not be subject to immediate volition. The essay in Chapter 6 illustrates this variable dimension of temporal forms in the context of global population and resource issues, a key contemporary factor in what Durkheim called dynamic density and a major challenge, according to Braudel, to the durability of any social structure in the *longue durée*. The essay shows how population and resource issues take on very different meanings and are linked to different aspects of foreign policy and international structure when viewed through different temporal lenses.

If structure is brought to life, as it were, through the dimension of time, its effects on social practices are inscribed in space: in the case of the modern international polity, the system of fixed, disjoint, and mutually exclusive territorial formations. But space is not given in nature. It is a social construct that people, somehow, invent, thereby helping to define what structure will actually look like when it is situated in space. Moreover, space serves not merely as an inert container for the effects of structure. It generates emergent properties of its own—the need for open diplomatic communication across mutually exclusive territorial formations, for example—which may lead states to modify the structural principles that define space—such as the invention of the concept of extraterritoriality, to continue with the same illustration. And so the loop closes. The duality of structure becomes operationalized. It is made time–space contingent. And the possibility of transformation is not foreclosed as an artifact of theoretical presupposition.

I brought these theoretical observations to bear on the institution of modern territoriality in 1993b, included in Chapter 7.* The emergence of modern territoriality did include the factors that power-based and rationalist theories stress, but by themselves their retrodictive value is severely limited. This was a multidimensional process that also included ecodemographic dynamics, at one end of the spectrum, and, at the other, the mental

---

* The modern variant of territoriality is one form by means of which the constituent units in international politics are differentiated from one another, a dimension that Waltz, it will be recalled, dropped out of his definition of structure.

equipment that people drew on and reimagined in the process of reflecting on the changing world around them. The essay shows how these multiple dimensions interacted to produce the specifically modern form of territoriality. Moreover, the essay locates the key to exploring any possible future transformation in the practice of "unbundling" territoriality as a means whereby states, from the start, have dealt with forces and factors that they cannot reduce to territorial solution, and in what I describe as the "multi-perspectival" political practices to which it may lead over time. States do not wither away as a result, the essay concludes, not even in the ever-more integrated European Union, but they come to assume multiple identities, play diverse roles, and for some purposes act in different, more collectively legitimated, capacities than in the past.

This essay took many years to write but the work gave me enormous pleasure: it afforded me the opportunity to reflect on diverse literatures from history (political, military, economic, cultural), the arts, the humanities, as well as several social sciences. More than any other publication of mine it resonated with and has been taken up by specialists in other fields and abroad. It reminded me, in short, of why I chose scholarship as a career.

Having said that, the essay falls short of one initial aspiration: it does not contain a theory of system transformation. Law-like generalizations can help account for aspects of such a transformation. But none, I now believe, seems feasible of its totality, the explanation of which will continue to rely on narrative protocols. The contingencies are too great, the role of unanticipated consequences too pervasive. And if constructivism means anything at all it means taking those facts of social life seriously. However, as Part III seeks to show, the same analytical features of constructivism that some may regard as a source of social scientific weakness also may well comprise a more robust basis for guiding real actors in making real decisions, especially at moments in history when no one can credibly claim that interests and preferences are exogenously given and fixed, but are up for grabs—that is to say, at moments of discontinuity such as the world has experienced since 1989.

5   Political structure and dynamic density

The concept of structure is central to the study of transformation. In international relations, Kenneth Waltz's formulation (1979) has been central to the study of structure. Accordingly, I began my probes into the subject of international transformation with a review of Waltz, the first result of which was this essay, originally published as 1983d.

Waltz's model of structure contains no transformational logic, I discovered, only a reproductive logic. Indeed, it allows for only two types of transformation (but explains neither): that produced by a shift in polarity (from a multipolar to a bipolar world, and back again); and that produced by a shift from anarchy to central rule. But this analytical posture requires Waltz either to ignore the interval between the collapse of the Roman Empire and the ascendancy of territorial states in Europe—roughly a millennium in duration; or to claim that the entire period since the collapse of Rome to 1945 was simply multipolarity of greater or lesser numbers. Despite a heroic attempt to patch up Waltz by trying to make a case, in effect, for the latter option (Fischer 1992), neither move is viable on logical or historical grounds.

The two major flaws in Waltz's formulation of international structure—its inability to explain transformation, and its inability even to describe the shift from the medieval system (which followed once the dust had settled on the collapse of imperial Rome) to the modern international system—stem from the same source. Waltz claims that what is normally the second of three components of structure in political systems—differentiation of units—drops out at the international level because the units are functionally alike, leaving only the deep organizing principle of anarchy and the distribution of capabilities among units. But differentiation does not drop out if it is defined as the basis on which units are segmented—which is how Durkheim, on whom Waltz explicitly draws, defined it. Reinserting differentiation into the model of structure has two consequences: it introduces a dimension of change (principles of segmentation), which in fact distinguishes the medieval from the modern—and possibly the modern from some postmodern—international system; and it introduces a determinant of change, because what Durkheim called the dynamic density of social relations worked to undermine medieval principles of political segmentation much as the "new economic historians" claim that the quantity, velocity, and diversity of economic transactions in late medieval times undermined the feudal structure of property rights.

Beyond a relatively small circle of hard-core realists who remain ambivalent about my challenge to Waltz, the response to this essay has been positive across a wide spectrum of international relations theorists, and has led to productive theoretical innovations. The most creative and extensive has been the work of Buzan, Jones, and Little (1993), and Buzan and Little (1996).

In *The Rules of Sociological Method*, Emile Durkheim sought to establish the "social milieu," or society itself, "as the determining factor of collective evolution." Society, in turn, he took to reflect not the mere summation of individuals and their characteristics, but "a specific reality which has its own characteristics." And the basis of this "specific reality," Durkheim held, was "the system formed by [individuals'] association, by the fact of their combination." Hence, "if the determining condition of social phenomena is . . . the very fact of association, the phenomena ought to vary with the forms of that association, i.e., according to the ways in which the constituent parts of society are grouped" (Durkheim 1895: 116, 103, xlvii, 112). In short, Durkheim attributed the range of possibilities for individual action in the short run and collective evolution in the long run to changing forms of social solidarity.[1]

Durkheim's formulation remains one of the canons in sociological theory, though over the years its practical influence waned and came to be felt largely indirectly, as through the analysis of "primitive social structures" by Lévi-Strauss (1967). Suddenly, it is enjoying a resurgence in the study of a social domain never contemplated by Durkheim: the international system. Foremost among its proponents is Kenneth Waltz, in his book *Theory of International Politics* (1979). For Waltz, the international system is not only an appropriate level of analysis in the study of international politics, but also the decisive unit of analysis: "Nations change in form and purpose; technological advances are made; weaponry is radically transformed; alliances are forged and disrupted." And yet, "similarity of outcomes prevails despite changes in the agents that produce them." Thus, "systems-level forces seem to be at work" (ibid.: 67, 39). How should one conceive of international politics in systemic terms? Waltz's first answer, taking up roughly one-third of *Theory*, is: "not in the reductionist manner of the past." He is concerned primarily with the form of reductionism that seeks to know a whole through the study of its parts. This practice, he argues, is characteristic of most previous attempts to construct international theory, including self-styled systems theories. For most of the latter, the system is simply an aggregation of pertinent attributes of units and their interactions: "the systems level thus becomes all product and is not at all productive" (ibid.: 50). To be productive, the systems level has to express systemic properties and to explain how these act "as a constraining and disposing force on the interacting units within it" (ibid.: 72). In contrast, for Waltz the international system has its own "specific reality," to use Durkheim's term, imparted by the structure of international anarchy. As a result of anarchy, self-help by political units is the fundamental basis of international association. The other two-thirds of the book are given over to elaborating and illustrating this model.

Waltz's structuralist model of international politics has generated a great deal of attention, positive as well as critical. Arguably, it is one of the most important contributions to the theory of international relations since his own *Man, the State, and War* (1959), enhancing in a fundamental manner the level of discourse in the field. Moreover, Waltz's posture is a welcome antidote to the prevailing superficiality of the proliferating literature on international interdependencies, in which the sheer momentum of processes sweeps the international polity along toward its next encounter with destiny. Nevertheless, as I hope to show in this essay, its own utility for the study of international transformation is severely limited.

Unlike many commentaries, which have rejected Waltz's structuralist effort categorically, I propose to assess it on its own terms, within its self-consciously Durkheimian problematic.[2] I do so because a clear understanding of the structure of any social totality, including the international polity, is an essential ingredient in the study of its continuity or transformation. In the first section I summarize Waltz's model of international system and situate it within its Durkheimian context. In the next two sections I show that Waltz pushes so much out of this model, to avoid what he calls reductionism and remain faithful to what he views as structuralist strictures, that he exogenizes a critical dimension of all social totalities as well as all possible sources of fundamental change—ironically, including one that drove Durkheim's own model. Hence, I conclude in the final section, Waltz's insistence on continuity over transformation in international politics comes as little surprise: his model allows for no other outcome. Along the way, I suggest modifications to the Waltzian model, still in keeping with its Durkheimian parameters, and I note the avenues of potential change that it would lead us to explore.

INTERNATIONAL POLITICAL STRUCTURE

Waltz starts off by making two important distinctions: between system and unit, and between structure and process. The terms are defined in a somewhat circular manner, but his intention is clear: "A system is composed of a structure and of interacting units. The structure is the system-wide component that makes it possible to think of the system as a whole" (1979: 79). Durkheim is helpful in disentangling these notions: "Whenever certain elements combine and thereby produce, by the fact of their combination, new phenomena, it is plain that these new phenomena reside not in the original elements, but in the totality formed by their union." A system, then, is this new totality formed by the union of parts, a totality enjoying a "specific reality which has its own characteristics" (Durkheim 1895: xlvii, 103). The structure depicts the organization of a system, or the laws of association by which units are combined to form the systemic totality. Processes are simply the patterned relations among units that go on within a system—relations that reflect in varying degrees the constraints imposed by the system's structure.

The model

With these distinctions established, Waltz turns to his central concern: demonstrating the impact of variations in international political structure on international outcomes, and explaining similarities of outcomes over time as an effect of structural continuity. His concept of political structure consists of three analytical components: (1) the principle according to which the system is ordered or organized; (2) the differentiation of units and the specification of their functions; and (3) the degree of concentration or diffusion of capabilities within the system.

Applying these terms to the international realm, Waltz argues first that its most important structural feature is the absence of central rule, or anarchy (1979: 88–93). No one by virtue of authority is *entitled* to command; no one, in turn, is *obligated* to obey. States are the constitutive units of the system. Waltz advances empirical arguments why this should be so (ibid.: 93–95), but it follows logically from his premises: because legitimate authority is not centralized in the system, states—as the existing repositories of the ultimate arbiter of force—ipso facto are its major units. The desire of these units, at a minimum, to survive is assumed. And the organizing principle of self-help is postulated: if no one can be counted on to take care of anyone else, it seems reasonable to infer that each will try to put itself in a position to be able to take care of itself.

As a result, the international system is formed much like a market: it is individualistic in origin, and more or less spontaneously generated as a by-product of the actions of its constitutive units, "whose aims and efforts are directed not toward creating an order but rather toward fulfilling their own internally defined interests by whatever means they can muster" (ibid.: 90). This situation does not imply the absence of collaboration: collaboration is one of the means that states can muster in pursuit of their interests, some of which will be shared with others. It does imply that collaboration occurs "only in ways strongly conditioned by" the structure of anarchy (ibid.: 116), which is to say that the acceptability of the means of collaboration takes priority over the desirability of its ends (ibid.: 107–110). Once formed, the international system, again like a market, becomes a force that the units may not be able to control; it constrains their behavior and interposes itself between their intentions and the outcomes of their actions (ibid.: 90–91).

With respect to the second component of international political structure, Waltz contends that, in a system ordered by self-help, the units are compelled to strive to be functionally alike—alike in the tasks they pursue. Obviously, they are not alike in their respective capabilities to perform these tasks, but capabilities are the object of the third component of structure, not the second. Accordingly, since no functional differentiation of states exists except that imposed by relative capabilities, the second component of political structure, according to Waltz, is not needed at the international level, and "drops out" (ibid.: 93–97).

The degree of concentration or diffusion of capabilities within the system is the third component of structure. Here Waltz again argues by way of analogy: just as economic outcomes change when the structure of markets shifts from duopoly to oligopoly to perfect competition, so too do international outcomes change depending upon whether two, several, or no preeminent powers inhabit the system. "Market structure is defined by counting firms; international-political structure, by counting states. In the counting, distinctions are made only according to capabilities ... What emerges is a positional picture, a general description of the ordered overall arrangement of a society written in terms of the placement of units rather than in terms of their qualities" (ibid.: 98–99).

Care should be taken to understand one subtle but critical point. Waltz strives for a "generative" formulation of structure.[3] He means for the three (or, internationally, two) components of structure to be thought of as existing at successive causal depth levels. Ordering principles constitute the "deep" structure of a system, shaping its fundamental social quality. They are not visible directly, only through their hypothesized effects. Differentiation, where it exists as a structural property, mediates the effects of the deep structure, but within a context that has already been circumscribed by the deep structure. It is expressed through broad and enduring social institutions, and therefore is more directly accessible to the observer. The distribution of capabilities comes closest to the surface level of visible phenomena, but its impact on outcomes is simply to magnify or modify the opportunities and constraints generated by the other (two) structural level(s). When all is said and done, however, this generative model eludes Waltz, with consequences that we shall explore at the appropriate point.

And so, Waltz concludes, "international structures vary only through a change of organizing principle or, failing that, through variations in the capabilities of units" (ibid.: 93). What outcomes are explained by international structure and structural variation, so defined?

"From anarchy one infers broad expectations about the quality of international-political life. Distinguishing between anarchic structures of different type permits somewhat narrower and more precise definitions of expected outcomes" (Waltz 1979: 70). Waltz stipulates and illustrates expected outcomes in three domains of international relations: the international security order, the international economic order, and the management of "global problems."

The security order

From the principle of self-help, it will be recalled, one can infer that states will try to put themselves in a position that will enable them to take care of themselves. They have two types of means at their disposal: "internal efforts (moves to increase economic capability, to increase military strength, to develop clever strategies) and external efforts (moves to strengthen one's own alliance or to weaken and shrink an opposing one)." As one or more states successfully undertake any such measure, "others will emulate them or fall by the wayside" (Waltz 1979: 118). As other states emulate them, power-balancing ensues. Thus, the international security order is governed by balance-of-power politics. "Balance-of-power politics prevails whenever two, and only two, requirements are met: that the order be anarchic and that it be populated by units wishing to survive" (ibid.: 121).[4]

Though Waltz is careless in maintaining the distinction, it should be noted that the theory predicts balan*cing*, not balan*ces*, of power, where balances are defined as equivalences. Whether actual balances form, and even more so whether any specific configuration or alignment forms, will only in part be determined by positional factors; it will also depend upon information and transaction costs, and a host of unit-level attributes.

Power-balancing can as readily produce war as it can lower its incidence. It is inherently indeterminate. However, its indeterminacy is reduced as the number of great powers in the system diminishes. Here is where the degree of concentration of capabilities enters the picture. Waltz contends that systemic stability—defined as the absence of systemwide wars—is greatest when the number of great powers is smallest. For then actors exist who have both systemic interests and the unilateral capabilities to manipulate systemic factors—comparable to price-fixing, which becomes easier the smaller the number of firms involved. Barring a universal empire, which would domesticate international politics altogether, the most favorable situation, according to Waltz, is a system dominated by two great powers. World War II produced such an outcome; it transformed a multipolar into a bipolar system—the only such transformational consequence ever to have been produced in all of modern history.

The economic order

The principle of self-help also shapes the fundamental contours of the international economic order. In a domestic realm, units are free to pursue economic specialization because any adverse effects of their resultant mutual dependence can be regulated by the authorities. Economic competition takes place, but it is embedded in a collaborative political framework. As a result, an elaborate division of labor is permitted to evolve among the individual parts that becomes a source of strength and welfare for the collectivity as a whole. Internationally, the principle of self-help compels states to strive to be functionally alike precisely because mutual dependence remains problematic and is a source of vulnerability to states. Economic collaboration takes place, but it is embedded in a competitive political framework. As a result, the international division of labor is slight in comparison, and reflects the relative strengths of the units and their respective capabilities to provide for their own welfare (Waltz 1979: 104–107, 143–144).[5] Hence, as Waltz has put it elsewhere, "in international relations [economic] interdependence is always a marginal affair" (Waltz 1970: 206). This is a general outcome that one expects, given the structure of anarchy.

Structural variation will produce changes in the international economic order. Waltz explores one such change. He contends that systemic interdependence, low to begin with, will be still lower the smaller the number of great powers. The reason is that "size tends to increase as numbers fall," and "the larger a country, the higher the proportion of its business it does at home" (1979: 145). Waltz is thereby led to his controversial contention that international economic interdependence has been lower in the postwar era of bipolarity than it was under multipolarity prior to World War I.[6] In support of his argument, Waltz notes that the external sector "loomed larger" for the great powers prior to World War I under multipolarity than it does today, and that international trade and investment then reflected a greater degree of inter-country specialization than it does today.[7]

What of the internationalization of production and finance and the worldwide integration of markets, of which both liberal and Marxist theorists make so much? Waltz is unimpressed. These theorists "dwell on the complex ways in which issues, actions, and policies have become intertwined and the difficulty everyone has in influencing or controlling them. They have discovered the complexity of processes and have lost sight of how processes are affected by structure" (ibid.: 145).

Lastly, Waltz is sanguine about this outcome on normative grounds. He believes that "close interdependence means closeness of contact and raises the prospect of occasional conflict," while lower interdependence is believed to diminish this prospect. "If interdependence grows at a pace that exceeds the development of central control, then interdependence hastens the occasion for war" (ibid.: 138). This general premise can be seen to follow from Waltz's theory. But its historical validity is dubious, or at least is highly conditioned by factors he fails to specify—Waltz may want to describe the origins of World War I in these terms, for instance, but it isn't clear what he would do, then, with the preceding "Hundred Years' Peace."

Managing "global problems"

Any political system develops means by which to order the relations of force, to organize production and exchange, and to deal with problems that are common to the members of the collectivity. The international political system is no exception. The third functional domain, including what Waltz calls "the four p's—pollution, poverty, population, and proliferation" (1979: 139)—he discusses under the rubric of "international management" or the management of "global problems." This is, he maintains, governed by "the tyranny of small decisions" (ibid.: 108).

The problem is structural. In a domestic society, individual behavior can be constrained by considerations concerning the desirability of the greater social good, as defined by some central agency. But the international system is not an entity that is capable of acting in its own behalf, for the greater social good. Thus, while a growing number of problems may be found at the global level, solutions continue to depend on national policies (ibid.: 109). But national policies are constrained by the structure of self-help. Therefore, the incidence and character of "international management" is determined by the acceptability of the means by which to respond to "global problems," as calculated by the separate units, not by the desirability of the end to be achieved. As a result, international management is likely to be supplied in suboptimal quantities even when all concerned agree that more is necessary. "A strong sense of peril and doom may lead to a clear definition of the ends that must be achieved. Their achievement is not thereby made possible ... Necessities do not create possibilities" (ibid.: 109).

To break out of the tyranny of small decisions, "we have to search for a surrogate of government" (ibid.: 196). International organization provides no answer. To manage the system effectively, a central agency would require the means to control and protect its client states, means that it could obtain only from those client states. However, the greater its potential managerial powers, "the stronger the incentives of states to engage in a struggle to control it" (ibid.: 112). The result, far from centralizing authority, would be power-balancing. "The only remedy for a strong structural effect is a structural change" (ibid.: 111). It should come as no surprise that for Waltz the likelihood of approximating government is greatest when the number of great powers is smallest. "The smaller the number of great powers, and the wider the disparities between the few most powerful states and the many others, the more likely the former are to act for the sake of the system" (ibid.: 198). Hence, Waltz's overall conclusion that in the world as it exists, not as we might wish it to be, "small is beautiful"—and "smaller is more beautiful than small" (ibid.: 134).

How durable is this international structure? Remarkably so, Waltz insists. There are only two ways to alter it, and neither occurs frequently or rapidly. Within-system change is produced by a shift in the configuration of capabilities. In the modern era, a multipolar configuration endured for three centuries even though the identity of the great powers changed over time. Bipolarity has lasted for more than three decades.* The other kind of change, a change *of* system, would be produced if the structure of anarchy were transformed into a hierarchy. In the modern system of states this has never occurred. Indeed, Waltz contends that its occurrence is prevented by the very structure of anarchy. In a hierarchical realm, the emergence of a potentially dominant force (a leading candidate in an election, for example) initially may trigger attempts to balance it. But if its chances of succeeding pass a certain threshold there is every likelihood that it will benefit from

---

* Waltz anticipated the end of bipolarity no better than anyone else—the hypothetical case he raised concerned the possible unification of Europe, which he did not view very likely (1979: 180). He now believes that multipolarity is reemerging (Waltz 1993).

"bandwagoning," assuring its success. By contrast, in an anarchical realm, the emergence of a potentially dominant force may well be accompanied by bandwagoning until it reaches a certain point. Then, if actual domination begins to seem possible, it is likely to evoke counterbalancing efforts (ibid.: 123–138). Bandwagoning in the one case, and balancing in the other, best secures the position of the constituent units in the respective realms, and thereby serves to maintain the deep structures of the respective realms.

DIFFERENTIATION

According to Waltz, "the texture of international politics remains highly constant, patterns recur, and events repeat themselves endlessly" (1979: 66). We have seen his explanation. But does it hold? One problem with it is that it provides no means by which to account for, or even to describe, the most important contextual change in international politics in this entire *millennium*: the shift from the medieval to the modern international system. The medieval system was, on Waltz's own account (ibid.: 88), an anarchy.[8] But the difference between it and the modern international system cannot simply be attributed to changes in the distribution of capabilities among units. To do so would be utterly nonsensical because we would not know which units to compare or on what basis to compare them. As Hedley Bull points out, contemporaries found it impossible to enunciate a fundamental constitutive principle or criterion of membership in the medieval international system— indeed, the term "international" as we understand it today did not exist. The major units were known as *civitates, principes, regni, gentes* and *respublicae*, the idea of statehood not yet having taken hold (Bull 1977: 29). To these must be added cities, associations of trades, commercial leagues, and even universities, not to mention papacy and empire—all of which, for certain purposes, were considered to be legitimate "international" political actors, though of course they varied in scope and importance. The right of embassy could be granted or denied to any of them, depending upon the social status of the parties involved and the business at hand (Mattingly 1964).

The problem is that an entire dimension of social totalities is missing from Waltz's model. It is missing because he drops the second analytical component of political structure, differentiation of units, when discussing international systems. And he drops this component as a result of giving an infelicitous interpretation to the term "differentiation"—used by Durkheim and sociologists generally to denote segmentation or individuation in society. Instead, Waltz confuses differentiation with differences. As we have seen, he claims that there are no functional *differences* among states that are not accounted for by capabilities, and so drops *differentiation* as a component of structure. But the modern system of states is distinguished from the medieval system precisely by the principles on the basis of which their constituent units are differentiated—meaning segmented or individuated— from one another. If anarchy tells us that the political system is a segmental realm, differentiation tells us on what specific principles the segmentation is determined. The second component of structure, therefore, does not drop out at the international level; it stays in, and it serves as an exceedingly important source of structural variation.

What are these principles of segmentation, and what are their effects? Taking my cue from no less a realist than Meinecke (1957), I refer to the medieval variant of this structural level as a "heteronomous" institutional framework, and to the modern variant as the institutional framework of "sovereignty."

The feudal "state," if this designation makes any sense at all (cf. Poggi 1978), consisted of chains of lord–vassal relationships. Its basis was the fief, which was an amalgam of conditional property and private authority. Property was conditional in that it carried with it explicit social obligations. And authority was private in that the rights of jurisdiction and administration over the inhabitants of a fiefdom resided personally in the ruler. Moreover, the prevailing concept of usufructure meant that multiple titles to the same landed property were the norm. As a result, the medieval system of rule comprised "a patchwork of overlapping and incomplete rights of government" (Strayer and Munro 1959: 115), which were "inextricably superimposed and tangled," and in which "different juridical instances were geographically interwoven and stratified, and plural allegiances, asymmetrical suzerainties and anomalous enclaves abounded" (Anderson 1974: 37–38).

This system of rule was inherently "international." To begin with, it was quite common for rulers in different territorial settings to be one another's feoffor and feoffee for different regions of their respective lands. The king of France, for example, "might send letters on the same day to the count of Flanders, who was definitely his vassal, but a very independent and unruly one, to the count of Luxembourg, who was a prince of the Empire but who held a money-fief (a regular, annual pension) of the king of France, and to the king of Sicily, who was certainly a ruler of a sovereign state but also a prince of the French royal house" (Strayer 1970: 83). In addition, the feudal ruling class was mobile in a manner not dreamed of since—able to travel and assume governance from one end of the continent to the other without hesitation or difficulty, because "public territories formed a continuum with private estates" (Anderson 1974: 32). Thus, "Angevin lineages could rule indifferently in Hungary, England or Naples; Norman in Antioch, Sicily or England; Burgundian in Portugal or Zeeland; Luxemburger in the Rhineland or Bohemia; Flemish in Artois or Byzantium; Hapsburg in Austria, the Netherlands or Spain" (ibid.). Hence, the very distinction between "internal" and "external" political realms, separated by clearly demarcated "boundaries," was not recognized until the early modern period—and is, in fact, an indicator of the medieval-to-modern transformation.

Lastly, the medieval system of rule was legitimated by common bodies of law, religion, and custom that expressed inclusive natural rights pertaining to the social totality formed by the constituent units. These inclusive legitimations posed no threat to the integrity of the constituent units, however, because the units viewed themselves as municipal embodiments of a universal moral community (Mattingly 1964: 41 ff.).

In sum, the medieval system was a quintessential system of segmental territorial rule; it was an anarchy. But it was a form of segmental rule that had none of the connotations of territorial exclusiveness conveyed by the modern concept of sovereignty. It was a heteronomous structure of territorial rights and claims.

Just as the medieval state represents a fusion of its particular forms of property and authority, so does the modern. The chief characteristic of the modern concept of private property is the right to exclude others from the possession of an object. And the chief characteristic of modern authority is its totalization, the integration into one public realm of parcelized and private authority. "The age in which 'Absolutist' public authority was imposed was also simultaneously the age in which 'absolute' private property was progressively consolidated" (Anderson 1974: 428). In contrast to its medieval counterpart, the modern system of rule consists of the institutionalization of public authority within mutually exclusive jurisdictional domains.

This shift may be most clearly observed through the lenses of legitimation. The concept of sovereignty is critical. Unfortunately, it has become utterly trivialized by recent usage, which treats sovereignty either as a necessary adjunct of anarchy or as a descriptive category expressing unit attributes, roughly synonymous with material autonomy.[9] But sovereignty was not an adjunct of anarchy in the medieval system of rule, as we have seen. And in its proper modern usage, it signifies a form of legitimation that pertains to a system of relations, as we shall now see.

The rediscovery from Roman law of the concept of absolute private property, and the emergence of mutually exclusive territorial state formations which stood in relation to one another much as owners of private *estates* do, went hand-in-hand. Together, their ascendancy occasioned what we might call a legitimation crisis of staggering proportions. How can one justify absolute individuation when one's moral frame of reference is inclusive natural rights? And if one does manage to justify absolute individuation, what basis is left for political community? The works we regard today as the modern classics in political theory and international legal thought were produced in direct response to this legitimation crisis. Of greatest interest for present purposes are the analogous solutions developed by Locke and Vattel, because they came to be the most widely accepted legitimations for their respective realms, bourgeois society, and the interstate system.

Here is how John Locke defined the first of his tasks in resolving the crisis: "I shall endeavour to shew, how Men might come to have a property in several parts of that which God gave to Mankind in common" (cited in Tully 1980: 95). He fulfilled this task by allowing for natural individuation of property to the extent "where there is enough, and as good left in common for others" (ibid.: 129). But the condition of scarcity ultimately limits natural individuation, and its advent is hastened by the introduction of money, which makes possible accumulation of property beyond what one needs and can use. Covetousness and contention ensue. Therefore, to "avoid these Inconveniences which disorder Mens properties in the state of Nature, Men unite into Societies" (ibid.: 150–151). As his second task, Locke endeavored to show what the basis was of the political community so constituted. This he accomplished by establishing a means–ends relation between the public good and the preservation of property: since individual property rights existed prior to the formation of civil society, "the power of Society, or Legislative constituted by them, can never be suppos'd to extend farther than the common good; but is obliged to secure every ones Property by providing against those . . . defects . . . that made the State of Nature so unsafe and uneasie" (ibid.: 163). In sum, for Locke the purpose of civil society lay in providing a conventional framework within which to protect natural individual property rights that, beyond a certain point in history, could not be vindicated in its absence—with property being defined broadly, to include that in which individuals have rights. And the legitimacy of the political community so established derived simply from the minimalist social needs of the separate "proprietors," without recourse to any "standard of right that stood outside and above" these bare facts (Macpherson 1962: 80).

This was precisely also Vattel's accomplishment in international theory. In *Droit des Gens*, published in 1758, Vattel wrote "the international law of political liberty" (Gross 1968: 65)—the political liberty, that is, of states. This law rested on natural rights doctrines. At the same time, Vattel brought to a successful resolution the floundering efforts of the better part of two centuries to establish a complementarity between the sovereign claims of the separate states and the idea of a community of states, rendered in such a way that the latter was not entirely discarded in favor of the former. As F. H. Hinsley has put it (1967: 245): "It was a condition of the discovery of the international version of sovereignty that the notion of Christendom be replaced by a different understanding of international society—one that was compatible, as the medieval understanding was not, with belief in the sovereignty of the state." In the manner of Locke, Vattel accomplished this by establishing a means–ends relation between international society and the preservation of the separate existence of its units. The minimalist social needs of sovereigns to maintain the order that made their separate existence possible became, for Vattel, the province of the community of states.

In sum, from the vantage point of their respective social totalities— domestic and international systems—private property rights and sovereignty may be viewed as being analogous concepts in three respects. First, they differentiate among units in terms of possession of self and exclusion of others. "Private," as R. N. Berki has put it aptly, "refers not so much to the nature of the entity that owns, but to the fact that it is an entity, a unit whose ownership of nature ... signifies the exclusion of others from this ownership" (1971: 99). Second, because any mode of differentiation inherently entails a corresponding form of sociality, private property rights and sovereignty also establish systems of social relations among their respective units. They give rise to the form of sociality characteristic of "possessive individualists" (Macpherson 1962), for whom the social collectivity is merely a conventional contrivance calculated to maintain the basic mode of differentiation and to compensate for the defects of a system so organized by facilitating orderly exchange relations among the separate parts. Third, the most successful theorists of the two realms—as measured by their impact on bourgeois society and statecraft, respectively—developed an autonomous legitimation of the political order based simply on the minimalist social needs of its component units—where autonomy characterizes the moral basis of the legitimation of sovereignty, not sovereignty itself. That is to say, these theorists derived an "ought" from an "is" where the "is" was neither transcendental nor purely subjective, but enjoyed an irreducible intersubjective existential quality.

Appropriately, the first specifically modern invention of diplomacy was the principle of extraterritoriality: having so profoundly redefined and reorganized political space, the possessive individualist states "found that they could only communicate with one another by tolerating within themselves little islands of alien sovereignty" (Mattingly 1964: 244).

In sum, when the concept of differentiation is defined properly, as Durkheim and other sociologists have defined it, the second level in Waltz's model of structure does not drop out. It stays in, and serves to depict the kind of institutional transformation characteristic of the shift from the medieval to the modern international system—and by extension of the argument, it serves as a dimension of possible future transformation from the modern toward a postmodern international system. Its inclusion also has a number of more immediate consequences, three of which I simply enumerate.

First, this structural level gives greater determinate content to the general constraints of anarchy deduced by Waltz. One illustration will suffice to make the point. According to Waltz, the core element of collaboration in an anarchical realm is "the exchange of considerations" (Waltz 1979: 113). Neither he nor Chester Barnard (1948: 151), whom he follows on this point, defines what is meant by the term "considerations," however. And from anarchy alone one cannot infer any specific meaning. But greater content is provided by the institutional frameworks of heteronomy and sovereignty, respectively. In the medieval system, the exchange of considerations was calculated *intuitu personae*, that is, taking into account the "majesty," "dignity," and other such individual and subjective attributes of the status and wealth of the parties to the exchange (Mattingly 1964). This is as foreign to the modern mind as is Aristotle's effort to calculate a just price for exchange by taking into account the social standing of the parties to it (Polanyi 1957), but it represents no less an "exchange of considerations" for it. In the framework of sovereignty characteristic of "possessive individualists," of course, "considerations" translates as rough quantitative equivalency—which, of course, is what Waltz mistakenly thinks he is deducing from anarchy.

Second, this structural level provides the basis for a more refined and compelling response than Waltz is able to give to liberal interdependence theorists who argue that because sovereignty (erroneously defined as unit autonomy) is becoming "relatively irrelevant," realism no longer offers an appropriate explanation of international outcomes. All that Waltz can, and does, say is that this is a unit-level issue which has no place in systemic theory. However, in view of the analogous relationship established above between private property rights and sovereignty, those who would dispense with the concept of sovereignty on the grounds of growing international interdependence must first show why the idea of private property rights should not have been dispensed with long ago in the capitalist societies, where they are continuously invaded and interfered with by the actions of the state. Yet we know that, at a minimum, the structure of private property rights will influence when the state intervenes; usually it also affects how the state intervenes. If this concept still has utility domestically, in the face of binding state action, then its international analogue ought, if anything, to be even more relevant. The reason for the continued significance of the concepts is that they are not simply descriptive categories. Rather, they are components of generative structures: they shape, condition, and constrain social behavior.

Lastly, incorporating this structural level allows us to reach beyond the confines of Waltz's model to examine "within-system" changes that are not the product of shifts in the distribution of capabilities among states—but without violating its Durkheimian premises. For example, the institutional framework of sovereignty differentiates units in terms of juridically mutually exclusive and morally self-entailed domains. However, the scope of these domains is defined not only territorially but also functionally, depending upon the range and depth of state activity in domestic social and economic affairs: the New Deal state and its counterparts abroad, to cite one instance, are more expansive than the laissez-faire state. It follows that the functional scope of the international system will also vary, depending upon the hegemonic form of state/society relations that prevails collectively at any given time. Therefore, the hegemonic form of state/society relations, or a lack thereof, constitutes an attribute of the international system and can be used as a systems-level explanatory factor. And a good thing that it can be so used, for despite his best efforts Waltz cannot explain the qualitative differences between the late-nineteenth-century and the post-World War II international economic orders simply by the facts of multipolarity then and bipolarity now. Their differences stem from the respective hegemonic forms of state/society relations prevailing in the two eras—"laissez-faire liberalism" then and "embedded liberalism" now [see Chapter 2].

In sum, the basis upon which any social totality is segmented into individual units, and the corresponding forms of association by which those units in turn are grouped together, is an irreducible element of its structure; there is no reason whatever to assume that the international totality differs in this regard. In the international realm, anarchy constitutes the deep structure. Its effects are mediated by prevailing forms of individuation: a heteronomous institutional framework in the case of the medieval system, and the more familiar framework of sovereignty in the case of the modern.

DYNAMIC DENSITY

There is not only a dimension of social totalities missing from Waltz's model. If he takes his Durkheimian premises seriously, then a fundamental determinant of change is missing as well. According to Durkheim, "growth in the volume and dynamic density of societies modifies profoundly the fundamental conditions of collective existence" (1895: 115). Both are capable of altering "social facts." By volume, Durkheim means the number of socially relevant units, which Waltz includes in his model by counting the number of great powers. But what of dynamic density? By this, Durkheim understands the aggregate quantity, velocity, and diversity of transactions that go on within society. But Waltz, as we have seen, banishes such factors to the level of process, shaped by structure but not affecting structure in any manner. The problem is that, having dropped out differentiation, Waltz has no means to relate dynamic density to his concept of structure for, if Durkheim is right, it is most closely related to differentiation.

On logical and historical grounds, the pressure of what Durkheim calls dynamic density is exerted most directly on prevailing property rights within a society. Formal theories of property rights, for example, routinely invoke such factors as crowding, the existence of externalities, and the incentives of optimal scale to explain and justify the reordering of individual property rights (Furubotn and Pejovich 1974). Lacking this dimension of structure, Waltz rejects the phenomenon as not having anything to do with structure. True, the only relevant question for Waltz's purposes is whether the pressure of dynamic density is ever so great as to trigger a change not simply in the individual property rights of states, but in the basic structure of property rights that characterizes the collective system of states. It happens that the shift from the medieval to the modern system represents one such instance. And it is not an unreasonable hypothesis that any transformation beyond the modern system would represent a similar instance.

In their enormously ambitious and provocative analytical economic history of the rise of the West from 1300 to 1700, North and Thomas (1973) discuss the medieval-to-modern shift in the following terms. Self-sustained economic growth in the West was made possible by the instituting of efficient economic organization. Efficient economic organization in turn entailed a societal restructuring of property rights that reduced the discrepancy between private and social rates of return. This restructuring of property rights was produced by a combination of diminishing returns to land, resulting from population pressures; a widening of markets, resulting from migration; and an expansion of the institutions providing justice and protection to achieve a more optimal size for commerce and warfare, as well as their reorganization to eliminate domestic competitors. The transformation of the state was driven on the supply side by rulers' pursuit of revenues: where the particular fiscal interests of state actors coincided with an economically efficient structure of property rights—as they did in the Netherlands and Britain—successful economic growth ensued; others became also-rans. In this instance, then, Durkheim's notion of dynamic density can be linked to a societal restructuring of property rights and political organization, which had the domestic and international consequences that we examined in the previous section.

North and Thomas's model, even if it were without problems on its own terms, cannot simply be extended into the future of the international system. For one thing, as the authors themselves point out, from the seventeenth century onward, differences in the efficiency of economic organization have become a major determinant of the consequences of the "natural" forces that they examine, so that the phenomenon of dynamic density today is infinitely more complex. For another, the restructuring of property rights and political organization that they describe were in large measure instituted from the top down by rulers gaining control of the emerging state formations; no analogue exists in the contemporary international system. However, neither of these qualifications warrants neglecting dynamic density as a possible determinant of future systemic change. They merely suggest that its manifestations and effects are likely to be different, and that indicators designed to detect them will have to reflect these differences.

A second reason for Waltz's neglect of dynamic density as a possible source of change reflects an error of commission rather than of omission. I mentioned earlier that Waltz strives for, but fails fully to achieve, a generative formulation of international political structure. As a result of this failure, one circuit through which the effects of dynamic density could register at the systems level is severed. In a generative structure, it will be recalled, the deeper structural levels have causal priority, and the structural levels closer to the surface of visible phenomena take effect only within a context that is already "prestructured" by the deeper levels. For example, we ask of the distribution of capabilities within the international system what difference it makes for the impact of the general organizational effects of the deep structure of anarchy, as mediated by the more specific effects of the institutional framework of sovereignty. That is how the *systemic* effects of changes in the distribution of capabilities are determined. We then go on to ask how these systemic effects condition and constrain outcomes.

However, when assessing possible sources of change, Waltz short-circuits his own model: he slips from a *generative* to a *descriptive* conception of structure. For example, in the face of demographic trends, quantitative and qualitative changes in global industrial production as well as in ecological and resource constraints—some of which surely could be coded as measures of systemic dynamic density—Waltz tends to conclude: yes, but the United States and the Soviet Union still are relatively better off than anybody else, and the United States is relatively better off than the Soviet Union; therefore these changes have no systemic effects and remain of no concern to systemic theory. But within a generative model of structure the question that Waltz *should* be asking is whether any of these changes, singly or in combination, make any difference not simply for the *relative* position of the superpowers, but for the *absolute* capacity of bipolarity to *mute* the underlying deleterious organizational effects of anarchy and sovereignty—how beautiful does small remain in the face of these forces? A generative model of structure demands this chain of reasoning, as Waltz acknowledges in his abstract description of it. I, for one, would be surprised to learn that some of the changes alluded to above [and explored in the following chapter] do not adversely affect the managerial capacity of bipolarity and, thereby, alter systemic outcomes.

In short, both errors of omission and commission account for Waltz pushing out of his model of systemic structure and into the realm of unit-level process a source of change that Durkheim regarded a key determinant in "the conditions of collective existence" (1895: 115).

CONCLUSION

In Waltz's model of the international system, structural features are sharply distinguished from unit-level processes, and structure is the productive agency that operates at the level of the system. Accordingly, only structural change can produce systemic change. But in Waltz's model nothing, in turn, produces structural change. The problem with his posture is that, in any social system, structural change ultimately has no source other than unit-level processes, and these somehow must be linked to structure if it is to be capable not merely of recording change after the fact, but explaining and predicting it. When Waltz banishes these factors from the domain of systemic theory he also exogenizes all sources of structural change. Durkheim typically is regarded as having been an extreme systemic deter-minist. But by means of the concept of dynamic density, he at least sought to endogenize some aspect of change of society into his theory of society. Not so Waltz.

Waltz reacts strongly against what he calls reductionist tendencies in international relations theorizing. In the conventional usage, as we noted above, he finds that the system is all product and is not at all productive. He takes great pains to rectify this imbalance. He goes too far, however. In his conception of systemic theory, unit-level processes become all product and are not at all productive. Hence, what Anthony Giddens says of Durkheim is said even more appropriately of Waltz: he adopts what is supposed to be a methodological principle, and turns it into an ontological one (Giddens 1978: 126). As a result, Waltz's theory of "society" contains only a reproductive logic, but no transformational logic. In his model, therefore, continuity is a product of premise even before it is hypothesized as an outcome.

6   Social time and ecodemographic contexts

It is universally acknowledged that studying the transformation of any social formation requires taking the dimension of time into account. Less well appreciated is the fact that time varies not only in duration but also in form. For example, temporality as increments of elapsed time differs from temporality as *la longue durée* not only in duration but also in the character of the units that make each up. Because international relations theory traffics largely in the world of elapsed time, an epistemological bias is built into our theories which makes it difficult to grasp potential elements of transformation in the world around us. This essay, published as 1986a, defines three temporal forms: incremental, conjunctural, and epochal. And it illustrates their characteristics by exploring the different features of global population and resource issues that come into focus when viewed through the lenses of each form.

These analytical issues are not much discussed in international relations theorizing. In the study of large-scale social change generally, they have been most extensively explored by the *Annales* school of historiography, especially the work of Braudel (1972, 1980), and Le Goff (1980, 1992). For a perspective rooted in German philosophy of history but which makes similar arguments, see Koselleck (1985).

Braudel argues that the ecodemographic dimension ultimately poses the greatest challenge to the long-term durability of social structures. Hence the choice of two of its components, the international implications of population and natural resource issues, as the illustrative subject matter of this essay.

A premise that is widely shared among analysts, irrespective of their methodological or ideological proclivities, is that effective policy responses to "global issues" concerning the human environment require that the time horizon of policy making be expanded (Dahlberg 1983). This is so for the obvious reason that the effects of decisions taken or foregone today may not materialize until well into the future, and it may take equally long to reverse these effects should that prove necessary.

But it is not only the length of time that changes as time horizons expand; entirely new and different factors also come into focus when we do so. Donald Kennedy considers this to be the major lesson derived from scenarios depicting so-called nuclear winter: "What we have learned from the things biologists and atmospheric physicists are telling us today is that the proper time scale is years, and that the processes to which we must look are unfamiliar both in kind and scale" (Kennedy 1984: xxxi).

This essay starts with Kennedy's insight about the epistemological dimensions of temporality in the attempt to better understand how global ecodemographic issues may affect the future international polity. The first section proposes and fleshes out the idea that temporality serves as a useful basis for conceptualizing policy challenges posed by population and natural resource issues. The second section illustrates the different population and resource issues that come into focus depending on the time frame within which they are viewed. The third section suggests that different time frames also have implications for epistemological approaches to policy making—how much and what kind of knowledge to insist upon before taking which types of action. The essay concludes with some implications of the significance of temporal factors in foreign policy making.

TIME FRAME AND ISSUE TYPES

Let us begin with a stylized illustration. Imagine a simple agricultural community, relying on a staple crop. To manage year-to-year fluctuations in temperature and precipitation, the community is likely to keep reserves on hand to compensate for possible temporary shortfalls. In the wake of a succession of climate-induced bad harvests, however, inventory formation by itself probably will be seen as inadequate, and the community is likely to take further steps such as planting a new crop mix and scattering its fields among different sites. Lastly, the onset of a progressively inhospitable climate is likely to elicit still more radical measures, possibly including migrating to more favorable climes (Bryson and Murray 1977; Rotberg and Raab 1981).

In this illustration, the duration of time that the community takes into consideration in making its decisions increases from one step to the next. But duration is neither the only change that takes place nor the most important. After all, annual fluctuations can go on literally forever without triggering any response over and above emergency stockpiling. In addition to the duration of time that our hypothetical community took into consideration, three other changes also occurred in the illustration: (1) the frameworks of social time within which the fluctuations in temperature and precipitation are assessed; (2) the nature of the issue that is perceived to require a response as this framework shifts; and (3) the type of responses that are seen appropriate as the framework shifts. Thus, the critical difference among the three time frames lies in what Emory and Trist (1973: 11) call the "temporal gestalten" that are embedded in them—or, more simply, their temporal forms.

Temporal forms reflect phenomena in the natural world, including the succession of seasons. But they are also social constructions (Sorokin 1964; Geertz 1973; Le Goff 1980). Specifically, they frame social perceptions of what we might call the temporal location of events and processes (Durkheim 1965: 14–15; Zerubavel 1982: 2). In our illustration, the raw datum, fluctuations in temperature and precipitation, is identical in each of the three time frames. But its temporal location changes from one to the next. Our hypothetical community assessed fluctuations initially within a year-to-year context; then as indicating the possibility of a climatic cycle; and finally as portending fundamental climate change. Thus, the same observable phenomenon was placed successively within three characteristic temporal forms. These may be described as incremental, conjunctural, and epochal time. Variations in temporal forms produced variations in social meaning and action.

To each temporal form there corresponds a particular conception of the elements that go to make up the socially relevant universe. An incremental time frame slices social time into a succession of discrete and infinitely divisible units. The corresponding view of the social universe visualizes its elements in terms of separate and distinct actors, palpable properties, and discontinuous events. A conjunctural time frame, in contrast, depicts the basic units in social time as cycles or some other representation of temporal movement. The corresponding view of the socially relevant universe focuses attention on the processes that underlie actors, properties, and events. Epochal time is removed still further from everyday experience. It is the temporal form considered basic by, for example, the historians of *la longue durée*. As Jacques Le Goff, one of the leading practitioners of the art, insists, *la longue durée* should be regarded not simply as lasting a long time but "as having the structure of a system," emerging at one point and dissipating at another (1980: xi). Climatologists, for example, delineate little and big ice ages, and ecologists refer to biotic regimes. In each case, the frame of reference is a structural arrangement that governs the functioning of some system within certain boundary conditions. Epochal time is measured by change in those structures: once they are transformed beyond the boundary conditions, a new historical era, climatological age, or ecological regime is said to come into existence.

We can now apply these notions to global population and resource issues. Which aspects of population and resources come into focus when viewed through the lenses of an incremental time frame? In terms of population, the central issue of concern to policymakers historically has been changes in the relative size and attributes of their own population as well as those of strategic and economic competitors and partners. By attributes we mean age, gender, health, ethnic composition, spatial distribution, and so on. This is what the classical geopolitics literature called the "manpower aspects" of population (Sprout and Sprout 1962). What is the corresponding depiction of resources? Here, the central issue has been the distribution of and access to strategically and economically important raw materials, including fuel, nonfuel minerals, food, water, and the like. These factors comprise what the 1952 Paley Commission called "the materials strength" of nations (President's Materials Policy Commission 1952). It is striking how anachronistic these characterizations seem today for foreign policy making in the industrialized parts of the world.

Now take the second temporal form, that of conjunctural movements. The postwar "baby boom" in the United States is an example of such a movement in population. It has affected far more than the relative size and attributes of the US population; it also affected the demand for and supply of housing, schools, employment, transportation, durable and consumer goods, as well as the cultural landscape, crime rate, and partisan politics. In the global context, an analogous phenomenon is the momentum that is built into rates of growth in world population. The core issue here is the balance between this demographic momentum, as it is known, and the rate at which economic opportunities, social amenities, and physical infrastructure can be supplied (World Bank 1984). On the resource side, the key issue of a conjunctural kind is the sustainability of resource bases, such as arable land, fisheries stocks, mineral deposits, gene pools, and the like, given current and anticipated levels of demand (Repetto 1986). These population and resource issues have become far more pronounced in the recent decades relative to the classical geopolitical conceptions.

When we shift to the temporal form of epochal time, still different dimensions of population and resources are drawn to our attention. On the population side, over the course of human history some social systems have proved to be too small to maintain themselves as autonomous or even effectively functioning entities, others too large; some have been too densely populated, others too sparsely. We may refer to this issue as the social carrying capacity of different organizational forms. This is a measure of the size of population clusters to be organized, relative to known and acceptable means of social organization (Hawley 1950; Bennett 1976). On the resource side, we may speak of the natural carrying capacity of physical and biological life support systems. This refers to the ability of the biosphere to perform the environmental services on which human (and other) life depends, including the maintenance of heat and energy balances, screening out solar radiation, recycling nutrients, and similar processes (Ehrlich et al. 1977). This is the domain of global ecopolitics, the arrival of which on the international policy agenda was signaled by the 1972 United Nations Conference on the Human Environment.

In sum, specifying temporal forms in this manner permits us to differentiate systematically among different types of population and resource issues, based not only on substantive attributes but also their epistemological properties. The next step in the analysis is to identify real world analogs of these generic issue types.

ISSUE TYPES AND POLICY PROBLEMS

In the previous section, I argued that when temporal forms are shifted, generically different aspects of the same issue, such as global population and resources, are identified. Here I propose to illustrate the different issue types by describing briefly some actual areas of international policy that fall within each. To keep the discussion manageable, it will be limited to those aspects of population and resource issues that could effect major changes in the overall international security and economic orders, respectively.

Relative size and attributes of populations

Notwithstanding the old saying that "God is always on the side of the biggest battalions," there has never been a simple one-to-one correspondence between national population size and international hierarchy. Whatever correspondence there may have existed in the past between the two has become weaker over time, owing to developments in the technology of warfare (Sprout and Sprout 1962). Moreover, there is little evidence that population size in and of itself constitutes a significant source of international conflict behavior (Choucri 1974).

Among the attributes of populations that have proved most potent in triggering violent conflicts are various segmental cleavages within societies: above all, ethnic, religious, and tribal cleavages (Choucri 1974; Enloe 1980), as well as maldistribution of wealth (Durham 1979; Kleinman 1980). Conflicts triggered by such cleavages may spill over into the international arena. Many regional conflicts today are of this sort, and no change in this situation appears imminent.

On the economic side, there appears to be little direct relation between population size per se, and place in the international division of labor. Here again, the attributes of populations rather than sheer numbers are the more significant demographic factor. Nevertheless, to the extent that the structure of world industrial production reflects relative labor costs, the combination of relative size and age of labor forces in the industrial and developing worlds will reinforce the growing role of high-technology and service activities in the industrialized countries and the importance of developing countries as producers and exporters of manufactured products. The same set of factors will keep up migratory pressure on porous national borders, such as between Mexico and the United States.

Resource distribution and access

Gaining control over or securing access to adequate supplies of essential raw materials has long been assumed a necessary condition of becoming and remaining a great power. Moreover, the struggle for raw materials has long been linked to foreign expansionist drives, including warfare and imperialism (Eckes 1979).

Five industrialized countries—the Soviet Union, the United States, Canada, Australia, and South Africa—possess most of the world's supplies of the twenty-five minerals that account for over 90 percent of the total value of all minerals consumed (Arad and Arad 1979: 64). Hence, it would take an extraordinary confluence of events to alter fundamentally the global balance of strategic power via the raw materials route. This is not to say, however, that conflicts over raw materials are inconceivable.

Resource war scenarios hinge in part on the degree to which the West is vulnerable because of its high degree of reliance on raw materials imports, though the United States in most instances relies on imports by volition rather than necessity. The regions of greatest concern in this connection are the Persian Gulf, which is both highly unstable politically and the source of a large share of the West's oil; southern Africa, from the Congo to the Cape, from which the West imports virtually every important nonfuel mineral (in many cases more than half of total consumption), and which also dominates the oil routes around the Cape; and the Indian Ocean, on which the other two border and which contains strategic and commercial sealanes of great importance to the West (US Congress 1980, 1981a, 1981b).

North–South resource war scenarios dominated policy debates in the 1970s, following the Organization of Petroleum-Exporting Countries (OPEC) embargo. The central question was whether the South can manipulate its control over raw materials in such a way as to compel the North to acquiesce to Southern political demands or to react against the South with the threat of force or force itself. The North was and remains most vulnerable in the area of petroleum, though less to OPEC power than to regional instability. Beyond that, a great deal depends on how the future of South Africa unfolds, but here, too, general instability rather than deliberate supply manipulation is the greater threat (Arad and Arad 1979; Sambunaris 1981; Gilpin 1982).

Intraregional conflicts may affect the supply of raw materials worldwide even if resources are not directly at issue, and intraregional resource conflicts could become globalized. With two exceptions, the most likely areas in which either might occur have already been mentioned. One of the exceptions is conflict attending resource-induced migration. The second exception is fresh water as a source of conflict. It is likely to become increasingly salient, possibly involving river diversion (148 of the world's 200 major river basins are shared by two countries), underground aquifers, and water augmentation systems (Thompson 1978).

On the economic side, no other raw material is likely to match the impact on the international economic order that petroleum had after 1973. This is so for three reasons. First, the ratio of minerals consumption to gross domestic product (GDP) has been decreasing steadily throughout the industrialized world, so that the importance of nonfuel minerals to overall economic activity there is declining (Tilton and Landsberg 1983). Second, the annual import bill for nonfuel minerals is much lower than for oil—in the case of the United States, on the order of roughly ten to one—so that it is inconceivable for the direct macroeconomic effects of any price increases to be even remotely comparable with the effects that oil price increases had during the 1970s. Third, the necessary conditions for successful cartelization of nonfuel minerals markets appear to be met in few if any cases: so that even if cartels were to be formed, they are not likely to be able to sustain themselves for any appreciable length of time (Russett 1984; Tilton and Landsberg 1983). Temporary interruptions of supplies, however, may well increase as time goes on due to the political instability of supplier countries and regions.

For the developing world, the critical resource other than petroleum, of course, is food. Aggregate food availability on a global basis is no longer a constraint on access to food anywhere. Access to food worldwide increasingly has become a matter of effective market demand—which is to say it is a function of social power and government policy, domestic and international (Johnson 1984).

The issues described above exemplify the kinds of policy problems that come into view when global population and resource-related factors are viewed through the lens of an incremental time frame. The relevant players and events can be identified with relative ease, and the parameters within which they operate in principle are knowable. For the industrialized world, they are increasingly policy issues of the past. When the focus shifts to a conjunctural time frame, very different kinds of policy problems appear.

Demographic momentum

From about 1750 until 1900, world population grew at about 0.5 percent per annum; from 1900 to 1950, the rate of population increase rose to 1 percent per annum; it reached 2 percent in the 1960s. In the industrialized countries, fertility fell to replacement levels or even below by the 1970s. In the developing countries, fertility continued to increase and the death rate to decrease. As a result, the rate of population increase in the developing world reached 2.4 percent per annum in the 1960s. Owing largely to the impact of China, it declined to roughly 2 percent thereafter, but remains between 2 and 4 percent for most low- and middle-income countries. Total world population by the 1980s stood at about 4.8 billion. According to World Bank calculations at that time (1984), the momentum built into the rate of increase would produce a world population of some 6.3 billion by the year 2000. Because the mothers-to-be themselves were already born, this projection was made with a fair degree of certainty. On standard assumptions, projections of total world population in the 1980s foresaw roughly 9.8 billion people on the planet by 2050. Even with rapid fertility decline, for the next several decades the world is likely to experience a demographic momentum at a rate and under conditions for which there is no precedent in history.

The most facile security-related scenario is that of rapid population growth leading to external aggression. In academic parlance, this notion is embodied in the "lateral pressure" model of international conflict (Choucri and North 1975); it used to be known as the struggle for *Lebensraum*. In either guise, its past predictive value is uncertain at best. It has proved virtually impossible to define the key causal terms, be they scarcity, density, size, or growth rates, in such a manner that predictions based on them are confirmed with any degree of consistency. It is almost always possible to adduce counter-examples where equal magnitudes failed to yield the predicted outcome (Kleinman 1980). Accordingly, Quincy Wright (1942), in his monumental study of the causes of war, concluded that the effect of population pressure was indeterminate. It is clear, however, that population pressure has, on occasion, served as a pretext or justification for external aggression, as by the geopolitical propagandists in the service of Hitler and Mussolini (Sprout and Sprout 1962: 407).

There is a second and closely related indirect link between population pressure and conflict potential. In the developing countries, populations are likely to encounter institutional barriers long before they encounter absolute physical scarcity—or, perhaps more accurately, segments of populations may encounter physical scarcity because of the existence of such institutional barriers as landholding patterns as well as government policies that favor one population segment at the expense of others. Population pressure then may spill over into international conflict behavior, as it did in the so-called soccer war between El Salvador and Honduras (Durham 1979). Yet it does so not because of population increases per se, but because institutional arrangements deny access to resources to those segments of populations that are often growing most rapidly (Durham 1979; Kleinman 1980). The external spillover may be inadvertent, or it may be deliberate by the state diverting domestic problems into the international arena.

It is also possible to imagine more widespread militarization resulting from large labor surpluses in developing countries, especially among young men. From 1980 to 2000, the working age population of developing countries is expected to increase by 1.15 billion, compared with a corresponding increase of 730 million during the prior twenty years. The record of the recent past is not encouraging with respect to the absorptive capacity of developing countries' economies on such a scale. For a variety of reasons—the hope of securing domestic stability, the mobilization of mass labor for infrastructural projects, the greater relative availability of security assistance from abroad as compared to economic assistance—the military side of many Third World governments may increase in importance as an employer of last resort.

Lastly, rapid urbanization in developing countries is often cited as a cause for concern. Third World cities have been growing at almost twice the rate of overall populations. UN statistics using the mid-1970s as the base project an urban agglomeration of some 31 million in Mexico City by the year 2000, 26 million in São Paulo, nearly 23 million in Shanghai, 19 million in Rio, some 17 million in Bombay and Jakarta, and so on, all of which represent unprecedented rates of urban growth (United Nations 1980). African cities, starting from a smaller base, will not reach those levels of absolute size, but are growing at an even more rapid pace. The security-related problem that is feared is social turmoil resulting from an insufficient capacity on the part of cities to service such large increments of population in so short a time. Social turmoil in turn may provide targets of opportunity either for domestic forces to internationalize the problem or for foreign forces to meddle in domestic affairs, though the limited evidence available to date is ambiguous (Bienen 1984; Harrod 1986).

Most of the direct economic effects of this demographic momentum will be felt by the individual countries concerned. Precisely what those effects will be is subject to analytical and empirical dispute as well as to ideological posturing (see Barney (1980) versus Simon (1981)). Nevertheless, no one argues seriously that countries already characterized by low levels of per capita income, heavy dependence on agriculture, an insufficient stock of social overhead capital and physical amenities, and weak institutional infrastructure will be better off with rapid population growth rates than with lower rates. And the fact is that many of the developing countries experiencing high rates of population growth fall into this category.

There are likely to be several kinds of international economic effects. First, demographic trends in developing countries will keep their real wages low relative to those in industrialized countries. This sets the stage for increased pressure on the industrialized countries through the mechanisms of international trade and migration, particularly from the middle-income developing countries. Second, barring dramatic international and domestic policy reversals, the recent African initiatives undertaken by international agencies, donor governments, and nongovernmental organizations are likely to be but the first in a series of increasingly permanent "emergency" relief efforts, not only in African but also in other low-income countries.

A third international economic effect that is frequently postulated is an increase in the global prices of raw materials due to population increases. This is a more dubious proposition. For nonfuel minerals, real production costs have been declining steadily, while current and prospective reserves continue to increase (Tilton and Landsberg 1983). Factors other than population pressure are likely to be responsible for price instability in world oil markets (Russell 1984), though population pressure will continue to raise the private and social costs of such noncommercial sources of energy as fuelwood and dung. Finally, while food prices limit access to food for some segments of populations, international food prices are not themselves population driven, nor is the share of the world's income devoted to agriculture increasing (Food and Agriculture Organization 1979).

Sustainability of resource bases

The question of sustainability in the case of resources concerns the natural resource capital required to maintain and improve human welfare in the future. For the purposes of the present discussion, we can divide these resource bases into (1) fossil fuel deposits, (2) nonfuel mineral deposits, and (3) biological resources.

In the area of fossil fuels, at some point during the next twenty-five years or so a transition away from oil is likely to commence, though it should be noted that the margin of error in calculating petroleum reserves has always been substantial. Other fossil fuels remain plentiful, as are prospective synthetic fuels based on fossil fuel sources; their viability depends on price and on environmental considerations. The same is true of nuclear power, the most widespread alternative energy source. Energy conservation continues to offer major supply possibilities (Russell 1984). The key policy problem for fossil fuels, then, is to devise adequate transition strategies.

In the case of nonfuel minerals, most analyses of the quantities likely to be added to current reserves during the next fifty years, even assuming no change in prices, agree that supplies should be adequate. This projection holds for a variety of plausible population scenarios and other changes on the demand side (Ridker 1979). However, constraints can be expected to arise from such factors as environmental controls, land use restrictions, and the cost of water. These could affect locational decisions of extraction and production, and thus the short-term security of supplies and stability of prices.

In contrast to the previous two, the situation is very different when it comes to what we might call biological resource bases: soils, aquatic systems, forests, biomass fuels, genetic materials, and the like. The problem here is twofold. First, long-term global trend data are either nonexistent or of little use. They are of little use because critical interdependencies—for example, the interrelationships among deforestation, soil cover, fresh water supplies, and the atmosphere—either are quite novel or have not been monitored in the past. Second, projections are problematic because in many instances they depend on assumptions made about the institutional arrangements that will govern these resource bases in the future. For example, Simon and Kahn (1984: 11) reach the casuistic conclusion that the "alarms" in the 1960s and 1970s warning of the impending death of the Great Lakes "have turned out totally in error," allegedly shown by the fact that "fishing and swimming conditions there are now excellent." They neglect to mention that the entire regulatory regime of the Great Lakes was transformed in the interval, largely in response to those "alarms."

At the global level, potentially large pools of genetic resources situated disproportionately in tropical forests have yet to be discovered, and many of the fractions that have been discovered are far from having either a market or a shadow price. As a result, there is no incentive to husband them. Tropical forests themselves are currently treated as though they were a one-time windfall rather than a renewable resource (Guppy 1984). Forestry elsewhere and fisheries everywhere are barely beyond the hunting and gathering stage. The same is true of biomass fuel sources in the developing countries. Large discrepancies exist worldwide between the private gains and social costs of overburdening agricultural soils and aquatic systems.

If one assumes that current institutional arrangements will remain as they are, then one is compelled to project unsustainable rates of exploitation with major and possibly deleterious effects globally: deforestation, species loss, soil erosion, siltation, salination, and other forms of biotic impoverishment, together with serious economic loss and conflict potential. If one assumes that prices will come to reflect replacement values, that property rights will be reconfigured to internalize externalities, and that states will compensate for any remaining market failures, then one reaches the conclusion of a virtually limitless and, presumably, harmonious future. On the historical record, neither set of assumptions merits much confidence.

Thus, the fossil fuels sector poses transition problems. The kinds of problems that may emerge in the nonfuel mineral areas are not likely to be shaped uniquely if at all by the sustainability issue in any foreseeable future, but rather by more situational factors affecting distribution and access. Biotic impoverishment would raise quite different kinds of problems. On the security side, seriously degraded resource bases could lead to domestic turmoil and regional conflicts. On the economic side, possible negative effects would range from opportunity costs (lost genetic resources), to greater vulnerability resulting from increasingly fragile resource bases (soil erosion), to economic dislocation produced by depletion of resource bases (forestry, fisheries).

In sum, the issues that emerge when one views global population and resources through a conjunctural time frame are demographic momentum and the sustainability of resource bases. These issues have become more pronounced in recent decades, relative to the more classical population and resources issues.

Let us turn now to how population and resources issues look in the temporal frame of epochal time.

Social carrying capacity

In the long run, the social carrying capacity of different organizational forms potentially affects cities, countries, and the state system itself.

With respect to cities, one obvious question is whether the large urban formations projected for the Third World are viable organizational entities, at a human cost that is acceptable. Urban growth gives rise to economies of scale and agglomeration. But it has not been determined whether there exists any particular urban size at which diseconomies come to outweigh them (Linn 1983; World Bank 1984). Even less is known about the relationship between urban size and political/administrative "economies" and "diseconomies." For economists there is no such thing as "over-urbanization," because self-correcting mechanisms would prevent it (Kelley and Williamson 1984). But what is self-correction for the economist may be social turmoil and conflict for the political scientist—not to mention for the individuals involved.

So it is with countries. Until recently, concerns were often heard about the long-term viability of small and mini-states in an age of ever-larger social formations. But in the light of projected population sizes for some countries, concern has shifted to whether some countries may become too large relative to their political and administrative capacity. The same kinds of conceptual conundrums hold here as for cities. In addition, the available statistics do not offer much guidance or inspire confidence. For example, on standard fertility assumptions the population of Kenya, at 18 million around 1980, is expected to grow to 120 million by 2050; but on the assumption of rapid fertility decline the total is projected to be 50 million fewer (World Bank 1984). Presumably this is a difference that would make a difference, even for a "soft" African state (Callaghy 1985), but it is impossible to say if it is a decisive one.

The institutional inadequacy of the system of states is an article of faith for many concerned with the sustainability of planetary ecosystems, though arguments in defense of the system of states are also frequent and elegant (see Bull 1977; Waltz 1979). This issue raises the scope and scale of social ecology, broadly defined (Hawley 1950), to entirely new levels, at which it has never had to be considered before. The critical question concerns how effective some of the institutional mechanisms can be, such as international regimes, by which states attenuate the effects of the international structure of anarchy.

Natural carrying capacity

Nothing better introduces this last set of issues than the hypothesized phenomenon termed "nuclear winter," which entered public debate in the early 1980s (Turco et al. 1983; Sagan 1983/84; Ehrlich et al. 1984). Nuclear winter crystallizes in the extreme the disruptions of planetary life support systems that could result from certain human intrusions into the biosphere, most of which are the cumulative by-products of normal, everyday activities.

The concept of nuclear winter refers to the projected effects on the biosphere of the particulate matter that would be the by-product of a nuclear exchange, in addition to the direct effects of blasts, fires, and radiation. In brief, this is the scenario generated by the scientific models: as a result of the dust, soot, and smoke produced by nuclear explosions, the amount of sunlight reaching the earth would be reduced. A prolonged darkness would ensue, followed by a drop in temperatures. The settling of the particulate matter, perhaps after a period of several months, would be accompanied by increased exposure to ultraviolet light, since the nuclear blasts would have resulted in ozone depletion. All the while, ionizing radiation from nuclear fallout would spread. This combination of atmospheric, climatic, and radiological effects would have a directly destructive impact on human, animal, and plant life. In addition, it would impair the normal functioning of natural ecosystems in the longer run. As a result, there would be interruptions in the services provided by these ecosystems, including photosynthesis, maintaining the gaseous composition of the atmosphere, regulating climates, producing fresh water, disposing of wastes, recycling nutrients, generating and preserving soils, and so on.

Far short of nuclear war or other cataclysmic changes, these life-supporting resources can be degraded by industrial processes and products, agricultural practices, the burning of fossil fuels, deforestation, and a host of other routine human activities. Much of the attention of policymakers has been devoted to immediate or acute problems, such as the health effects of air and water pollution and toxic waste disposal. Far less attention has been paid to the degradation of natural life support systems. These problems in the first instance are predominantly local or national in scope. But some, such as acid rain, also have transborder effects. Moreover, even local problems may have cumulative effects that may ultimately be global in scope; the buildup of carbon dioxide in the atmosphere is one case in point. Some problems, such as ozone depletion, are global in effect to begin with.

The buildup of carbon dioxide is typical of the kinds of issues that fall into this category. It is the product of the cumulative effects of dispersed processes, no single instance of which may seem—or may be—important in and of itself. It is the kind of issue that evolves slowly, and therefore does not force itself to the top of the policy agenda. In addition, there are enormous uncertainties concerning its dynamic and above all its full range of potential consequences. Carbon dioxide buildup may have a direct impact on weather and climate via the so-called greenhouse effect, and it potentially can alter the balance of nature because of its impact on photosynthesis. The performance of environmental services would be affected worldwide.

In sum, this last temporal form, epochal time, draws our attention to certain aspects of the organization of communities—social, on the one hand, and natural, on the other. With respect to population, it raises the issue of the social carrying capacity of organizational systems; with respect to resources, it raises the issue of the natural carrying capacity of planetary life support systems. They are by far the most elusive but also the most profound of all population and resources issues, and are likely to become more central policy concerns in the next century.

IMPLICATIONS FOR POLICY MAKING

The US national defense establishment, including its civil defense branch, traditionally viewed the consequences of nuclear war in terms of how much devastation would be caused by any given primary blast and its collateral damage, such as local radioactive fallout. Gradually, delayed effects of fallout transported over long distances were discovered, but their potential magnitude and scale continued to occasion surprises. Only later was official concern also drawn to such problems as the electromagnetic pulse effects of nuclear blasts on command and control capabilities. And the issues raised by nuclear winter expanded the horizon still further, in terms of duration and the types of phenomena that were taken into consideration. We might say, then, that in assessing the possible effects of nuclear war, military planners moved slowly from an incremental time frame, to a conjunctural time frame, and most recently to an epochal time frame.

As such shifts take place, new policy problems are discovered and new responses devised. But our discussion suggests that new problems differ from the old not only substantively but also epistemologically. A world composed of discrete time increments and distinct actors having palpable properties is inherently more knowable than one composed of aggregate processes that work themselves out only over the course of the unfolding of some dynamic. Complex systems and their laws of transformation are the most difficult of the three to comprehend with any degree of certainty. Here, I briefly suggest some of the implications of these epistemological differences for devising global population and resource policies.

In the world that we see through an incremental time frame, the relevant players and events are readily identified, their attributes assessed, and judgments made about their long-term significance. Precise prediction of specific outcomes may not be possible, but the basic parameters of situations can be known and their likely trajectories projected. In principle, information is plentiful. The key analytical problem for policy making in this domain, therefore, is the standard one of choice under the constraint of how much time and energy can be devoted to any particular decision. Care must be taken that cognitive and institutional mechanisms that policymakers use to reduce information to manageable proportions do not at the same time distort it.

For example, David Baldwin (1985) has shown that there is a tendency in foreign policy circles to underestimate the utility of economic instruments of statecraft and, by implication, to overrate the efficacy of force. Even a casual reading of congressional hearings concerning possible resource wars, cited in the previous section, supports Baldwin's observation. Moreover, those same sources also indicate that policymakers may discount such potential triggers of resource-related conflicts as competition over fresh water supplies in favor of a preoccupation with strategic minerals; that during the cold war the East–West aspect of strategic minerals was weighted far more heavily than any other, though the justification for doing so was often questionable; and that, as an indigenous source of conflict, such attributes of populations as ethnic cleavages or economic stratification are poorly understood. In short, even in the world of incremental time frames policymakers bring to bear conceptual baggage that not only simplifies but distorts information about population and resources. The classical geopolitical lenses are still powerful devices.

Formulating policy in response to phenomena that appear within a conjunctural time frame is subject to more fundamental epistemological constraints to begin with. There are more unknowns here. Factors that are assumed to remain constant within an incremental time frame are variable here. And it is inherently more difficult to produce an intended effect on ongoing processes than it is on actors and discrete events. What are some of the shortcomings of policy making in this domain?

On the population side, US foreign policy concerns have been limited largely to family planning. There has been little official strategic or economic thinking devoted to the broader demographic issues that we examined above, or to the social, economic, and political arrangements on which their impact will hinge. As for securing sustainable resource bases, the United States has relied chiefly on the institution of the market. This has worked reasonably well in the nonfuel minerals sector. It might also work in the realm of commercial fuels if governments, including the US government, allow the market to operate effectively. But by definition, market forces are not going to take care of the problem of noncommercial fuels. In the area of world food security, further progress depends not so much on aggregate supply as on implementing institutional and policy changes, largely within food-deficient countries. Lastly, in the realm of biological resources public policy is required to compensate for the absence of pricing mechanisms in some instances, and for the disjunction between the private and social costs in others, to facilitate the emergence of conditions under which market forces can play an effective role in the future. In short, areas of policy concerning the underlying forces that shape current trajectories are still very poorly developed.

The population and resource issues that emerge within an epochal time frame reflect an agenda that is still in the making. At the intergovernmental level, the process was begun at the UN's Stockholm environment conference in 1972, and further elements were added at subsequent UN conferences on population (in 1974 and 1984) and human settlements (in 1976). The core problem that increasingly has come into focus concerns the effects of human scale on the productive and regenerative capacities of ecosystems. The key epistemological problem for decision-making is the trade-off between potentially high risks and inadequate knowledge about them. The problem is compounded by the fact that complete information in many instances may never be at hand, and even adequate information in some instances may be produced either too late or perhaps only as a by-product of the very outcomes that one is seeking to avoid. What is called for, therefore, is a "bias shift" in decision making, away from a conventional problem-solving mode, wherein doing nothing is favored on burden-of-proof grounds, toward a risk-averting mode, wherein prudent contingency measures would be undertaken to avoid risks that we would rather not face or to compensate for them if they arose—much as we do in the realm of national security.

The collective knowledge base on which more informed decisions can be based must be expanded. This involves additional research, monitoring, modeling, information exchange, and the like. The major difficulty here, aside from expense, is the adversarial context within which knowledge will be produced and used—akin to debates between the tobacco industry and the public health establishment in the United States, but without the possibility of closure being imposed by a central arbiter. Furthermore, in most instances, the costs of responding will be direct and visible whereas the benefits are likely to be diffuse and longer term. As a result, mechanisms will have to be evolved to cope with the inevitable "free rider" problems and to establish schemes of burden sharing. Both are extraordinarily difficult to achieve in the decentralized international polity. The national policies of individual states, and even more so collective policies of the international community as a whole, remain in a very early stage of development in this domain.

CONCLUSION

The ecology of international conflict and of international economic relations is changing today, as it always has. The major difference between the past and present in this regard is that the ever-evolving interplay between socioeconomic forces and biophysical factors has reached a planetary scale. To the extent that policymakers exhibit any concern at all with the issues arising from this transformation, they would prefer to handle them as conventional issues. The more visionary advocates outside of government, for their part, prefer to believe that conventional aspects of these issues no longer exist, or are not as important, as the novelty that they seek to have us embrace. If the former is akin to apprehending the future through a rearview mirror, in McLuhan's inimitable phrase, the latter is an instance of looking right over the horizon altogether and not keeping one's eyes on the road directly ahead. The gap between the two is enormous; and it must be narrowed if policy responses are to deal effectively with emerging global realities.

It has been a premise of this essay that the manner in which we conceptualize policy problems has direct practical consequences, and as these conceptualizations change over time so, too, will policy processes and outcomes. I have suggested that the dimension of time serves as a particularly useful basis for conceptualizing global population and resource issues. Ultimately, any set of categories is arbitrary. But the conceptualization developed here permits us, through one and the same analytic operation, to display the diversity of the socially relevant meanings of global population and resource issues, and to group these diverse meanings in such a way that they immediately convey policy strategies.

Focusing on the dimension of time has two other advantages over possible alternative bases of conceptualization. First, temporal forms are not idiosyncratic to the observer. They are, to borrow Durkheim's apt term, *"représentations collectives"* that express *"réalités collectives"* (1965: 13). That is to say, they are dimensions of social structure. Second, in the light of the current global ecological transition, there are few deeply embedded aspects of social structure that it is more important to bring closer to the surface of conscious concern. Of all the inchoate mental imageries that shape society's approach to international order, few can do greater real world damage to our collective future than the effects of assessing ecological developments around us within the wrong time frame. We have seen the lingering effects of the classical geopolitical conception of population and resources issues, and, more generally, the difficulties policymakers have in grasping conjunctural and epochal dimensions of these issues.

Having said all that, I must conclude by acknowledging that this essay has made but a modest beginning. My discussion has considerably simplified the complex relations that go on within and among temporal forms. I have focused on only three characteristic such temporal forms; of course there are others. Even more seriously, my discussion may give the impression that the three are distinct and separate. They are distinct, but they are not separate. As Emory and Trist (1973: 11) have put it: "Any person or group is at any instant in many 'presents', each corresponding to what is a phase of the temporal gestalten in which he or it is embedded." Obviously there is only one present, but different time frames place it in different temporal locations and thus alter its signification. Finally, I have ignored the systematic relationships that may exist among the different time frames, whereby acting on phenomena that are highlighted within one affects phenomena in the others, or whereby trade-offs and perhaps even contradictions may exist between what is desirable in one time frame as opposed to what is desirable in others. These are important issues that will have to be dealt with—all in good time.

7 Territoriality at millennium's end

Along with structure and time, space is the third dimension in which transformation unfolds. The modern international polity embodies a historically specific form of political space: distinct, disjoint, and mutually exclusive territorial formations. Presumably, then, a postmodern world polity would be one in which this form of organizing political space is fundamentally modified or has lost its social efficacy. This essay, first published as 1993b, devises an analytical framework for studying the possible emergence of postmodern international political forms by reexamining the process whereby modern territoriality itself first came to be.

Insofar as structure, time, and space are inseparable dimensions of historicity, this essay is related closely to the previous two. In the shift from the medieval to the modern European polity, events in incremental time combined with forces of a conjunctural and secular scale, to generate a level of dynamic density of sufficient magnitude to cause the medieval system of rule to unravel, ultimately triggering new principles of political differentiation. Material and functional considerations loomed large in this complex of processes, but irreducible elements of social epistemology also played a critical role in delegitimating medieval practices and institutions and in imagining successor forms. Chief among these epistemic factors was a change in prevailing conceptions of spatial differentiation that affected virtually all aspects of social life, from the visual arts and language to the organization of homes and cities. Their common feature was viewing their referent world from the vantage of a single, fixed point of view—or single-point perspective.

The essay suggests that signs of postmodern forms of organizing international political space, if they existed, would be found in the unbundling of territoriality whereby states deal with issues they deem to be inescapably transterritorial in scope, and that a key indicator of such a shift would be the emergence of multi-perspectival political practices and doctrines for the governance of those spaces. The European Union most closely approximates a multi-perspectival polity: no longer fully national but not destined to become a single supranational form. More modest instances also exist in the domain of economic globalization, ecology, and possibly even security relations

The year 1989 has already become a convenient historical marker, invoked by commentators to indicate the end of the postwar era. An era is characterized by the passage not merely of time but also of the distinguishing attributes *of a time*, attributes that structure expectations and imbue daily events with meaning for the members of any given social collectivity. In that sense, what the journalist Theodore H. White observed in 1945 is true once again: the world, he wrote, is "fluid and about to be remade" (White 1978: 224). Arguments will continue for many years about the determinants of the collapse of the old postwar order and the contours of the new post-postwar order. But even among diverse theoretical traditions there exists a shared vocabulary describing "the world" that has become fluid and is being remade: in its simplest, irreducible terms, the world of strategic bipolarity.

The same cannot be said of another "world" that may also be undergoing processes of historical change: the modern system of states. This world exists on a deeper and more extended temporal plane, and its remaking would involve a shift not in the play of power politics so much as of the stage on which that play is performed. Here, no shared vocabulary exists in the literature to depict change and continuity.

Take efforts to express the emerging architecture of the European Union (EU) as a case in point. "It is a negative characteristic which first imposes itself," the Marxist theorist Etienne Balibar concedes. "The state today in Europe is *neither national nor supranational*, and this ambiguity does not slacken but only grows deeper over time" (Balibar 1991: 16, emphasis in original). From the other end of the political spectrum, *The Economist* agrees and gropes for metaphor: in place of older federative visions, it sees "a Europe of many spires," a European "Mont Saint Michel". For their part, Eurocrats speak of overlapping layers of European economic and political "spaces," tied together, in the words of former Commission President Jacques Delors, by the community's "spiderlike strategy to organize the architecture of a Greater Europe" (quoted in Riding 1991: A1).

These formulations are not terribly precise or definitive. Still, they are improvements over the treatment Europe typically receives in the standard academic literatures. In Kenneth Waltz's classic neorealist treatise (1979), the European Community earned only a few fleeting references, and then only to argue that it would never amount to much in the "international structure" unless it took on the form of a unified state. In the instrumental rationality of game theory and transaction cost analysis, macrostructures are treated as relatively unproblematic consequences of the interplay of micromotives, and hence generate little interest as independent social facts (see Garrett 1993, for example). And regional integration theory long ago acknowledged its own obsolescence in the face of the new European reality (Haas 1976). In none of these theoretical perspectives is there so much as a hint that the institutional, juridical, and spatial complexes associated with the EU may constitute nothing less than the emergence of the first truly postmodern international political form.

Prevailing perspectives may have difficulty describing and explaining the process of European transformation, but none suggests that it is not occurring. At the level of the global economy, in contrast, the phenomenon of transformation not only strains the available vocabulary but, on some accounts, its very occurrence remains in doubt.

There has been a remarkable growth in transnational microeconomic links over the past thirty years or so, comprising markets and production facilities that are designated by the awkward term "offshore" (Ruggie 1996a: chap. 6). The popular image of globally integrated markets—functioning "as if they were all in the same place," in real time and around the clock (Stopford and Strange 1991: 40)—is most closely approximated in world currency markets, and secondarily in capital markets. Transactions take place in national facilities, which may be *housed* in New York, Tokyo, and European financial centers, but they are considered to *take place* in nonterritorial space. On the manufacturing side, sourcing, production, and marketing increasingly are organized within "global factories" (Grunwald and Flam 1985), orchestrated by administrative hierarchies that span the globe, with the most rapidly growing segment of world trade, as a result, being made up of intrafirm or related-party transactions as opposed to the conventional arm's-length exchange that is the staple of economic models and policy. Moreover, an increasing share of the goods that are traded in this offshore world actually are services: whereas in merchandise trade, factors of production stand still and goods move across borders, in traded services typically the factors of production do the moving while the good (service) is produced for the consumer on the spot.

The orthodox liberal view that these developments imply the growing irrelevance of states is, as Thomson and Krasner correctly insist (1989: 198), "fundamentally misplaced." Indeed, states are anything but irrelevant even in the ever-more-integrated EU. But the conventional realist grounds for rejecting the transformational potential of these developments is equally misplaced: the belief that because global markets and transnational corporate structures are not in the business of replacing states, they entail no potential for fundamental change in the system of states (see Kapstein 1991/92; Krasner 1991). No theoretical or historical warrant for this institutional substitutability theorem has ever been established.

Illustrations of conceptual blinders of this sort can be multiplied many times over in other issue-areas. The global ecological implosion inherently invites epochal thinking, yet most studies of global environmental policy focus on negotiation processes and the dynamics of regime construction or treaty compliance while ignoring the possibility of fundamental institutional change in the very system of states. Similarly, in the field of security studies, no epochal thought has been expressed by any serious specialist since 1957, when John Herz published his classic essay, "Rise and Demise of the Territorial State" (Herz 1957)—despite the fact that changes in military technology and in the relations of force are widely acknowledged to have been driving factors of political transformation throughout human history (McNeill 1982; Tilly 1990).

The long and the short of it is that we are not very good as a discipline at studying the possibility of fundamental discontinuity in the international system; that is, at addressing the question of whether the modern system of states may be yielding in some instances to postmodern forms of configuring political space. We lack even an adequate vocabulary; and what we cannot describe, we cannot explain. It is the purpose of this essay, in Clifford Geertz's apt phrase (1973: 13), to help us "find our feet" in this terrain, which is the necessary first step of any scientific endeavor, no matter how hard or soft the science.

In the next section, I summarize briefly the major features of the lively debate about postmodernism that has been taking place in the humanities. It is suggestive in many respects, but it does not solve our problem entirely because the modern state and system of states barely figure in it. The bulk of this essay therefore is devoted to a relatively modest and pretheoretical task: to search for a vocabulary and for the dimensions of a research agenda by means of which we can start to ask systematic questions about the possibility of fundamental international political transformation today. The central attribute of modernity in international politics has been a peculiar and historically unique configuration of territorial space. I shall proceed by reexamining the transformation whereby this spatial formation first came to be.

THE ENDS OF MODERNITY

The concept of postmodernity suggests a periodizing hypothesis, an epochal threshold, the end of "an historical project" (Wellmer 1985: 337). That much is clear. But, what is the universe of discourse and practices to which it pertains? To that question numerous possible answers exist, not all of which are of equal interest for present purposes.

When the term "postmodernity" first gained currency in the 1970s and 1980s, it referred largely to recent developments in the realm of aesthetics or style: the nostalgic eclecticism in architectural forms, the prevalence of pastiche and abrupt juxtapositions of imagery in art, the deconstructivist impulse in literature. Simultaneity and superimposition replaced sequence; the subject was decentered, dismembered, and dispersed; and language was made to turn in on itself to create a void of infinite signification where the quest for meaning had previously unfolded (Hassan 1987 presents a widely used schema differentiating modern from postmodern aesthetic practices). In the field of international relations, these expressions of postmodernity have been largely symptomatic, as Pauline Rosenau (1990) has shown, illustrating changed practices of discourse and narrative rather than treating them as possible indicators of a changed historical condition.

In the humanities, it was not long before postmodernity came to be associated not merely with matters of style but also with a new historical condition: according to Andreas Huyssen (1984: 8), a "slowly emerging cultural transformation in Western societies." This transformation concerns the fate of what Juergen Habermas calls the "project" of modernity, first formulated by the eighteenth-century philosophers of the European Enlightenment; that is, systematic efforts "to develop objective science, universal morality and law, and autonomous art, according to their inner logic" (Habermas 1981: 9). The Enlightenment was animated by the desire to demystify and secularize, to subject natural forces to rational explanation and control, as well as by the expectation that doing so would promote social welfare, moral progress, and human happiness. But the optimism, certitude, and categorical fixity of this project were shattered—by Nietzsche, Freud, Wittgenstein; Darwin, Einstein, Heisenberg; Braque, Picasso, Duchamp; Joyce, Proust, Beckett; Schoenberg, Berg, Bartok; two world wars, a Great Depression, Nazi death camps, Stalin's Gulags, Hiroshima and Nagasaki—long before Lyotard, Foucault, and Derrida pronounced and celebrated its demise.

Although the terrain is high culture, the battle that ensued between the "Frankfurters and French fries," as Rainer Naegele describes it irreverently, has been fought largely on political grounds. Habermas has endeavored to hold on to the *intentions* of the Enlightenment in order to complete its project. According to Huyssen (1984: 31), Habermas "tries to salvage the emancipatory potential of enlightened reason which to him is the *sine qua non* of political democracy. Habermas defends a substantive notion of communicative rationality, especially against those who will collapse reason with domination, believing that by abandoning reason they free themselves from domination." Jean-François Lyotard is hostile to the very thought: "We have paid a high enough price for the nostalgia of the whole and the one," he shouts; "let us wage a war on totality; let us be witnesses to the unpresentable; let us activate the differences" (1984: 81–82). Even Habermas's admirers express doubts about the viability of his quest (cf. Huyssen 1984; Jay 1985).

The two distinctively modern programs for mastering international relations are deeply implicated in this project of modernity: realist balance-of-power thinking and idealist institutionalism, both of which have their origins in the eighteenth century. On the realist side, the Treaty of Utrecht (1713) enshrined the notion of a self-regulating equilibrium as a core feature of European society and stipulated that its defense should be of concern to one and all (Anderson 1963). According to Martin Wight (1973: 98), for realist theorists of the day "the sovereign states followed their ordered paths in a harmony of mutual attraction and repulsion like the gravitational law that swings planets in their orbits." On the idealist side, the eighteenth century opened with the Abbé de Saint-Pierre's institutionalist plan to secure "*Perpetual Peace*," and closed with Kant's (Hinsley 1963).

The concept of postmodernity also has been projected beyond the cultural realm, into the political economy, initially by Marxist analysts. Frederic Jameson led the way (1984, 1989). For Jameson, postmodernism depicts "the third great original expansion of capitalism around the globe (after the earlier expansions of the national market and the older imperialist system)" (1984: 80). The production and manipulation of signs, images, and information are the raw materials of this new "mode of production" as well as the means by which its expansion is achieved. But this is an expansion,

Jameson suggests, that in effect "internalizes": just as the Bonaventure Hotel in Los Angeles or the Eaton Center in Toronto seeks to internalize its exterior, aspiring "to be a total space, a complete world, a kind of miniature city," so too does global capitalism today internalize within its own institutional forms relationships that previously took place among distinct national capitals. This results in a "postmodern hyperspace," as Jameson terms it, "a heteronomy of fragments which nevertheless remains unified by virtue of expressing the logic of late capitalism" (1984: 80–81).[1]

Several other works have elaborated on Jameson's notions of a postmodern capitalist mode of production and its consequences (Harvey 1989; Castels 1989). They resonate at a superficial level with the brief description of global microeconomic changes at the outset of this essay, as well as with the images of spaceship earth, global warming, nuclear winters, and the like, by means of which the ecosphere is popularly visualized. But they remain silent on the issue of the state and the system of states, which in the end is not surprising in light of the fact that they are cast in a modes-of-production framework.

Nevertheless, these works are suggestive at a deeper level, in their emphasis on the space–time implosion experienced by the advanced capitalist societies. Harvey, for instance, notes that "space and time are basic categories of human existence. Yet we rarely debate their meanings; we tend to take them for granted, and give them common-sense or self-evident attributions" (1989: 201). Ultimately, he contends, the current transformation in capitalist production relations is merely one specific expression of a reconfiguration in social space–time experiences to a degree not witnessed since the Renaissance. Harvey concurs with Jameson, however, that "we do not yet possess the perceptual equipment to match this new hyperspace . . . in part because our perceptual habits were formed in that older kind of space I have called the space of high modernism" (ibid.).

And so the postmodernist debate has shifted in barely two decades from the domain of aesthetics, to culture more broadly, to political economy. Correspondingly, the meaning of "modern" in "postmodern" has shifted from what it is in modern art, the modern novel, or modern architecture, first, to the so-called age of Enlightenment; next, to the structure of capitalist production relations; and then to the very epoch in Western history that was initiated by the Renaissance. It is the last of these space–time complexes that concerns me here, because it also marks the transformation that produced the modern mode of organizing political space: the system of territorial states. However, since no perceptual equipment exists, as Jameson remarks, through which to grasp what he calls "global hyperspace," I hope to advance our understanding of the possible rearticulation of international political space by looking for clues in the past, to discover how the modern political form itself was produced.

MODERN TERRITORIALITY

Historically, the self-conscious use of the term "modern" to denote "now" dates from the sixteenth century (Williams 1989). The epochal sense of modern to denote "modernity" dates from the eighteenth century, when the threshold demarcating its beginning was put at roughly 1500 (Koselleck 1985: 243). Writing in the eighteenth century, Lord Bolingbroke defined an epoch by the chain of events being so broken "as to have little or no real or visible connexion with that which we see continue ... The end of the fifteenth century seems to be just such a period as I have been describing, for those who live in the eighteenth, and who inhabit the western parts of Europe" (cited in Wight 1977: 111).

One of the chains in which visible connection to the past was ruptured was the organization of political space. The fact of that rupture is well enough known. But, what, if any, categories and modes of analysis does it suggest for the study of international transformation more generally? To that, the main task of this essay, I now turn.

Differentiation

Let us begin at the very beginning: politics is about rule. Adapting a formulation by Anthony Giddens (1981: 45), we can define the most generic attribute of any system of rule as comprising legitimate dominion over a spatial extension. I use the term "spatial extension" advisedly, to drive home the point that it need not assume the form of territorial states. The social facticity of any spatial extension in turn implies some mode of differentiating human collectivities from one another. By this I do not mean the progressive structural differentiation that was long a staple of macro-sociological theorizing and which is now thoroughly discredited (Tilly 1985). I mean the notion of differentiation that John Locke had in mind when he asked "how men might come to have a property in several parts of that which God gave to mankind in common" (Locke 1947: 134).[2] There are at least three ways in which prior or other systems of rule have differed in this regard from the modern territorial state.

First, systems of rule need not be territorial at all. That is to say, the basis on which the human species is socially individuated and individuals, in turn, are bound together into collectivities can take (and historically has taken) forms other than territoriality. For example, anthropologists quaintly used to characterize as "primitive government" those systems of rule wherein the spatial extension was demarcated on the basis of kinship. Indeed, they held that a critical stage in societal evolution was precisely the shift from consanguinity to contiguity as the relevant spatial parameter (Morgan 1877). Territory was occupied in kin-based systems, to be sure, but it did not *define* those systems.

Second, systems of rule may be territorial but need not be territorially *fixed*. Owen Lattimore's work on nomadic property rights is relevant here. Writing of Mongol tribes, Lattimore pointed out that no single pasture would have had much value for them because it soon would have become exhausted. Hence, driven by what he called "the sovereign importance of movement," the tribes wandered, herding their livestock. But, they did not wander haphazardly: "They laid claim to definite pastures and to the control of routes of migration between these pastures" (Lattimore 1962: 535). Accordingly, "the right to move prevailed over the right to camp. Ownership meant, in effect, the title to a cycle of migration" (Lattimore 1940: 66). The cycle was tribally owned and administered by the prince.

Third, even where systems of rule are territorial, and even where territoriality is relatively fixed, the prevailing concept of territory need not entail *mutual exclusion*. The archetype of nonexclusive territorial rule, of course, is medieval Europe [see Chapter 5], with its "patchwork of overlapping and incomplete rights of government" (Strayer and Munro 1959: 115), which were "inextricably superimposed and tangled," and in which "different juridical instances were geographically interwoven and stratified, and plural allegiances, asymmetrical suzerainties and anomalous enclaves abounded" (Anderson 1974: 37–38). The difference between the medieval and modern worlds is striking in this respect.

Briefly put, the spatial projection of the medieval system of rule was structured by a nonexclusive form of territoriality, in which authority was both personalized and parcelized within and across territorial formations and for which inclusive bases of legitimation prevailed. The notion of firm boundary lines between the major territorial formations did not take hold until the thirteenth century; prior to that date, there were only "frontiers," or large zones of transition (Wallerstein 1974: 32). As noted in Chapter 5, the medieval ruling class was mobile in a manner not dreamed of since, able to assume governance from one end of the continent to the other without hesitation or difficulty because "public territories formed a continuum with private estates" (Anderson 1974: 32). In this connection, Georges Duby writes, wryly, of Henry Plantagenet: "This was Henry, count of Anjou on his father's side, duke of Normandy on his mother's, duke of Aquitaine by marriage, and for good measure—but only for good measure—king of England, although this was of no concern to the country in which he spent the best part of his time" (Duby 1980: 286). In addition, the medieval system of rule was legitimated by common bodies of law, religion, and custom expressing inclusive natural rights. But these inclusive legitimations posed no doctrinal threat to the integrity of the constituent political units because the units viewed themselves as municipal embodiments of a universal moral community (Mattingly 1964: 41). Hence the "heteronomous shackles," in Friedrich Meinecke's vivid phrase, on the autonomy—indeed, on the very ability of thinkers to formulate the concept—of the state.[3]

The antonym of Meinecke's term is "homonomous." The distinctive signature of the modern—homonomous—variant of structuring territorial space is the familiar world of territorially disjoint, mutually exclusive, functionally similar, sovereign states.

The chief characteristic of the modern system of territorial rule is the consolidation of all parcelized and personalized authority into one public realm. This consolidation entailed two fundamental spatial demarcations: between public and private spheres and between internal and external spheres.[4] The public sphere was constituted by the monopolization on the part of central authorities of the legitimate use of force. Internally, this monopolization was expressed through the progressive imposition of what was called the "king's peace," or the sole right of the king's authority to enforce the law. As Norbert Elias notes (1983: 202), this idea was "very novel in a society in which originally a whole class of people could use weapons and physical violence according to their means and inclinations." Externally, the monopolization of the legitimate use of force was expressed in the sovereign right to make war. Philippe Contamine (1984: 169) has put it well: " 'The king's war' and 'the kingdom's war' must, in the end, be identical." Finally, the inclusive bases of legitimation that had prevailed in the medieval world, articulated in divine and natural law, yielded to the doctrine of sovereignty, and *jus gentium* slowly gave way to *jus inter gentes*.

To summarize, politics is about rule. And the distinctive feature of the modern system of rule is that it has differentiated its subject collectivity into territorially defined, fixed, and mutually exclusive enclaves of legitimate dominion. As such, it appears to be unique in human history (for an excellent survey, see Sack 1986). Without the concept of differentiation, then, it is impossible to define the modern era in international politics—modes of differentiation are the pivot in the epochal study of rule. Hence the irony of Waltz's continued insistence that the dimension of differentiation "drops out" from the neorealist model of international structure, on the dubious ground that the differentiation of a collectivity into its constituent units is an attribute of the units rather than the collectivity [see Chapter 5 and Waltz 1986].

The obvious next issue to address is how one accounts for this peculiar form of sociopolitical individuation. Now, providing an account of things in contemporary international relations research typically means specifying their causes. That in turn requires that we have a theory—in this case, a theory of international transformation. But we have no such theory. As I have suggested, we can barely even describe transformation in the international polity. Hence, I mean something far less ambitious by the phrase "providing an account of." The modern system of states is socially constructed. The issue I address below is simply what were the raw materials that people used and drew upon in constructing it? I find that developments in three dimensions of European collective experience were particularly salient, and that the three dimensions are irreducible to one another: namely, material environments, strategic behavior, and social epistemology.

Material environments

The study of the *longue durée* has become a special province of the *Annales* school of historiography (Braudel 1980). The starting point of the *Annales* approach is the "ecodemographic" context of human collectivities, on the premise that it poses the biggest long-term challenge for social structures. It then moves on to various constructed environments and to patterns of routine social practices. If we were to view the emergence of the modern European mode of structuring territorial space from this vantage point, what sorts of developments would catch our eye?

Consider the material side of life throughout the thirteenth and into the fourteenth century: human ecology, the relations of production, and the relations of force. Climatologically, the early phase of the period remained favored by the so-called little optimum of the early Middle Ages (Herlihy 1974; Ladurie 1971). Population grew markedly. Land clearing, draining, and diking progressed rapidly, increasing the size of the cultivated area and breaking down barriers to communication within territorial formations while expanding their external frontiers (Jones 1981: chap. 4). Although the overwhelming proportion of the population continued to live in rural areas, medieval cities grew, and some (Milan, Paris, Venice) may have reached 150,000 inhabitants (Herlihy 1974: 30; Hohenberg and Lees 1985).

A sustained economic expansion took place as well. Productivity increased; more and more goods were produced for sale or exchange; and trade revived, not merely in luxury goods but increasingly in staples. That last point is crucial. In the words of Eric Jones (1981: 90), "the peculiarities of European trade arose because of the opportunities of the environment. Climate, geology and soils varied greatly from place to place. The portfolio of resources was extensive, but not everything was found in the same place." Furthermore, economic transactions increasingly became monetized, the impact of which was felt throughout the entire fabric of social relations (Elias 1983), while developments in "invisibles," including the great fairs, shipping, insurance, and financial services, further lubricated commerce and helped to create a European-wide market (Jones 1981).

In the realm of force, the feudal cavalry was coming to be undermined by the longbow, pike, and crossbow and the feudal castle, subsequently, by gunpowder (McNeill 1982). The monetization of economic relations, together with the commutation of feudal services into money payments, in turn made it possible for territorial rulers to retain mercenaries. Generating revenue through taxation augmented the trend toward standing armies. The more effective internal pacification that resulted provided a more secure economic environment, which in turn increased both private and public returns (Jones 1981; Elias 1983).

Nevertheless, territorially defined, territorially fixed, and mutually exclusive state formations did not emerge at this point. It was not that simple. What happened instead was that this period of expansion and diversification was arrested suddenly and ferociously in the mid-fourteenth century. Famines, wars, and plagues decimated the population of Europe, reducing it by at least one-third and probably more. Entire localities disappeared; deserted lands reverted to heaths and swamps. The economy went into a deep and seemingly permanent depression and pillaging, robbing, and civil unrest again became endemic. Recovery did not return until the second half of the fifteenth century (Hays 1989; cf. Tuchman 1978).

These changes in the material world, both positive and negative, were so profound, however, that existing social arrangements were strained to the point of collapse.

Strategic behavior

Indeed, economic growth and diversification from the thirteenth to the fourteenth century had encountered institutional limits well before they were snuffed out by the Black Death and the Hundred Years' War. These limits included the feudal structure of property rights and forms of labor control; inadequate investment, especially in agriculture; the maze of secular and ecclesiastical jurisdictional constraints that pervaded medieval society; and the socially parasitic nature of the multiplicity of territorial rulers. One way to characterize the impact of the material changes discussed above on the prevailing institutional order is to say that they altered the matrix of constraints and opportunities for social actors, giving rise to new situations of strategic interaction among them. This is the subject matter of the "new economic history," initially associated with the work of North and Thomas (1973). Consider the following illustrations.

First, the drastic demographic declines of the fourteenth century affected relative factor prices, favoring agricultural workers and industrial producers while disadvantaging the land-owning class—the very basis of feudal society.

Second, the fourteenth-century calamities created opportunities for "entrepreneurial politicians" to prove their social utility by providing a variety of social services, ranging from disaster relief to more effective institutional arrangements for the conduct of commerce. According to Jones (1981: chap. 7), the forces favoring institutional change responded more imaginatively to the calamities than the forces that sought to impede it (also see Milgrom, North, and Weingast 1990).[5]

A third example involves the relationship between medieval juridical authorities and the trade fairs—a relationship that in some respects resembles that between the transnational economy and national jurisdictions today. The medieval trade fairs were encouraged by local lords; some took place only a stone's throw from the feudal castle. The fairs were favored for the simple reason that they generated revenue. In the case of the famous Champagne fairs, Verlinden (1963: 127) writes that revenues were gained from "taxes on the residences and stalls of the merchants, entry and exit tolls, levies on sales and purchases, dues upon weights and measures, justice and safe-conduct charges upon the Italians and Jews" (also see Bautier 1971). Moreover, local lords at any time could have closed down any fair in their domain—much as states today can close down offshore markets and producers—though other lords in other places probably would have been only too pleased to provide alternative sites.

In no sense could the medieval trade fairs have become substitutes for the institutions of feudal rule. Yet the fairs contributed significantly to the demise of feudal authority relations. They did so because the new wealth they produced, the new instruments of economic transactions they generated, the new ethos of commerce they spread, the new regulatory arrangements they required, and the expansion of cognitive horizons they effected all helped undermine the personalistic ties and the modes of reasoning on which feudal authority rested. As Marvin Becker has put it (1981: 15), the medieval trade fairs were a place in which "the exchange system was freed from rules and rituals" (also see Coleman 1986). Like the exchange system, the system of governance also ultimately unraveled. Once momentum shifted from fairs to towns, greater institutional substitutability did come to exist because, in the words of the medieval maxim, "Town air brings freedom" (*Stadtluft macht frei*)—that is to say, the towns actually exercised jurisdiction over and evoked the allegiance of their new inhabitants (Rorig 1967; Le Goff 1976).

Fourth, and finally, Hendrik Spruyt (1994) has shown that the erosion of the medieval system of rule, the growth of trade, and the rise of the towns triggered new coalitional possibilities among kings, the aristocracy, and the towns. Indeed, Spruyt explains the pattern in political forms that succeeded medieval rule—territorial states in some places, city-states in others, and city-leagues elsewhere still—by the specific nature of the coalitions that formed. In short, the exogenous shocks of the fourteenth century fundamentally strained the prevailing social order and created a new matrix of constraints and opportunities for social actors.

Some new economic historians want to go further, however, to imply that the modern system of states resulted *directly* from this process because the state represented the optimal size of political units that was required to provide efficient property rights and physical security. Smaller units simply "had to grow," North and Thomas contend (1973: 17). In the economic realm, this drive for juridical expansion of the state is said to have come, on the demand side, from a desire for efficient property rights, which would reduce the discrepancy between private and social rates of return. On the supply side, expansion, they argue, was driven by the fiscal interests of rulers for higher revenues. In the security realm, new weapons technology and a shift in advantage to the offense allegedly drove the desire for larger and fiscally more capable political formations (McNeill 1982).

The theory that the modern state was functionally determined in this manner has at least two serious shortcomings. First, its retrodictive value is severely limited: centralizing monarchies emerged in the West, to be sure; but city-states were consolidating in Italy and principalities as well as city-leagues in Germany, thus preventing their formation into larger (and by the logic of the new economic history, presumably more efficient) political units. Meanwhile, eastern Europe merely sank back into the somnambulance of another round of serfdom. Moreover, as Spruyt (1994) demonstrates, two other successor forms to the medieval system of rule, the Italian city-states and the Hanse, in fact were viable political alternatives to the territorial state, fully able to levy taxes and raise armies, for the better part of two centuries.[6] In social life, two centuries is no mere time lag.

Second, there is a substantial logical and empirical gap between the existence of some functional pressure for political units to grow, and their blossoming specifically into a system of territorially defined, territorially fixed, and mutually exclusive state formations. To assert that the specificities of the modern state system *also* were functionally determined entails a claim of staggering historical and intellectual proportions, which the new economic history cannot possibly vindicate. We shall now see why.

Social epistemes

Michael Walzer points the way. "The state," he once wrote (1967: 194), "is invisible; it must be personified before it can be seen, symbolized before it can be loved, imagined before it can be conceived." The process whereby a society first comes to imagine itself, to conceive of appropriate orders of rule and exchange, to symbolize identities, and to propagate norms and doctrines is neither materially determined, as vulgar Marxists used to claim, nor simply a matter of instrumental rationality, as the irrepressible utilitarians would have it.

German social theorists in a line from Max Weber to Juergen Habermas have viewed society as comprising webs of meaning and signification. In the French tradition, from Durkheim to Foucault, there has been a continuing exploration of *mentalités collectives.* No single concept captures both sets of concerns, the one being more semiotic, the other more structural. For lack of a better term, I shall refer to their combination as expressing the "epistemic" dimension of social life, and to any prevailing configuration of its constituent elements as a "social episteme" (with due apologies to Foucault 1970). The demise of the medieval system of rule and the rise of the modern resulted in part from a transformation in social epistemology. Put simply, the mental equipment that people drew upon in imagining and symbolizing forms of political community itself underwent fundamental change.

At the doctrinal level, students of international law and organization have long noted the impact on the concept of sovereignty of the novel religious principle *cujus regio ejus religio,* which placed the choice between Protestantism and Catholicism in the hands of local rulers, and the corresponding secular principle *Rex in regno suo est Imperator regni sui,* which stipulated that the political standing of territorial rulers in their domains was identical to that of the Emperor in his (Gross 1968; Hinsley 1967). Sir Ernest Barker exclaimed that in these two phrases "we may hear the cracking of the Middle Ages" (quoted by Gross 1968: 56–57). Moreover, the rediscovery of the concept of absolute and exclusive private property from Roman law no doubt aided in formulating the concept of absolute and exclusive sovereignty [see Chapter 5].

At a deeper level of political metaphysics, historians of political thought have long noted the impact on the emerging self-image held by European territorial rulers of a new model of social order that reflected recent changes in views of the natural world: society as a collection of atomistic and autonomous bodies-in-motion in a field of forces energized solely by scarcity and ambition. This is the model within which such distinctively modern theorists as Machiavelli and subsequently Hobbes framed their thinking (Walzer 1967; Wolin 1960; Macpherson 1962; Pocock 1975).

It may be possible to claim, though I think hard to sustain, that these doctrinal and perhaps even the metaphysical changes were determined by power and greed—or "efficiency" considerations, to use the more clinical term favored in the literature. However, the new forms of spatial differentiation on which the novel political imageries were constructed are another matter: they mirrored a much broader transformation in social epistemology that reached well beyond the domain of political and economic life.

Consider, for example, analogous changes in the linguistic realm, such as the growing use of vernaculars (Febvre and Martin 1984), and the coming to dominance of the "I-form" of speech—which Franz Borkenau (1981) described as "the sharpest contradistinction between I and you, between me and the world." Consider analogous changes in interpersonal sensibilities, as in new notions of individual subjectivity and new meanings of personal delicacy and shame (Elias 1978). These changes, among other effects, led to a spatial reconfiguration of households, from palaces to manor houses to the dwellings of the urban well-to-do, which more rigorously demarcated and separated private from public spheres and functions.[7]

Arguably, the single most important of those developments occurred in the visual arts: the invention of single-point perspective. Previous visual representation exhibited two spatial characteristics. First, artists rendered their subjects from different sides and angles "rather than from a single, overall vantage" (Edgerton 1975: 9). Second, variation in figure scale was determined by the symbolic or social importance of the person or object represented and "not by any principle of optical inversion" (White 1987: 103). As Harold Osborne explains, in single-point perspective (the invention of which is generally credited to Filippo Brunelleschi about 1425) "the pictorial surface is regarded as a transparent vertical screen, placed between the artist and his subject, on which he traces the outlines [of the visual field] *as they appear from a single fixed viewpoint*" (1970: 840, emphasis added). The corollary to the fixed viewpoint, from which the world is seen, is the horizon vanishing point, at which objects recede out of view.

By virtue of this development, precision and perspective became prized; Brunelleschi, for example, also made major contributions to optics and cartography. But of greatest significance is the fact that this was precision and perspective from a particular point of view: a *single* point of view, the point of view of a *single* subjectivity, from which all other subjectivities were differentiated and against which all other subjectivities were plotted in diminishing size and depth toward the vanishing point.

If there is one common element in the various expressions of differentiation that we have been discussing, this novel perspectival form is it. Every civilization tends to have its own particular perspective, Edgerton concludes in his classic study, its own dominant symbolic form for conceiving and perceiving space, and single-point perspective "was the peculiar answer of the Renaissance" (1975: 158). But what was true in the visual arts was equally true in politics: political space came to be seen and defined *as it appeared from a single fixed viewpoint*. The concept of sovereignty, then, represented merely the doctrinal counterpart of the application of single-point perspectival forms to the spatial organization of politics.[8]

This transformation in the spatial organization of politics was so profound—literally mind-boggling—that contemporaries had great difficulty grasping its full implications for many years to come. Mattingly, for example, recounts the efforts of Francis I as late as 1547 to reform the apparatus of the French state by fixing the number of *secrétaires d'État* at four. Rather than separating their duties according to the logical distinction, by modern standards, between domestic and foreign relations, however, each of the four was assigned one quadrant of France *and* the relations with all contiguous and outlying states (Mattingly 1964: 195).

To conclude, material changes may have awakened both a need and a desire for this broad transformation in the prevailing social episteme, which produced fundamentally new spatial forms. And entrepreneurial rulers could and did try to exploit those new images and ideas to advance their interests. Nevertheless, the breadth and depth of these changes argue, at the very least, in favor of a relative autonomy for the realm of social epistemology. Walzer has put it well: "If symbolization does not by itself create unity (that is the function of political practice as well as of symbolic activity), it does create *units*—units of discourse which are fundamental to all thinking and doing, units of feeling around which emotions of loyalty and assurance can cluster" (1967: 194–195, emphasis in original).

Accordingly, I turn next to the domain of social practice, wherein the new unity was achieved. I highlight two aspects of it in particular: the process of social empowerment, which facilitated the consolidation of territorial rule; and the process of "unbundling" territoriality, which made it possible for the new territorial rulers, who viewed their individual subjectivity as constituting a self-sufficient moral and political domain, to form a society of similarly situated states.

Social empowerment

The disarticulation of the medieval system of rule meant that parametric conditions would have to be fixed at three levels in the newly formed social aggregations of power: the domestic social structure, the territorial formation, and the collectivity of territorial units. In each case, the relative success of the contending parties was shaped not simply by the material power they possessed or the interests they pursued but also by a process of social empowerment that reflected the ongoing transformation of social epistemes. I focus below on the territorial state and its collectivity.[9]

At the level of territorial state formations, the key parametric condition to be fixed was precisely where in society (that is, around which power aggregation) the right to rule would crystallize. Let us return for a moment to the western European monarchies around the middle of the fifteenth century. Their future looked bleak. In Castile, whose king sometimes claimed the title Emperor, the crown was among the weakest in all of Europe; the towns were dominant. In Aragon, the towns were weak and the nobility was in control, pledging allegiance to their king with this unimpressive oath: "We, who are as good as you, swear to you, who are no better than we, to accept you as our king and sovereign lord, provided you observe all our liberties and laws: but if not, not" (quoted in Johnson and Percy 1970: 56). In France, the monarchy had to be saved in 1429 by a farmer's daughter who was guided in her quest by visions and voices from "higher" sources; but not even that intervention helped, and when the Hundred Years' War finally ground to a halt more than two decades later, the country lay in ruins. England, already weak and divided, became further torn by the deadly Wars of the Roses. And so it went.

The turn came suddenly. By the end of the century, strong centralized administration had "almost completely transformed the political life of western and west-central Europe," in Johnson and Percy's words (1970: 73). The new political units had become a palpable reality, no longer simply an aspiration, a trend, or a struggle. In France, moreover, a weak central monarchy ended up absorbing a stronger duchy of Burgundy in the process.

How can this shift be explained? One way to put it is that a fundamental shift was occurring in the purposes for which power could be deployed by rulers and be regarded as socially legitimate by their subjects. Accordingly, central rulers became more powerful *because of* their state-building mission. Internally, the use of force became fused with the provision of public order, steadily discrediting its deployment for private extraction and accumulation. Externally, the use of force became fused with statecraft, discrediting its deployment for primitive expansion and aggrandizement (Pocock 1975; Guenée 1985).

This process of empowerment also helps to account for the pattern of successes and failures in centralizing efforts noted above. The monarchs in the West tended to hitch their fate to those new objectives, and large-scale exclusive state formations emerged. West-central Europe and Italy, on the other hand, still had to cope with those meddlesome remnants of heteronomy, the Holy Roman Empire and the Papacy. While they lacked the power to prevail, so long as they retained a degree of social efficacy it remained difficult to formulate clearly the concept, let alone create the institution, of an exclusive state formation. Here city-states and principalities became the expression of homonomous territoriality. In the east, these social changes never took hold in the first place. Tilly (1975: 22) points out that even in the western kingdoms the leaders of prior institutions and some ordinary people "fought the claims of central states for centuries," right into the seventeenth century, but over time the issue at stake increasingly became the terms of central rule, not the fact of it.

At the level of the collectivity of states, the critical parameter to fix concerned the right to act as a constitutive unit of the new collective political order. The issue here was not who had how much power, but who could be designated *as* a power (Ashley 1984: 259). Such a designation inherently is a collective act. It involved the mutual recognition of the new constitutive principle of sovereignty. Martin Wight points out (1977: 135) that "it would be impossible to have a society of sovereign states unless each state, while claiming sovereignty for itself, recognized that every other state had the right to claim and enjoy its own sovereignty as well." Reciprocal sovereignty thus became the principled basis of the new international order.

To be sure, the new organizing principle of reciprocal sovereignty was challenged in and hammered home by wars; but even in the evolution of European wars we can see signs of it taking hold. As already noted, private wars ceased to be tolerated, and war making came to be universally regarded as an attribute of sovereignty. Even more interesting, European warfare thereafter seems to exhibit a progression in the dominant types of war.

The first form we might call "constitutive" war. Here the very ontology of the units—that is to say, what kind of units they would be—was still at issue. The Wars of Religion are the prime instance. As characterized by Reinhart Koselleck (1985: 8), the Peace of Augsburg (1555) finally froze its fronts in place by means of a new moral understanding: "The compromise, born of necessity, concealed within itself a new principle, that of 'politics,' which was to set itself in motion in the following century." Still, an international politics that was morally separated and autonomous from the realm of religion did not become fully and firmly established until the Peace of Westphalia (1648), ending the Thirty Years' War.

This first phase was followed by warfare in which the nature of the units was accepted but their territorial configuration remained contested. We might call these "configurative" wars. The Wars of Succession of the early eighteenth century—Spanish, Polish, and Austrian—and the Seven Years' War (1756–1763) illustrate this type. Among other factors, these conflicts revolved around the principles of territorial contiguity versus transterritorial dynastic claims as the basis for a viable balance of power. In the end, territorial contiguity won out, at least in the European core (Anderson 1963; Kaiser 1990).

The third phase in the evolving types of warfare consists of the familiar strategic and tactical wars ever since, wars that we might call "positional"— interrupted by periodic quests for universal empire, which have been successfully repulsed on each occasion (Dehio 1962; Gilpin 1981).

Finally, when the concept of state sovereignty expanded to become the concept of national sovereignty, the use of mercenaries in warfare declined and ultimately was eliminated altogether. Armed forces subsequently became an expression of the nation (Thomson 1994).

The critical threshold in this transition was the passage from constitutive to configurative wars, for it first acknowledged the principle of reciprocal sovereignty. When all was said and done, Europe ended up with a great many not-so-powerful states, including the nearly two hundred German principalities, which could not possibly have vindicated their right to exist by means of material power, but which were socially empowered by the collectivity of states to act as its constitutive units (cf. Strang 1991).

Thus, the process of social empowerment was part of the means by which the new units of political discourse were inscribed in social life to produce new units of political order.

The paradox of absolute individuation

Our story ends in a paradox. Having established territorially fixed state formations, having insisted that these territorial domains were disjoint and mutually exclusive, and having accepted these conditions as the constitutive bases of international society, what means were left to the new territorial rulers for dealing with problems of that society that could not be reduced to territorial solution?

This issue arose in connection with the use of common spaces, such as contiguous and transborder waterways as well as the oceans [see Chapter 4]. How does one possess something one does not own? And, still more problematic, how does one exclude others from it? Inland waterways could be split down the middle and typically were, though often not until other and more violent means had been exhausted. Ocean space beyond defendable coastal areas posed a more substantial problem. Spain and Portugal tried a bilateral deal whereby Spain claimed a monopoly of western ocean trade routes to the Far East and Portugal the eastern, but they failed to make their deal stick. At the request of the Dutch East India Company, a young lawyer by the name of Hugo Grotius launched a distinguished career by penning a pamphlet entitled, and proclaiming the contrary doctrine of, *Mare Liberum*, which did stick.[10]

The really serious problem arose not in the commons, however, but right in the heart of the mutually exclusive territorial state formations: no space was left within which to anchor even so basic a task as the conduct of diplomatic representation without fear of relentless disturbance, arbitrary interference, and severed lines of communication.

In medieval Europe, the right of embassy was a method of formal and privileged communication that could be admitted or denied depending upon the social status and roles of the parties involved and the business at hand (Mattingly 1964). Ambassadors had specific missions, for which they enjoyed specific immunities. For a variety of misdeeds and crimes, however, ambassadors were tried and sentenced by the prince to whom they were accredited, as though they were a subject of that prince. This solution ceased to be acceptable, however, once the right of embassy became a sign of sovereign recognition and ambassadors were in place permanently. The short-term response was to grant more and more specific immunities to resident ambassadors as the situation demanded. During the century or so of religious strife, however, that option too came to be undermined by, among other factors, the so-called embassy chapel question.

As the term implies, this had to do with the services celebrated in an ambassador's chapel, at which compatriots were welcome, when the religions of the home and host sovereigns differed. For example, Edward VI insisted that the new English prayer book be used in all his embassies; Charles V would tolerate no such heresy at his court. It was not uncommon for diplomatic relations to be broken over the issue in the short run. In the long run, however, that proved too costly a solution; the need for continuous and reliable communication among rulers was too great. A doctrinal solution was found instead. Rather than contemplate the heresy of a Protestant service at a Catholic court and vice versa, it proved easier to pretend that the service was not taking place in the host country at all but on the soil of the homeland of the ambassador. And so it gradually became with other dimensions of the activities and precincts of embassy. A fictitious space, "extraterritoriality," was invented. Mattingly captured the paradox well (1964: 244): "By arrogating to themselves supreme power over men's consciences, the new states had achieved absolute sovereignty. Having done so, they found they could only communicate with one another by tolerating within themselves little islands of alien sovereignty." Adda Bozeman adds (1960: 482–483) that these islands of alien sovereignty were seen, however, "not only as the foreign arm of each separate government, but also as the nucleus of the collective system of . . . states . . . outside of which no sovereign could survive."

What we might describe as an "unbundling" of territoriality, then, of which extraterritoriality was the first and most enduring instantiation, over time has become a generic contrivance used by states to attenuate the paradox of absolute individuation. International regimes, common markets, political communities, and the like constitute additional institutional forms through which territoriality has become unbundled (cf. Kratochwil 1984). In sum, nonterritorial functional space is the place in which territorial rulers situate and deal with those dimensions of collective existence that they recognize to be irreducibly transterritorial in character. It is here that international society is anchored, and in which its patterns of evolution may be traced.

Patterns of change

Mattingly, in his magisterial study (1964: 105–6), acknowledges that "the taproots of the modern state may be followed as far back as one likes in Western history [even] to the cities of antiquity whereof the hazy images continued to provide some statesmen in every medieval century with an ideal model of authority and order." But, as he shows persuasively, the modern state did not *evolve* from these earlier experiences; it was *invented* by the early modern Europeans. This suggests a final issue for consideration: the patterns exhibited by epochal change. Three are indicated by the medieval-to-modern transformation.

First, unanticipated consequences played a major role in determining the ultimate outcomes of long-term changes. The Crusades were not designed to suggest new modes of raising revenues for territorial rulers, but they ended up doing so (Finucane 1983). The modern state was not logically entailed in the medieval papacy; yet, according to Strayer (1970: 22), by the example of effective administration it set, "the Gregorian concept of the Church almost demanded the invention of the concept of the State." Society did not vote for capitalism when it endorsed the civilizing impulses of commerce; but the bourgeoisie, the social carriers of commerce, embodied it (Hirschman 1977). Monarchs did not set out to weaken their constitutional powers by selling offices or convening assemblies to raise taxes; they sought only to increase their revenues.[11] In short, the reasons for which things were done often had very little to do with what actually ended up being done or what was made possible by those deeds (cf. Gould 1985).

Second, fundamental transformation may have had long-standing sources, but when it came, typically it came quickly by historical standards. Moreover, it came amid crisis and disintegration of the previous order— amid a generalized loss of predictability and understanding of, in Tracy Strong's words (1974: 245), "what might count as politics, of what counts as evidence and what as fact, and of what is contentious and what might appear secure." Once the system of modern states was consolidated, however, the process of fundamental transformation ceased: "[states] have all remained recognizably of the same species up to our own time," Tilly concludes (1975: 31), though their substantive forms and individual trajectories of course have differed substantially over time (Mann 1988). Paleontologists describe this pattern of change—stable structures, rupture, new stable structures—as "punctuated equilibrium."[12]

Finally, change has never been complete or all-encompassing. As Spruyt (1994) makes clear, the medieval system of rule in the first instance was succeeded by several viable forms of territorial governance: large-scale territorial states, city-states, and city-leagues. And, critically, the process that ultimately selected out the territorial state embodied a different logic than the process that produced both the state and its alternative forms. Also note that the formal demise of the Holy Roman Empire—a relic of medievaldom that historians insist never was holy, nor Roman, nor an empire—did not occur until 1806—as close in time to the formation of the European Economic Community as to the Peace of Westphalia, which is typically said to have formally inaugurated the modern international polity. Finally, sociopolitical collectivities of long historical standing retain efficacy today without being contained in territorial states, ranging from transnational networks of ethnic and religious affinity to the Commonwealth of Nations. Designating dominant historical forms, therefore, is a matter of balance: of judging ascendancy and decline, relevance and spurious signification. Nonetheless, it is the case that the modern state has succeeded in driving out substitutable alternatives more effectively than any other prior form.

HISTORICIZING POSTMODERNITY

At the close of the fifteenth century, Europe stood poised to reach out to and then conquer the globe. By the beginning of the twentieth century, this "Columbian epoch," as Sir Halford Mackinder characterized it (1904), was coming to an end. In his seminal essay, Mackinder addressed two distinct dimensions of the new "global" epoch. The first attracted the most attention but is the less important for present concerns: the strategic consequences of the essential unity of the world's oceans, which gave rise to the great heartland/rimland and land-power/sea-power debates that became the stuff of geopolitics, right down to the postwar theory of containment. The second, which subsequent commentators have largely ignored, concerned the spatial and temporal integration of previously separate and coexisting world systems, each enjoying a relatively autonomous social facticity and expressing its own laws of historicity, into a singular post-Columbian world system.

In this essay, I have looked for a vocabulary and the dimensions of analysis that would allow us to ask sensible questions about possible postmodern tendencies in the world polity. I have done so by unpacking the process whereby the most distinct feature of modernity in international politics came to be: a particular form of territoriality—disjoint, fixed, and mutually exclusive—as the basis for organizing political life. In conclusion, I summarize briefly the main findings of this endeavor and point toward some methodological as well as substantive implications for future research.

First, the summary: The concept of differentiation is the key that allowed us to uncover the historically specific and salient characteristics of modern territoriality. Accepting that the international polity, by definition, is an anarchy, that is, a segmented realm, on what basis is it segmented? On what basis are its units individuated? What drove the peculiarly modern form of individuation? And what were its implications for the international collectivity? The mode of differentiation within any collectivity, I suggested, is nothing less than the pivot of epochal shifts in systems of rule.

The modern mode of differentiation resulted from changes in several domains of social life, which are irreducible to one another. These domains included material environments (ecodemographics, relations of production, relations of force); the matrix of constraints and opportunities within which social actors interacted (the structure of property rights, divergences between private and social rates of return, coalitional possibilities among major social actors); and social epistemes (political doctrines, political metaphysics, spatial constructs). Each was undergoing change in accordance with its own endogenous logic. But these changes also interacted, sometimes sequentially, sometimes functionally, sometimes simply via the mechanism of diffusion, that is, of conscious and unconscious borrowing. Whereas individual strands of change can be traced back almost at will, at a certain point the new forms crystallized fairly quickly and shaped all subsequent developments.

The domain of social epistemes, the mental equipment by means of which people reimagined their collective existence, played a critical role. The specificity of modern territoriality is closely linked to the specificity of single-point perspective. Social epistemes did not act as some ethereal *Zeitgeist* but through specific social carriers and practices. Social epistemes affected outcomes via the mechanisms of social empowerment and delegitimation and by informing such doctrinal contrivances as extraterritoriality, on which the society of territorial state formations came to rest.

Our case also offers some methodological insights for the study of transformation today. One methodological point follows directly from the relative autonomy of the diverse domains wherein past change occurred. Clearly, different bodies of contemporary international relations theory are better equipped to elucidate different domains of contemporary change and continuity. Neorealism is very good on the endogenous logics of the relations of force, but it is even more reductionist than most modern Marxisms when it comes to appreciating the role of social epistemology. The microeconomics of institutions provides great insight into strategic behavior, but it is silent on the origins of the social preferences that give it substantive meaning. Cultural theories are virtually alone in addressing the role of spatial imageries, but typically they neglect the effect of micromotives, and so on. Each, therefore, can become a "grand theory" only by discounting or ignoring altogether the integrity of those domains of social life that its premises do not encompass. Nor are the various bodies of extant theory in any sense additive, so that we could arrive at a grand theory by steps. In short, while there may be law-like generalizations *in* the medieval-to-modern transformation, there are none *of* it. Accordingly, understanding that transformation—and presumably any analogous shift that may be taking place today—requires an epistemological stance that is quite different from the imperious claims of most current bodies of international relations theory. It requires, as Quentin Skinner characterizes it (1985: 12), "a willingness to emphasize the local and the contingent, a desire to underline the extent to which our own concepts and attitude have been shaped by particular historical circumstances, and a correspondingly strong dislike... of all overarching theories and singular schemes of explanation."

A second methodological point follows directly from the first. If it is true that the intellectual apparatus by which we study fundamental change is itself implicated in a world that may be changing, how valid and viable is that intellectual quest to begin with? This is particularly vexing in attempts to understand the prospects of postmodernity, insofar as prevailing scientific approaches are part and parcel of the very definition of modernity (see Benhabib 1984). Not being a philosopher of science, my answer perforce is somewhat unschooled. Nevertheless, I find fault with the postmodernist epistemologues and the dominant positivists alike.

For the postmodernists, modern scientific method represents either force or farce. In its stead, they retreat into a fetishistic obscurantism that they impute to poststructuralist/postmodernist method. But their "move"—to use one of their "privileged" terms—is deeply misguided, as a simple example will show. In the cultural transformations toward postmodern forms, few insights are accorded greater significance than Einstein's theories of relativity. This is because relativity, by revolutionizing human understanding of space and time, shattered one of the fixed and even absolute pillars of modern thought. Yet Einstein's theories were soon confirmed: the special theory by laboratory experiments and the general theory during the eclipse of 1919, all in accordance with fairly straightforward scientific methods. What Einstein did was to formulate an entirely new and different *ontology* of the physical world. Indeed, he never even accepted the implications for *epistemology* that others drew from his work, as illustrated by his often-cited rejoinder to the uncertainty principle, that God does not play dice with the universe. My point is this: it is entirely possible to say things of importance about postmodernity, and even to have contributed to the historical condition of postmodernity, without degenerating into what passes for postmodernist method.

As for the dominant positivist posture in our field, when it comes to the study of transformation it is reposed in deep Newtonian slumber wherein method rules, epistemology is often confused with method, and the term "ontology" typically draws either blank stares or bemused smiles. I choose the Newtonian analogy deliberately and with care. Gerald Feinberg's depiction helps to show why it is useful (1978: 9): "Newtonian mechanics by itself did not attempt to explain what forces might exist in nature, but rather described how motion occurred *when the force was known*" (emphasis added). As noted in the Preface, merely by substituting "structures" or "preferences" for "forces" in that sentence, one obtains an apt rendering of prevailing international relations theories today. They describe how "motion" occurs—*given* a set of structures or preferences. Accordingly, these theories cannot, ontologically, apprehend fundamental transformation, for the issue of "what forces [structures/preferences] might exist in nature" is precisely what the study of transformation is all about.

Our examination of the emergence of modern territoriality also has substantive implications for the study of potential transformation in the international system today. A full application of the historically grounded conceptual framework sketched out here is well beyond the scope of this essay. Nevertheless, I close with an overall analytical lead, as well as some working hypotheses about each of the illustrative cases with which I began.

The preceding analysis suggests that the unbundling of territoriality is a productive venue for the exploration of contemporary international transformation. Historically, as we have seen, this is the institutional means through which the collectivity of sovereigns has sought to compensate for the "social defects" that inhere in the modern construct of territoriality.[13] This negation of the exclusive territorial form has been the locale in which international society throughout the modern era has been anchored. The terrain of unbundled territoriality, therefore, is the place wherein any rearticulation of international political space would be occurring today.

Take first the European Union, in which the process of unbundling territoriality has gone further than anywhere else. Neorealism ascribes its origins to strategic bipolarity; microeconomic institutionalism examines how the national interests and policy preferences of the major European states are reflected in patterns of EU collaboration; and neofunctionalism anticipated the emergence of a supranational statism. Each contains a partial truth. From the vantage of the present analysis, however, a very different attribute comes into view: the EU may constitute the first "multiperspectival polity" to emerge since the advent of the modern era. That is to say, it is increasingly difficult to visualize the conduct of international politics among community members, and to a considerable measure even domestic politics, as though it took place from a starting point of fifteen separate, single, fixed viewpoints. Nor can models of strategic interaction do justice to this particular feature of the EU, since the collectivity of members as a singularity, in addition to the central institutional apparatus of the EU, has become party to the interstate strategic interaction game. To put it differently, the identity of each of the fifteen members—and identities are logically prior to preferences—increasingly endogenizes the collectivity they comprise. To be German, French, Dutch, and so on—even to be British—increasingly also means to be an EU member. In this context, European Union leaders may be thought of as entrepreneurs of collective identities—former Commission President Delors, for example, self-consciously exploited the tension between community widening and community deepening so as to catalyze the further reimagining of European collective existence. There is no indication, however, that this reimagining will result in a federal state of Europe—which would merely replicate on a larger scale the typical modern political form.

The concept of multiperspectival forms offers a lens through which to view other possible instances of international transformation today. Consider the system of increasingly integrated transnational microeconomic relations, described briefly at the outset of this essay. Perhaps the best way to describe it, when seen from our vantage point, is that these links have created a "global region" in the world economy—a decentered yet integrated space-of-flows, operating in real time, which exists alongside the spaces-of-places that we call national economies. The conventional spaces-of-places continue to engage in external economic relations with one another, which we call trade, foreign investment, and the like, and which are more or less effectively mediated by the state. In the nonterritorial global economic region, however, distinctions between internal and external once again are exceedingly problematic, and any given state is but one constraint in corporate strategic calculations. This is the world in which IBM is Japan's largest computer exporter, and Sony is the largest exporter of television sets from the United States. It is the world in which Brothers Industries, a Japanese concern assembling typewriters in Bartlett, Tennessee, brings an antidumping case before the US International Trade Commission against Smith Corona, an American firm that imports typewriters into the United States from its offshore facilities in Singapore and Indonesia. It is the world in which even the US Pentagon is baffled by the problem of how to maintain the national identity of "its" defense–industrial base (Moran 1990). This nonterritorial global economic region is a world, in short, that is premised on what Lattimore called the "sovereign importance of movement," not of place. The long-term significance of this region, much like that of the medieval trade fairs, may reside in its novel behavioral and institutional forms and in the novel space–time constructs that these forms embody, not in any direct challenge that it poses as a potential substitute for the existing system of rule.

Consider also the transformative potential of global ecology. The human environment is of central importance for future planetary politics in numerous respects. Central among them is its potential to comprise a new and very different social episteme—a new set of spatial, metaphysical, and doctrinal constructs through which the visualization of collective existence on the planet is shaped. This episteme would differ in form from modern territoriality and its accoutrements insofar as the underlying structural premise of ecology is holism and mutual dependence of parts. The difficulty is in tapping this social epistemological dimension empirically. Nonetheless, it may be possible to infer from state behavior whether and to what extent it is coming to express new and different principles of international legitimacy, for example. The concept of international custodianship is one candidate for closer scrutiny. Under it, no other agency competes with or attempts to substitute for the state, but the state itself acts in a manner that expresses not merely its own interests and preferences but also its role as the embodiment and enforcer of community norms (Allott 1983)—a multiperspectival role, in short, somewhat in the manner of medieval rulers vis-à-vis cosmopolitan bodies of religion and law. Another possible approach is to examine the impact of real or simulated environmental catastrophes on the thinking of policymakers and especially on the popular imagination at large: Chernobyl, the Antarctic ozone hole, and global warming scenarios come to mind.

Finally, this analysis also potentially enriches the field of international security studies. To cite but one example, no one in any position of authority anywhere in Europe responded to the most profound geopolitical changes of the postwar era—the collapse of the Soviet Union's East European empire, of the Soviet Union itself, and German reunification—by advocating, or quietly preparing for, a return to competitive bilateral alliances. All of the options on the table concerning the external mechanisms for achieving security in Europe, East and West, were multilateral in form [see Chapter 4]. This development suggests a hypothesis for further exploration. Within the industrialized world, and partially beyond, we may be witnessing emerging fragments of international security communities alongside more traditional modes of organizing international security relations elsewhere. These security communities are not integrated in the manner that the ill-fated European Defense Community would have been, but they are more extensively institutionalized than the "pluralistic security communities" of integration studies in the 1950s (Deutsch et al. 1957) [see also Chapter 9]. Once more the term "multiperspectival" seems appropriate. Within the scope of these security communities the imbalances of advantage that animated positional wars throughout the modern era now are resolved by more communitarian mechanisms instead. Such mechanisms do not imply the abolition of the use of force; they do imply, however, that the use of force is subject to greater collective legitimation.

It is truly astonishing that the concept of territoriality has been so little studied by students of international politics; its neglect is akin to never looking at the ground that one is walking on. I have argued that disjoint, mutually exclusive, and fixed territoriality most distinctively defines modernity in international politics and that changes in few other factors can so powerfully transform the modern international polity. What is more, I have tried to show that unbundled territoriality is a useful terrain for exploring the condition of postmodernity in international politics, and I have suggested some ways in which that might be done. The emergence of multiperspectival institutional forms was identified as a central dimension in understanding the possibility of postmodernity.

On reflection, though, the reason territoriality is taken for granted is not hard to guess. Samuel Beckett put it well in *Endgame*: "You're on earth, there's no cure for that." Unbundled territoriality is not located some place else; but it is becoming another place.

Part III

The question of agency
Making history in the new era

"Men [people] make their own history," Marx wrote in the *Eighteenth Brumaire*, "but they do not make it just as they please; they do not make it under circumstances chosen by themselves, but under circumstances directly found" (Tucker 1978: 595). The two major bodies of international relations theory today, neorealism and neoliberal institutionalism, fundamentally are about "circumstances" which states "find" in the object world around them and which constrain their behavior. Based on a particular rendering of those circumstances, and by assuming the interests or preferences of states to be given and fixed, these theories seek to explain patterns of outcomes and sometimes prescribe behavior.

Constructivism, in contrast, is interested as much in the "making" of circumstances, to extend Marx's aphorism, as in their being "found"— without, however, lapsing into subjectivism or idealism. It takes "making" to have at least two meanings: What do people make of their circumstances in the sense of understanding them? And what do they make of their circumstances in the sense of acting on whatever understanding they may hold?

This issue concerns the so-called agent–structure debate in social theory (see Wendt 1987 and Dessler 1989 for good discussions in the context of international relations). The essays in the two previous sections explore some of the generic issues in international institutionalization and transformation that are raised by a constructivist approach, including the question of agency. The essays in this section focus on a concrete problem of agency at a particular juncture: how to secure a stable post-cold war international order. They were inspired by two concerns: the practical need to refashion key policy assumptions and frameworks that had guided the major powers' foreign policies since World War II; and the incoherence or muted responses this challenge occasioned in the two major bodies of international relations theory.

For example, NATO features prominently in "what now?" scenarios concerning European and transatlantic security relations. But highly regarded realists have argued with equal certitude and based on the same core premises that NATO has become irrelevant and is likely to collapse; remains alive by dint of inertia but will wither away gradually; and is as important as ever and should expand (see, respectively, Mearsheimer 1990;

Waltz 1993; Kissinger 1994; Kissinger may not qualify as a "neo" realist, but thus far his position seems the most likely to be vindicated by events). Neoliberal institutionalists, for their part, to date have said relatively little systematically about security relations in general or NATO in particular, though contemporary versions of older liberal traditions, in the form of the "democratic peace" (Doyle 1986) and "collective security" (Kupchan and Kupchan 1991), speak to both.

Leaving aside some of the deeper epistemological issues discussed in the introductory chapter of this volume, the problem is that the validity claims of neorealism and neoliberal institutionalism presuppose the existence of the very factors that states have struggled to redefine since 1989: stable sets of interests or preferences regarding key aspects of the international order. Of course, factors related to power and expected utility play significant roles in that redefinition. But the process itself consists not merely of an *enactment*—which is how agency is depicted in the standard theories—but, as Frank Ninkovich puts it (1994: xv), "an active process of interpretation and construction of reality," involving discursively as well as tactically competent actors. The constructivist approach is intended to shed light on this process.

Each of the essays in the following three chapters teases out an ideational element from the mix of factors determining state behavior regarding the future international security order and seeks to demonstrate its consequences. The essay in Chapter 8 focuses on American "identity" in shaping US policy; that in Chapter 9 on the sense of a transatlantic "security community" in relation to the future of NATO; and that in Chapter 10 on the strategic implications of the multilateral norm of nondiscrimination in the context of UN peace operations.

Although I had long been involved on the peripheries of policy circles, truth in advertising requires me to confess that these essays did not simply flow deductively from a fully articulated prior theoretical view on this issue. I had none. And the process of devising one was somewhat unorthodox. Its proximate cause was a *force majeure*: when the Berlin wall came down the six o'clock news invaded my life. As Director of the University of California's prestigious Institute on Global Conflict and Cooperation, which is headquartered in San Diego, I became that quiescent, sybaritic, but also heavily defense-dependent community's resident expert on the future world order and developments related, in fact or fancy, thereto.

In trying to make some larger sense of dramatic daily events for local television and op-ed commentaries, and reflecting especially on the relevance of my work on multilateralism, I soon developed a more ambitious agenda to explore the possible contours of the post-cold war international order. This endeavor resulted in my book, *Winning the Peace* (1996a), which addressed America's role in the new era. By placing the current juncture within the corresponding contexts of 1919, 1945, and the early cold war years, I found that a self-perception of American "exceptionalism" was and remains central to defining the US role.

The essay in Chapter 8 builds directly on that argument. It demonstrates that, especially but not exclusively in the absence of an overarching external threat, American leaders on prior occasions in this century have sought with some success to frame US policy toward the reconstruction of the international order in terms of organizing principles that resonate with America's sense of self as a nation, specifically with America's civic form of nationalism. More importantly, the essay contends that their doing so represents not merely the cloaking of "given" material interests in rhetorical garb, but that in several significant instances, including the creation of the UN and the choice of NATO's indivisible security commitments, this identity factor shaped the very definition of interests the United States subsequently pursued. Thus, the essay suggests that a transformative strategy of utilizing American power to move regional balances toward regimes of cooperative security relations will elicit greater domestic support for a constructive US international security policy than a case-by-case material interests-based approach. The specific form of these regimes will differ, of course, for different parts of the world due to their specific geopolitical complexions.

One of the key differences between the present and previous attempts in this century to reconstruct the international order is the institutional legacy earlier efforts have left behind. NATO is the most important case in point. Notwithstanding realist views to the contrary, NATO has never been merely a traditional alliance; its indivisible and generalized security commitments owed as much to the idea of collective security as to the conventional alliance form (see Chapters 4 and 8; also Ruggie 1996a: 80–88). And over time the transatlantic region has evolved into a "security community." Chapter 9 views the future of NATO through this prism. Karl Deutsch and his colleagues defined the concept as comprising institutionalized expectations of peaceful change, which they deemed to be most dependable the more they reflect cognitive bonds of "'we-feeling,' trust, and mutual consideration" (1957: 36). The issue of NATO expansion takes on a particular meaning with these desiderata in mind. Specifically, I contend in this essay that the European Union has become a "core area" (Deutsch's term) of the transatlantic security community in its own right. Therefore, the structure of NATO should be further adapted to reflect that fact, its relationship to the West European Union consolidated, and eastward expansion should be more of a West European-led process.

The final essay addresses the issue of UN peace operations, for which a demand will continue to exist in certain regional conflicts. Peacekeeping is nowhere mentioned in the UN charter. It was itself invented at the time of the 1956 Suez crisis in response to changed international circumstances—the emergence of the so-called third world—that created a need as well as an opportunity. Early post-cold war euphoria raised expectations that UN peace operations would move beyond the traditional peacekeeping modality. That euphoria proved unrealistic. But the sense of futility that followed Somalia and Bosnia exaggerated in the opposite direction. It is too simplistic to say that the UN failed because the interests of the major powers did not permit it to succeed, and premature to declare impartial intervention in any form an oxymoron. These assessments leave unexamined critical ideational factors. Neither member states nor the UN secretariat articulated *doctrinally* a new type of UN peace operation for post-cold war limited conflicts, beyond peacekeeping but short of all-out warfighting. And the reasons had far more to do with different national *military cultures* among the major powers, especially the United States, Britain, and France, than it did with fundamental national interests. As a result, traditional peacekeeping was simply coupled haphazardly with ad hoc "robust" mechanisms and thrown into conflict situations for which it was not suited. Not surprisingly, it failed. The essay in Chapter 10 examines the doctrinal confusions attending robust UN peace operations, and outlines a formulation that tries to do justice to both their normative and strategic requirements while remaining cognizant of the outer limits of political acceptability.

Collectively, these essays suggest that "making history" in the new era is a matter not merely of defending the national interest but defining it, nor merely enacting stable preferences but constructing them. These processes are constrained by forces in the object world and instrumental rationality is ever present. But they also deeply involve such ideational factors as identities and aspirations as well as leaders attempting to persuade their publics and one another through reasoned discourse while learning, or not, by trial and error. In sum, nothing makes it clearer than the question of agency at times such as ours why the constructivist approach needs to be part of the theoretical tools of the international relations field.

8 Interests, identity, and American foreign policy

For successive generations born after World War II, few facts about political life seemed as certain as an internationalist US foreign policy. Indeed, from the time of the Vietnam war on, the potential dangers of American over-extension abroad aroused greater concern than its opposite. Clearly, the Soviet threat—or bipolarity, in structural realist parlance—helped pull the United States into active international involvement. What will happen now that the Soviet Union and bipolarity are gone? Will the United States revert to neo-isolationism in security policy and the political affairs of the world?

This essay (1997b) argues that the answer lies at least as much in the domain of identity—America's sense of self as a nation—as in the realm of interests defined by polarity. That was true in 1919 and 1945. It was true even during the cold war: identity factors shaped America's definition of interests in choosing the specific form of NATO's security guarantees, in US support for the European Defense Community and other regional as well as global "collective security" mechanisms—including UN peacekeeping, and the creation of the UN in the first place.

When the remaking of the international order has been at stake, in 1919, 1945, as well as post-1947—and as it is once again today—systemic attributes provide only a limited guide to US foreign policy. Structural and functional precepts become national interests only when they tap into, and resonate with, ideas, principles, and norms rooted in the nation's sense of self.

As a nation, the United States was not only born free, Robert Keohane once remarked (1983a: 9), it was also "born lucky." It found itself far removed from the continuous jostling of European power politics, protected by vast oceans on either side while adjoined by relatively weak and usually friendly neighbors to the north and south, largely self-sufficient in raw materials, able to expand into continental scale, and a magnet attracting a steady influx of newcomers eager to break with their past and make a fresh start. Accordingly, the United States, before the turn of this century, luxuriated in the posture, as described by John Quincy Adams, of being "the well-wisher to the freedom and independence of all . . . the champion and vindicator only of her own" (quoted in LaFeber 1989: 80). Thus, America's traditional aversion to "entangling alliances," first expressed in George Washington's farewell address, flowed naturally from its geopolitical constitution (Gilbert 1961).

Beginning around the time of the Spanish-American war, however,

American leaders felt the world closing in on the United States. In September 1901, President William McKinley delivered a major address on America's new role in the world, at the new century's first world's fair, in Buffalo, New York. "God and men have linked nations together," he stated. "No nation can longer be indifferent to any other" (quoted in Fromkin 1995: 23). The next day McKinley was assassinated, making Theodore Roosevelt, or TR, president. TR picked up McKinley's banner and carried it a step further in his first state of the union message. "The increasing interdependence and complexity of international political and economic relations," he declared, "render it incumbent on all civilized and orderly powers," the United States included, "to insist on the proper policing of the world" (quoted in Dallek 1983: 34–35). But the dilemma was how to interest an increasingly powerful but reluctant America—Congress and public alike—in that mission.

And so began an epic struggle for nearly the next half century about how to secure sustained American political engagement in world affairs to promote a stable international order, and one that was favorable to the pursuit of US interests. TR lost the struggle prior to World War I as did Woodrow Wilson in 1919. The interwar period saw a reversion to American isolationism in security policy and erratic behavior in the international economic realm. Before World War II had even ended, Franklin Roosevelt devised intricate and heterodox plans to secure American engagement, but they were never fully tested. For by 1947, as *Newsweek* predicted at the time, the Truman Doctrine "had clearly put America into power politics to stay" (quoted in McCullough 1992: 549). Perceptions of the Soviet military threat coupled with anticommunist ideological fervor, in short, resolved a historic American dilemma.

What will happen now that the cold war is history? Does not this dilemma become unresolved again? And is not a new framing of America's political role in the world necessary as a result? In raising these question I intend neither to predict the recrudescence of 1930s-style isolationism nor to prescribe rabid American interventionism. But I do suggest that sustaining American engagement in the maintenance of world order is likely to become a more difficult task in the years ahead than during the past half century, and that it is well worth our while, therefore, to look back at pre- and early-cold war attempts to resolve the dilemma, before America's determination to counter the Soviet threat became taken for granted.

Several factors imply future difficulties. First, no functional equivalent to the "pull-factor" the Soviet threat exerted on US foreign policy is likely to emerge anytime soon (Deibel 1992). The risk of American overcommitment, a constant concern of many during the cold war, is reduced thereby, but the possibility of undercommitment increases. And it is reinforced by the lingering effects of the Weinberger–Powell "all-or-nothing" doctrine governing the use of force that gained dominance in the wake of Vietnam (Gacek 1994).

Second, unless it is counteracted, public opinion will reinforce this tendency. Drawing on the quadrennial foreign policy polls conducted by the Chicago Council on Foreign Relations, William Schneider (1997: 27–28) finds that in the latest survey, conducted in October 1994, most measures of public support for American international engagement were at all-time lows since immediately after Vietnam—including "defending our allies' security" and "protecting weaker nations against foreign aggression." In a *Times Mirror* survey taken in June 1995, the view that the United States should "mind its own business internationally and let other countries get along the best they can on their own" was rejected by just 51 percent of the public while 41 percent agreed, the highest level of agreement since the survey's inception in 1974.

Economic liberals believe that the forces of economic globalization are sufficiently strong to counter the tendencies described above. They may be right in the long run, but in the near term there are grounds for skepticism. The perceived negative effects of globalization occasion far greater concern among the American public, which widely believes that outsourcing to low-wage countries is responsible for downward wage pressures, wider income gaps, and heightened labor market uncertainties in the American economy.[1] Recent electoral politics have begun to tap those concerns. Ross Perot's 1994 presidential bid appealed largely on "social protectionist" grounds: declining economic opportunities and grave social uncertainties for the middle classes produced by the "giant sucking sound" of high-wage jobs moving out. Perot gained 19 percent of the vote, the biggest third-party success since TR's Bull Moose run in 1912. Pat Buchanan in the 1996 Republican primaries lashed out against "stagnant wages of an alienated working class," promised to "insulate" wages from externally-induced downward pressure, and proposed a "social tariff" to accomplish that end (quoted in Kuttner 1995: 26). Organized labor has been supportive of just about any form of protectionism for two decades. In short, a potentially sizable electoral coalition exists, populist rather than partisan in nature, ready for a more mainstream politician who promises social protection against the economic insecurity it associates with the forces of globalization.[2]

Yet another indicator of greater difficulties ahead is provided, albeit obliquely, by Henry Kissinger in his recent book, *Diplomacy*. Without the Soviet threat, realism by itself cannot suffice to frame US foreign policy, Kissinger concludes ruefully. In the new era, a foreign policy strategy based on case-by-case interest calculations is simply too unreliable. Hence, realism, Kissinger contends, must be coupled with an animating "vision" which provides the American public with a sense of "hope and possibility that are, in their essence, conjectural" (1994a: 835)—and for which he, the master practitioner of the realist craft, now looks to the "idealism" that he spent his career mocking.

In short, it seems reasonable to proceed on the premise that sustained engagement by the United States for the sake of a stable international order will prove more problematic in the years ahead than it was during the cold war. That observation, in turn, poses the question to which this essay is addressed: what can we learn from previous efforts by US leaders to prevail at comparable historical junctures—when the remaking of the international order was at stake, but in the absence of an overarching threat? Exploring this critical policy concern also sheds light on a significant theoretical issue: prior efforts to achieve American engagement in the cause of world order entailed the role of imagery, ideas, and justifications. A study of these efforts permits us, therefore, to analyze the interaction between ideational factors and interests, whether defined in power-related or functional terms.

The discussion is organized as follows. The first section briefly retells the story of the strategies of engagement American leaders pursued in 1919, 1945, and in the early cold war years. This recapitulation demonstrates that what Kissinger recommends for the years ahead in fact characterizes the most promising strategy of the past: it linked the pursuit of American interests to a transformative vision of world order that appealed to the American public's sense of collective self.

The second section explores the nature of that appeal. I seek to show that there is a certain congruence between the vision of world order invoked by American leaders when "founding" a new international order has been at stake, and the principles of domestic order at play in America's understanding of its own founding, in its own sense of political community. Furthermore, I indicate why it is inappropriate to dismiss the invocation of these principles as "mere rhetoric" or to squeeze it into the container of idealism.

The concluding section draws out the argument's implications for the conduct of US foreign policy in the new era, incorporating some of the lessons of the past.

STRATEGIES OF ENGAGEMENT

By means of what strategies did previous generations of American leaders seek to persuade a reluctant country that the United States should become actively involved to secure and maintain a stable international order? Which worked, and which did not? This section recapitulates the debates at three prior junctures in this century when the remaking of the international order was at stake, as it is today: the period just before, during, and after World War I; the foreign policy designs constructed during World War II for the postwar era; and the early cold war years.

TR and Wilson

All of the essential elements of the story were present in its very first instance. One of the folk tales handed down about the Versailles treaty fight in the US Senate is that it represented a titanic clash between internationalism and isolationism in which the forces of darkness prevailed over the forces of light. The tale may have its rhetorical uses, but it is incorrect. The fight was between two forms of internationalism that were not able or did not choose to find common ground, as a result of which both lost: realist unilateralism and liberal multilateralism. Isolationism won by default (Knock 1992).

Theodore Roosevelt initially treated America's becoming a world power in unproblematic terms. The United States would simply have to act like other great powers, because it, like they, was affected by and in turn affected a power balance that was increasingly global in scope. Influenced by theorists of maritime geopolitics Alfred T. Mahan and John W. Burgess, TR was especially concerned about the British navy's steady loss of dominance and with it, he feared, its maritime policing role, including its contribution to safeguarding the Monroe Doctrine (Stephanson 1995: 83–87). McKinley had followed up the Spanish-American war with a brief imperialist fling, acquiring several naval stations across the Pacific to the Philippines. TR issued his corollary to the Monroe Doctrine, whereby the United States no longer simply warned European powers to stay out of hemispheric affairs but claimed America's right to intervene in them; and he built a navy worthy of a world power, sending it on a symbolic round-the-world cruise.

And yet, as war approached in Europe, TR, by then no longer president, was unsuccessful in urging American military preparedness on balance-of-power grounds. Nor was there widespread support for his call to arms once war broke out. "I have no influence whatever in shaping public action," he complained to the British foreign secretary, "very little influence indeed in shaping public opinion" (quoted in Cooper 1983: 286). As Robert Dallek explains (1983: 35), "most Americans in Roosevelt's day were unprepared to accept his realism as a guideline for current and future actions abroad."

Indeed, McKinley and Roosevelt had already begun to discover the utility of unorthodox foreign policy instruments when realist ways were unavailable, some of which would later form the core of Woodrow Wilson's program. Finding no Congressional support for joining Europe in a scramble to partition China, the McKinley administration instead called on the powers to adopt a nondiscriminatory "open door" commercial policy in China, and to preserve its territorial and administrative form. In 1905, TR, who privately ridiculed international arbitration as "that noxious form of silliness which always accompanies the sentimental refusal to look facts in the face," successfully mediated the Russo-Japanese war, for which he won the Nobel peace prize (ibid.: 56). And it is little remembered that TR was the first American leader to propose a league of nations: a "World League for

the Peace of Righteousness," he called it in an October 1914 article, to function as "a posse comitatus of powerful and civilized nations" (Cooper 1983:
281).

Roosevelt's foreign policy legacy remained ambiguous, however, because,
on his own reckoning, he failed to resolve the dilemma of how to get the
United States to assume the role of great power. Wilson shared TR's objective of securing sustained American engagement in the political and security
affairs of the world. But he took a different tack toward it.

With election day 1916 approaching, and with the United States still a
non-belligerent, Wilson, in a major campaign speech, decried the European
balance-of-power system, not so much on idealist as on geopolitical
grounds: "Now, revive that after the war is over, and, sooner or later, you
will have just such another war. And this is the last war of the kind, or of
any kind that involves the world, that the United States can keep out of"
(quoted in Knock 1992: 97). German submarine attacks on American
merchant ships demonstrated that neutrality could no longer protect the
United States. And with the balance-of-power system having just produced
war again in Europe, Wilson concluded: "We must have a society of
nations." He elaborated these ideas in his well-received January 1917 "Peace
without Victory" address to the Senate, proposing a postwar league of
nations as the institutional expression, not of a balance but "a community
of power" (ibid.: 112). When Wilson asked Congress, on 2 April 1917, to
declare war on imperial Germany, he stated solemnly that if Americans
must shed blood, it would be "for democracy, for the right of those who
submit to authority to have a voice in their own governments, for the rights
and liberties of small nations, for a universal dominion of right by such a
concert of free peoples as shall bring peace and safety to all nations and
make the world itself at last free" (ibid.: 121–122). These were "American
principles," Wilson affirmed. Finally, Wilson's famous Fourteen Points,
proclaimed a year later, combined his previous proposals into a comprehensive program for postwar peace: sovereign equality and national
self-determination, mutual guarantees of political independence and territorial integrity, free trade, freedom of the seas, transparent diplomacy, and the
spread of democracy to autocratic—and for Wilson, therefore, militaristic—
governments, coupled with a reduction of armaments and the institution of
collective security. Success, he explained, would lessen the need for future
American sacrifice.

Thus, in their analysis of *why* the United States should be involved in the
political affairs of the world Roosevelt and Wilson differed relatively little
(Ninkovich 1994). But they differed profoundly in the means they chose
toward that end. Where Roosevelt tried to "normalize" America to get it to
act as he believed a great power should, Wilson appealed to American principles—to American "exceptionalism." Indeed, with his posse analogy, TR,
too, had tried to enlist a distinctly American experience in his cause, the old
West before law and order were instituted, but to no avail. The public

preferred Wilson's version until late in the day. "Existing evidence," the respected Wilson scholar, Lawrence Gelfand, has written (1983: 89), "essentially the considered judgment of seasoned politicians and journalists in the fall of 1918 and well into the spring of 1919, pointed toward solid public support for American membership in the League of Nations."

In the end, of course, Wilson lost the treaty fight. Public anxiety became aroused by growing fears about American boys repeatedly being sent overseas to fight for the League—"every time a Jugoslav wishes to slap a Czechoslav in the face," TR charged on one occasion (quoted in Knock 1992: 229). But the fight was lost in the Senate, which had shifted to Republican control in the 1918 midterm elections. There were barely a dozen hard-core irreconcilables in the Senate—so-called because they were opposed to American membership in a League of any form. They alone, therefore, could not defeat the League. Henry Cabot Lodge (R-Mass.), Chairman of the Foreign Relations Committee, and once TR's mentor, was prepared to vote for the League and deliver enough Republican votes to ratify the treaty, provided that Wilson accepted Lodge's "reservations." Fourteen in number (like Wilson's Fourteen Points), they covered much ground. But in essence it came down to this nonnegotiable issue: in Lodge's words, to "release us from obligations which might not be kept, and to preserve rights which ought not to be infringed" (ibid.: 258–267). In other words, Lodge claimed that the League might pressure the United States—it could not require—to take actions the United States might not wish to take, and pose a hindrance when it did wish to act. But Lodge's stance was not isolationism; it was unilateralism.

It is far from certain that Lodge's reservations would have done irreparable harm to Wilson's concept of the League; for example, Wilson himself rejected putting American troops at the League's disposal. But he would not or could not compromise.[3] Compounding that irony, Lodge, like his protégé TR, worked assiduously throughout his career to have the United States play a major-power role in world affairs. And yet at this critical moment, by insisting on strict unilateralist means in place of Wilson's soft multilateralism, he, too, undermined his own objective and helped usher in an era of isolationism.[4]

The core lesson that Franklin Roosevelt, Harry Truman, and Dwight Eisenhower drew from this experience was not only that isolationism is "bad" and internationalism "good" for the sake of international stability and the pursuit of US interests, but, more subtly, that unilateralism had opened the door to isolationism. The link between unilateralism as principle and isolationism as result was this. Having rejected the League, the country insisted, as Senator William Borah, an interwar isolationist leader, put it, that the United States "does propose to determine for itself when civilization is threatened, when there may be a breach of human rights and human liberty sufficient to warrant action, and it proposes also to determine for itself when to act and in what manner it shall discharge the obligation which time and circumstances impose" (quoted in Jonas 1966: 7). The next step—and, to the early post-World War II generation of US leaders, an inevitable step in view of America's geopolitical constitution—was to set such a high threshold for what constituted a vital or important American interest that no threat to international peace and security triggered an American response. Not being required, by virtue of any institutionalized undertaking or commitment, to assume any practical stand regarding the forces pushing the world toward war again in the 1930s, the United States took none. Only the direct attack on Pearl Harbor, twenty-seven months into World War II, "broke this emotional deadlock," as Dallek characterizes it (1983: 7).

FDR

In a manner of speaking, Theodore Roosevelt and Woodrow Wilson were theorists of international relations in their own right. In contrast, Franklin Delano Roosevelt was a tinkerer—"the juggler," as he once gleefully described himself (Kimball 1991). His plans for anchoring American participation in the creation and maintenance of a stable postwar order exhibit that skill. But insofar as FDR pioneered the use of public opinion data in the White House, those plans were closely attuned to what his personal pollster, Hadley Cantril, described as "the state of mind of the American people" (1967: 79).[5]

Roosevelt's hybrid design for the postwar international economic order, which I have dubbed the "embedded liberalism compromise" [see Chapter 2], has been extensively studied. The United States sought a global version of the "open door," which required breaking down the discriminatory trade and monetary blocs, zones, and instruments that had prevailed in the 1930s, as well as lowering barriers to international economic transactions. At the same time, the international edifice of the open door had to accommodate the domestic interventionism of the New Deal. And therein lay the compromise: unlike the economic nationalism of the thirties, the postwar international economic order would be multilateral in character. But unlike the *laissez-faire* liberalism of the gold standard and free trade, its multilateralism would be predicated on the interventionist character of the modern capitalist state, including the United States, which its public had come to expect.

Roosevelt also conducted a campaign aimed at eliminating European empires, again with strong domestic support, though he was restrained by the need to avoid weakening Britain's resolve in the war and to ensure British and French postwar cooperation (Kimball 1991: 127; Hilderbrand 1990: 170–181;, Smith 1994: 126). And his administration was responsible for the initiation of major international human rights agreements.

FDR's design for the security order was more contested at the time and remains more poorly understood even today, largely because it involved the United Nations (Widenor 1982)—a name he chose personally and proudly announced to Churchill. His juggling act here confused and displeased both Wilsonian liberals and realists. But it resonated with the American public and, given the available options, it made strategic sense.

Not long before Roosevelt left for the February 1945 Yalta conference with Stalin and Churchill, at which the organization of postwar security relations was one of the major subjects of discussion, Cantril sent him a summary of prevailing public opinion toward international affairs. "The present internationalism rests on a rather unstable foundation," Cantril wrote. "It is recent, it is not rooted in any broad or long-range conception of self-interest, it has little intellectual basis" (1967: 76). It was not, therefore, to be taken for granted.

Roosevelt's initial impulse, like Churchill's and Stalin's, had run along regional spheres-of-influence lines. FDR favored a "four policemen" scheme, adding China as a counterweight to the Soviets in Asia. But he soon concluded that the American people would find such a scheme too cynical, and he feared that Congress might use it as an excuse to shirk American involvement in the postwar stabilization of Europe and Asia. "The only appeal which would be likely to carry weight with the United States public," Roosevelt explained to British Foreign Secretary Anthony Eden, "would be one based upon a world-wide conception" (quoted in Kimball 1991: 96). At the same time, Roosevelt could not, as he told Soviet Foreign Minister Vyacheslav Molotov, "visualize another League of Nations" (quoted in Divine 1967: 61). It had proved unworkable abroad, and carried too much negative baggage at home. And so he proposed a universal United Nations in which the major powers would play a special role.

FDR had two major strategic objectives in establishing the United Nations. First, and above all else, he saw it as an institutional tripwire that would force American policymakers to take positions on potential threats to international peace and security, and to justify those positions, one way or the other—not simply to look the other way, as they had done in the 1930s (Dallek 1979). Second, FDR believed that a stable postwar security order also required, in the words of John Lewis **Gaddis** (1982: 9), "offering Moscow a prominent place in it; by making it, so to speak, a member of the club." Gaddis calls this the strategy of "containment by integration"—in contrast to the subsequent American strategy of containing the Soviets by exclusion and exhaustion. But this strategy required a club to which both Washington and Moscow belonged. FDR hoped that the UN Security Council, especially the institution of the permanent five, would perform that function.

FDR also believed that the United Nations had to have "teeth" and be able to enforce its decisions by military means if others failed if it was to possess credibility among the public, serve these geopolitical objectives, and provide deterrent value vis-à-vis potential aggressors. But, he assured the American people, "we are not thinking of a superstate with its own police force and other paraphernalia of coercive power." Instead, the United States and the other major powers, he said, planned to devise a mechanism for "joint action" by national forces (Hilderbrand 1990: 65).

What, in analytical terms, was the nature of this construction? In effect, and perhaps consciously, FDR tried to reconcile the leagues of Wilson and TR—the one a universal organization of formal equals, the other a big power club.[6] As Wilson's Assistant Secretary of the Navy, FDR witnessed first hand the clash between Wilson and TR, FDR's distant cousin whom he saw often and admired much. Better than most contemporaries or later commentators, FDR understood that Wilson and TR, at bottom, had sought the same end of securing sustained American engagement, which he, too, embraced. He also appreciated how and why their preferred means differed. With the searing isolationist experience as interlude, there was no doubt in FDR's mind about which tack to take: the multilateralism of Wilson, not the unilateralism of TR. But he departed from Wilson instrumentally. Wilson, the committed liberal internationalist, rejected what he regarded as old world power politics as a legitimate instrument within a new world-led collective security scheme. FDR, "the juggler," grafted a collective security scheme onto a concert of power.[7] That move circumscribed the scope of the UN's collective security mechanisms, to be sure, but FDR had no desire, nor did he think it possible, for such a mechanism to operate beyond the firm grasp of the great powers.

By 1944, the lesson that not even the United States could insulate itself against being dragged into war together with FDR's painstaking politicking had thoroughly discredited isolationism. In the Congressional elections that year virtually all isolationists in both parties lost their seats—despite the fact that in the 1942 midterm elections the Republicans had their best showing since the 1920s, coming very close to taking control of the House and, eleven months after the attack on Pearl Harbor, managing to reelect all but 5 of 115 members with isolationist records (Divine 1967: chap. 5). But in 1944, the Republican Party lined up in support of the UN, led by Wendell Willkie, author of a best-selling tract entitled *One World*, who campaigned for its presidential nomination; John Foster Dulles, Wall Street lawyer and the party's leading foreign policy voice; and New York Governor Thomas E. Dewey, the party's eventual nominee.

Wilsonian liberals were critical of FDR, however. They doubted whether he had fashioned "a truly internationalist organization."[8] But that was not his intention. In any case, Wilson, the paragon of liberal internationalism, rejected provisions in the covenant that would have put American forces at the League's disposal; FDR devised an arrangement that made possible United States military participation in UN peace operations.

Realists were aghast, but for a different reason. George Kennan, serving in the Moscow embassy, urged "burying" the proposals for the UN. "We are badly enmeshed in our own unsound slogans," he admonished Washington in an unsolicited cable (quoted in Hilderbrand 1990: 250), referring to the idea of collective security and being unable to grasp Roosevelt's heterodox design. The realist barrage of criticism continued into the postwar years, and included "some of the most influential thinkers in this country on the proper conduct of American foreign policy"—in addition to Kennan, Walter Lippmann, Hans Morgenthau, and Reinhold Niebuhr (Smith 1994: 103).

But FDR's chief target had been the public, not intellectuals, through every medium imaginable, from high-level briefings to films and comic books. We have no means by which to measure the effects of these efforts. But as the war in Europe was drawing to a close and just prior to the UN's founding conference in San Francisco, a Gallup poll reported that 81 percent of Americans favored US entry into a "world organization with police power to maintain world peace"; and of those responding affirmatively, 83 percent described entry as "very important." A confidential poll taken for the State Department showed similar results: eight of ten surveyed supported the commitment of American forces to the United Nations to help keep peace (Divine 1967: 251; Cantril 1967: 77). Did these views concerning America's second try at linking itself to the cause of world order reflect merely the triumph of hope over experience, as Dr. Johnson said about second marriages? It seems not. For the same polls also indicated that nearly 40 percent of the public believed the United States would find itself involved in another war within a quarter century (Divine 1967: 251).

We can only speculate what might have happened to FDR's scheme had the cold war not ensued. But with the Senate ratifying the UN charter by 89–2, and with Congress deciding that once it had also ratified the agreement making US troops available to the UN, on its call, the president required no additional Congressional authorization to commit those troops to specific UN missions, the scheme certainly achieved its immediate objective. At least for the moment, the United States was anchored into the international order.

Truman and Eisenhower

If the outbreak of the cold war largely made moot Roosevelt's designs in the security sphere, by bifurcating the permanent five, it also provided an even more effective—indeed, sometimes too effective—substitute. Framed by bipolarity and animated by anticommunism, the "discourse of national security," as Emily Rosenberg (1993) describes it, took hold. But multilateralism in security relations did not simply vanish. Its core analytic features—that threats to peace are indivisible and require a collective response—formed the basis of America's security policy toward Europe— and, more problematically, was extended via the domino theory to other cold war theaters.[9]

In responding to West European security needs, President Truman had four sets of options available: US unilateral security guarantees to one, several, or an organization of European states; US bilateral alliances with the most directly threatened European states; a "dumbbell" model, whereby a guarantee or agreement linked North American and European alliances; or an arrangement that promised equal protection under a common security umbrella for an indivisible grouping of states, including the United States. Each would have satisfied Europe, and each would have served notice on the Soviets that the United States was committed to the security of Europe. Truman chose the last: a NATO containing Article 5 commitments—that a war against one is a war against all, calling for a collective response—a direct descendant of Articles 10 and 16 of the League covenant, on which Lodge had skewered Wilson.

Truman's choice of instrument, to repeat, was not determined by the need to respond to the Soviets. But it had considerable domestic appeal: in addition to deterring the Soviets, the NATO security arrangement, coupled with the impetus that the Marshall Plan gave to European economic unification, promised to transform the "old" European order: making it economically and militarily better able to take care of itself, rendering it less war-prone and therefore less likely to drag the United States into yet another European war, and ultimately making Europe more like the United States. Indeed, Congress with near unanimity adopted a resolution endorsing "the creation of a United States of Europe" (Hogan 1987: 38–39). In short, what Wilson had sought circuitously to accomplish via the League, Truman approached more straightforwardly through NATO: an "ersatz collective security" scheme, in Ninkovich's words (1994: 170), backed by the United States until it could become self-sustaining. Arthur Vandenberg (R-Mich.), chairman of the Senate Foreign Relations Committee, eagerly sponsored legislation paving the way for negotiations of a "collective self-defense organization" consistent with the UN charter.[10] "Why should a Democratic President get all the kudos in an election year?" he asked (quoted in Kaplan 1986: 112).

In the Senate, Robert A. Taft of Ohio—"Mr. Republican," towering intellect, isolationist, but also fierce anticommunist—opposed NATO because he saw it exactly for what it was. "I do not like the obligation written into the pact which binds us for twenty years to come [the initial duration of the treaty] to the defense of any country, no matter by whom it is attacked and even though the aggressor may be another member of the pact" (Taft 1951: 88–89). Taft was prepared to let his isolationism be overruled by his even greater antipathy toward the Soviets, he stated, in favor of US bilateral security ties to specific European countries or a unilateral guarantee to all of Western Europe. But NATO he found too much to swallow, even in the cause of anticommunism.

Some realist practitioners expressed similar concerns. Kennan did not believe that US military commitments of any kind to Europe were necessary. But if they had to be made, Kennan preferred that they take a "particularized" and not a "legalistic-moralistic" form: that is, specific in nature, limited in time, and contingent on discrete exigencies (Stephanson 1989: 140; Mayers 1988: 152–155; Lundestad 1980: 172–173, 188–189).[11] For Kennan,

NATO was barely an improvement over the UN in this regard. Moreover, Kennan feared that the universalistic language of NATO's security commitments inherently entailed an impetus for NATO to expand—which, of course, it did and continues to do—a prospect the United States, he believed, could ill afford.[12] Kennan lost that debate, and his position contributed directly to his departing the State Department. "Believing that he had exorcised the spirit of idealistic Wilsonianism," Ninkovich writes (1994: 152), "[Kennan] found himself fighting a losing battle with its strategic doppelganger."

The Republican-controlled Senate ratified the North Atlantic Treaty by 82–13, suggesting "that a national consensus had been reached" (Kaplan 1988: 37). Indeed, Jacob K. Javits (R-N.Y.) introduced legislation in 1950 to establish an East Asian NATO, but the situation on the ground there made that impossible (LaFeber 1989: 474).[13] Nevertheless, when the Korean war broke out "the decision to conduct the American response through United Nations machinery was never at any time seriously debated in Washington, and for all practical purposes it was an automatic reaction" (Stairs 1970: 308; also see Ninkovich 1994: 190).

The Eisenhower administration pushed these proclivities further, seeking opportunities to institute what the president repeatedly described as "collective security." Collective security was "a *must* for the future of our type of civilization," Eisenhower declared, while his Secretary of State, John Foster Dulles, claimed that it was "the only posture which was consistent with US national security policy as a whole"—referring to the liberal character of America's political institutions (both quoted in Ninkovich 1994: 212–213).[14] As the first Supreme Allied Commander in Europe, Eisenhower had been an early and ardent advocate of a unified European Defense Community (EDC)—indeed, more so than most European leaders—and he had helped persuade President Truman of its desirability. As president himself, he pushed actively for its establishment (Duchin 1992). The Joint Chiefs of Staff came to accept EDC, as did Congress, which proposed to make military aid to EDC countries conditional on the adoption of the treaty. Dulles told the North Atlantic Council in 1953 that if Europe failed to ratify EDC, "grave doubts" would arise in the United States concerning the future of European security, and that America would be obliged to undertake an "agonizing reappraisal" of its role in Europe (ibid.).

After EDC's defeat in the French National Assembly, the allies quickly reached consensus on restoring German sovereignty and rearming it within an institutionally more robust NATO. But Eisenhower did not abandon his earlier aspirations. He turned to nuclear energy to strengthen the security dimension of European integration, facilitating the creation of EURATOM (Helmreich 1991). He also planned ways of sharing nuclear weapons with the European NATO allies, and toward the end of his term apparently explored ways of providing an independent nuclear force to a consortium of NATO allies comprising France, Britain, and West Germany (Weber 1993: 258).

In a similar though less consequential institutional move, Eisenhower occasioned and facilitated the invention of UN peacekeeping when he opposed three of America's closest allies, Britain, France, and Israel, at Suez. Eisenhower described the UN action as yet another element in the collective provision of security. For realist commentators it was the height of folly, "permitting the very foundations of American policy [to be] swept away," Kennan complained bitterly, "the victim of an empty legalism" (Kennan 1956: A8; also see Morgenthau 1956: 36; Wolfers 1962: 198).

The Kennedy administration broke this historical pattern. Whereas US leaders from FDR to Eisenhower had "groped for a definition of the world role their country should play," David Fromkin writes (1995: 7), "pursued by doubts that they had got it right," Kennedy's best and brightest "took it for granted that the United States was a superpower with global interests and responsibilities." The country, apparently, agreed. It remained to be seen if America was, indeed, prepared to pay any price, bear any burden, as the young president proclaimed. But, notably, by the time Kennedy came along opinion pollsters had lost interest in asking the public about the desirability of an active US role in the world, so invariant were the affirmative responses (Holsti 1992: 460). Their interest soon would be rekindled by Vietnam, after America grasped the full meaning of Kennedy's proclamations.[15]

Let us bring this discussion to a close with an analytical reprise.

Internationalist leaders from the turn of the century on down have sought to devise strategies of international engagement for the United States. They have differed little about why such engagement was deemed necessary; differences lie in their preferred means toward that end. Realists, beginning with TR, have sought to "normalize" America, urging it to act like other great powers do. Prior to the cold war Americans were unresponsive, perhaps because they did not see America as a normal great power, and for good reason: in geopolitical terms alone there had never been a great power like it. But even after the advent of the cold war, judging by Truman's and Eisenhower's concerns, Americans seemed to require more persuasive reasoning. The outbreak of the cold war may have "put America into power politics to stay," as *Newsweek* had put it in 1947, but Truman and Eisenhower both wondered how long that would last.

Wilson, far from seeking to normalize America, drew on its sense of difference—on American exceptionalism—linking the quest for sustained US international engagement to America's self-defining ideas at home. FDR, Truman, and Eisenhower also sensed that realism, by itself, was an inadequate base and so they, too, embraced similarly grounded reformist aspirations for the international arena, linking US engagement to a broader vision of world order which they felt would resonate with the American public. Unlike Wilson, however, they had no aversion to balance-of-power politics. Thus, FDR built a universal security organization onto a concert of great powers, while Truman and Eisenhower coupled America's transformational agenda abroad with the process of bipolar power-balancing.

But there are many aspects of American exceptionalism, as Lipset has documented empirically (1996). Precisely which of them have endured in these prior foreign policy quests? Why? And do the answers have any bearing on the future? These questions take us into the realm of identity politics.

IMAGINING "US"

The common element in the world order postures of Wilson, FDR, Truman, and Eisenhower is a set of distinctive organizing principles: security cooperation by means of more comprehensive and institutionalized arrangements than the traditional system of bilateral alliances; an "open door" world economy comprising uniform rules of trade and monetary relations together with minimum state-imposed barriers to the flow of international economic transactions; anti-colonialism grounded in self-determination; anti-statism grounded in individual rights; and the promotion of democracy. In contrast with TR's and Lodge's unilateralist prescriptions based in realism, these are multilateral principles that entail a mildly communitarian vision of world order.[16]

These organizing principles express general milieu preferences, that is, preferences concerning the overall contours and direction of international relations. They do not predict specific day-to-day policy choices. Reconciling universals with particular circumstances, domestic and international, is always contingent and problematic. Nevertheless, we have seen that at the three prior instances in this century when the remaking of the international order was at stake—in 1919, 1945, and post-1947—these American leaders reached for these principles. Perceived interests, of course, influence milieu preferences and even more so whether or not these preferences are enacted in any particular instance. But a country that is as powerful as the United States and, relatively speaking, as well insulated from the vicissitudes buffeting most other countries often has more than one means available to satisfy its interests. Hence, America's balance of choice versus necessity, to borrow a phrase from the classical realists, often leaves substantial freedom of choice. In exercising that choice, these leaders believed—or at least behaved in a manner consistent with the belief—that multilateral world order principles enjoyed a particular resonance with the American public that other ideas (especially "normalization") would not evoke, and thus would help institute sustained US international engagement.

There would not be much news in an argument that leaders' concerns with evoking domestic support shapes foreign policy, and that some efforts to persuade succeed while others fail. But I postulate a more specific hypothesis to account for the recurrent recourse to multilateralism: there is a certain congruence between these principles for the "founding" (construction or reconstruction) of an international order and the principles of order at play in America's understanding of its own founding as a political community. Multilateral organizing principles are singularly compatible with America's own form of nationalism, on which its sense of political community is based. Below, I first explicate this argument; I present some evidence in its support; and I indicate why it would be wrong to dismiss it on the grounds that it represents mere rhetoric or idealism.

American nationalism

A nation, by definition, is an imagined community. It is imagined because, Benedict Anderson (1983: 15) notes, "the image of their communion" lives in the minds of its members, bonding people who will never know one another while depicting non-members, including those known personally, as alien. America's form of nationalism differs from that of most other nations, however. Most nations claim an "organic" basis in either land or people, and these are the usual referents of a nation's foundational myths. The American form of nationalism, in contrast, has no such organic basis. "America— wanting a land which always bore its name or a people who always identified themselves as 'Americans'—is the imagined community *par excellence*" (Campbell 1992: 251). Accordingly, the very act of communion—the principled basis on which the American community was constituted and is continually reconstituted—has played the decisive role in America's definition of itself as a nation.

"No assembly of men can constitute a nation," the conservative philosopher Joseph de Maistre wrote in antipathy to French revolutionary ideas of nationhood. "An attempt of this kind ought even to be ranked among the most memorable acts of folly" (quoted in Finkielkraut 1995: 13). Yet that is precisely how America formed itself as a nation. Thus, America traditionally has viewed itself as a willful community, or an elective community—"making a new nation out of literally any old nation that comes along," as G. K. Chesterton remarked (1922: 14). In principle, anyone can become an American. But that fact is made possible, in turn, only because the American concept of political community rests on, not the exclusive organic specificities of traditional nations, but, in the words of political theorist Tracy Strong (1980: 50), "a universal or general foundation open in principle to everyone."

American nationalism, then, is a civic nationalism embodying a set of inclusive core values: intrinsic individual as opposed to group rights, equality of opportunity for all, anti-statism, the rule of law, and a revolutionary legacy which holds that human betterment can be achieved by means of deliberate human actions, especially when they are pursued in accordance with these foundational values. Being an American is defined as believing and doing these things.[17]

The multilateral world order principles invoked by Wilson, FDR,

Truman, and Eisenhower bear a striking affinity to America's sense of self as a nation: an expressed preference for international orders of relations based on "a universal or general foundation open in principle to everyone," not on discriminatory or exclusionary ties. The anti-colonial, self-determination, and human rights strains require little elaboration. The "open door" world economy is an equal opportunity principle—which, in a limited sense, is how the McKinley administration already meant it when it presented the open door notes regarding the future of China to the great powers at the turn of the century. In (re)constructing the security order, the appeal to, and of, collective efforts in support of general principles, as opposed to bilateral alliances based on particularistic grounds, expresses a similar normative orientation. In short, the multilateral world order principles that American leaders have invoked when the remaking of the international order has been at stake reflect the idea of America's own foundational act of political communion.

What evidence exists to support this claim? American exceptionalism has been documented at least from the time of Tocqueville; Lipset's recent survey of this country's atypical political culture, institutions, and practices has a long and distinguished pedigree.[18] American advocacy for multilateral world order principles is also well documented and is broadly accepted as an accurate rendering of US milieu preferences outside the security sphere. In the study of security relations, which has been dominated by realists, any imputed role for multilateral principles has been and remains controversial, far more likely to be dismissed as rhetoric or idealism than taken seriously—an issue to which we return momentarily. No direct evidence exists of the relationship I have hypothesized between America's inorganic nationalism and multilateralism, however, because it has never been explicitly studied. Below, I present some (necessarily) indirect evidence, which lends support to the plausibility of the hypothesis.

Nation and world

The fact that, and the manner in which, the United States has made "a new nation out of literally any old nation that comes along" produces a bias in favor of multilateral organizing principles for constructing/reconstructing the international order. The foreign policy implications of domestic ethnic politics provide one source of supportive evidence for this claim; and the deepening scholarly understanding of the structure of public opinion on foreign policy issues more generally suggests that the hypothesis merits further attention. I take up each in turn.

Evidence of a relationship between inter-ethnic accommodation at home and multilateral organizing principles abroad itself comes in several clusters. First, multilateral principles on key occasions that are of interest to us have served to manage potential instability in domestic ethnic politics. For example, before the United States entered the World War I the British ambassador in Washington reported to London Wilson's fears that America's taking sides in the war might unleash serious domestic ethnic clashes. (Fromkin 1995: 118). Wilson's "Peace Without Victory" speech, in which he proposed settling the war short of the unconditional surrender of Germany, reflected this concern, as did his desire to base the postwar security order on the common defense of general principles rather than on discriminatory bilateral alliances (Knock 1992).

Similarly, after World War II, "multilateralism favored everybody's homeland" (Cowhey 1993: 169). The domestic ethnic politics of country-by-country allocations of US aid and security guarantees at best would have been highly complex, and at worst highly divisive. As it was, the multilateral approach of the Marshall Plan and NATO made it possible to assist Western Europe as a whole. That had the effect of transforming the domestic politics of ethnic identities into more of a median voter issue, thereby avoiding inter-ethnic rivalries and enhancing bipartisan support for the policy.

An even greater push to "go multilateral" may be generated in the future by what the Israeli political scientist Yossi Shain (1994, 1994–95) calls US diasporas in the era of multiculturalism. Shain notes that more ethnic communities than ever have become empowered in the United States, including groups of Asian and Latin American origins as well as African Americans. Their foreign policy influence is likely to grow in a post-cold war world, Shain argues, in which fewer international-structurally determined friends and foes exist. The choice for US policymakers in such an environment is between fragmenting relevant areas of foreign policy along an ever-larger number of ethnic lines or transforming ethnically defined preferences into multilateral directions. History suggests that, except for special bilateral relationships, the latter course is the more likely.

The relationship between American nationalism, multiculturalism, and foreign policy orientations has also been explored in a recent study of public opinion (Citrin *et al.* 1994). It adduced two findings of interest to us: that the advent of multiculturalism has not undermined the prevailing sense of American nationalism; and that multilateralism is a viable foreign policy instrument to accommodate heightened multicultural awareness.

No state in the Union is more ethnically diverse than California. When asked if there are unique American qualities, and if so what they are, 80 percent in a statewide poll responded affirmatively. Of those who did, 85 percent mentioned specific traits "familiar to the readers of de Tocqueville"—including individual rights, equal opportunity, and cultural diversity (ibid.: Table 2, p. 12).[19] In a national poll, respondents divided roughly 5:3 between "assimilationist" and "distinct cultures" views as their preferred model for America. "Strikingly, whites, blacks, and Hispanics did not differ in their responses to this question" (ibid.: 13–15). Nativist impulses, not surprisingly, were most pronounced on the issue of immigration, as it always has been throughout American history. But the perceived threat was far more likely to be defined in economic terms (loss of jobs, higher taxes to pay for welfare and social services) than cultural. The researchers also constructed composite "nativist" and "multicultural" indices. "Clearly, both outlooks are [statistical] minority viewpoints" (ibid.: 20, also Table 5, p. 21). Blacks and Hispanics scored higher on multiculturalism, but it was decisively a minority viewpoint within those groups as well.

On the issue of foreign policy, the study concludes that the more numerous competing forms of ethnic and cultural identity in the United States today may make the task of forging new domestic coalitions in support of an activist foreign policy more complex in the years ahead. But the essence of America's collective identity—the authors' term for it is "cosmopolitan liberal"—"remains a relative bedrock that could provide support for diverse foreign policy positions" (ibid.: 26).[20] High among the positions for which support exists is "instrumental," though not "ideological," multilateralism.

In sum, one relatively direct link between the character of American nationalism and the political efficacy of multilateral world order principles exists through the mechanism of accommodating differences of ethnos, race, and religion among Americans in keeping with the concept of civic, as opposed to organic, nationhood.

A more general source of evidence comes out of the new consensus in research on public opinion and foreign policy. For some fifteen to twenty years after World War II, the so-called Almond—Lippmann view held sway among students of this subject (Holsti 1992; *ISQ* 1986). This view included three propositions: that public opinion toward foreign policy issues is highly volatile, offering little systematic guidance to policymakers; that it lacks coherence to the point of amounting to "non-attitudes;" and that it had little impact on policy in any case. Among the major foreign policy specialists who subscribed to this view were George Kennan and Hans Morgenthau.

The new consensus, in essence, has turned these propositions on their heads (see especially Page and Shapiro 1992). The public is no better informed than was previously assumed, but it is believed to manage its information efficiently. Foreign policy attitudes are highly stable, the new consensus holds, and change "in ways that are regular, predictable, and indeed generally sensible, given the values that citizens hold and the information made available to them" (Shapiro and Page 1994: 217). Moreover, attitudes are now believed to be highly structured. "The American public makes sharp distinctions among [foreign] policies, favoring some and opposing others. Moreover, these distinctions tend to be coherent and consistent with each other: they fall into regular patterns that make sense and that fit with an overall system of values" (ibid.: 218). Lastly, although precise specifications are few, it is now believed that public opinion does affect the making of foreign policy. Influence flows in both directions: Leaders use information about attitudes "for the purpose of leading, persuading, or manipulating the public" (ibid.: 232). And there is evidence that the public reciprocates, for example, at times to restrain extreme positions that political leaders may hold (Nincic 1992; Holsti 1992). In short, the recent literature depicts the public as being not much better informed but more rational—even wiser—than was previously believed.

Of greatest interest to us here is how public opinion toward foreign policy issues is structured. Consider first the number of dimensions along which opinion is believed to fall. In the early postwar period, it was assumed that a single internationalist—isolationist dimension sufficed, and survey questions were posed accordingly. By the late 1970s, and especially once Ronald Reagan came to office, it was deemed desirable to differentiate liberal from conservative variants of internationalism. The former was soon recast as multilateralism, the latter as unilateralism, and both were contrasted with isolationism (Holsti and Rosenau 1979; Wittkopf 1986). But that distinction, in turn, left ambiguous where views on the role of force fit in. Debates continued about how many new categories were required and whether they were appropriately considered attitude "types" or underlying "dimensions" that generate types. Multilateralism initially was introduced as an attitude type, but more recently it has been identified empirically, by means of factor analysis, as an underlying dimension by William Chittick and colleagues (Chittick, Billingsley, and Travis 1995). Indeed, they distinguish multilateralism from other attitudinal dimensions by virtue of a factor they term "identity." By identity they mean how inclusive the referent community is or how transcultural the values are that respondents' foreign policy attitudes encompass (for example, support for narrow particularistic interests versus support for universal human rights). In this scheme, nativism is closely associated with a preference for unilateralism in foreign policy, and a more expansive identity with multilateralism.

There is also some evidence to suggest that a hierarchy exists in the structure of foreign policy opinions. Hurwitz and Peffley (1987; also see Hurwitz, Peffley, and Seligson 1993) tested a model suggesting that attitudes on specific foreign policy issues reflect more general foreign policy "postures" (isolationism, for example). These postures, in turn, are constrained by general beliefs or "core values" (such as patriotism or the [im]morality of warfare). Because the questions included in their survey concerned US–Soviet relations at a single point in time during the cold war the model cannot help us directly here, but the idea of such a hierarchy is highly suggestive.

In sum, it is not possible at this time to perform direct public opinion-based tests of the relationship I have imputed between the inorganic form of American nationalism and multilateral world order principles. But what we do know about the structure of public opinion certainly does not contradict the existence of such a relationship and, indeed, lends it some support. That multilateralism features prominently in foreign policy attitudes is no longer in dispute; the only question is whether it functions merely as a category of attitudes that rises or falls with events, or as an underlying dimension that reflects identity factors and generates attitudes. Furthermore, our imputed relationship is consistent with the hierarchical model of foreign policy attitudes—where core beliefs constrain postures, and postures predict attitudes.

To conclude, the manner in which certain domestic ethnic differences are accommodated as well as the structure of public opinion on foreign policy issues suggest that our hypothesis is, at minimum, plausible. Sense of self as nation, and preferences for world order principles, both reflect a bias in the direction of greater openness, inclusiveness, and nondiscrimination than one would expect in the case of a country solidly rooted in an organic specificity of nationhood.

A third evidentiary source—and by far the most direct—would open up if one could assume that the leaders who were doing the things described in the previous section knew what they were doing, and that they knew what they were saying when, as Wilson did, they described multilateral world order principles as "American principles." But that source is still inadmissible because we know that leaders do and say things for a variety of reasons other than those they state. So I turn next to the vexing role of ideational factors and political discourse in the framing of US world order policy.

Ideas, idealism, and interests

Because we are entering hotly contested terrain here, I want to be very clear about the specification of my argument and its scope. In the first section, I argued that at the three previous instances in this century of reconstructing the international order, American leaders advocated multilateral organizing principles as a "vision," borrowing Kissinger's term, to animate the support of the American public. After the outbreak of the cold war this vision, in the security sphere, was folded into the process of balancing the Soviet Union, but it did not disappear. In the present section, I argued that this vision evokes organizing principles that are embedded in America's own inorganic form of nationalism, and I offered the best evidence available in support of my contention. What I want to show now is that the conventional tendency to dismiss such instances of political persuasion as being "mere rhetoric" or to attribute them to "idealism" is problematic in the cases under consideration.

Let us begin with the issue of rhetoric. Based on what is known about Wilson, when he addressed the Senate in 1917 and spoke of the "American principles" for which the nation would fight imperial Germany the odds are that he believed what he said. Nonetheless, it is theoretically possible that material interests alone drove the decision and that he was dressing it up in rhetorical garb. But is the same likely to be true of FDR's explaining to Anthony Eden why he believed that the American public would not support a spheres-of-influence approach to the organization of post-World War II security relations and that a universal form, therefore, should be established?

Is it plausible of Eisenhower when he wrote to his brother Milton that "the establishment of collective security by cooperation is a *must* for the future of our type of civilization"? Or when he wrote in his diary that "we must seek . . . collective security for the free world. Any alternative promises little more than tragic failure"? (FDR was quoted above; the Eisenhower quotations are from Ninkovich 1994: 212–213, italics are Eisenhower's). Leaders do not usually practice mere rhetoric in private dealings with close war-time allies, let alone in letters to siblings or in their own diaries.

Perhaps rhetoric is not the appropriate term, then. Perhaps idealism is at work. The case against characterizing these episodes as expressions of idealism consists of several parts. To begin, of the four presidents involved in our story only Wilson has ever been accused of being an outright idealist—and he not entirely correctly, as John Milton Cooper shows persuasively in his joint biography of TR and Wilson (1983).[21] It is true that the others were accused of succumbing, at times, to something realists called the Wilsonian legacy and, thus, of being indirect idealists by descent—as we saw above, FDR regarding the UN, Truman at the time of the creation of NATO, and Eisenhower during the EDC debate and at Suez. But that charge, in turn, triggers two responses.

First, the author of the Wilsonian legacy doctrine, E. H. Carr in his classic polemic, *The Twenty Years' Crisis* (1946), lumped together the shrinking band of liberal internationalists with just about every other strand of idealism in interwar America, and pinned them all on the alleged lingering effects of Wilsonianism. But by far the largest segment of American idealists at the time were isolationists, not Wilsonian internationalists. The Kellogg–Briand pact, which promised, implausibly, to end war by treaty, was one of Carr's prize illustrations. Yet, as Jonas points out (1966: 49), William Borah, Republican of Idaho, "did more than any other man to bring about approval of the Kellogg–Briand Pact by the Senate in 1929." And Borah had been a leading irreconcilable in 1919, forming what he called a "Battalion of Death" to prevent ratification of the League's covenant. Such anomalies, however, have not deterred successive generations of critics from perpetuating the "Wilsonian legacy" myth.

Second, there is scant evidence that any of these leaders acted contrary to American interests, at least as they perceived them. Wilson was trying to solve the same geopolitical puzzle that drove Theodore Roosevelt: the world is closing in on the United States, how do we engage in it? The post-World War II group was equally interest driven. The issue becomes complicated, however, because the same domestic ideational factors that were reflected in the world order vision these leaders articulated *also* shaped their conception of American interests. Consider, again, FDR's conversation with Eden about spheres of influence. Some abstract entity called the United States might well have found its postwar security interests fully satisfied by the four policemen scheme FDR had initially favored. But what FDR said to Eden, in effect, was that the *real* United States, given his understanding of what it was and where it was, would not accept, or might drop out of, a postwar security order based on spheres of influence. And so off to the UN it was. Similarly, Truman was not convinced that the various available alternatives to NATO's indivisible security commitments would suffice, then and even less so in the future, to keep the US engaged in Europe, as a result of which American interests, to Kennan's horror, became defined in considerably more expansive terms than the mere abstract strategic logic of the situation alone would have dictated. And Eisenhower, while accepting this expansive conception of US interests, also feared that some of them would seem so remote to the American public that only collective legitimation would prove successful, and that only collective efforts would avoid exhausting America's treasury and morale.

But are we not left then, in the final analysis, with the old realist saw that the American people are idealist, and that sophisticated leaders are forced to play on that idealism to get anything done? That may or may not be true in general terms; the contention is too sweeping to tackle fully here. But within the scope of the present argument, I would make the following observation. This issue is an issue in the first place because of America's geopolitical constitution. If the United States were landlocked in the middle of a dense strategic complex made up of relative equals, in which the external sector loomed large, chances are that the challenge these American leaders struggled with would have been resolved long ago. But even today, as Eric Nordlinger demonstrated in his provocative last book (1995), it is possible to travel a long way down the road of isolationism without appearing foolish.[22] Keenly aware of that fact, this cadre of leaders acted on Weber's dictum that ideas are interests, too. Moreover, their belief that these American ideas also would enjoy some efficacy abroad does not betray undue naiveté because, as noted, the American nationalism on which the ideas drew itself is founded on principles that are more universalistic and transcultural than those of most other nations.

It is ironic that the American public's attitudes regarding why and how it would consent to helping construct or reconstruct the international order, so deeply rooted in America's fundamental geopolitical reality, should be confused with idealism by none other than realist theorists of geopolitics.

These issues are not easily resolved, nor is it easy to persuade those who hold very different views. My objective here is more modest. I contend that within its specified scope conditions—American policy postures toward the construction/reconstruction of the international order—the standard objections one would anticipate to my argument do not trump. The world order visions articulated by American leaders on these occasions cannot be summarily dismissed as rhetoric, nor can they be readily swept into the convenient dustbin of idealism. What is more, the interaction of ideational factors and material interests at these junctures was highly complex: ideas not only shaped how interests were pursued, but in some cases helped define the interests the United States subsequently did pursue. Finally, the conceptual bridge that FDR, Truman, and Eisenhower built between America's sense of exceptionalism, on the one hand, and the international order, on the other, is a remarkable achievement—not only for keeping the United States engaged, but also for helping to transform Europe and to institute multilateral organizing principles globally to a far greater extent than would have been the case otherwise: in economic policy, decolonization, human rights, democracy promotion, and even in the sphere of security relations.

CONCLUSION

This interplay between ideas and interests in the framing of US policy toward "remaking" the international order has a number of practical implications for the post-cold war era.

Sustained American engagement to help create and maintain a stable international order historically has not been part of the natural international order of things. Our discussion has shown that achieving it has been a non-trivial task. The Cold War era may well prove an interlude in a more enduring American dilemma: how to be politically not only in the world but of it when no overarching external threat exists. Adjusting US foreign policy to the post-Cold War international context entails, therefore, more than modifying the scope and intensity of specific commitments to fit with narrow, case-by-case strategic assessments. It also requires that some framework of policy be devised that makes sense to the American people and which specifies milieu goals that they will aspire to.

One major difference between the earlier instances of remaking the international order and now is, of course, the institutional legacy FDR and his successors left behind—which to some extent functions in ways that would not surprise them. The war in Bosnia–Herzegovina is a case in point, albeit belatedly and grudgingly so. On the eve of the 1992 presidential election the Bush administration had little desire to become militarily involved. Once in office, the Clinton administration, despite its campaign rhetoric, focused on domestic issues and followed suit. But the institutional tripwire FDR had planted ultimately kicked in. When the United States did become involved it was in large measure to salvage the ill-fated UN operation and, even more importantly, the reputation of NATO.

But relatively few such tripwires exist in the security sphere, and the future effectiveness of those that do exist cannot be taken for granted. Our analysis suggests the outlines of a US policy posture toward the post-cold war international security order: to build on existing institutional bases by coupling continued US engagement to strategies of transformation designed to achieve greater indigenous sustainability. US security policy in Europe and East Asia, the two major cold war theaters, as well as toward UN peace operations in third world regional disputes, can all be fruitfully approached with this aim in mind.

NATO is central to all "what now?" considerations regarding the future of the transatlantic security community (see Chapter 9 below). US political attention has focused almost entirely on NATO expansion into Central and Eastern Europe. But building up the capacity of the European Union (EU) to act militarily within NATO and having eastward expansion be more of a European-led process, coupled with the EU's own expansion, would more effectively ensure a sustainable basis for this security community. It would be more equitable toward the United States, and thus enjoy greater long-run domestic support in this country; it would be less likely to create a self-fulfilling prophecy vis-à-vis Russia—triggering a Russian threat where none now exist; and it would more effectively lock in economic reforms, democratic transitions, and the protection of minority rights in Eastern and Central Europe than a US-led expansion of NATO, which has little day-to-day practical leverage over any of these developments. There is no better venue to begin this process than to prepare the West European Union, the EU's fledgling security arm, to assume from NATO's Bosnia mission the inevitable long-term peacekeeping role.

No NATO equivalent exists in East Asia. The US bilateral alliances with South Korea and Japan, instituted at the time of the Korean war, served as the cornerstones of US containment policy. With the end of the cold war these alliances have become politically exposed in the United States ("why are we defending our most successful economic competitors?") and in the region (especially US ground forces on Okinawa). Furthermore, the case for a continued US military presence in East Asia has to be made to the American public almost entirely on balance-of-power grounds ("engaging" an emerging China, reassuring neighbors about one another), which is typically not a compelling basis, as we have seen. Japan has taken modest steps to deepen and diversify its self-defense role, but remains constrained by regional suspicions. The strategy that follows from our analysis is for the United States to use its alliances as a means to promote greater regional security cooperation. This would involve incorporating into the emerging regional power balance as many mechanisms as possible that promise to enhance transparency and help build confidence, with the aim of achieving viable regional frameworks for conflict resolution in the medium term and moving toward the ideal of a regional security community in the long run. Modest regional and subregional building blocks are beginning to take hold. Potentially the most important is the ASEAN (Association of Southeast Asian Nations) Regional Forum (ARF) (see Dibb 1995; Leifer 1996). The Australian security specialist, Paul Dibb, points out that solidifying these mechanisms will not be easy, due to the absence of a cooperative tradition in, as well as the sheer strategic complexity of, the region. But at the same time, he believes, "there is the sense [in the region] that an opportunity exists that should be exploited before it is too late" (Dibb 1995: 67).

Finally, after a brief post-cold war euphoria, the United Nations is in a precarious state. Member countries were quick to assign it new tasks but not to upgrade its capabilities—or even, notably in the case of the United States, to pay the bills. Clearly, the UN performed poorly in Somalia and Bosnia. But if Soviet armies had marched across the central front in Europe in the early 1950s, NATO would not have performed well either because it had not yet been equipped to. It took considerable time, effort, and money for it to become the effective military institution that we now take for granted. The point is simply this: to whatever extent member states wish to ratchet up the UN's role they must also upgrade its capabilities.

Support for the UN among the American public remains high—in 1995, according to a Republican polling firm, 69 percent of the public supported relying on UN forces to deal with conflicts that did not directly threaten the United States, compared with 17 percent in favor of unilateral US action (UNA–USA 1995). Schneider's analysis of the 1994 Chicago Council survey (1997: 27) found that "support for strengthening the United Nations as 'a very high foreign policy goal of the United States' was 51 percent, its highest level in 20 years," and the only significant internationalist indicator to rise. Moreover, "a majority supported US participation in international peace-keeping forces. Fewer than 1 in 5 said we should not take part" (ibid.). The public was split over whether the United States should accept a UN commander or insist on its own. Ironically, at 54 percent, the UN enjoyed higher approval ratings among the American public than any branch of the US government (UNA–USA 1995).

But these views, it seems, either are not as salient in voting or simply not as well organized politically as opposition to the UN. The Republican Congress has been hostile, the Democratic administration chastened though generally supportive. The US military has become quietly engaged with the UN, however, convinced that "gray area" conflicts—beyond the scope of traditional peacekeeping but short of all-out warfare—are here to stay, and that outside the NATO and East Asian contexts collective responses through the UN in many instances will prove the most viable and sustainable option. As argued in greater detail in Chapter 10, below, for the UN to become an effective collective instrument in gray-area peace operations, major doctrinal innovations are necessary, predeployment planning and more standardized training must be instituted, and its capacity to field and command forces enhanced.

9   NATO and the transatlantic security community

History is "made," for better or worse, by decisions such as whether and how to expand NATO to include countries in Central and Eastern Europe. Decisions of this sort can define the basic contours of an entire era. It is more than a little disturbing, therefore, that the issue of NATO expansion looks so perplexing when viewed through the lenses of conventional international relations theory. According to structural realists, NATO already should, or soon will, have faded into irrelevance (Mearsheimer 1990; Waltz 1993). Neoliberal institutionalism stresses, correctly, that demand for NATO's services is as strong as ever (Keohane and Martin 1995), but the countries that are objectively in greatest need of those services are not even in the queue for expanded membership (the Baltics, Ukraine, Belarus). Finally, even though a stable and friendly Russia is America's single most vital interest in that region, advocates of NATO expansion inspired by both bodies of theory acknowledge that it potentially could pose a threat to future US–Russia relations.

The essay in this chapter (1997a) looks to a more communitarian tradition of theorizing to make the case for a different NATO strategy. Drawing on the insights of Karl Deutsch and his colleagues (1957), it argues that NATO plays a critical role today in completing the transformation of the traditional conduct of European power-politics that was initiated by the Truman and Eisenhower administrations. The future of the transatlantic security community, as well as its expansion into Central and Eastern Europe, are best served by consolidating NATO's West European pillar, and by having expansion be more of a West European-led process.

Few observers challenge the proposition that a tightly coupled security community exists today among the nations of North America, the European Union, and NATO. No country within this transatlantic region expects to go to war with any other. Apart from Greece and Turkey, none devotes financial or organizational resources to the possibility of war with any other—or, as far as we know, even has military contingency plans for such an eventuality. Observers do differ, however, on whether this security community can be sustained, let alone expanded, in the new era, in the absence of the cohesive bond that the Soviet threat once exerted (Harries 1993; Mearsheimer 1990).

NATO is central to all "what now?" considerations regarding the transatlantic security community. In American political circles, attention has focused almost entirely on the issue of NATO expansion into Central and Eastern Europe as "the key security question facing the West" (Glaser 1993:

10). This preoccupation is largely driven by three factors: a widely-held belief that expansion is the most effective means of sustaining NATO and, thereby, of maintaining a vital US role in European security relations; a genuine desire to reduce security anxieties of Central and East European states by including them in a broader security community; and, perversely on the part of some in Congress, because almost no matter how it is packaged current scenarios for NATO expansion entail an anti-Russian element.

In contrast, I argue that deepening the relationship between NATO and the European Union (EU) is more critical to the long-term future of the transatlantic security community than immediate NATO expansion; that pushing ahead with expansion prior to deepening, far from sustaining the transatlantic security community, potentially undermines it; that a US-led NATO expansion permits EU members to get off the hook of adjusting their own institutions and practices to accommodate their Eastern neighbors; that a European-led eastward expansion delivers greater promise, poses fewer risks, and is more equitable vis-à-vis the United States; and that such an overall strategic package is closely in keeping with initial plans for NATO that its American founders had in mind.

The adoption by NATO's foreign ministers of the Combined Joint Task Forces concept at their Berlin meeting in June 1996 marked an important step in the right direction. But it was just that: one step. It left many pressing questions unanswered and the momentum for at least partial early expansion unimpeded.

The concept of security communities is largely alien to the standard logic of strategic studies, the conceptual lenses through which the future of NATO is typically considered. Hence, I begin by briefly summarizing the main attributes of security communities. I then go on to explore their relationship to the future structure of NATO.

SECURITY COMMUNITIES

The concept of security community was devised by students of regional integration in the 1950s, at a time when the original six in Europe were in the process of creating the European Common Market, to describe a state of affairs toward which they believed Europe was heading (Deutsch et al. 1957; for a suggestive update, see Adler and Barnett 1996). A security community was defined as a group of political units whose relationships exhibit "dependable expectations of peaceful change," that is, the "assurance that members will not fight each other physically, but will settle their disputes in some other way" (ibid.: 5). Expectations of peaceful change tend to be most dependable, the historical research suggested, the more they reflect cognitive bonds of "'we-feeling,' trust, and mutual consideration" among the constituent units—a *sense* of community, in short (ibid.: 36). The development of such bonds, in turn, is aided by a number of background conditions, in particular a "compatibility of the main values" as to the political, economic, and legal institutions and practices (ibid.: 46, 66).

Historically, security communities have tended to form around "core areas": at the national level, Prussia in the process of nineteenth-century German unification, Piedmont in Italy; internationally, Sweden in the pluralistic Scandinavian security community that began to take hold in the early years of this century, the United States in the more tightly coupled transatlantic security community since the 1950s.[1] These core areas take initiatives, act as stabilizers, and provide the potential for mutual economic rewards as well as the high levels and diverse flows of social communications that facilitate the growth of we-feeling and trust.

Security commitments typically follow and complement economic and cultural ties in the formation of security communities. Indeed, military alliances have turned out to be "a relatively poor pathway" unless they were embedded in a broader project of political, economic and social integration (ibid.: 190). The creation of NATO itself followed the Marshall Plan by two years. US policymakers saw the Marshall Plan as the primary vehicle for European reconstruction—its necessary condition, as it were—and only gradually moved toward NATO as a reinforcing security mechanism—the sufficient condition. Similarly, Spain's admission into NATO in 1982 was meant to complement its entry into the European Economic Community (now European Union).

In explaining the existence of the transatlantic security community today, it is difficult to determine precisely the relative causal weights that are attributable to the Soviet threat, transatlantic security commitments, West European economic integration, and common bonds of civil society, market economy, and constitutional democracy. But without the first NATO itself almost certainly would not have been established. Accordingly, it would be astonishing if the significant decline of the external threat were not reflected in demands, on both sides of the Atlantic, for new forms of transatlantic security ties. At the same time, the EU has emerged as a "core area" in its own right, far more capable than in the past to assume roles and generate benefits by which core areas sustain security communities. In short, no issue is more critical to the future viability of the transatlantic security community than realigning the division of responsibilities within NATO between the United States and Western Europe.

STRENGTHENING THE EUROPEAN PILLAR

As noted above, in the 1950s the United States served as the core area around which a transatlantic security community was constructed. There was no alternative. The United States accounted for roughly half of the world's total economic output, and it was the only nation capable, politically and militarily, of pulling together the Western alliance. Today, however, with a larger population and economic size than the United States, the EU offers the potential for establishing a more balanced relationship.

Moreover, as François Heisbourg (1992) correctly notes, continued success of European unification is *the* critical factor in determining whether Western Europe itself remains a functioning security community or reverts to a pre-1914 balance-of-power system, with all the potential sources of instability that would entail. Outside a successful EU, there is no guarantee that the Franco-German partnership would hold, for example, or that Germany would not pose heightened security concerns in the Eastern half of the continent, including Russia. At best, Western Europe without a successful EU would be fragmented and inward-looking, and it would likely cast doubt on the future of NATO itself.

In addition, the EU is better equipped than NATO to deal with many of the non-military tasks the United States, in particular, has sought to place on NATO's shoulders vis-à-vis Central and Eastern Europe. The benefits of associate status and, even more so, membership in the EU—from lower entry barriers for exports to transfer payments—provide it with far greater day-to-day leverage over the states in its orbit to reinforce economic and democratic reforms and encourage the protection of minority rights. And the desire to sustain European integration is by far the most effective deterrent against EU members being drawn into opposing sides of ethnic or any other kinds of conflicts on the EU's periphery.[2] NATO lacks concrete leverage for such tasks. Indeed, it has shown itself to be incapable of resolving the most serious ethnic conflict among its members (Cyprus), while accommodating member states that have, at one time or another, been decidedly non-democratic in character (Greece, Portugal).

Finally, the quest for NATO membership by Central and East European countries is not driven primarily by specific threats to their security. Poland and Hungary have shortened the terms of military conscription, and the Polish as well as Czech armies have reduced some divisions and disbanded others (Brown 1995: 37)—hardly actions of states that feel militarily threatened. Rather, as Czech President Václav Havel has eloquently described it (1994: 4), these countries are asking for affirmation that they belong to the West: "If we in 'postcommunist countries' call for a new order, if we appeal to the West not to close itself off to us, and if we demand a radical reevaluation of the new situation, then this is not because we are concerned about our own security and stability . . . We are concerned about the destiny [in our countries] of the values and principles that communism denied, and in whose name we resisted communism and ultimately brought it down." But that desire is far more effectively met by practical economic, social, and political ties with their West European neighbors in the EU than by the mere extension of NATO security guarantees.

In short, these are compelling reasons why policymakers should attend to the challenge of recalibrating the division of responsibilities within NATO between North America and Europe. This challenge is more critical to the future of the transatlantic security community than NATO enlargement. NATO's European pillar must be strengthened and its relationship with the EU better articulated. What might a new organizing concept look like?

An indivisible transatlantic security link remains essential, for reasons Henry Kissinger (1994b: A27) puts well: "Without America, Europe turns into a peninsula at the tip of Eurasia, unable to find equilibrium much less unity . . . Without Europe, America will become an island off the shores of Eurasia condemned to a kind of pure balance-of-power politics that does not reflect its national genius." In addition, the United States possesses military capabilities that even a fully united Europe needs but would be hard pressed to match.[3]

These considerations suggest the desirability of NATO moving toward a division of labor whereby the United States provides security guarantees, strategic systems, logistical and intelligence capabilities, and limited ground troops to a more balanced collective defense and peacekeeping effort, one in which Europe is obliged—and also permitted—to organize itself to play a larger role than is now the case. The June 1996 Berlin meeting of NATO foreign ministers marked progress in this direction.

Most significantly, the foreign ministers adopted provisions for a new command-and-control concept known as Combined Joint Task Forces (CJTF), first accepted in principle at NATO's January 1994 Brussels summit (NATO 1996; for background, see Barry 1996). The CJTF arrangement is intended to give NATO headquarters structures that are more flexible and forces that are more mobile for contingency operations beyond NATO's traditional collective defense role, inscribed in Article 5 of the North Atlantic Treaty. Nucleus staffs for CJTFs will be established by "dual hatting" selected personnel within existing NATO commands.

By facilitating the use of NATO military capabilities and assets in a manner that is "separable but not separate" from NATO's integrated command, CJTFs make it possible for the Western European Union (WEU), the EU's designated defense component, to lead NATO-supported crisis management and peacekeeping missions, and for these missions to include as participants countries that are neither NATO nor EU member states. (The CJTF arrangement technically is in place in NATO's Bosnian Implementation Force [IFOR], though the overall operation remains under US command.) Such operations will require unanimous approval by the North Atlantic Council, but not actual participation of all NATO members. At one and the same time, then, CJTFs contribute to diversifying NATO's mission, building a European security and defense identity within NATO, enhancing NATO's Partnership for Peace with the countries of Central and Eastern Europe as well as the former Soviet republics—and, as a result, CJTFs have been a key factor in France's military *rapprochement* with NATO. Small wonder that Robert Hunter, US envoy to NATO, hailed this as "the alliance's most significant modernization" (quoted in Fitchett 1996: 7).

Several complex issues remain to be worked out, however. Among them is the elaboration of European command arrangements within NATO for

WEU-led operations, and provisions for the identification and release of the "separable but not separate" capabilities and assets to them. Their most vexing aspect concerns the role of the United States in operations led by the WEU in which the United States plays only a limited or no direct role. It arises in at least three ways, each more problematic than the previous.

First, many of the assets the WEU would utilize are American assets, including aircraft, communications equipment, and intelligence systems. Acceptable methods for allocating costs and liability will have to be devised, but should not prove inordinately difficult. However, the United States will also want to monitor the use of its assets, and the line between monitoring and exacting operational approval is murky. Second, even though the United States may not be otherwise involved in a mission, the operation of many of these assets will require American personnel. Such differential involvement in missions is bound to generate differences in perceptions of threats and preferences for action—as was the case in the UN's Bosnia operation, in which France and Britain, but not the United States, had forces on the ground. Resolving these differences is a non-trivial task. Third, because any WEU-led contingency operation could escalate and pose a threat to NATO territory, the lines of command of such non-Article 5 operations must lead back seamlessly to NATO's command structure, at the top of which sits an American general whose superiors are in Washington, DC. It is not clear how far down into WEU-led operations fears about potential escalation will reach.

These potential sources of tension will exist if the United States *supports* a WEU-led contingency operation but elects not to participate in it; a NATO Policy Coordination Group has been established to manage them in actual cases. But what if the United States were *opposed*? In that event, said by the United States to be unlikely, presumably there would be no operation. This arrangement is acceptable all around today because Europe lacks the requisite military capabilities and assets. But it is hard to imagine a US veto as a permanent solution for the EU's security and defense identity (ESDI) if and as Europe comes to acquire a greater capacity to act.

Moreover, keep in mind that these institutional innovations in NATO concern only non-Article 5 operations—that is, crisis management and peacekeeping, but not the collective defense of NATO's core territory. Two latent issues regarding the scope of ESDI lurk down the road, however, and if they emerge into the open they will implicate Article 5 as well.

As matters now stand, ESDI does not exist in any practical terms apart from the possibility of WEU-led CJTFs, presumably using Eurocorps and other Euro-designated NATO forces.[4] Hence, ESDI is limited to non-Article 5 operations. All EU member states, including France, accept this minimalist ESDI concept at this time. But will they remain satisfied with it when serious anomalies emerge? For example, under this concept the EU will remain unable to promise benefits of collective defense to its members who are not also members of NATO—even if they have associated themselves with the

WEU, which has its own Article 5 provision and which Maastricht designated the EU's defense component.[5] And yet, should NATO expand as planned, EU member states that are also members of NATO will be required to defend new non-EU states. That eventuality poses an acute dilemma: If ESDI remains permanently subordinated to NATO and the EU is obliged to accommodate differential zones of security within it while helping to protect non-members, the EU's own evolution as a political union would be truncated. But if the EU were to activate its own collective defense commitments through the WEU it would compete with and threaten to undermine NATO and the transatlantic security ties. NATO planners and policymakers prefer to think of these issues as being premature, so there has been little public discussion of the Herculean task of devising a solution that avoids either extreme.[6]

The other fundamental ESDI-related issue that enters the collective peripheral vision of NATO officialdom from time to time, only to disappear again, concerns the role within ESDI of British and French nuclear forces. As long ago as January 1992, then-French President François Mitterrand, feeling expansive about the prospects of European security cooperation, mused aloud about a European doctrine for a joint nuclear deterrent (*The Economist* 1992: 48). Understandably, in view of conflicted interests in Europe, including in Britain and France, as well as across the Atlantic, the status quo prevails. If ESDI were to become a greater reality, however, Mitterrand's musings might have to be revisited. But the issue could surface even before then. American analysts in the tradition of *realpolitik* are persuaded that Germany, as part of the process of becoming a "normal" great power, will seek to acquire "the full spectrum of great power capabilities, including nuclear weapons" (Layne 1993: 37; also see Waltz 1993). Germany today shows no such inclination. Nevertheless, it is possible to imagine that it could become desirable all around to devise such a joint deterrent as part of ESDI to lock in Germany's present posture. Any movement in that direction would deeply implicate NATO's Article 5.

This set of issues concerning the relationship between NATO and the EU, then, go to the very heart of both organizations and are truly among the most intellectually complex and politically charged the alliance has ever faced. Serious missteps in any direction could undermine the transatlantic security community. Accordingly, they deserve far more attention than they have received, especially in the United States. Moreover, none of these issues is made easier by NATO expansion, on which American attention has been riveted. In fact, expansion makes several more difficult to resolve.

THE PERILS OF PREMATURE EXPANSION

The idea of NATO expansion to include, in the near future, at least Poland, Hungary, and the Czech Republic enjoys broad bipartisan support in Washington. It is seen as a less pressing issue in most allied capitals in

Europe but no NATO member is opposed. The standard arguments, pro and con, are well rehearsed by now and require only capsule summaries.[7]

Three main arguments have been advanced in favor of expansion. The first contends that it will deter any residual or future threats of Russian aggression in Central and Eastern Europe, and reassure the countries of that region that they will be defended from it. Skeptics counter that this move has all the makings of a self-fulfilling prophecy, potentially creating the very condition it is intended to hedge against. As Philip Zelikow, a former Bush administration official, puts it regarding one of the three likely early admits (1996: 13): "There are no acute areas of political tension between Poland and Russia, other than those created by the NATO enlargement issue itself."

The second argument in support holds that expansion is necessary to avoid the existence of a security vacuum between Germany and Russia—an area Kissinger (1993: 24) has described as a strategic "no-man's land." Skeptics respond that the notion of a security vacuum is a metaphor, not a well-tested hypothesis, and thus is a dubious guide to policy. Moreover, by including a small number of new states within its defense perimeter NATO would specifically exclude and, thereby, possibly degrade the security of others that have greater reason to be worried to start with—notably the Baltic states and Ukraine. No current scenario for NATO expansion includes these countries. The term "Koreanization" has gained currency to depict this result, referring to Dean Acheson's failure, in his January 1950 National Press Club speech, explicitly to include South Korea within the US defensive perimeter.

The third argument has to do with locking in democratic gains and economic reforms as well as containing ethnic conflicts. We have already noted that NATO lacks instruments to accomplish these tasks whereas the promise of EU membership offers considerable leverage. Skeptics add that by far the strategically most significant ethnic minority in the entire region are the Russians left behind in the former Soviet Republics—again notably in the Baltics and Ukraine. Current plans for NATO expansion would do nothing to relieve that problem and, on the contrary, could worsen it by encouraging nationalist factions in Moscow to demand greater protection for ethnic Russians in the "near abroad" as NATO advances toward them.

Faced with these not insubstantial rejoinders, proponents of NATO expansion have begun to think seriously about, and propose solutions for, the second-order problems their recommended expansion would create. These proposals consist largely of special arrangements, programs, and promises for the excluded areas, the security of which NATO expansion might worsen, and/or an agreement or even treaty with Russia, in which NATO expansion is bound to pose domestic political problems (for Eastern Europe, see Asmus and Nurick 1996; Larrabee 1996; for Russia, Brzezinski 1993; Kissinger 1994b). These proposals would merit consideration if the security rationale for immediate NATO expansion were compelling. On balance, however, it is difficult to reach that conclusion. In addition, whereas promises to the Baltic states and possibly Ukraine might gain Congressional support, any meaningful agreement with Russia is more problematic precisely because NATO expansion appeals to some in Congress on anti-Russian grounds.

Further, NATO's Partnership for Peace, which began as an expedient, has become a permanent fixture of considerable practical utility. It comprises all Central and East European states as well as the former Soviet Republics, including Russia; it carries out joint military planning and exercises and has developed other means to adapt the national military forces and equipment of interested Partner states to NATO standards; it encourages civilian control over militaries; and several Partner states, including Russia, are participating in IFOR. NATO's June 1996 Berlin meeting agreed to further enhance the Partnership. Early NATO expansion to include a few could jeopardize these gains for many. That risk, too, might be worth taking if the rationale in favor of admitting the few were compelling; but it is not.

It should be noted that few of the risks attending the projection of Western security guarantees eastward—in particular, the danger of creating a self-fulfilling prophecy with regard to Russia, and potentially worsening the security situation of excluded states—are posed by a European-led process: via the WEU, or by EU enlargement coupled with simultaneous NATO expansion. It is the centrality of the American component of a NATO-only expansion that creates the problems. Clearly, a WEU-led process would require that further progress first be made on some of the unresolved ESDI issues discussed above. And EU enlargement would require the West Europeans to pay the greater price. But the ESDI changes are desirable in their own right, as we have seen. And there is every reason to expect Western Europe to take the lead responsibility for integrating the East, just as the United States did for the West in the postwar years.

This last point suggests the next. All the attention that the possibility of NATO expansion has attracted has let the EU off the hook. Opening up EU markets to the exports of Central and East European countries would do more to support their economic and political transitions than any act or utterance by NATO. No single external measure would do more to sustain reforms in Poland than reform of the EU's Common Agricultural Policy. Yet American policymakers as well as leaders in Central and Eastern Europe have blandly accepted the EU's contention that its enlargement is so complex and so costly that, *ipso facto*, it cannot take place for some years. As Zelikow shrewdly observes (1996: 15): "It is hard to avoid the impression that NATO membership is valued [by East and West Europeans alike] mainly as an alternative, largely symbolic gesture of inclusion." Washington's bipartisan triumphalist attitude toward NATO expansion permits Europe to get away with this.

Finally, as currently planned, NATO expansion would pose a potential threat to NATO's most distinctive feature, historically unprecedented for any alliance: its Article 5 commitment that an attack against one will be viewed as an attack against all, triggering the appropriate collective response. Recall that even during the cold war, facing a common enemy, and with five American divisions on the central front backed by a vast and lethal arsenal of nuclear weapons, NATO witnessed a running debate about the credibility of this commitment to Europe on the part of the United States—whether the United States would risk New York, Chicago, or Los Angeles for Paris, Rome, or London. Why should anyone believe that the United States would do so now for Warsaw, Budapest, or Prague?

NATO has five options to deal with this problem. First, it can suspend or eliminate Article 5 obligations altogether, as recommended recently by a former Clinton administration official (Kupchan 1996). Doing so would be a radical step because it would deprive NATO of the very feature that makes it unique—and of the indivisible security link between the United States and Europe. Second, NATO can ignore the problem and knowingly accept the fact that Article 5 commitments to the countries of Central and Eastern Europe are not credible. But doing that would undermine the indivisibility of Article 5 guarantees throughout the alliance. Third, NATO can extend partial commitments to Central and East European states that would not include Article 5 guarantees. It is unclear what the East would be getting, though, that it does not already have through the Partnership for Peace. Fourth, NATO can extend full commitments and undertake measures to firm up their credibility. But most advocates of NATO expansion are not prepared to recommend the most credible means of accomplishing that end—the physical coupling provided by placing NATO troops, including Americans, on the new front lines—because that, clearly, would be too provocative toward Russia, and too costly, besides.

That leaves the European option. If extending NATO's Article 5 obligations lacks credibility in part because there is no common enemy to defend *against*, an EU-led expansion would redirect the focus onto what its member states should be prepared to defend one another *for*: a European community not merely in a metaphorical sense, and no longer strictly in an aspirational sense, but increasingly in terms of the grubby details of everyday existence. A greater capacity for the EU to pursue a broader array of collective security tasks through the WEU—utilizing NATO's CJTFs for the foreseeable future—would become one of those grubby details.

In sum, our examination of the issues attending NATO expansion also points to the desirability of strengthening NATO's European pillar. It suggests an expansion strategy that is West European-driven, tied to EU accession. Such a strategy holds greater practical promise for the East and poses fewer risks, East or West. What is more, as we shall see next, it would also be more consistent with long-standing American objectives in Europe, which have been not to dominate but to transform its international politics.

THE PAST AS PROLOGUE

The fact that the United States came to the defense of Western Europe after World War II, despite its interwar isolationism, was not startling. The United States, too, felt threatened by the prospect of Soviet expansion. But the form of America's initiative was unusual. As noted in Chapter 8, both Presidents Harry Truman and Dwight Eisenhower, in addition to responding to the Soviet threat, also sought to transform the international politics of Western Europe, moving from a conventional balance-of-power system toward a security community that would ultimately be capable, in alliance with the United States, of sustaining itself.

It was John F. Kennedy's administration that coined the phrase "strengthening NATO's European pillar"—ironically, *after* reversing its predecessors' policies that had been aimed at precisely that objective. The reversal had to do largely with the strategic management of nuclear weapons. The Kennedy team devised doctrines that were very different from Eisenhower's "massive retaliation"—"to blow hell out of them in a hurry if they start anything," as Eisenhower once explained it. The new doctrine of "flexible response" was far more complex and subtle, and required far greater centralization of control over nuclear weapons. Secretary of Defense Robert McNamara criticized independent European nuclear deterrents in a major policy statement delivered at Ann Arbor in 1962, on the grounds that they were incompatible with the requirements of fighting "restrained" nuclear wars (Jervis 1989). This new nuclear policy generated corresponding institutional shifts in NATO's command arrangements. Further American-induced moves toward what is today called a European security and defense identity stopped. And France subsequently pulled out of NATO's military structure.

But that chapter in strategic history ended in 1989. European security no longer hinges on the centralized management of a balance of terror. Many of its dictates, therefore, have lost their meaning, many of its mindsets their relevance. Accordingly, the United States can now safely move toward a new version of the Truman–Eisenhower posture toward European security and the Atlantic alliance. The key is to build up NATO's European pillar—for its own sake, and to help project stability into Central and Eastern Europe.

10 UN forces: whither—or whether?

The end of the cold war created new possibilities for UN peace operations, but they were not nearly as unproblematic or unlimited as the early post-cold war euphoria anticipated. After Somalia and Bosnia many observers question if any opportunity at all remains, but now the sense of limits seems exaggerated. The United Nations is severely constrained by systemic factors, to be sure. But it remains unclear whether these operations were inherently destined to be defeated by such constraints, because governments and the UN Secretariat also poorly understood and managed more volitional aspects of the operations, over which they have greater control.

Chief among the volitional areas in which some improvement is possible are devising a more systematic doctrinal formulation for "gray area" peace operations—the terrain between traditional peacekeeping and all-out warfighting—and rationalizing the organization of command functions at UN headquarters. The essay in this chapter (1996b) recommends feasible changes in both. Their result would not turn the UN into a fully operational global collective security organization—that remains out of reach even if it were deemed desirable—but in terms of institutional evolution, they would be on par with the invention of peace-keeping itself.

The United Nations Security Council picked the hard way to determine the limits of UN military operations: embarrassment and even humiliation on the ground in Somalia and Bosnia, followed by outright retreat in the first and an inevitable hand-off to NATO in the second. How much credibility the UN has left beyond the domain of traditional peacekeeping is not clear. At the same time, the sentiment of retrenchment and retreat that has set in at the United Nations, many national capitals, and the media is premature. For, as a Hungarian scholar has noted, "the disgrace of the UN lies not so much in the fact that it could not get the job done in Bosnia, but that it still recycles the same old arguments about the hamstrungness of the organization, stopping short of actually spelling out what it is that the UN can do" (Sekerez 1996: 11). Some of the same muddled reasoning that first pushed the UN into this range of conflicts, in short, is now pushing it back out.

Critical assessments of so-called "gray area" UN peace operations— beyond peacekeeping but short of all-out warfighting—have tended to focus on two sets of factors. One is the ambiguous and often shifting political objectives assigned to such missions by the Security Council. The other concerns the UN's own administrative shortcomings. Both, of course, have been serious impediments to the UN's success. But there is also a third, mediating factor that has received far less attention than it deserves: lack of any doctrinal understanding of "gray area" operations together with a very poorly developed UN command structure. This essay identifies the key dimensions of both in the hope that doing so will clarify the choices that governments and UN officials must make concerning the future of "robust" UN peace operations. It may well be that, in the end, these operations have little or no future. But that fact should be established by far more rigorous examination and its analytical bases better understood than is now the case.

The first section briefly summarizes the model of UN military enforcement that the founders had in mind. The second section discusses the doctrinal confusion exhibited by recent robust UN peace operations, and sketches out the contours of an analytical model that may prove useful. The third section takes up the issue of command and control.

THE ENFORCEMENT SYSTEM

The enforcement provisions of the UN charter were designed by the major powers with the unraveling 1930s in mind: Manchuria, Ethiopia, and how the policy of appeasement, in David Fromkin's words (1995: 372), had "made the Germany of 1936, which could have been defeated by practically anybody in Europe, into the Germany of 1939, which could be defeated by practically nobody in Europe." Chapter VII of the charter provides for an escalating ladder of collective responses to interstate aggression, ranging from diplomatic isolation, to economic sanctions, and ultimately military actions. The key to the UN's credibility as a deterrent against aggression, it was widely believed in the waning months of World War II, was the last of these: unlike the League of Nations, the UN would have "teeth."

Creating an international military force in some form was a central concern at the four-power Dumbarton Oaks conference held in the summer of 1944 (Hilderbrand 1990). There were two alternatives: a standing international force or ad hoc arrangements providing national contingents when needed. Initially, almost all postwar planners favored a true international police force. But as time went on they drew away from the idea because of such practical difficulties as how to recruit, equip, base, train, transport, and command an international force, and also due to the realization that ad hoc arrangements were likely to arouse less domestic political opposition. President Franklin Roosevelt rejected the notion of "a superstate with its own police force and other paraphernalia of coercive power," favoring instead a mechanism for "joint action" by national forces (ibid.: 65).

Three UN charter provisions on military enforcement emerged from Dumbarton Oaks, representing a radical departure from previous peacetime experience. Under the first, largely reflecting US language, each member undertook to make available to the UN Security Council, "on its call" when needed to maintain international peace and security, armed forces, facilities, and other assistance, including rights of passage, in accordance with special agreements that were to be negotiated as soon as possible (Article 43). The agreements would specify the number and types of forces, as well as the kinds of facilities and other assistance, which each member was prepared to make available, and they were subject to the usual treaty ratification process of each member state.

The second provision reflected American and, even more so, Soviet interest in the special role of air forces. To enable the UN to take "urgent military measures," members that had the capability were asked to designate, on a stand-by basis, air contingents for combined international enforcement action (Article 45). They were to be governed by the same special agreements. The Soviet Union's interest presumably reflected the enormous losses they suffered at the hands of the invading German army during the war, and the desire to have all the help possible to intercept any future attack before it struck deep into its homeland. On the American side, the major advocate, not surprisingly, was the air force (Smith 1970: 49–51). But there was also great interest on political grounds because the use of air power, US policy-makers believed, would reduce the domestic difficulties involved in "sending our boys overseas" (Hilderbrand 1990: 142).

Third, at the suggestion of Britain, it was agreed to establish a Military Staff Committee comprising the national chiefs of staff of the Security Council's five permanent members (Article 47). The British drew on the successful precedent of the Combined Chiefs of Staff system with the United States for their joint campaigns in World War II. The Military Staff Committee was to advise and assist the Security Council on military matters within its jurisdiction, including the "strategic direction" of any armed forces placed at the Council's disposal. Questions regarding the actual command and control of such forces were left to be worked out subsequently.

In February 1946, the Security Council directed the Military Staff Committee, as its first task, to devise plans for the force agreements stipulated in Article 43. The committee met some 157 times during the next fifteen months, and reached agreements-in-principle on many issues. But by mid-1947 it became clear that its efforts had fallen victim to the escalating cold war. The negotiations foundered on the relative strength and composition of forces to be contributed by each of the permanent five. The final US position advocated—astonishingly, in retrospect—a combined total of 20 ground divisions or around 200,000 men, 1,250 bombers, 2,250 fighters, 3 battleships, 6 carriers, 15 cruisers, 84 destroyers, and 90 submarines. The Soviet Union favored a smaller combined force, consisting of 12 ground divisions, 600 bombers, 300 fighters, 5–6 cruisers, 24 destroyers, and 12 submarines (Bowett 1964: 12–18). Perhaps it was possible somehow to reconcile these two positions (Grove 1993: 180). But the Soviets, no doubt worried about Western dominance of UN enforcement activities, also divined a "principle of equality" pertaining to forces in the charter—in accord with which each of the permanent five would have been limited to the same type and size, thereby reducing all to the lowest level offered by any one of them. This interpretation was particularly problematical for the air component, because it would have lowered all contributions to the level of China's, which barely had an air force. It seems that, having solidified its control over the buffer states on its western borders, the Soviet Union no longer saw any pressing need for a collective air deterrent. Attempts to form UN stand-by forces were formally abandoned in August 1948.

The North Korean invasion of South Korea in June 1950 triggered the innovation of UN-authorized "coalition forces," utilized again in the Persian Gulf war forty years later. The Korean operation flew the UN flag whereas Operation Desert Storm did not, but the practical difference was negligible. It is unimaginable that General Douglas MacArthur, commander of UN forces in Korea, paid much heed to the UN when he ignored even his Washington superiors—and ultimately had to be sacked by President Truman for what amounted to insubordination.

There is no telling what might have happened if the stand-by forces negotiations had gone differently and agreements been reached. Even in a best-case scenario, the permanent five soon would have confronted the need to formulate novel doctrines for joint military operations because even at that time relatively few of the conflicts the UN faced were instances of clear-cut interstate aggression, fitting the model of military enforcement embedded in Chapter VII of the charter. Furthermore, they would have had to deal with the unresolved issues of command and control. In other words, the UN would have encountered much earlier in its life the practical military problems that came to afflict its peace operations once they were unshackled by the end of the cold war.

OPERATIONAL DOCTRINE

Neither the UN nor its member states strictly speaking have fully known what they have been doing in "gray area" peace operations, or how to do it. Frustration and failure, therefore, have been inevitable.[1] The problem is this. The UN distinguishes between two types of collective peace operations employing military forces: enforcement and peacekeeping. But its role in a rapidly growing number of conflicts has conformed to neither. As a result, these operations have wandered about in a conceptual void (Ruggie 1993d)—in Somalia and Bosnia with tragic consequences for their participants and for the UN itself. This problem would exist regardless of whether the UN were to have its own rapid deployment force, draws on dedicated stand-by forces, or is obliged to continue the practice of waiting for countries to volunteer troops. The critical issue is not where forces come from, but the objectives and rules of engagement governing their employment and deployment.

Enforcement is easy to grasp, and it was the use of force that the UN's architects envisaged. A specific act of aggression, or a more general set of hostile actions, are collectively identified as a threat to international peace and security and the aggressor state is subjected to an array of sanctions until its violation is reversed. Ultimately, enforcement can involve flat-out war-fighting—the "all necessary means" of Resolution 678, authorizing what became Operation Desert Storm. The UN does not have an institutionalized military enforcement capability of this sort and is unlikely soon to acquire one. Large-scale UN military enforcement, therefore, is almost certain to remain episodic and, as in the Korean and Gulf wars, consist of UN authorization and general political oversight together with execution by ad hoc coalitions of the willing.

Peacekeeping is nowhere mentioned in the UN charter. It was a practical invention, the doctrinal expression of which was a reflection of the 1956 Suez experience. Above all, peacekeeping is predicated on the consent of the parties, which typically have agreed to cease hostilities before a peacekeeping mission is deployed. Moreover, peacekeepers fight against neither side but play an impartial interpositionary role, monitoring a cease-fire or controlling a buffer zone. Indeed, they do not fight as such. They carry only light arms and are authorized to shoot only in self-defense—and, on occasion, in the defense of their mission if it comes under direct attack. Unlike fighting forces, then, peacekeepers are not intended to create the peace they are asked to keep. They accept the balance of forces on the ground and work within it. Ironically, this military weakness may be an advantage in that it reassures all parties that the peacekeeping force cannot affect the strategic balance to their disadvantage. In short, peacekeeping is a device to guarantee transparency, to reassure all sides that each is carrying out its promises.

Symbolizing the new post-cold war spirit, in January 1992 the UN Security Council met for the first time ever at the level of heads of state or government. The summit asked Secretary General Boutros Boutros-Ghali to prepare a keynote strategy document for UN peace operations in the new era. Entitled *An Agenda for Peace* (UN 1992), it set out to define more diverse and robust roles for the UN. Two proposed departures from previous practice were critical. First, *An Agenda for Peace* defined peacekeeping as "the deployment of a United Nations presence in the field, *hitherto* with the consent of all the parties concerned" (para. 20). Here was a clear signal that the UN might, in some instances, seek to deploy peacekeepers without local consent. Second, the document noted that cease-fires had often been agreed to in the past but not always complied with, making it necessary for the UN to try and restore a cease-fire. But because this task on occasion exceeded the capability of peacekeeping forces, Boutros-Ghali continued, "I recommend that the [Security] Council consider the utilization of peace-enforcement units in clearly defined circumstances and with their terms of reference specified in advance" (para. 44). Here the Secretary General was calling for a new United Nations military role altogether, beyond peacekeeping, but short of all-out warfighting.

At the same time, the UN found itself confronting types of conflicts it had not encountered since the Congo operation in the early 1960s, which had nearly destroyed the organization. Of twenty-one peace operations established between 1988 and the end of 1994, thirteen involved what were (or became) primarily intrastate rather than interstate conflicts (UN 1995: 3). Many took place amid the rubble of contested or collapsed domestic authority (Angola, Cambodia, Somalia), and/or they involved large ethnic minorities left exposed when federal political structures disintegrated (former Yugoslavia, Caucasus).

Boutros-Ghali's proposals should have led immediately to joint efforts by the UN and its member states, especially the most capable and interested national militaries, to determine and assess their doctrinal implications and practical feasibility. Instead, the traditional peacekeeping modality was simply ratcheted up and projected into uncharted terrain—euphemistically termed "semi-permissive environments." There it was supplemented by such ad hoc "peace-enforcement" components as the US Quick Reaction Force and Army Rangers in Somalia, or NATO's air-strike capability in Bosnia-Herzegovina. But countries participating in these newer UN peace operations did so on the basis of very different understandings, sometimes without realizing that this was so.

Cambodia was the first of these operations (Doyle and Suntharalingham 1994). Doctrinal differences were muted, however, thereby possibly inducing a false sense of confidence. This was due to four factors. First, the major parties involved had decided that the conflict should be terminated; the Paris agreements reflected their consensus. Second, none of the internal factions could fundamentally alter the military balance of forces on the ground, which the UN, in turn, might have been tempted to re-equilibrate. The Khmer Rouge repeatedly employed terror tactics to do so but, beyond its own area of control, it was held in check by the Vietnamese-installed Cambodian government faction. The latter also intimidated and even murdered political opponents but was unable itself to dominate. This balance of forces created enough space for the UN operation to pursue its major non-military objectives, including the repatriation of refugees and conducting a nation-wide election to constitute a legitimate government. Third, all participants in the UN mission were resolute that the UN should not try to enforce its mandate. Accordingly, they simply accepted the fact that the mission would be unable to carry out several major military objectives it had been assigned: achieving a complete cease-fire, followed by cantoning, disarming, and demobilizing 70 percent of the four internal factions' forces—and it pushed on with those civilian objectives that it had a chance to achieve. Fourth, and perhaps most poorly understood, the very failure to disarm the factions may have strengthened the rest of the mission. For it provided the individual factions with means they controlled to protect their interests in case any of the others broke out of the agreement, and thus gave each enough confidence to permit the mission to keep moving ahead.

Doctrinal confusion impeded—and ultimately defeated—the UN's Somalia mission. During its US-led phase, from December 1992 through May 1993, the operation was authorized, under the enforcement provisions of the UN charter, "to use all necessary means to establish as soon as possible a secure environment for humanitarian relief operations" (*New York Times* 1992: A14). The United States responded by committing up to 28,000 troops. As described by General Colin L. Powell, Chairman of the US Joint Chiefs of Staff, the US forces' mission statement reflected prevailing American military doctrine: an overwhelming force applied decisively over a limited period of time, after which the remaining political and humanitarian tasks would be handed off to the United Nations (Gordon 1992: A5; Lewis 1992: 15). Even so, the United States rejected a UN request that it pacify and disarm the warring clans. Paradoxically, after US forces were drawn down and control of the operation was turned over to the UN under what most participants believed was a more traditional peacekeeping mandate, the Security Council escalated the mission's objectives to include disarming the tribal factions and, in retribution for a fatal attack on Pakistani peacekeepers, implicitly authorized a manhunt for General Mohammed Farah Aidid and an offensive against his clan's leaders.

This escalation dismayed several troop contributing countries. Italy threatened to withdraw its 2,600-member contingent, Prime Minister Carlo Azeglio Ciampi accusing the UN of moving toward "a military intervention almost as an end in itself, against the wishes of those who are carrying it out" (quoted by Cowell 1993: A1). US military leaders were unhappy for a different reason: they felt that the escalation demanded a corresponding increase in tanks and armored vehicles, but Secretary of Defense Les Aspin turned down their request (Cushman 1993: A14).

In the end, three types of forces with three different missions and three separate command and control structures were deployed simultaneously in the streets of Mogadishu: a traditional UN peacekeeping force, supporting the provision of humanitarian assistance; a US Quick Reaction Force, only tenuously connected to UN command, for more muscular reinforcement; and to hunt General Aidid, a 400-strong detachment of US Army Rangers, commanded out of Tampa, Florida and completely autonomous from the UN. "The UN will be powerless," one of its officials predicted. "They won't know who's fighting who" (quoted by Lorch 1993: A3). He was right. An unsustainably ambiguous and even contradictory set of tasks and means to pursue them so eroded support for the mission that first the United States and then the United Nations were forced to abandon their military operations—and despite humanitarian successes in the countryside, leaving Mogadishu in much the state they found it.

Doctrinal confusion was even worse in the case of Bosnia. The United States viewed the issue of possible military intervention in the former Yugoslavia through the lenses of the "all-or-nothing" doctrine that came to govern its use of force in the wake of Vietnam (Gacek 1994). As defined by the US Joint Chiefs of Staff (1992), the "all" part of this doctrine stipulates the swift, decisive, comprehensive, and synchronized application of preponderant military force to shock, disrupt, demoralize, and defeat opponents. Because US policymakers did not consider America's vital interests to be directly affected by the disintegration of Yugoslavia while the US military regarded the Serbian-dominated Yugoslav army (JNA) to be one of the more potent in Europe, even demonstration strikes were ruled out—as when the JNA shelled Dubrovnik in 1991, at which time, according to a recent account by Warren Zimmermann (1995), who was then US ambassador to Yugoslavia and had advised against military involvement, they might have deterred Serbian escalation. In 1992, General Colin Powell angrily rejected former British Prime Minister Margaret Thatcher's suggestion that the West launch limited air strikes to deter further Bosnian Serb shelling of Sarajevo: "As soon as they tell me it is limited, it means they do not care whether you achieve a result or not. As soon as they tell me 'surgical,' I head for the bunker" (quoted by Gordon 1992: A1).

The "all-or-nothing" doctrine, however, left the United States with the "nothing" option for a growing number of conflict situations that conformed neither to traditional peacekeeping nor all-out warfighting. On the eve of a presidential election, the Bush administration required little persuading not to become militarily involved in Bosnia. The Clinton administration decided early on to limit US military involvement to NATO air strikes—except to protect UN troops if they were forced to withdraw or to implement a peace settlement, as under the Dayton accords.

While American and British scholars speculated in the immediate post-cold war years about putative norms of humanitarian intervention in internal conflicts, France actively sought to shape UN peace operations to give expression to certain of those norms (Guillot 1994). The French approach combined pursuit of negotiated settlements at the diplomatic level with the protection of civilian populations, by non-consensual military means if necessary, from aggression by local warring factions. Thus, France advocated creating "safe areas" within which civilians could be shielded and humanitarian aid distributed; "humanitarian corridors" through which these areas would be supplied; together with armed protection of humanitarian convoys engaged in "innocent passage" through the corridors. Most notably, the proposal to establish the UN safe areas in Bosnia (Sarajevo, Tuzla, Gorazde, Bihac, and Srebrenica) came from France.

In Bosnia these French notions ran afoul of two factors. First, unless "humanitarian intervention" in an internal conflict supports and protects civilians on all sides, it will be regarded as a hostile act by the disadvantaged faction. The Bosnian Serbs frequently harassed and even attacked UN troops in the safe areas for that reason. Second, if the intervening force is regarded as favoring one faction and is also out-gunned by the disfavored, it merely offers itself up as a target. When the safe areas were created in Bosnia-Herzegovina, the UN Secretary-General's military advisors estimated that it would take 34,000 troops to deter Serb aggression; governments provided the UN with 7,600, hoping that a symbolic UN presence and Serb fears that an attack on it might trigger NATO airstrikes would suffice (Gordon 1993)—and even at that level the full complement took more than a year to arrive. France tried to compensate for these deficiencies through heroics—as in General Philippe Morillon's stand to keep Srebrenica from falling—denunciations—as in General Jean Cot's very public complaints about the humiliations suffered by UN troops at the hands of the Bosnian Serbs—and threats—that the UN either use greater force or suffer the withdrawal of French forces: "*tirer ou se tirer* (to shoot or to get out)" (Guillot 1994: 39; personal interviews with Generals Morillon and Cot in New York). Until mid-1995, these efforts were in vain.

Britain expended greater effort than any other country to devise a new doctrine for post-cold war peacekeeping, but its attempt to achieve clarity in the event further confounded the UN's Bosnian operation. Like the United States and France, Britain began with the view that this operation constituted neither traditional peacekeeping nor warfighting, that it was a "gray area" operation. When Lt. General Sir Michael Rose arrived in Bosnia as UN force commander the press viewed his experience in British Special Forces, together with his own early actions to break the siege of Sarajevo in February 1994, to signify that the UN was now prepared to use greater force in securing compliance with its mandates (Pomfret 1994; Gordon 1995).

Gradually, however, the new British doctrine took shape, and it moved sharply away from these expectations. Termed "Wider Peacekeeping," the doctrine categorically rejected the very notion of "gray area" operations as "spurious historically [and] dangerous doctrinally" (Dobbie 1994: 3).[2] There are only two types of UN military operations, it held, peacekeeping and enforcement, which it deemed a subset of warfighting. Moreover, what divides the two "is not the level of violence," as is typically assumed, "but simply consent" (ibid.). Thus, wider peacekeeping was said to share with traditional peacekeeping the defining feature of being consent-based. By the time he left his command, General Rose had come around to echo this dichotomy: "Patience, persistence and pressure is how you conduct a peacekeeping mission . . . If someone wants to fight a war here on moral or political grounds, fine, great, but count us out . . . I'm not going to fight a war in white-painted tanks" (quoted in Cohen 1994: A7).

But what, then, was "wider" about "wider peacekeeping"? In terms of the use of force, apparently that it did not rule out selective purposes other than self-defense. As General Rose explained, "Hitting one tank is peacekeeping. Hitting infrastructure, command and control, logistics, that is war" (ibid.). Yet how can hitting even one tank be justified under the requirement of consent, except in self-defense? Here the British doctrine drew a novel distinction between "operational" and "tactical" levels of consent. Through continuous negotiations with the appropriate leadership at the theater level, overall consent for an operation must be maintained at all times, it said.

Accordingly, "wider peacekeeping" ruled out the *strategic* use of force. At the same time, within a framework of operational consent, the doctrine permitted the *tactical* use of force in defense of the mission as well as in self-defense. Moreover, when force is used for these purposes it must be "appropriate, proportionate, demonstrably reasonable and confined in effect to the specific and legitimate target intended" (Mallinson n.d.).[3]

Insofar as the UN Secretariat ever expressed a common doctrine for the Bosnian military operation, this was it.[4] The results were not salutary. So-called operational consent carried over poorly to the field level, leaving UN forces deployed in highly vulnerable positions. Their small numbers and restrictive rules of engagement often made it difficult for the troops to defend themselves, let alone their mission. And when the mission was reinforced by the "peace enforcement" component of NATO airstrikes, as urged repeatedly by the United States, the troops became, predictably, hostages to retaliation.

In sum, the major powers held very different precepts regarding the appropriate form of UN military intervention in the Bosnian conflict, while the UN's civilian and military command more or less came around to reflect Britain's concept of "wider peacekeeping." If these precepts were not entirely at cross-purposes, they decidedly did not add up to a coherent and sustainable doctrine. In mid-1995, a pervasive sense of failure and embarrassment, coupled with the opportunity created by Croatia's successful sweep through its Serb-inhabited Krajina region as well as a move by the US Congress unilaterally to lift the arms embargo on Bosnia, led Britain and France to field a more heavily armed UN Rapid Reaction Force, NATO to launch Operation Determined Force, and the United States to take the lead in forging the agreement of 8 September 1995, which led ultimately to the Dayton accords.

A doctrinal basis for robust UN peace operations must be formulated if the UN is to have a future in the terrain between traditional peacekeeping and warfighting. The British "wider peacekeeping" team focused on *consent* as the decisive factor. But the problem is precisely cases wherein consent is sporadic, or in which domestic authority is contested or has collapsed—and in which no party has been collectively branded an aggressor. A recent US Army field manual marks an advance, but it, too, remains unsatisfactory in the end (US Department of the Army 1994). It distinguishes between "peace operations" and "warfighting." Rejecting the doctrinal strictures of "wider peacekeeping," it further differentiates between two types of peace operations: peacekeeping and peace enforcement. The major differences between those two is said to involve not only the consent of the parties, but also the role of force and the degree of impartiality in its application. Thus, in peace enforcement "consent is not absolute and force may be used to coerce or compel"—but not to *defeat* any belligerent (ibid.: 12). In a word, this American doctrinal effort assigns greater weight to the *strategic objectives* of force than its British counterpart. The manual acknowledges that peace enforcement "strains the perception of impartiality," thus requiring diligence to retain even-handedness (ibid.: 13). Moreover, "since misunderstanding can be disastrous," field commanders are encouraged to appeal to higher authorities for clarification and advice concerning these demarcations (ibid.). But it fails to indicate what those higher authorities should say when they are called upon.

To be successful, efforts at forging a common doctrinal understanding will have to reflect the institutional culture of the United Nations as well as the political consensus among the UN's masters on the Security Council. But such efforts also must reflect the insights of strategic theory and experience far more than has hitherto been true. The literature on this subject, though devised for different purposes and contexts, nevertheless suggests a number of *ceteris paribus* maxims that can guide efforts to rethink the UN's role in "gray area" conflicts—or demonstrate its limits. We briefly summarize several.

The most elementary point—but one that recent UN missions have ignored or violated with abandon—is that any successful use of force short of simply imposing a surrender must alter the decision calculus of the target unit enough for it to change its objectionable behavior. But symbolic gestures, "moral deterrence," or token deployments are highly unlikely to yield that result when the target units are fighting for their own survival, to subjugate or eliminate rivals, monopolize the extractive potential of the state, or if they are locked in a security dilemma (Jervis 1978; Walter 1996), wherein none has any guarantee that others will not take advantage of it and thus all act as though the others will do so—characteristics of many postcold war conflicts. Such "soft" measures have their desired utility only if the intervening force has firmly established a very high level of credibility; they cannot themselves produce that credibility.

Next, numerous Security Council resolutions, especially on Bosnia, have made reference to the concept of "deterrence" without exhibiting the slightest regard for its requirements. Deterrence is about discouraging a target unit from attempting specified actions before they are taken, essentially by manipulating its calculation of the costs and benefits of proceeding. It is well understood in the literature that deterrence using conventional weapons is more difficult to achieve than nuclear deterrence because it leaves far greater room for ambiguity and miscalculation (Mearsheimer 1983)—a situation worsened by the vast growth in global arms markets since the end of the cold war. In the former Yugoslavia, NATO airstrikes at the time of Dubrovnik might have deterred further Serb escalation, as Ambassador Zimmermann contends, especially in light of the fact the Serbs seemed to be testing how far they could go without suffering serious costs. But there was never any chance that the extremely vulnerable blue helmets in the so-called "safe areas" in Bosnia could act as a deterrent against Bosnian-Serb attacks; the Security Council's use of that term in the authorizing resolution represented either an egregious act of folly or outright callousness (see Jakobson 1996 for a more extensive analysis).

Timothy Crawford (1996) has adapted the distinction between "basic" and "extended" deterrence to the context of UN peace operations. Here, basic deterrence is understood as the ability of UN forces to deter an attack against themselves, while extended deterrence refers to their ability to deter an attack against third parties (humanitarian missions, civilians in "safe areas"). The distinction is important because basic deterrence is known to be relatively easier to achieve than extended deterrence. The main reason is simply that, in the case of basic deterrence, the stakes for the deterring force are higher and so, too, therefore, is the credibility of its deterrence threats. The mandates of recent UN forces implicitly and sometimes explicitly have included extended deterrence roles without acknowledging this step-level difference. Moreover, if a force is unable to achieve basic deterrence, as was true of UNPROFOR in Bosnia, it is virtually inconceivable that it could succeed in providing the more demanding extended deterrent role.[5]

Yet another well-established proposition in the literature is that deterrence, though difficult, is a relatively easier task than compellence—Thomas Schelling's term (1966) for coercing a target unit to cease or change an action that it has already undertaken. Again, the reason is straightforward: the willingness of states or groups to bear costs in order to achieve gains is usually lower than the pain they will endure to avoid losses. This suggests that explanations of UN failure that stress some absolute lack of "muscle" at least in part may have misconstrued the problem: a relatively modest-sized force may be more successful at achieving deterrence than a much larger force is at achieving compellence. Thus, beyond a certain threshold of credibility, further force requirements are relative to strategic objectives. Accordingly, proposals for UN rapid deployment capabilities discussed by the Netherlands, some Nordic countries, and Canada may well make sense—and not merely for small conflicts, which is how they are usually considered, but also for certain tasks even in potentially larger ones.

Finally, Robert Pape (1992) has demonstrated that if compellence by military means becomes necessary, it is relatively easier to achieve through denial than through punishment. Denial functions by preventing the target unit from attaining its goals, punishment by raising its overall costs or risks. Punishment, according to Pape, "is likely to succeed only when the [target's] resolve is low" (ibid.: 437). For denial to succeed, however, it is necessary for the intervening forces to be able to persuade the local belligerent that they have the ability and the will to ruin the feasibility of its strategy, and that its further expenditures of resources is, therefore, futile. It is difficult to discern precisely toward what end UN forces in Bosnia engaged in "appropriate, proportionate, and demonstrably reasonable" military counter-attacks, including air strikes. But they were unlikely ever to achieve or even to threaten denial. Inflicting damage is insufficient; it must be damage to the target's capabilities "in ways that undermine [its] expectation of military success" (ibid.: 464), and—contra General Rose's injunction—thus must include supply lines and communications networks.

In sum, without a more solid doctrinal basis UN peace operations will have no future in the terrain between traditional peacekeeping and warfighting. And the UN can have no solid doctrinal basis for such operations unless strategic thinking and requirements are taken more seriously in authorizing and executing missions than they have been in the past. Any such doctrine is likely to fall within the general category of what Alexander George (1991) calls "forceful persuasion." It must be married to the preference and need by the UN to retain impartiality when no party to a conflict has been declared the aggressor—rather than, on balance-of-power grounds, helping to bring about the conflict's termination by allying itself with one to achieve the defeat of the other. And its chief military attribute resides in the objectives toward which force is employed, which do *not* include defeating belligerents. The outlines of a UN-based "forceful persuasion" model may be sketched briefly, though both logical and practical problems remain to be resolved.

The political aims of such a strategy are to prevent local combatants from achieving collectively censured ends or employing collectively censured means, and to establish that a negotiated settlement is the better option. Consent is highly desirable and ongoing communication with the parties necessary. But consent is not absolute and force may be used to deter or compel. When it is, it must be used impartially, meaning without a priori prejudice or bias and in response to violations of agreements, Security Council mandates, or norms stipulated in some other fashion (Daniel and Miles 1996). Ideally, the timely show of sufficient international force would deter the local use of force altogether. If the time for deterrence has passed, or should deterrence fail, the international force would be employed to dissuade local combatants from continuing military action by neutralizing specific sources of offensive activity. As a last step, international force would seek to deny military victory to local combatants by means of strikes at their strategic vulnerabilities.

To achieve these aims, the international force above all must be militarily credible. At the high end of the spectrum, it would be virtually indistinguishable from warfighting units in all respects *except* their political and military objectives. But neither its size nor technical or operational capabilities can be defined generically. Nor is it possible to stipulate in the abstract when, militarily speaking, a UN-organized force will suffice and when a larger and heavier coalition force is necessary. That will depend on the balance of power on the ground as well as on where, on the ladder of escalation, the force is required to intervene.

Thus, UN retrenchment and retreat back to the familiar grounds of traditional peacekeeping are no better informed by the specific requirements of "gray area" peace operations than was the initial push into this terrain. Devising a shared conception among governments of how to do what they had asked the UN to do is a necessary first step toward a better understanding. Constructing viable implementation mechanisms is the next.

COMMAND AND CONTROL

In any military operation, personnel, equipment, and procedures must be integrated in such a way as to achieve unified direction of effort in the field, guided by and in support of overall strategic objectives (Palin 1995). Recent UN operations have exhibited anything but those characteristics.[6]

Problems exist throughout the entire chain of command: the Security Council routinely adopts mandates that do not provide militarily meaningful guidelines to missions; troop contributing countries have no systematic input into the designing of mandates unless they happen to be Security Council members; there is no duly constituted military authority at UN headquarters to command overall operations and serve as the interface between political authorities and force commanders; and the Secretary General acts as both the Council's executive agent in military operations and neutral mediator. In theater, force commanders are required to perform operational tasks without adequate strategic guidance or plans. Their options in employing the troops and equipment provided by governments are subject to constraints by national authorities, which they do not always make known in advance. And national contingent commanders often seek instructions from their capitals before acting on orders by UN force commanders—a practice that is hardly surprising but delays and can jeopardize the success of field actions while further undermining unity-in-command. Linking UN peace operations with non-UN "peace enforcement" components has also proved difficult: attempts to couple UN and NATO commands through a "dual key" arrangement for NATO airstrikes in Bosnia led to confusion and mutual recrimination, degrading the mission of both; decoupling UN and US command structures in Somalia produced calamity. As a result, UN military units have been unable to act strategically, quickly, and on a sustained basis.

These issues are unlikely to be fully resolved any time soon; national political cross-currents are simply too strong. Nevertheless, modest steps toward improvement should be possible. But to achieve them the two most commonly advocated options must be jettisoned in the process: giving greater authority to the Secretary General and reviving the Military Staff Committee. Under traditional peacekeeping, UN headquarters plays a management role, vested in the Secretary General. The newer peace operations, however, also require effective performance of critical command functions. The current system of military advisors leaves their functioning entirely at the discretion of the Secretary General, who may or may not ask for or accept their advice, or share it with the Security Council, and which in any event is too weak to perform the grand-strategic and operational planning roles that more robust operations demand but which are now lacking.

Because these planning roles should serve as a link between political decision-makers and field operations, the military advisors should be responsible to the Security Council and enjoy a sphere of institutional independence from the Secretary General.

The charter, as noted above, assigned the "strategic direction" of UN forces to the Military Staff Committee, advising the Security Council, with operational command and control issues to be worked out subsequently. Simply reviving this instrument is not a satisfactory solution either, because its fixed and representational character—senior military officers from the permanent five—renders it inappropriate for day-to-day command purposes. For example, China has not voted affirmatively in the Security Council for any UN use of force in any conflict that could be construed as having an internal dimension—which includes the majority of conflicts that have ended up on the UN docket since the end of the cold war. Citing Article 2.7 of the charter, China fears external intervention in disputes that it considers within its own domestic jurisdiction, including Tibet and Taiwan. Faced with strong Security Council sentiment in favor of a mission, China has abstained. One would expect China's categorical position to be carried over from the political forum of the Security Council to what should be a professional military planning and executive arena by its delegate on the Military Staff Committee.

In addition, the major troop contributing countries, many of which are not, or only rarely, on the Security Council, should have a greater say in the determination of mandates and changes therein, as well as in devising and reviewing operational plans. Greater involvement in the formative stages of missions should help reduce the extent that national authorities interject themselves at the field level. The chief problems here are that it is not always known *ex ante* who the troop contributing countries to a particular mission will be, and that any arrangement based on them would lack permanence.

These considerations suggest a hybrid arrangement, taking the relevant UN charter provisions quite literally. The Military Staff Committee would be responsible for generally advising and assisting the Security Council on issues relating to the military requirements of the Council's responsibilities (Article 47.1), and provide general "strategic direction" to UN peace operations (Article 47.3). For command functions in actual operations, the Council would ask the military most capable and most involved countries to form an operational planning and command structure, under the Council's authority and staffed by the Department of Peacekeeping Operations (Article 47.3: "Questions relating to the command of such forces shall be worked out subsequently").

Finally, to reduce the incidence of national contingent commanders consulting their capitals as a matter of routine before acting on virtually any orders from UN force commanders, senior officers of the larger contributing forces in any given mission could be made part of the field headquarters staff of that mission, performing liaison and advisory functions outside the operational chain of command. This model draws on the precedent set by General John Shalikashvili as commander of Operation Provide Comfort, protecting the Kurdish population of Northern Iraq in the wake of the Gulf war. Troop contributing nations would be asked to deal through this mechanism on matters affecting their contingents, and if warranted by an operation's size they could provide their national representative officers with a staff to support these functions—thereby turning what is now a vice undermining missions into a virtue strengthening them.

CONCLUSION

The end of the cold war created new possibilities for UN peace operations, but they were not nearly as unlimited or unproblematic as the early post-cold war euphoria promised. After Somalia and Bosnia, however, many observers have wondered whether any range of opportunity remains. Clearly, the UN did not perform those missions successfully. But consider this counterfactual comparison: if Soviet armies had marched across the central front in Europe in the early 1950s, NATO's performance would have deeply embarrassed the alliance. It took the impetus of the Korean war as well as considerable time, effort, and money for NATO to generate its formidable military structure.

UN member states do not aspire to have the UN resemble NATO in this regard. But the point is simply this: to whatever extent member states wish to ratchet up the UN's role they must also upgrade its capabilities—just as NATO's were in the 1950s. This essay has argued that for any form of UN military operations beyond the traditional peacekeeping modality to succeed, it will be necessary to develop a shared doctrinal understanding of the nature of these operations and institute improvements in the arrangements for command and control.

Powerful political obstacles do stand in the way. In the United States, the Republican Congress and presidential aspirants have been hostile, the Democratic administration chastened. At some point, however, we can expect the US military to weigh in and facilitate a more reasoned discourse. For the military, slowly shedding its Vietnam-induced all-or-nothing doctrine, itself has become persuaded that "gray area" conflicts are here to stay at least for the foreseeable future, and that in many instances collective responses, through the UN and other mechanisms, are the most viable and sustainable option.[7]

Notes

INTRODUCTION: WHAT MAKES THE WORLD HANG TOGETHER?

1 The so-called relative gains problem stressed by neorealists requires a partial qualifier, which I simply note here and return to below.

2 The "social communications" model of national and international political community formation developed by Karl Deutsch and his associates also deserves mention (Deutsch et al. 1957), though it was relatively weak in identifying specifically political mechanisms of the process.

3 The main features of *Theory* were outlined in Waltz (1975).

4 See, for example, *The Children of Light and the Children of Darkness* (1944) and *Christian Realism and Political Problems* (1953).

5 Some formulations assume states to be unitary actors, whereas others seek to include domestic factors through the mechanism of two-level games.

6 To return to an issue raised in note 1 above, in this limited and negative sense Grieco could claim that neorealism embodies a relational ontology. But Grieco subsequently has weakened his claim (1993), and in any case negative positionalism would be just about the most atomistic of all possible relational ontologies, and would not be accepted as such by social constructivists. More on this in the third section of this chapter.

7 Some realists, it should be noted, want no part of this consensus; see, for example, Mearsheimer (1994/5).

8 Structuration theory proposes a formulation of the "agent-structure" problem in which agents (e.g., states) and structures (e.g., of the international system) are mutually constituted, in the sense that neither has logical priority over the other and neither can exist or be understood apart from the other. The agent-structure problem, in turn, is a subset of issues concerning the social construction of social reality.

9 In Chapter 3, following Searle (1984) and Kratochwil (1989), I further differentiate between two types of social facts: collective states of mind about objects and states of affairs in the world, and those social facts which require human institutions for their existence.

10 Searle (1995: 7–8) makes the important point that an "ontologically subjective" fact can be "epistemologically objective" in the sense that its existence, within limits, can be established by systematic inquiry

11 On numerous occasions, I have been asked why I have neglected the literature now known as sociological institutionalism (for a good review, see Finnemore 1996b). My answer is twofold. First, sociological institutionalism initially emerged in the shadow of Immanuel Wallerstein's world systems analysis, which was as prone to neglecting intersubjective phenomena as is neo-utilitarianism—

indeed, in some ways the two are methodologically quite similar, as Robert Brenner (1977) noted in his classic critique of what he called "neo-Smithian Marxism." More recently, as sociological institutionalism has become more truly sociological, it nevertheless has concerned itself almost entirely with the diffusion of cultural norms from the core to the periphery, but provides little handle on the genesis of those norms in the first place, which has been one of my main concerns.

12 It may be possible to extend two-level game models in the attempt to accommodate some of the domestic factors, though it is not clear how satisfactory the result would be. But the international factors remain beyond neo-utilitarian reach; see the reference to debates between rational-choice theory and the theory of communicative action in the following section of this essay, Ideational Causation.

13 A major weakness of this empirical work is that it establishes the diffusion of institutional norms more effectively than of actual behavior.

14 This is not to say that interesting results cannot be produced by the analysis. For example, John Ferejohn's chapter in the Goldstein–Keohane volume not only is first-rate in its own right, but it serves as an exemplar of sophisticated research in the rationalist mode that reaches out to include institutional and cultural factors without stripping them of their integrity. The volume also includes several excellent chapters that have nothing to do with neo-utilitarian models, including those by Ikenberry, Halpern, Jackson, Sikkink, and Katzenstein. My concern is the Goldstein–Keohane framework of ideational factors.

15 This perspective draws on the work of Stephen Toulmin (1972) and Donald Campbell (1987). See Adler (1991) for an excellent discussion.

16 Keohane seems to be entertaining moves in a similar direction, if I understand his recent remarks on the desirability of a supplementary "extra-rationalistic research program" (Keohane 1996). He specifically mentions wanting to accommodate acts of persuasion, for which, he notes, there is no need in what he calls "intra-rationalistic analysis."

17 As noted in Chapter 7, the practice of retrojecting actors' responses to incentives that make sense only under modern market rationality into the differently constituted economies of pre-modern Europe accounts for the fact that the so-called new economic history does such a poor job at retrodicting actual outcomes in the origins of capitalist economies and territorial states.

18 This point is not uncontroversial. For example, King, Keohane, and Verba find the idea of non-causal explanation "confusing" (1994: 75), though it is hardly alien to the philosophy of social science My point would not be compromised, however, if these "accounts" were called something other than noncausal explanations, as long as it is understood that they go well beyond even compound definitions, well beyond even very thick descriptions, and function in a logical domain that precedes the scope of causal relations as we normally understand that term. This set of issues is related to, but not identical with, Weber's notion of *Verstehen*, to which I return below. (For additional problems with the concept of causality in international relations theory, see Chapter 3.)

19 A partial exception is Keohane's metaphorical account of sovereignty as a "cartel-type" solution to a collective action problem that states initially faced, as a result of which they agreed to refrain from intervening in the affairs of others "conditional on others' restraint" (1995: 172–173). On that analytical basis, Keohane devises a rationalist–institutionalist interpretation of changes in sovereignty today, in which states under conditions of high interdependence may use sovereignty as a bargaining resource to establish a legal grip on aspects of transnational processes that they cannot otherwise control.

20 In Chapter 5, I discuss briefly the meaning of "feudal anarchy," which functioned very differently than the modern form.
21 It is possible to imagine an international relations theory that pays no regard to the specific forms of the units or the structures that combine them into a system. For example, Krasner (1997: 3) has suggested an analytical formulation whereby "rulers want to stay in power, and being in power they want to promote the security, prosperity, and values of their constituents." But a theory based on such assumptions would be exceedingly abstract, highly indeterminate, and might prove unfalsifiable—what would falsify it other than behavior that is consistent with rulers not wanting to stay in power or not trying to promote the interests and values of their constituents?
22 There are several grounds on which to criticize Waltz's use of Durkheim. In Chapter 5, I merely note that Waltz ignored even Durkheim's own materialist and system-level cause of transformation—what Durkheim called "dynamic density"—in reaching his conclusion that the international system does not fundamentally change over time.
23 The term is Schluchter's, according to whom Weber in this connection built in part on Georg Simmel.
24 For a fuller discussion, see Chapter 3. It must be noted that Weber, unlike Wilhelm Dilthey, on whose work he drew, held that *Verstehen* is not opposed to but serves causal explanation, as he understood the latter.
25 Chapter 4 includes an extensive illustration of this critical point in the context of nominal versus normative definitions of multilateralism.
26 Searle (1997) critiques a corresponding attempt by David Chalmers to bridge the brain–mind divide on similar grounds.
27 See, for example, Campbell's comment that Alexander Wendt and I "seem to be exhibiting a fear, a (Cartesian) anxiety" in the face of postmodernist challenges, this after taking me to task for my criticism of what I regarded as certain nihilistic tendencies in postmodernism (1996: 16–17).

1 THE NEW INSTITUTIONALISM IN INTERNATIONAL RELATIONS

1 In fact, it is also inconsistent with the historical record of how states came into being. One of the "main findings" of Karl Deutsch and his associates speaks to this point (1957: 24): "Another popular belief that our findings make more doubtful is that the growth of the state, or the expansion of its territory, resembles a snowballing process, or that it is characterized by some sort of bandwagoning effect . . . In this view, as villages in the past have joined to make provinces, and provinces to make kingdoms, so contemporary states are expected to join into ever larger federations . . Our findings do not support this view."
2 Two important exceptions are Lindberg (1970) and Keohane and Nye (1974).
3 In borrowing Vernon's phrase (1971), I do not mean to imply that he succumbs to the syndrome.
4 Thus, my only quarrel with the otherwise exceedingly suggestive article by Keohane and Nye (1974) is that it pays insufficient attention to the vectors that bound the policy spaces within which transgovernmental relations and international organizations exist, and within which organizational tasks and consequences assume their meaning as well as significance.
5 A related discussion has preoccupied students of international law for some time. For views that are compatible with the views expressed here, see Falk (1964) and especially Gottlieb (1972).

2 EMBEDDED LIBERALISM AND THE POSTWAR ECONOMIC REGIMES

1 Major primary-producing countries, by and large, did not establish their own central banks until the 1930s—this includes Argentina, Canada, India, New Zealand, and Venezuela.

2 For example, France decided in 1928 to accept only gold in settlement of the enormous surplus it was accruing; and in 1929 the US "went off on a restrictive monetary frolic of its own" even though it was in surplus (Cleveland 1976: 6). Four years later, in his inaugural address, President Roosevelt proclaimed the primacy of domestic stabilization, as he did again a few months later when, on the eve of the World Economic Conference of 1933, he took the United States off gold.

3 Nurkse was speaking of "the great majority of countries." Those who chose bilateralism as an instrument of imperialism and/or economic warfare were unlikely to be accommodated within any multilateral regime. However, mere state trading or even the participation of centrally planned economies, while posing special problems, were not seen to be insuperable obstacles to postwar multilateralism (see Feis 1947; Mikesell 1947).

4 John H. Williams, vice-president of the Federal Reserve Bank of New York, was a leading spokesman for the New York financial community, which resented having lost control over international monetary affairs when authority shifted from the FRBNY to the US Treasury under Secretary Morgenthau. Their plan, which had some support in Congress, called simply for a resurrection of the gold-exchange standard, with the dollar performing the role that sterling had played previously. They opposed the New Deal "gimmickry" of the White Plan, and of course liked Keynes's Clearing Union even less (Van Dormael 1978: chap. 9).

5 In the case of Britain, the other major actor in the negotiations concerning postwar economic arrangements, opposition from the Left was based on the desire to institute national economic planning, which would necessarily entail discriminatory instruments of foreign economic policy. Opposition from the Right stemmed from a commitment to imperial preferences and the imperial alternative to a universal economic order. Speaking for many moderates, Hubert Henderson of the Treasury was opposed because he doubted the viability of a "freely working economic system," that is, of laissez-faire: "To attempt this would be not to learn from experience but to fly in its face. It would be to repeat the mistakes made last time in the name of avoiding them. It would be to invite the same failure, and the same disillusion; the same economic chaos and the same shock to social and political stability; the same discredit for the international idea" (from a memorandum prepared by Henderson in December 1943, quoted in Gardner 1980: 30).

6 The third panel of the Bretton Woods triptych was the World Bank, which to some extent may also be said to reflect this conjunction of objectives. True, the grandiose concept of an international bank to engage in countercyclical lending and to help stabilize raw materials prices, which both White and Keynes had entertained at one point, was shelved due to opposition on both sides of the Atlantic. Nevertheless, for the first time, international public responsibility was acknowledged for the provision of investment capital, supplementing the market mechanism.

7 The differential impact on the two regimes is explained largely by the asymmetry that prevailed in the monetary domain and the somewhat more balanced configuration in trade. In the case of money, the United States possessed the fungible resources that everyone required, including some two-thirds of the

world's monetary gold supply, which it acquired as an unbalanced creditor country before World War II. At the same time, the US saw no situation in which it might become dependent on the regime as a debtor. The case of trade is inherently more symmetrical because the mutual granting of access to markets is the key resource. It is also a domain in which the domestic constraints within the United States differed little from domestic constraints elsewhere.

8 For example, Article XII calls for quantitative restrictions, but as time passed import surcharges were usually imposed. In an extremely peculiar but telling non-use of Article XII, France imposed emergency measures against imports after the 1968 disturbances, while enjoying a strong reserve position and only "fearing" a potential balance-of-payments problem. France asked for "sympathy and understanding" from its GATT partners and got both. The exceptional nature of the circumstances was stressed all around, the danger of precedent was flagged, and the measures were approved—and soon thereafter discontinued by France. According to Curzon and Curzon (1976: 222) the case shows "the complicity which exists between governments when one of them is forced to take unpopular trade measures because it has a domestic problem on its hands." They intend the depiction of the reaction by France's trading partners as "complicitous" to be a criticism; in point of fact, it captures the very essence of a regime.

9 We are speaking here, of course, of ideal–typical contrasts. In the real world, other factors are also at work, and the notion of declining American hegemony is imprecise and easy to exaggerate (see Strange 1982).

3 EPISTEMOLOGY, ONTOLOGY, AND THE STUDY OF INTERNATIONAL REGIMES

1 Braudel's unit of analysis is what he terms "civilizations" in their "ecodemographic context." The general approach is discussed in Braudel (1980); the original empirical study was Braudel (1972). See also Chapter 7.

2 See Dallmayr and McCarthy (1977) for a good selection of readings that begins with Weber, includes the neopositivist response, the Wittgensteinian school, phenomenology, and ethnomethodology, and ends with hermeneutics and critical theory.

3 One of the distinctive characteristics of strategic interaction is that ultimately it rests upon a *unilateral* calculation of verbal and nonverbal cues: "A's expectation of B will include an estimation of B's expectations of A. This process of replication, it must be noted, is not an interaction between two states, but rather a process in which decision-makers in one state work out the consequences of their beliefs about the world; a world they believe to include decision-makers in other states, also working out the consequences of their beliefs. The expectations which are so formed are the expectations of one state, but they refer to other states" (Keal 1984: 31).

4 Account should also be taken of the fact that different types of norms— implicit versus explicit, constraining versus enabling, and so on—function differently in social relations (see Ullman-Margalit 1977, and Hart 1961). Compliance, too, is a variegated and complex phenomenon, as discussed by Young (1979).

5 Krasner (1985) is one of the few contemporary realists to take seriously the relationship between power and norms. We can agree with much of what Krasner has to say about the efficacy of norms, principles of legitimacy, and movements of thought—indeed, he even invokes hermeneutics. And yet, in the

end, we remain perplexed at how he reconciles this position with his fervent commitment to logical positivism.

4 MULTILATERALISM AT CENTURY'S END

1 Gilpin (1981: 15): "Although . . peaceful adjustment of the systemic disequilibrium is possible, the principal mechanism of change throughout history has been war, or what we shall call hegemonic war (i.e., a war that determines which state or states will be dominant and will govern the system)."

2 According to Steve Weber (1993: 214), in 1989 "some foreign policy thinkers in Paris reverted to old ideas, suggesting a new alliance with Poland, the emerging Eastern European states, and perhaps the Soviet Union as well in opposition to Germany. These flirtations with bilateral treaties and a new balance of power have been mostly left by the wayside." By historical junctures comparable to 1989, I mean 1848, 1919, and 1945. After 1848, what was left of the Concert of Europe rapidly degenerated into a system of competitive alliances; after World War I, France in particular sought the protection of bilateral alliances against Germany; and after World War II, several West European countries sought bilateral alliances with the United States and with one another. Among the useful sources for the first two periods are Albrecht-Carrié (1958), Carr (1961), Degenhardt (1981), and Taylor 1971).

3 Latin America seems to fall somewhere in between. According to Bloomfield and Lowenthal (1990: 868), "While the United States was ignoring and undermining multilateralism in the Western hemisphere, the Latin American nations themselves were moving towards greater co-operation, or *concertacion*, as they call it, to some degree as a response to United States policy."

4 For an early rendition of this refrain see Bergsten (1972); and most recently, *The Economist* (1991).

5 Contrary to folklore, Woodrow Wilson was not prepared to commit the United States to specific and automatic military obligations under the League of Nations; his collective security scheme would have relied on public opinion, arms limitations, and arbitration more than on enforcement mechanisms. Senator Henry Cabot Lodge's fundamental objection to the League of Nations was that its permanence and universalism would entail limitless entanglements for the United States abroad. Lodge favored stronger and more specific security guarantees to France and against Germany (see Ambrosius 1987: 51–106).

6 See Doyle (1986: 19–47). Some of the more predatory expressions of the Nazi arrangements came very close to, if they did not actually constitute, the imperial form.

7 Obviously, the existence of nuclear weapons, economic interdependence, externalities, or other technical factors can and probably does affect the social constructions that states choose. I am not imputing causality here, simply clarifying a concept.

8 Bilateral balancing need not imply equality; it simply means establishing a mutually acceptable balance between the parties, however that is determined in practice. For an extended discussion of this issue, see Polanyi (1957).

9 The distinction between coordination and collaboration was proposed by Stein (1983); also see Snidal (1990) and Martin (1993). The international property rights of states invariably are taken for granted, however, even though their stable definition is logically and temporally prior to the other two collective action problems. I have therefore added this dimension.

10 Note also the following analysis of the Treaty of Paris (1815) offered by historian Richard Langhorne (1986: 317): "There appeared at clause 6, in what was

certainly Castlereagh's drafting, [a shift in] emphasis from a specific guarantee to a scheme for the continuous management of the international system by the great powers."

11 The counter to my argument, of course, would be that "systemic factors" determine or at least shape the preferences and behavior of hegemons. That, too, is plausible as a general hypothesis. As it concerns this particular instance, however, I attach greater credibility to the actual postwar plans of the Third Reich and to what, since 1917, we knew Leninist world order designs to be than I do to the explanatory or predictive value of systemic theory. For methodological discussions of counterfactuals, see Nash (1991) and Fearon (1991).

12 The UN with US support acquired a more modest collective security role in the form of peacekeeping in the 1950s and a nuclear nonproliferation role via International Atomic Energy Agency safeguards and the nonproliferation treaty in the 1960s.

13 The requirement that the Europeans cooperate in reconstruction on a multilateral basis produced the Organization for European Economic Cooperation in 1948; it eventually became the Organization for Economic Cooperation and Development (OECD)—the chief mechanism through which economic bureaucrats of all the advanced capitalist countries coordinate the conduct of day-to-day policies. As for European integration, by 1947 the idea had gained strong support in US media and political circles. Senator Fulbright and Representative Boggs went so far as to introduce identical resolutions into the Congress that year, asking it to endorse "the creation of a United States of Europe within the framework of the United Nations." The bills were passed overwhelmingly. European integration was seen as a more promising idea for European economic recovery than individual national efforts alone, and it offered safeguards for the reindustrialization of Germany, which in turn was increasingly seen as being necessary for European recovery and for the success of the newly articulated US policy of containing the Soviet Union (Hogan 1987).

14 Jervis has pointed out that the decisive event in instituting the peculiar form of bipolarity known as the cold war was the Korean War. High US defense budgets, a large US armed presence in Europe to back the North Atlantic Treaty security guarantees, and anticommunist commitments all across the globe took hold only after that war. What is more, Jervis argues, "there were no events on the horizon which could have been functional substitutes for the war"—and which, therefore, would have been capable of producing those features of the international security environment (1980: 563).

5 POLITICAL STRUCTURE AND DYNAMIC DENSITY

1 It should be noted that for Durkheim the designation "social fact" does not refer to all phenomena that take place within society, but only to those that exist exterior to individuals, are not subject to modification by a simple effort of will on the part of any specific individuals, and function as a constraint on individual behavior.

2 Durkheim is referenced four times in the index to Waltz's book; in a footnote (1979: 115), Waltz promises to elaborate on Durkheim's typology of social ordering principles in a future work.

3 The distinction here is between generative and descriptive structures. Descriptive structures are simply abstract summaries of patterned interactions within a system. For example, national capabilities are measured and hierarchies of state power are depicted. Trade and capital flows are measured and

hierarchies of economic power are deduced. Most uses of the concept of structure in international relations theory employ this meaning. In the realm of
generative structures, the concern is "with principles, not things" (Leach 1961:
7). The object is to discover the underlying principles that govern the patterning
of interactions, to infer their syntax. Saussurean linguistics probably was the
first self-conscious expression of generative structuralism in the social sciences,
and had a major impact on the study of linguistics and cultural anthropology.
For useful surveys, see Glucksman (1974) and Kurzweil (1980).

4 Waltz thus rejects the traditional view that a balance-of-power system requires
a minimum number of effective actors larger than two—preferably five, so that
one can act as balancer. This, he points out, "is more a historical generalization
than a theoretical concept" (1979: 164). Balancing takes place in a bipolar world
no less than in a multipolar world, except that the methods of balancing are
largely internal rather than external.

5 These notions closely parallel Durkheim's distinction between organic solidarity, linking highly differentiated units in a complex society, and mechanical
solidarity, linking like units in a segmental society. Organic solidarity represents
a qualitatively higher form and quantitatively greater extent of interdependence
(Durkheim 1893).

6 Waltz's original argument was with Richard Cooper (1968). Cooper shows,
among other things, that the price sensitivity of factors has been much higher in
the post-World War II period than prior to World War I. That may be economically interesting, Waltz maintains, but it is politically unimportant. The quick
reallocation of factors of production in response to relatively small margins of
advantage in fact demonstrates, according to Waltz, that those ties do not need
to be maintained, that they do not reflect mutual dependence stemming from
functional differentiation (1979: 141–142).

7 Economists would point out that intrasectoral trade, which accounts for an
ever-increasing share of total world trade, also reflects an international division
of labor. Waltz's response would be that it increases interdependence at the level
of the firm while decreasing it for the state, compared to what it would be given
an equivalent level of intersectoral trade.

8 Anarchy, recall, is defined as the absence of central rule. On the concept of
"feudal anarchy" see Gianfranco Poggi (1978: 31): "It arose from the fact that
the system of rule relied, both for order-keeping and for the enforcement of
rights and the redress of wrongs, on self-activated coercion exercised by a small,
privileged class of warriors and rentiers in their own interest." Moreover, any
standard text will document that neither the papacy nor the empire constituted
agents of centralized political authority (cf. Strayer and Munro 1959). Strayer
(1970) demonstrates nicely the balancing consequences triggered by threats of
supranationality from the papacy, most profoundly in this instance: "the
Gregorian concept of the Church," he contends, "almost demanded the invention of the concept of the state" (ibid.: 22).

9 Waltz's own definition of sovereignty is not helpful either: "To say that states
are sovereign is not to say that they can do as they please . . . To say that a state
is sovereign means that it decides for itself how it will cope with its internal and
external problems" (1979: 96).

7 TERRITORIALITY AT MILLENNIUM'S END

1 Marxist theorists of postmodernity encounter an inherent contradiction, to
borrow their own term, by the very nature of the enterprise. One of the features
of postmodernity on which virtually all other schools of thought agree is that it

invalidates the possibility of producing metanarratives, or *metarécits*, more fashionably—that "totalizing" and "logocentric" practice of modernity on which Lyotard urges us to wage war. Of course, few narratives are more "meta" than Marxism. Jameson's somewhat feeble response (1989) is that a system that produces fragments is still a system.

2 Luhman (1982) developed a nonteleological formulation of differentiation that I have found useful, in which he distinguishes among segmentation, functional differentiation, and stratification, sequenced temporally. I use the term here in the sense of segmentation.

3 This term is attributed to Meinecke by Scott in his introduction to Meinecke (1957; first published in 1924). According to the Oxford English Dictionary "heteronomous" refers to systems wherein the parts are subject to different laws or modes of growth and "homonomous" to systems wherein they are subject to the same laws or modes of growth. In the original, biological sense of the terms, the fingers on a hand would exhibit homonomous growth—for an international relations meaning, read "states are functionally alike"—and the heart and hands of the same body heteronomous growth—read "states are functionally different."

4 According to Perry Anderson (1974: 429), "the age in which 'Absolutist' public authority was imposed was also simultaneously the age in which 'absolute' private property was progressively consolidated." Jones (1981: 147) reaches a similar conclusion via a different route: "Productive activities that had been subject to collective controls were becoming individualized. This is a staple of the textbooks. But that Europe moved from the guilds and the common fields toward *laissez-faire* is only half the story. The missing half is that just when production was becoming fully privatized, services were becoming more of a collective concern, or where they were already communal, now the government was being involved." Jones is referring to the provision of such services as internal pacification, internal colonization of uncultivated lands, disaster management, and the like. The gradual differentiation between internal and external, as seen through the lens of changing norms and practices of diplomatic representation, is portrayed brilliantly by Mattingly (1964).

5 Perhaps the drollest illustration cited by Jones (1981), but nonetheless a significant one, actually comes from a later century, when the Austrian Hapsburgs built a *cordon sanitaire* some 1,000 miles in length, promising to shut out the plague that persisted in the Ottoman empire. Their feat had no epidemiological effect, but it generated considerable administrative effort and social mobilization and contributed, thereby, to state building.

6 Tilly notes a methodological problem that the "new economic historians" have glossed over: there are many more failures than successes in the history of European state building. "The disproportionate distribution of success and failure puts us in the unpleasant situation of dealing with an experience in which most of the cases are negative, while only the positive cases are well-documented" (1975: 39). Tilly explores a greater variety of state-building experiences in a more recent work (1990). Spruyt's critique is even more damning, however. He points out that because successor forms to the medieval system of rule other than territorial states have been systematically excluded from consideration, there is no fundamental variation in units on the dependent-variable side in theories of state building (Spruyt 1994).

7 Consider the situation as late as the fourteenth century, described in the following excerpts from Tuchman (1978): "Even kings and popes received ambassadors sitting on beds furnished with elaborate curtains and spreads" (ibid.: 161); "Even in greater homes guests slept in the same room with host and

hostess" (ibid.), and often servants and children did too (ibid.: 39); "Never was man less alone . . . Except for hermits and recluses, privacy was unknown" (ibid.: 39). See also Herlihy (1985), and Duby (1988). Martines (1979: 271) documents that "Francesco di Giorgio Martini (1439–1502)—the Sienese engineer, architect, painter, sculptor, and writer—was one of the first observers to urge that the houses of merchants and small tradesmen be constructed with a clean separation between the rooms intended for family use and those for the conduct of business." The differentiation between person and office also evolved during this period. As Strong notes (1974: 240), "the possibility that one human being could separately be both a human being and a king—a notion on which our conception of office depends—is first elaborated by Hobbes in his distinction between natural and artificial beings in the Leviathan."

8 McLuhan (1962) made several offhand remarks about an alleged parallel between single-point perspective and nationalism. He thereby misdated the advent of nationalism by several centuries. Moreover, he was less concerned with developing the parallel than with attributing its cause to the cognitive impact of the medium of movable print. Nevertheless, I have found McLuhan's thinking enormously suggestive. The relationship between changing perspectival forms and the organization of cities and towns has been explored extensively; see, among other works, Martines (1979) and Argan (1969).

9 For a provocative depiction of social empowerment domestically, see Hirschman (1977: 130, emphasis in original): "Weber claims that capitalist behavior and activities were the indirect (and originally unintended) result of a desperate search for individual salvation. My claim is that the diffusion of capitalist forms owed much to an equally desperate search for a way of avoiding society's ruin, permanently threatening at the time because of precarious arrangements for internal and external order." Thus, according to Hirschman, the ultimate social power of the bourgeoisie benefited from a shift in social values whereby commerce became socially more highly regarded—not because of any perceived intrinsic merit or interest in commerce but for the discipline and restraint it was believed to impose on behavior in a period of severe turbulence and grave uncertainty. Additional support for Hirschman's argument may be found in Pocock (1975: 193): "It looks, then, as if Machiavelli was in search of social means whereby men's natures might be transformed to the point where they became capable of citizenship."

10 Grotius's immediate aim was to establish the principle of freedom to conduct trade *on* the seas, but in order to establish that principle he had first to formulate some doctrine regarding the medium through which ships passed as they engaged in trade. The principle he enunciated, and which states came to adopt, defined an ocean's regime in two parts: a territorial sea under exclusive state control, which custom set at three miles because that was the range of land-based cannons at the time, and the open seas beyond, available for common use but owned by none (Aster Institute 1985).

11 North and Weingast demonstrate this point nicely, both formally and empirically, for seventeenth-century England—all but the overall logic they attribute to the process, which "interprets the institutional changes on the basis of the goals of the *winners*" (1989: 803, emphasis added). The problem with this interpretation is that the goals of the *losers*—the insatiable quest for revenues on the part of rulers—and not of the winners, drove the process that ultimately made possible the imposition of constitutional constraints on the prerogatives of monarchs.

12 See Eldredge and Tattersall (1982). Eldredge, in a personal conversation with the author, attributed the basic insight for the punctuated equilibrium model,

which he helped to develop, to the historian Frederick Teggart (1925). This is ironic in the light of the influence that the Darwinian model of biological evolution has had on social thinking, including historiography. Bock (1980: 165) has described large-scale social change in similar terms: "In place of a continuous process of sociocultural change, the records clearly indicate long periods of relative inactivity among peoples, punctuated by occasional spurts of action. Rather than slow and gradual change, significant alterations in peoples' experiences have appeared suddenly, moved swiftly, and stopped abruptly." In the context of international relations, see Krasner (1984, 1988).

13 Once again, I have in mind a Lockean understanding (1947), namely those "Inconveniences which disorder Mens properties in the state of Nature," the avoidance of which is said to drive "Men [to] unite into Societies." Those "social defects" may be thought of as generic forms of international "collective action problems," of which various types of externalities, public goods, and dilemmas of strategic interaction are but specific expressions.

8 INTERESTS, IDENTITY, AND AMERICAN FOREIGN POLICY

1 Economists do not agree on the magnitudes, mostly because prevailing models are insufficiently well specified to differentiate trade effects from other changes that are occurring simultaneously. But they assume that the effects are smaller than the public presupposes. The strongest case for adverse effects is made by Wood (1994); also see Bhagwati and Kosters (1994) and Rodrik (1997).

2 During the interwar years, extensive US international commercial ties and humanitarian involvement had little or no effect on America's willingness to be systematically engaged in the political and security affairs of the world. See Jonas (1966).

3 The legislative finale was bizarre. Republican irreconcilables voted *with* the Democrats to defeat the various Republican reservations. Then, on a straight up-or-down vote, the irreconcilables rejoined the Republican majority against the treaty. "Irreconcilables had feared that Democrats would eventually approve reservations, possibly even Lodge's, as a way of saving the treaty. Instead of pursuing that course, Democratic senators enabled the irreconcilables to achieve their goal of keeping the United States out of the League" (Ambrosius 1987: 208).

4 Knock contends that the primary reason for Lodge's actions is to be found in domestic politics. Seen from a Republican vantage, control of the Senate "was as slim as could be, perhaps ephemeral. What would become of the party—indeed, of the country—if Wilson got his League, if the Democrats could boast of [quoting from a letter by former Republican Senator Albert J. Beveridge to Lodge] 'the greatest constructive world reform in history'?" (Knock 1992: 240).

5 Cantril, funded by private sources, started his work for Roosevelt in early 1941. One question FDR had Cantril repeat frequently was: "So far as you personally are concerned, do you think President Roosevelt has gone too far in his policies of helping Britain, or not far enough?" Cantril later summarized the findings over time: "In spite of the fact that United States aid to Britain constantly increased after May of 1941, the proportion of people who thought the President had gone too far, about right, or not far enough remained fairly constant. This was precisely the situation he wanted to maintain during these critical months; hence his eagerness to learn the results of our periodic soundings" (Cantril 1967: 44).

6 Indicating that it may have been a conscious effort, FDR put in place the following foreign policy team after the 1940 election: at the State Department

both Secretary Hull and Undersecretary Sumner Welles were Wilsonian Democrats. At the War Department, "the secretaries of the armed forces were TR Republicans; indeed, the new navy secretary . . . had been one of TR's Rough Riders . . . The new Vice President was from TR's faction of the Republican party, the Progressives, as was William Donovan, who was about to head the forerunner of the CIA" (Fromkin 1995: 410, 420, 428).

7 Kimball (1991: 103) addresses the connection between Roosevelt's thinking and the post-1815 concert.

8 Freshman Senator J. William Fulbright took to the Senate floor only days after charter ratification to lament this flaw in Roosevelt's design (Woods 1992: 611).

9 On the generic features of multilateralism, see Chapter 4. The link between Wilsonian geopolitical analysis and the domino theory is discussed at length by Ninkovich (1994).

10 It is little remembered today that the NATO debate in Congress took place amid an avalanche of resolutions proposing to free the United Nations from the ill effects of the Soviet veto. The State Department opposed these efforts and steered the debate toward Article 51 of the UN charter, co-drafted by Arthur Vandenberg, which permitted the creation of collective self-defense organizations. Vandenberg and other key legislators were concerned that NATO be consistent with the UN charter. Once it was, Vandenberg believed—apparently in all sincerity—that the United States could now act "within the Charter, but outside the [Soviet] veto" (quoted in Hudson 1977: 63). The pre-war isolationist Vandenberg, according to Lawrence Kaplan (1988: 36), "had been converted to internationalism on the strength of the United Nations providing collective security for all." Also see Folly (1988).

11 In his memoirs, Kennan (1967: 406–407) recalled favoring a dumbbell arrangement, but one in which the two sides of the Atlantic would be linked, not by a treaty, merely by a US–Canadian guarantee of assistance in case of Soviet attack.

12 Later generations of realists have ignored NATO's genesis struggle and the unprecedented security commitments that triggered it, preferring to think of NATO, unproblematically, as simply another alliance. Their doing so rests on Arnold Wolfers' classic essay, "Collective Defense versus Collective Security" (1962: 181–204). Wolfers argued, correctly, that NATO was not an instance of collective security but of collective defense. It does not follow, however, that there are no principled differences between NATO's form of collective defense and old-fashioned alliances. Furthermore, Wolfers betrayed considerable confusion about his own distinction. Insisting that NATO was simply a multi-member alliance, Wolfers nevertheless called the 1945 Act of Chapultepec, which led to the Rio Pact, "not . . . an alliance but . . . a regionally circumscribed system of collective security for the Americas" (ibid.: 190). Oddly, the core concept of Chapultepec—that an attack on one is an attack against all, calling for a collective response—is identical to the North Atlantic Treaty, but Wolfers did not bother to explain the discrepancy in his assessments.

13 The Southeast Asian Treaty Organization (SEATO) established not long after the French defeat at Dienbienphu was little more than a traditional alliance, embodying none of the multilateral features of NATO.

14 Neither Eisenhower nor Dulles gave any indication that they were aware of the textbook model of collective security to which realists have always taken strong exception. They meant cooperative and institutionalized means of pursuing security—though later in the 1950s, trading on the success of NATO, Dulles applied the term indiscriminately to any and all security pacts in which the US was involved.

15 Recall Eisenhower's warning in 1953, as the French position in Indochina was deteriorating: "No Western power can go to Asia militarily, except as one of a concert of powers, which concert must include local Asiatic peoples" (quoted in Brown 1983: 81).

16 These principles are multilateral insofar as they express a preference for open and non-discriminatory orders of relations among states, based on diffuse reciprocity. As observed in Chapter 4, it goes without saying that the United States, as a leading world power, has never sought to endow multilateral organizations with significant independent authority, so these two forms of multilateralism—orders of relations among states and formal organizations that operate within such orders—must not be confused with one another.

17 To avoid any possible misunderstanding, note that I am describing a dominant belief system—America's foundational myth—not an empirical reality that has held equally well for all Americans at all times.

18 Lipset makes it clear that he means "distinctiveness," not exceptionalism in the sense of somehow being better. That is also how I use the terms here."

19 Advocates of multiculturalism themselves are turning away from what Garry Nash has termed "promiscuous pluralism" (quoted in Hollinger 1995: 82), in search for a "stretching of the we." Indeed, David Hollinger, a participant observer of multiculturalist movements, senses no irony in recommending that multiculturalists locate this wider "we" in "the civic character of the American nation-state," a "nationality [that is] based on the principle of consent and is ostensibly open to persons of a variety of ethno-racial affiliations"—a "civic nation . . . built and sustained by people who honor a common future more than a common past" (ibid.: 85, 84).

20 Liberal here refers a belief in the validity of such principles as liberty, individualism, popular sovereignty, and the like, not to partisan–political orientation.

21 Characterizing Wilson as an idealist, in contrast to TR, does not fully capture their positions, according to Cooper (1983: xiv): "In domestic affairs the two men professed to reverse these positions; in foreign affairs, they were by no means polar opposites."

22 Nordlinger represents a contemporary version of the "City on the Hill" strain of isolationism that has been present in American political life almost from the start. This holds that the United States should lead the world by example that others will want to emulate, as a result of which the United States can shape the international order without significant intervention in it. Indeed, many who have held this view contend that intervention abroad would only serve to degrade the purity of the American model at home. Clearly, this strain of isolationism also draws on American "exceptionalism" for its inspiration.

9 NATO AND THE TRANSATLANTIC SECURITY COMMUNITY

1 Deutsch and his colleagues distinguished between "amalgamated" and "pluralistic" security communities: those that become one single entity, and those that maintain the separate identities of their constituent units. NATO's Article 5 commitments and integrated military command structure do not fit neatly into this typology. NATO goes well beyond the normal pluralistic security community though it is not intended to comprise the amalgamated form. Hence I use the term "tightly-coupled."

2 When the Yugoslav crisis broke out in 1991, Germany supported Slovenia and Croatia, France the Yugoslav federation and, thus, Serbia. After Germany's precipitous recognition of Croatia, which led Bosnia-Herzegovina to seek immediate recognition, Germany and France, as described by Ole Wæver (1995:

8-9), "spent half a year talking each other into a joint position, which was not very impressive and not of much help to the Yugoslav peoples, but it had the one big merit of encapsulating the conflict, of preventing it from spreading and pulling in more powers."

3 These include, as John Duffield enumerates (1994/95: 781), "satellite surveillance; command, control, communication, and intelligence; logistics; long-range airlift and sealift; all-weather aviation; amphibious capabilities; large-deck aircraft carriers; and missile defenses."

4 The Eurocorps originated as a Franco-German brigade in 1990; it has since been joined by Belgium, Luxembourg, and Spain, is now 50,000 strong, and held its first maneuvers in November 1994. Also in 1994, France, Italy, Portugal, and Spain agreed to form a Mediterranean air and sea contingent called Euroforce; and Britain and France agreed to establish a joint airborne command.

5 Once NATO was established, the original WEU members also became members of NATO and delegated to NATO the task of collective defense. New EU members are eligible for WEU membership whether or not they are NATO members. But to avoid the chain-reaction effect of NATO obligations being triggered by its members' WEU commitments to non-NATO states, the two organizations have agreed to operate on the understanding that no eligible state will seek full membership in the WEU unless it is also prepared to join NATO. The newest EU members (Austria, Finland, and Sweden) are not, and so remain WEU observers.

6 Not surprisingly, the most trenchant questions have been raised by French security specialists; see, for instance, Gnesotto (1996).

7 The most thorough case for immediate expansion has been made by the RAND team of Asmus, Kugler, and Larrabee (1993, 1995), the most incisive case against by Brown (1995).

10 UN FORCES: WHITHER—OR WHETHER?

1 Writing in September 1992 (1992c: 5), before the UN's setbacks in Somalia and Bosnia, I observed that "it is a miracle of no small magnitude that disaster has not yet befallen one of these peacekeeping missions." The UN subsequently ran out of miracles and also failed to institute more prosaic measures.

2 The British Army Field Manual, which Dobbie helped draft, coupled the phrase "spurious historically" with the less inflammatory "misleading doctrinally" (Dobbie n.d.: II-5).

3 Mallinson also helped direct the UK's "wider peacekeeping" doctrine.

4 The UN never formally adopted a doctrine, but statements by the Secretary General and the Undersecretary General for Peacekeeping came to reflect these "wider peacekeeping" notions. For example, the latter used the distinction between operational and tactical consent to explain UN actions and inactions on the ground in Bosnia in a plenary presentation at the Eighth Annual Meeting, Academic Council on the United Nations System, Graduate Center of the City University of New York, 19 June 1995

5 American troops in Somalia under Operation Restore Hope achieved both ends; the subsequent parallel UN and US missions there, and UN ground forces in Bosnia, even when backed by NATO pin-prick airstrikes, accomplished neither. The preventive deployment in Macedonia "worked," but only research in Serbian sources can establish whether it worked as a deterrent.

6 This section draws on my participation as an expert consultant in a United Nations intergovernmental working group on command and control of peace-

keeping operations. The views expressed are entirely my own, and go well beyond the consensus view of the group and the UN Secretariat, as expressed in the final document (UN 1994).

7 I base this conclusion in part on the experience of co-directing a series of work-shops on "US Participation in Multinational Peace Operations," co-sponsored by Columbia University's School of International and Public Affairs and the National Defense University in Washington, DC.

Publications by John Gerard Ruggie

1972a: "Collective goods and future international collaboration," *American Political Science Review* 66(3): 874–893.

1972b: "The structure of international organization: contingency, complexity and post-modern form," *Papers, Peace Research Society (International)* 18: 73–91.

1973: "International technology and international action" (with Ernst B. Haas), in Eugene B. Skolnikoff (ed.) *Priority Research on Technology-Related Transnational and Global Policy Problems*, Cambridge MA: Center for International Studies, MIT.

1974a: "The state of the future: technology, collective governance and world order," unpublished PhD thesis, Department of Political Science, University of California, Berkeley.

1974b: "Contingencies, constraints, and collective security: perspectives on UN involvement in international disputes," *International Organization* 28(2): 493–520.

1975a: *International Responses to Technology: Regimes, Institutions and Technocrats*, co-editor with Ernst B. Haas, published as a special issue of *International Organization* 29(3).

1975b: "International responses to technology: concepts and trends," *International Organization* 29(3): 557–583; also in Sheila Jasanoff (ed.) *Comparative Science and Technology Policy*, Cheltenham UK: Edward Elgar (1997).

1975c: "Complexity, planning and public order," in Todd R. LaPorte (ed.) *Organized Social Complexity*, Princeton: Princeton University Press.

1975d: "Environmental and resource interdependencies: reorganizing for the evolution of international regimes" (with Ernst B. Haas), in *Report of the Commission on the Organization of Government for the Conduct of Foreign Policy*, Washington DC: US Government Printing Office.

1976a: "On the creation of a new international economic order: issue-linkage and the Seventh Special Session of the UN General Assembly" (with Branislav Gosovic), *International Organization* 30(2): 309–345; derivative article published as "The catalyst," in *CERES, The FAO Review on Development* 9 (January/February).

1976b: "The 'new international economic order': origins and evolution of the concept" (with Branislav Gosovic), *International Social Science Journal* 28(4): 639–646.

1978a: "Changing frameworks of international collective behavior: on the complementarity of contradictory tendencies," in Nazli Choucri and Thomas Robinson (eds) *Forecasting in International Relations*, San Francisco: W. H. Freeman.

1978b: "The North–South dialogue: problems and prospects of developing nations," *Millennium. Journal of International Studies*, Special Edition: 92–96.

1980a: "On the problem of 'the global problématique': what roles for international organizations?" *Alternatives* 5 (4): 517–550; also in Richard A. Falk, Samuel S. Kim, and Saul H. Mendlovitz (eds) *The United Nations and a Just World Order*, Boulder: Westview (1991).

1980b: Review of Stephen D. Krasner, "Defending the national interest: raw materials investments and US foreign policy," *American Political Science Review* 74(1): 296–299.

1981a: "The politics of money," *Foreign Policy* 43: 139–154.

1981b: "Information exchange and international change: the case of INFOTERRA" (with Ernst B. Haas), *International Relations* (London) 7(1): 979–997.

1982a: "International regimes, transactions, and change: embedded liberalism in the postwar economic order," *International Organization* 36(2): 195–231; also in Stephen D. Krasner (ed.) *International Regimes*, Ithaca NY: Cornell University Press (1983); and Oran R. Young (ed.) *The International Political Economy and International Institutions*, vol. 2 , Cheltenham UK: Edward Elgar (1996).

1982b: "A political commentary on Cancun," *Third World Quarterly* 4(3): 508–514.

1982c: "What message in the medium of information systems?" (with Ernst B. Haas), *International Studies Quarterly* 26(2): 190–219.

1983a: (editor) *The Antinomies of Interdependence: National Welfare and the International Division of Labor*, New York: Columbia University Press.

1983b: "International interdependence and national welfare," in *Antinomies of Interdependence*.

1983c: "Political structure and change in the international economic order: the North–South dimension," in *Antinomies of Interdependence*.

1983d: "Continuity and transformation in the world polity: toward a neorealist synthesis," *World Politics* 35(2): 261–285; also in Robert O. Keohane (ed.) *Neorealism and its Critics*, New York: Columbia University Press (1986).

1983e: "Human rights and the future international community," *Daedalus* 112 (Fall): 93–110.

1984a: *Power, Passions, and Purpose. Prospects for North–South Negotiations*, co-editor with Jagdish Bhagwati, Cambridge MA: MIT Press.

1984b: "Another round, another requiem? Prospects for the global negotiations," in *Power, Passions, and Purpose*.

1984c: "National interests and global institutions: strategic choices" (with Edward C. Luck), in *The United Nations in World Affairs· Options for the United States*, New York: UNA–USA.

1985a: "The United States and the United Nations: toward a new realism," *International Organization* 39(2): 343–356; also in Paul F. Diehl (ed.) *The Politics of International Organizations. Patterns and Insights*, Chicago: Dorsey Press (1989); and in Peter A. Toma and Robert F. Gorman (eds) *International Relations: A Primer on Understanding Global Issues*, Pacific Grove, CA: Brooks/Cole (1991).

1985b: "The United States, the United Nations, and the future" (with Peter Fromuth), in *Report of the Twenty-Sixth Annual Strategy for Peace Conference*, Muscatine, IA: Stanley Foundation.

1986a: "Social time and international policy: conceptualizing global population and resource issues," in Margaret P. Karns (ed.) *Persistent Patterns and Emergent Structures in a Waning Century*, New York: Praeger.

1986b: "International organization: a state of the art on an art of the state" (with Friedrich Kratochwil), *International Organization* 40(4): 753–775; also in Paul F. Diehl (ed.) *The Politics of International Organizations: Patterns and Insights*, Chicago: Dorsey Press (1989); in Friedrich Kratochwil and Edward D. Mansfield (eds) *International Organization. A Reader*, New York: HarperCollins (1994); and in Oran R. Young (ed.) *The International Political Economy and International Institutions*, vol. 1, Cheltenham UK: Edward Elgar (1996).

1987: "The North American political economy in the global context: an analytical framework" (with David Leyton-Brown), *International Journal* 42(1): 3–24.

1989a: "International structure and international transformation: space, time and method," in James N. Rosenau and Ernst-Otto Czempiel (eds) *Global Changes and Theoretical Challenges: Approaches to World Politics for the 1990s*, Lexington, MA: Lexington Books.

1989b. "The folly of our 'wait and see' on Soviets," *Los Angeles Times*, 9 May 1989.

1990a· "US strategy in a changing world," *Disarmament* (United Nations) 13(4)· 16–44.

1990b: "New European policy needed now," *San Diego Union*, 25 February 1990.

1990c: "Global changes should prompt integration of [Latin America's] economies," *San Diego Union*, 1 July 1990.

1990d: "Is America pursuing the right 'New World Order'?" *San Diego Union*, 2 December 1990.

1990e: "A critical look at Gulf strategy," *San Francisco Chronicle*, 8 December 1990.

1991a: "Embedded liberalism revisited: institutions and progress in international economic relations," in Emanuel Adler and Beverly Crawford (eds) *Progress in Postwar International Relations*, New York: Columbia University Press.

1991b: "Countdown to war?" *San Diego Union*, 13 January 1991.

1991c: "Use UN to ease into a global role," *Japan Times* (Tokyo), 10 April 1991.

1991d: "A new global security role for Germany and Japan," *San Diego Union*, 28 April 1991.

1992a: "Multilateralism: the anatomy of an institution," *International Organization* 46(3): 561–598; also in Ruggie (1993a); and in Friedrich Kratochwil and Edward D. Mansfield (eds) *International Organization. A Reader*, New York: HarperCollins (1994).

1992b: "Trade deals: a prelude to trade war?" *New York Newsday*, 19 January 1992.

1992c· "No, the world doesn't need a United Nations army," *International Herald Tribune*, 26–27 September 1992; also in *UN Special* (Geneva), No. 505, February 1993.

1992d: "When America talks, thugs listen," *Los Angeles Times*, 1 December 1992.

1993a: (editor) *Multilateralism Matters. The Theory and Praxis of an Institutional Form*, New York: Columbia University Press.

1993b: "Territoriality and beyond: problematizing modernity in international relations," *International Organization* 46(1): 139–174.

1993c: "Unravelling trade: global institutional change and the Pacific economy," in Richard Higgott, Richard Leaver, and John Ravenhill (eds) *Pacific Economic Relations in the 1990s: Cooperation or Conflict?*, Sydney, Australia: Allen and Unwin/Boulder CO: Lynne Rienner.

1993d: "Wandering in the void: charting the UN's new strategic role," *Foreign Affairs* 72(5): 26–31; also in William H. Lewis (ed.) *Peacekeeping: The Way Ahead?*, Washington DC: National Defense University (McNair Paper no. 25, November); *Foreign Affairs Agenda 1994*, New York: Council on Foreign Relations (1994); and Charles W. Kegley, Jr, and Eugene R. Wittkopf (eds) *The Global Agenda: Issues and Perspectives*, New York: McGraw-Hill (1995); Japanese translation in *Chuo Koron*, February 1994.

1993e: "Management and mismanagement at the United Nations," *Hearing Before the Subcommittee on International Security, International Organizations and Human Rights*, Committee on Foreign Affairs, House of Representatives, 103rd Congress, First Session, 5 March 1993 (US Government Printing Office).

1993f: "The Carteritis virus knocks Clinton off his feet," *New York Newsday*, 6 June 1993.

1994a: "Third try at world order? America and multilateralism after the Cold War,"

Political Science Quarterly 109(4): 553–570; also in Demetrios James Caraley and Bonnie B. Hartman (eds) *American Leadership, Ethnic Conflict, and the New World Politics*, New York: Academy of Political Science (1997).

1994b: "Peacekeeping and US interests," *Washington Quarterly* 17(4): 175–184; also in Brad Roberts (ed.) *Order and Disorder after the Cold War*, Cambridge MA: MIT Press (1995).

1995a: "At home abroad, abroad at home: international liberalization and domestic stability in the new world economy," *Jean Monnet Chair Papers*, 20, Florence: European University Institute; revised version in *Millennium: Journal of International Studies* 24(3): 507–526; excerpted as "Trade, protectionism and the future of welfare capitalism," in *Journal of International Affairs* 48(1): 1–11.

1995b: "The false premise of realism," *International Security* 20(1): 62–70.

1995c: "Peace in our time? Causality, social facts, and narrative knowing," *American Society of International Law, Proceedings, 89th Annual Meeting*: 93–100.

1996a: *Winning the Peace: America and World Order in the New Era*, New York: Columbia University Press.

1996b: "The United Nations and the collective use of force—whither or whether?" *International Peacekeeping* 3(4): 1–20; also in Michael Pugh (ed.) *The UN, Peace and Force*, London: Cass (1997); also published as occasional paper by the United Nations Association of the United States of America.

1997a: "Consolidating the European pillar: the key to NATO's future," *Washington Quarterly* 20(1): 109–124; also in *Quaderni Forum* (Florence) 9(4): 49–57.

1997b: "The past as prologue? Interests, identity, and American foreign policy," *International Security* 21(4): 89–125.

1997c: "Globalisierung und der gesellschaftliche Kompromiss des regulierten Liberalismus: Das Ende einer Ära?" ("Globalization and the embedded liberalism compromise: the end of an era?") in *Jahrbuch Arbeit und Technik* (1997).

References

Abel, T. F. (1948) "The operation called *Verstehen*," *American Journal of Sociology* 54(1): 211–218.

Adler, E. (1991) "Cognitive evolution: a dynamic approach for the study of international relations and their progress," in E. Adler and B. Crawford (eds) *Progress in Postwar International Relations*, New York: Columbia University Press.

—— (1992) "The emergence of cooperation: national epistemic communities and the international evolution of the idea of nuclear arms control," *International Organization* 46(1): 101–145.

—— (1997) "Seizing the middle ground: constructivism and world politics," *European Journal of International Relations* 3 (3) 319–359.

Adler, E. and Barnett, M. N. (1996) "Governing anarchy: a research agenda for the study of security communities," *Ethics and International Affairs* 10: 63–98.

Adler, E. and Haas, P. (1992) "Conclusion: epistemic communities, world order, and the creation of a reflective research program," *International Organization* 46(1): 367–390.

Aggarwal, V. K. (1985) *Liberal Protectionism: The International Politics of Organized Textile Trade*, Berkeley: University of California Press.

Albrecht-Carrié, R. (1958) *A Diplomatic History of Europe Since the Congress of Vienna*, New York: Harper and Row.

—— (1968) *The Concert of Europe*, New York: Walker.

Alexander, C. (1965) "A city is not a tree," *Architectural Forum*, 122: March and April.

Alker, H. A., Jr (1981) "Dialectical foundations of global disparities," *International Studies Quarterly* 25(1): 69–98.

—— (1990) "Rescuing 'reason' from the 'rationalists': reading Vico, Marx and Weber as reflective institutionalists," *Millennium: Journal of International Studies* 19(2): 161–184.

—— (1996) *Rediscoveries and Reformulations. Humanistic Methodologies for International Studies*, New York: Cambridge University Press.

Allott, P. (1983) "Power sharing in the law of the sea," *American Journal of International Law* 77(2): 1–30.

Ambrosius, L. E. (1987) *Woodrow Wilson and the American Diplomatic Tradition*, New York: Cambridge University Press.

Anderson, B. (1983) *Imagined Communities: Reflections on the Origin and Spread of Nationalism*, London: Verso Books.

Anderson, M. S. (1963) *Europe in the Eighteenth Century, 1713–1783*, London: Longmans.

Anderson, P. (1974) *Lineages of the Absolutist State*, London: New Left Books.

Arad, R. W. and Arad, U. B. (1979) "Scarce natural resources and potential conflict," in Arad et al. (eds) *Sharing Global Resources*, New York: McGraw-Hill.

Argan, G. C. (1969) *The Renaissance City*, New York: George Braziller.

Ashley, R. K. (1984) "The poverty of neorealism," *International Organization* 38(2): 225–286

—— (1987) "The geopolitics of geopolitical space: toward a critical social theory of international relations," *Alternatives* 12(3): 403–434.

—— (1988) "Untying the sovereign state: a double reading of the anarchy problématique," *Millennium: Journal of International Studies* 17(2): 227–262.

Asmus, R. D. and Nurick, R.C. (1996) "NATO enlargement and the Baltic States," *Survival* 38 (2): 121–142.

Asmus, R. D., Kugler, R. L., and Larrabee, F. S. (1993) "Building a new NATO," *Foreign Affairs* 72(4): 28–40.

—— (1995) "NATO expansion: the next steps," *Survival* 37(1): 7–33.

Aster Institute (1985) *International Law: The Grotian Heritage*, The Hague: Aster Institute.

Axelrod, R. (1984) *Evolution of Cooperation*, New York: Basic Books.

Axelrod, R. and Keohane, R. O. (1985) "Achieving cooperation under anarchy: strategies and institutions," *World Politics* 38(1): 226–254.

Baldwin, D. A. (ed.) (1985) *Economic Statecraft*, Princeton NJ: Princeton University Press.

—— (1993) *Neorealism and Neoliberalism. The Contemporary Debate*, New York: Columbia University Press.

Balibar, E. (1991) "Es Gibt Keinen Staat in Europa: Racism and politics in Europe today," *New Left Review* 186: 16–24.

Barnard, C. I. (1938) *The Functions of the Executive*, Cambridge MA: Harvard University Press.

—— (1948) *Organization and Management*, Cambridge MA: Harvard University Press.

Barnett, M. (1996) "Identity and alliances in the Middle East," in P. J. Katzenstein (ed.) *The Culture of National Security: Norms and Identity in World Politics*, New York: Columbia University Press.

Barney, G. O. (ed.) (1980) *The Global 2000 Report to the President of the US*, New York: Pergamon Press.

Barry, C. (1996) "NATO's combined joint task forces in theory and practice," *Survival* 38(1): 81–97.

Bator, F. M. (1957) "The simple analytics of welfare maximization," *American Economic Review* 47(1): 22–59.

Bautier, R. H. (1971) *The Economic Development of Medieval Europe*, H. Karolyi (trans.), London: Harcourt Brace Jovanovich.

Becker, M. B. (1981) *Medieval Italy: Constraints and Creativity*, Bloomington: Indiana University Press.

Benedick, R. E. (1991) *Ozone Diplomacy. New Directions in Safeguarding the Planet*, Cambridge MA: Harvard University Press.

Benhabib, S. (1984) "Epistemologies of postmodernism: a rejoinder to Jean-François Lyotard," *New German Critique* 33: 103–126.

Bennett, J. W. (1976) *The Ecological Transition*, New York: Pergamon Press.

Berger, P. L. and Luckman, T. (1966) *The Social Construction of Reality*, Garden City NY: Doubleday.

Berger, T. U. (1996) "Norms, identity, and national security in Germany and Japan," in P. J. Katzenstein (ed.) *The Culture of National Security: Norms and Identity in World Politics*, New York: Columbia University Press.

Bergsten, C. F. (1972) "The new economics and US foreign policy," *Foreign Affairs* 50(2): 199–222.

Berk, R. A. (1988) "Causal inference for sociological data," in N. J. Smelser (ed.) *Handbook of Sociology*, Newbury Park CA: Sage.

Berki, R. N. (1971) "On Marxian thought and the problem of international relations," *World Politics* 24(1): 80–105

Bernert, C. (1983) "The career of causal analysis in American sociology," *British Journal of Sociology* 34(2): 230–254.

Bhagwati, Jagdish (1997) "Fear not," *New Republic*, 19 May: 36–41.

Bhagwati, J. N. and Irwin, D A. (1987) "The return of the reciprocitarians," *The World Economy* 10(2): 109–130.

Bhagwati, J. N. and Kosters, M. (eds) (1994) *Trade and Wages*, Washington DC: American Enterprise Institute.

Bhaskar, R. (1979) *The Possibility of Naturalism*, Atlantic Highlands NJ: Humanities Press.

Bienen, H. (1984) "Urbanization and Third World stability," *World Development* 12(7): 661–692.

Black, C and Falk, R. A. (eds) (1972) *The Future of the International Legal Order*, Princeton: Princeton University Press.

Blackhurst, R., Marian, N. and Tumlir, J. (1977) "Trade liberalization, protectionism and interdependence," *GATT Studies in International Trade* 5: 18–19.

Blau, P (1963) "Critical remarks on Weber's theory of authority," *American Political Science Review* 57(1): 305–316.

Block, F. (1977) *The Origins of International Economic Disorder*, Berkeley CA: University of California Press.

Bloomfield, A. (1959) *Monetary Policy Under the International Gold Standard*, New York: Federal Reserve Bank of New York.

—— (1963) "Short-term capital movements under the pre-1914 gold standard," *Princeton Studies in International Finance* 11.

Bloomfield, R. J. and Lowenthal, A. F. (1990) "Inter-American institutions in a time of change," *International Journal* 45(4): 867–888.

Blyth, M. (1997) "Any more good ideas?" *Comparative Politics*.

Bock, K. (1980) *Human Nature and History. A Response to Sociobiology*, New York: Columbia University Press.

Borkenau, F. (1962) *World Communism. A History of the Communist International*, Ann Arbor: University of Michigan Press.

—— (1981) *End and Beginning On the Generations of Cultures and the Origins of the West*, Richard Lowenthal (ed.), New York: Columbia University Press.

—— (1995) *An Agenda for Peace, 1995*, New York: United Nations.

Bowett, D. W. (1964) *United Nations Forces: A Legal Study*, New York: Praeger.

Bozeman, A. G. (1960) *Politics and Culture in International History*, Princeton NJ: Princeton University Press.

Braudel, F. (1972) *The Mediterranean and the Mediterranean World in the Age of Philip II* (2 vols), S. Reynolds (trans.), New York: Harper and Row.

—— (1980) *On History*, S. Matthews (trans.), Chicago: University of Chicago Press.

Brenner, R. (1977) "The origins of capitalist development: a critique of neo-Smithian Marxism," *New Left Review* 104: 25–92.

Briggs, A. (1968) "The world economy: interdependence and planning," in C. L. Mowat (ed.) *The New Cambridge Modern History*, vol. 12, Cambridge: Cambridge University Press.

Bronowski, J. (1965) "The discovery of form," in Guyorgy Keps (ed.) *Structure in Art and in Science*, New York: Braziller

Brown, M. E. (1995) "The flawed logic of NATO expansion," *Survival* 37(1): 34–52.

Brown, S. (1983) *The Faces of Power*, New York: Columbia University Press.

Bruner, J. (1986) *Actual Minds, Possible Worlds*, Cambridge MA: Harvard University Press.

Bryson, R. A. and Murray, T. J. (1977) *Climates of Hunger*, Madison WI: University of Wisconsin.

Brzezinski, Z. (1993) "A bigger—and safer—Europe," *New York Times*, 1 December 1993: A23.

Buchanan, J. M. (1968) *The Demand and Supply of Public Goods*, Chicago: Rand McNally.

Buchanan, J. M. and Tullock, G. (1962) *The Calculus of Consent*, Ann Arbor: University of Michigan Press.

Bull, H. (1968) "The Grotian conception of international society," in H. Butterfield and M. Wight (eds) *Diplomatic Investigations*, Cambridge MA: Harvard University Press.

—— (1977) *The Anarchical Society: A Study of Order in World Politics*, London: Macmillan.

Bull, H. and Watson, A. (eds) (1984) *The Expansion of European Society*, London: Oxford University Press.

Burley, A. M. (1993) "Regulating the world: multilateralism, international law, and the projection of the new deal regulatory state," in J. G. Ruggie (ed.) *Multilateralism Matters· The Theory and Praxis of an Institutional Form*, New York: Columbia University Press.

Burley, A. M. and Mattli, W. (1993) "Europe before the court: a political theory of legal integration," *International Organization* 47(1): 41–76.

Butterfield, H. and Wight, M. (1968) *Diplomatic Investigations· Essays in the Theory of International Politics*, London: Allen and Unwin.

Buzan, B. (1981) "Negotiating by consensus: developments in technique at the UN conference on the Law of the Sea," *American Journal of International Law* 75(2): 324–348.

—— (1993) "From international system to international society: structural realism and regime theory meet the English School," *International Organization* 47(3): 327–352.

Buzan, B. and Little, R. (1996) "Reconceptualizing anarchy: structural realism meets world history," *European Journal of International Relations* 2(4): 403–438.

Buzan, B., Jones, C., and Little, R. (1993) *The Logic of Anarchy: Neorealism to Structural Realism*, New York: Columbia University Press.

Byson, R A. and Murray, T. J. (1977) *Climates of Hunger: Mankind and the World's Changing Weather*, Madison: University of Wisconsin Press.

Callaghy, T. M. (1985) "The patrimonial administrative state in Africa," prepared for "Symposium on African State in Transition," Georgetown University, 22–23 February 1985.

Campbell, D. T. (1987) "Evolutionary epistemology," in G. Radnitsky and W. W. Bartley (eds) *Evolutionary Epistemology, Theory of Rationality and the Sociology of Knowledge*, La Salle IL: Open Court.

Campbell, D. (1992) *Writing Security: United States Foreign Policy and the Politics of Identity*, Minneapolis: University of Minnesota Press.

—— (1996) "Political prosaics, transversal politics, and the anarchical world," in M. J. Shapiro and H. R. Alker (eds) *Challenging the Boundaries*, Minneapolis: University of Minnesota Press.

Cantril, H. (1967) *The Human Dimension: Experiences in Policy Research*, New Brunswick NJ: Rutgers University Press.

Caparaso, J. A. and Pelowski, A. L. (1971) "Economic and political integration of

Europe: a time-series quasi-experimental analysis," *American Political Science Review* 54(2): 418–433.

Carr, E. H. (1946) *The Twenty Years' Crisis 1919–1939*, New York· Harper.

—— (1961) *International Relations Between the Two World Wars*, New York: St Martin's Press.

Castells, M. (1989) *The Informational City*, Oxford: Basil Blackwell.

Chamberlain, J. P. (1923) *The Regime of International Rivers*, New York: Carnegie Endowment for International Peace.

Chesterton, G. K. (1922) *What I Saw in America*, New York: Dodd, Mead.

Chittick, W. O., Billingsley, K. R., and Travis, R. (1995) "A three-dimensional model of American foreign policy beliefs," *International Studies Quarterly* 39(3): 313–331.

Chomsky, N. (1964) *Current Issues in Linguistic Theory*, The Hague: Mouton.

Choucri, N. (1974) *Population Dynamics and International Violence*, Lexington MA: Lexington-Heath.

Choucri, N. and North, R. C. (1975) *Nations in Conflict*, San Francisco: W. H Freeman.

Christensen, T. J. and Snyder, J. (1990) "Chain gangs and passed bucks: predicting alliance patterns in multipolarity," *International Organization* 44(2): 137–168.

Citrin, J., Haas, E. B., Muste, C., and Reingold, B. (1994) "Is American nationalism changing? Implications for foreign policy," *International Studies Quarterly* 38(1): 1–31.

Clarke, W. M. (1990) "The midwives of the New Europe," *Central Banking* 1(1): 49–51.

Claude, I. L., Jr (1956) *Swords into Plowshares: The Problems and Progress of International Organization*, New York: Random House.

—— (1966) "Collective legitimization as a political function of the United Nations," *International Organization* 20(3): 367–379.

—— (1967) *Power and International Relations*, New York: Random House.

Cleveland, H. V. B. (1976) "The international monetary system in the interwar period," in B. M. Rowland (ed.) *Balance of Power or Hegemony: The Interwar Monetary System*, New York: New York University Press.

Cohen, B. (1983) "Balance of payments financing: evolution of a regime," in S. D. Krasner (ed.) *International Regimes*, Ithaca NY: Cornell University Press.

Cohen, R. (1994) "UN general opposes more Bosnia force," *New York Times*, 28 September 1994: A7.

—— (1995) "UN commander set to leave Bosnia after a year of triumph and disaster," *New York Times*, 22 January 1995: A6.

Coleman, J. (1986) "The civic culture of contracts and credit," *Comparative Study of Society and History* 28(3): 778–784.

Connolly, W. (1983) *The Terms of Political Discourse*, 2nd edn, Princeton NJ: Princeton University Press.

Contamine, P. (1984) *War in the Middle Ages*, M. Jones (trans.), New York: Basil Blackwell.

Conybeare, J. A. C. (1987) *Trade Wars: The Theory and Practice of International Commercial Rivalry*, New York: Columbia University Press.

Cook, T. D. and Campbell, D. T. (1979) *Quasiexperimentation*, Chicago: Rand McNally.

Cooper, J. M. (1983) *The Warrior and the Priest: Woodrow Wilson and Theodore Roosevelt*, Cambridge MA: Harvard University Press.

Cooper, R. N. (1975) "Prolegomena to the choice of an international monetary system," *International Organization* 29(1): 63–98.

—— (1968) *The Economics of Interdependence*, New York: McGraw-Hill.

Cowell, A. (1993) "Italy, in UN rift, threatens recall of Somalia troops," *New York Times*, 16 July 1993: A1.

Cowhey, P. F. (1993) "Elect locally, order globally: domestic politics and multilateral cooperation," in J. Ruggie (ed.) *Multilateralism Matters: The Theory and Praxis of an Institutional Form*, New York: Columbia University Press..

Cox, R. W. (1977) "Labor and hegemony," *International Organization* 31(3): 385–424.

—— (1983) "Gramsci, hegemony and international relations: an essay in method," *Millennium· Journal of International Studies* 12(2): 162–175.

—— (1986) "Social forces, states, and world orders: beyond international relations theory," in R. O. Keohane (ed.) *Neorealism and its Critics*, New York: Columbia University Press.

Cox, R. W. and Jacobson, H. K. (eds) (1973) *The Anatomy of Influence*, New Haven: Yale University Press.

Craig, G. A. and George, A. L. (1983) *Force and Statecraft*, New York: Oxford University Press.

Crawford, T. (1996) "The illogic of minimum force: doctrine and deterrence in Bosnia and beyond," Columbia University. unpublished paper.

Curzon, G. and Curzon, V. (1976) "The management of trade relations in the GATT," in A. Shonfield (ed.) *International Economic Relations of the Western World, 1959–1971*, vol. I, London: Oxford University Press for Royal Institute of International Affairs.

Cushman, J. H., Jr (1993) "How powerful US units will work," *New York Times*, 8 October 1993: A4.

Dahlberg, K. A. (1983) "Contextual analysis: taking space, time, and place seriously," *International Studies Quarterly* 27(3): 257–266.

Dallek, R. (1979) *Franklin D. Roosevelt and American Foreign Policy*, New York: Oxford University Press.

—— (1983) *The American Style of Foreign Policy*, New York: Oxford University Press.

Dallmayr, F. R. and McCarthy, T. A (1977) *Understanding and Social Inquiry*, Notre Dame: University of Notre Dame Press.

Daniel, D. C. F. and Miles, M. E. (1996) "Is there a middle option in peace support operations? Implications for crisis containment and disarmament," paper prepared for United Nations Institute for Disarmament Research, Geneva, Switzerland.

Danto, A. C. (1985) *Narration and Knowledge*, New York: Columbia University Press.

Degenhardt, H. W. (1981) *Treaties and Alliances of the World*, 3rd edn, Essex: Longmans.

Dehio, L. (1962) *The Precarious Balance*, New York: Knopf.

Deibel, T. (1992) "Strategies before containment: patterns for the future," *International Security* 16(4): 79–108.

Der Derian, J. (1987) *On Diplomacy*, Oxford: Blackwell.

Dessler, D. (1989) "What's at stake in the agent–structure debate?" *International Organization* 43(3): 441–473.

Deutsch, K. W. et al. (1957) *Political Community and the North Atlantic Area*, Princeton: Princeton University Press.

De Vries, M. G. and Horsefield, J. K. (1969) *The IMF, 1945–1965*, vol. II, Washington DC: International Monetary Fund.

Dibb, P. (1995) "Towards a new balance of power in Asia," *Adelphi Paper No. 295*, London: Oxford University Press.

Diebold, W., Jr (1952) "The end of the ITO," *Princeton Essays in International Finance* 16 (Princeton NJ).

—— (1988) "The history and the issues," in W. Diebold, Jr (ed.) *Bilateralism, Multilateralism and Canada in US Trade Policy*, Cambridge MA: Ballinger.

Divine, R. A (1967) *Second Chance The Triumph of Internationalism in America During World War II*, New York: Athenaeum.

Dobbie, C. W. G. (1994) "Wider peacekeeping: an approach to peacekeeping post cold war," paper distributed at United Nations High-Level Meeting on Peacekeeping, Ottawa, Canada, 29 April–1 May 1994

—— (n.d.) *Wider Peacekeeping*, unpublished.

Doyle, M. W. (1986) *Empires*, Ithaca NY: Cornell University Press

Doyle, M. W. and Suntharalingham, N. (1994) "The UN in Cambodia: lessons for complex peacekeeping," *International Peacekeeping* 1(2): 117–147.

Drucker, P. (1986) "Japan and adversarial trade," *Wall Street Journal*, 1 April 1986: 32.

Duby, G. (1980) *The Three Orders. Feudal Society Imagined*, A. Goldhammer (trans.), Chicago: University of Chicago Press.

—— (1988) "A history of private life," in *Revelations of the Medieval World*, A. Goldhammer (trans.), Cambridge MA: Belknap.

Duchene, F (1994) *Jean Monnet: The First Statesman of Interdependence*, New York: Norton.

Duchin, B. R. (1992) "The 'agonizing reappraisal': Eisenhower, Dulles, and the European Defense Community," *Diplomatic History* 16(2): 201–221.

Duffield, J. S. (1992) "International regimes and alliance behavior," *International Organization* 46(4): 369–388.

—— (1994/5) "NATO's functions after the Cold War," *Political Science Quarterly* 109(5): 763–788.

Durham, W. H. (1979) *Scarcity and Survival in Central America: Ecological Origins of the Soccer War*, Stanford CA: Stanford University Press.

Durkheim, E. (1933) [1893]*The Division of Labor in Society*, G. Simpson (trans.), New York: Macmillan.

—— (1938) [1895]*The Rules of Sociological Method*, E. G. Catlin (ed.), New York: Free Press.

—— (1951) *Suicide*, New York: Free Press.

—— (1953a) *Sociology and Philosophy*, D. F. Pocock (trans.), London: Cohen and West.

—— (1953b) [1911] "Value judgments and judgments of reality," in E. Durkheim *Sociology and Philosophy*, D. F. Pocock (trans.), London: Cohen and West.

—— (1953c) [1898] "Individual and collective representations," in E. Durkheim *Sociology and Philosophy*, D. F. Pocock (trans.), London: Cohen and West.

—— (1965) [1912] *The Elementary Forms of Religious Life*, New York: Free Press.

Dworkin, R. (1986) *Law's Empire*, Cambridge MA: Harvard University Press.

Eckes, A. E., Jr (1979) *The United States and the Global Struggle for Minerals*, Austin TX: University of Texas Press.

Eckstein, H. (1973) "Authority patterns: a structural basis for political inquiry," *American Political Science Review* 67(4): 1142–1162.

The Economist (1991) "Echoes of the 1930s," 5 January 1991: 15–16, 18.

—— (1991) "Many-spired Europe," 18 May 1991: 16.

—— (1992) "La force d'Euro-frappe?," 18 January 1992: 48.

Edgerton, S. Y., Jr (1975) *The Renaissance Rediscovery of Linear Perspective*, New York: Basic Books.

Ehrlich, P. R., Ehrlich, A., and Holdren, J. (1977) *Ecoscience. Population, Resources, Environment*, San Francisco: W. H. Freeman.

Ehrlich, P. R. *et al.* (eds.) (1984) *The Cold and the Dark. The World After Nuclear War*, New York: W. W. Norton.

Eichengreen, B. (1987) "Conducting the international orchestra: Bank of England leadership under the classical gold standard," *Journal of International Money and Finance* 6(1): 5–29.

Eldredge, N. and Tattersall, I. (1982) *The Myths of Human Evolution*, New York: Columbia University Press.

Elias, N. (1978) *The Civilizing Process*, New York: Urizen Books.

—— (1983) *Power and Civility*, New York: Pantheon.

Elrod, R. B. (1976) "The Concert of Europe: a fresh look at an international system," *World Politics* 28(2): 159–174.

Elshtain, J. B. (1987) *Women and War*, New York: Basic Books.

—— (1996) "Is there a feminist tradition on war and peace?" in T. Nardin (ed.) *The Ethics of War and Peace*, Princeton: Princeton University Press.

Emory, F. E. and Trist, E. L. (1973) *Towards a Social Ecology: Contextual Appreciation of the Future in the Present*, London: Plenum.

Enloe, C. H. (1980) *Ethnic Soldiers: State Security in Divided Societies*, Athens: University of Georgia Press.

Etzioni, A. (1966) "The dialectics of supranational unification," *International Political Communities*, Garden City: Anchor Books.

Falk, R A. (1964) "International jurisdiction: horizontal and vertical conceptions of legal order," in R. A. Falk (ed.) *The Role of Domestic Law in the International Legal Order*, Syracuse: Syracuse University Press.

—— (1969) "The interplay of Westphalia and charter conceptions of international legal order," in R. A. Falk and C. Black (eds) *The Future of the International Legal Order*, vol. I, Princeton: Princeton University Press.

Fearon, J. D. (1991) "Counterfactuals and hypothesis testing in political science," *World Politics* 43(2): 169–195.

Febvre, L. and Martin, H. J. (1984) *The Coming of the Book*, D. Gerard (trans.), G. N. Smith and D. Wootton (eds), London: Verso.

Feinberg, G. (1978) *What is the World Made of? Atoms, Leptons, Quarks, and Other Tantalizing Particles*, Garden City NY: Anchor Press/Doubleday.

Feis, H. (1947) "The conflict over trade ideologies," *Foreign Affairs* 25(2): 217–228.

—— (1966) *1933: Characters in Crisis*, Boston: Little, Brown.

Field, A. J. (1979) "On the explanation of rules using rational choice models," *Journal of Economic Issues* 13(1): 49–72.

—— (1981) "The problem with neoclassical institutional economics: a critique with special reference to the North/Thomas Model of pre-1500 Europe," *Explorations in Economic History* 19(2): 174–198.

—— (1984) "Microeconomics, norms, and rationality," *Economic Development and Cultural Change* 32(4): 683–711.

Finkielkraut, A. (1995) *The Defeat of the Mind*, J. Friedlander (trans.), New York: Columbia University Press.

Finnemore, M. (1996a) *National Interests in International Society*, Ithaca: Cornell University Press.

—— (1996b) "Norms, culture, and world politics: insights from sociology's institutionalism," *International Organization* 50(2): 349–347.

—— (1996c) "Constructing norms of humanitarian intervention," in P. J. Katzenstein (ed.) *The Culture of National Security: Norms and Identity in World Politics*, New York: Columbia University Press.

Finucane, R. C. (1983) *Soldiers of the Faith: Crusaders and Moslems at War*, London: J. M. Dent.

Fischer, M. (1992) "Feudal Europe, 800–1300: communal discourse and conflictual practices," *International Organization* 46(2) 427–466.

Fitchett, J. (1996) "New look for NATO: a balance of strategic aims," *International Herald Tribune*, 4 June 1996: A1.

Folly, M. H. (1988) "Breaking the vicious circle: Britain, the United States, and the genesis of the North Atlantic Treaty," *Diplomatic History* 12(1): 59–77.

Food and Agriculture Organization (1979) *Agriculture: Toward 2000*, Rome: Food and Agriculture Organization.

Forsythe, D. (1991) *The Internationalization of Human Rights*, Lexington MA: Lexington Books.

Foucault, M. (1970) *The Order of Things*, New York: Random House.

Fox, W. T. R. (1944) *The Super-Powers: The United States, Britain, and the Soviet Union*, New York: Harcourt, Brace.

Frieden, J. (1994) "International investment and colonial control: a new interpretation," *International Organization* 48(4): 559–593.

Fromkin, D. (1995) *In the Time of the Americans: The Generation that Changed America's Role in the World*, New York: Knopf.

Furubotn, E. G. and Pejovich, S. (eds) (1974) *The Economics of Property Rights*, Cambridge MA: Ballinger.

Gacek, C. M. (1994) *The Logic of Force· The Dilemma of Limited War in American Foreign Policy*, New York: Columbia University Press.

Gaddis, J. L. (1982) *Strategies of Containment*, New York: Oxford University Press.

Gallicchio, M. S. (1988) *The Cold War Begins in Asia*, New York: Columbia University Press.

Gardner, R. N. (1980) *Sterling–Dollar Diplomacy in Current Perspective*, New York: Columbia University Press.

Garrett, G. (1993) "International cooperation and institutional choice: the European Community's internal market," in J. G. Ruggie (ed.) *Multilateralism Matters: The Theory and Praxis of an Institutional Form*, New York: Columbia University Press..

Garrett, G. and Weingast, B. (1993) "Ideas, interests, and institutions: constructing the European Community's internal market," in J. Goldstein and R. O. Keohane (eds) *Ideas and Foreign Policy*, Ithaca: Cornell University Press..

Geertz C. (1973) *The Interpretation of Cultures*, New York: Basic Books.

Gelfand, L. E. (1983) "The mystique of Wilsonian statecraft," *Diplomatic History* 7(2): 87–102.

George, A. L. (1979) "Case studies and theory development: the method of structured, focused comparison," in P. G. Lauren (ed.) *Diplomacy: New Approaches in History, Theory, and Policy*, New York: Free Press.

—— (1991) *Forceful Persuasion*, Washington DC: United States Institute of Peace Press.

—— (1994) "Coercive diplomacy: definition and characteristics," in A. George and W. E. Simons (eds) *The Limits of Coercive Diplomacy*, 2nd rev. edn, Boulder CO: Westview.

Giddens, A. (1978) *Emile Durkheim*, New York: Penguin.

—— (1979) *Central Problems in Social and Political Theory*, Berkeley/Los Angeles: University of California Press.

—— (1981) *A Contemporary Critique of Historical Materialism*, Berkeley: University of California Press.

Gilbert, F. (1961) *To the Farewell Address Ideas of Early American Foreign Policy*, Princeton NJ: Princeton University Press.

Gill, S. (1995) "Globalisation, market civilisation, and disciplinary neoliberalism," *Millennium: Journal of International Studies* 24(3): 399–424.

Gilligan, C. (1993) *In a Different Voice: Psychological Theory and Women's Development*, Cambridge MA: Harvard University Press.

Gilpin, R. (1975) *Power and the Multinational Corporation*, New York: Basic Books.
—— (1981) *War and Change in World Politics*, New York: Cambridge University Press.
Gilpin, S. (1982) "Minerals and foreign policy," *Africa Report* 27(3): 16–22.
Glaser, C. L. (1993) "Why NATO is still best: future security arrangements for Europe," *International Security* 18(1): 5–50.
Glucksman, M. (1974) *Structuralist Analysis in Contemporary Social Thought*, London: Routledge and Kegan Paul.
Gnesotto, N. (1996) "Common European defense and transatlantic relations," *Survival* 38(1): 19–31.
Goffman, E. (1973) *The Presentation of Self in Everyday Life*, Woodstock NY: Overlook Press.
Goldstein, J. and Keohane, R. O. (eds) (1993) *Ideas and Foreign Policy*, Ithaca NY: Cornell University Press.
Gordon, M. R. (1992) "US is sending large force as warning to Somali clans," *New York Times*, 5 December 1992: A5
—— (1993) "Allies seem to hope Serbs won't attack," *New York Times*, 24 May 1993: A7
—— (1995) "UN commander set to leave Bosnia, after a year of triumph and disaster," *New York Times*, 22 January 1995: A6.
Gottlieb, A. and Dalfen, C. (1973) "National jurisdiction and international responsibility: new Canadian approaches to international law," *American Journal of International Law* 67: 229–258.
Gottlieb, G. (1972) "The nature of international law: toward a second concept of law," in R. A. Falk and C. Black (eds) *The Future of the International Legal Order*, vol. IV, Princeton: Princeton University Press.
Gould, S. J. (1985) "Not necessarily wings," *Natural History* 10/85.
—— (1988) "This view of life," *Natural History* 94(10): 12–25.
Gourevitch, P. (1986) *Politics in Hard Times*, Ithaca NY: Cornell University Press.
Gowa, J. (1989) "Bipolarity, multipolarity, and free trade," *American Political Science Review* 83(4): 1245–1256.
Graham, T. (1979) "Revolution in trade politics," *Foreign Policy* 36: 49–62.
Graham, T. and Mullins, A. F. (1991) "Arms control, military strategy, and nuclear proliferation," paper presented to Nuclear Deterrence and Global Security in Transition conference at Institute on Global Conflict and Cooperation, University of California, La Jolla, 21–23 February 1991.
Grieco, J. M. (1988) "Anarchy and the limits of cooperation," *International Organization* 42(3): 485–508.
—— (1990) *Cooperation Among Nations*, Ithaca: Cornell University Press.
—— (1993) "Understanding the problem of international cooperation: the limits of neoliberal institutionalism and the future of realist theory," in D. A. Baldwin (ed.) *Neorealism and Neoliberalism: The Contemporary Debate*, New York: Columbia University Press.
Gross, L. (1968) "The peace of Westphalia, 1648–1948," in R. A. Falk and W. Hanrieder (eds) *International Law and Organization*, Philadelphia: Lippincott.
Grove, E. (1993) "UN armed forces and the military staff committee: a look back," *International Security* 17(4): 172–182.
Grunwald, J. and Flamm, K. (1985) *The Global Factory: Foreign Assembly in International Trade*, Washington DC: Brookings Institution.
Guenée, B. (1985) *States and Rulers in Later Medieval Europe*, J. Vale (trans.), New York: Basil Blackwell.
Guillot, P. (1994) "France, peacekeeping and humanitarian intervention," *International Peacekeeping* 1(1): 30–43.

Guppy, N. (1984) "Tropical deforestation: a global view," *Foreign Affairs* 62(4): 928–965.

Haas, E. B. (1958) *The Uniting of Europe*, Stanford: Stanford University Press.

—— (1961) "International integration: the European and the universal process," *International Organization* 15(3): 366–392.

—— (1964) *Beyond the Nation State*, Stanford: Stanford University Press.

—— (1976) *The Obsolescence of Regional Integration Theory*, Research Monograph no. 25, Berkeley: Institute of International Studies, University of California.

—— (1983a) "Words can hurt you: or, who said what to whom about regimes," in S. D. Krasner (ed.) *International Regimes*, Ithaca NY: Cornell University Press.

—— (1983b) "Regime decay: conflict management and international organization, 1945–1981," *International Organization* 37(2): 189–256.

—— (1986) "What is nationalism and why should we study it?" *International Organization* 40(3). 707–744.

—— (1990) *When Knowledge is Power*, Berkeley: University of California Press.

—— (1997) *Nationalism, Liberalism, and Progress*, Ithaca: Cornell University Press.

Haas, P. M. (1990) *Saving the Mediterranean*, New York: Columbia University Press.

—— (ed.) (1992a) "Knowledge, power, and international policy coordination," *International Organization* 46 (special issue): 1.

—— (1992b) "Epistemic communities and international policy coordination," *International Organization* 46(1): 1–36.

—— (1992c) "Banning chlorofluorocarbons: epistemic community efforts to protect stratospheric ozone," *International Organization* 46(1): 187–223.

Haas, P. M., Keohane, R. O., and Levy, M. (eds) (1993) *Institutions for the Earth*, Cambridge, MA: MIT Press.

Habermas, J. (1979) *Communication and the Evolution of Society*, Boston: Beacon Press.

—— (1981) "Modernity and postmodernity," *New German Critique* 22: 3–14.

—— (1984) *Theory of Communicative Action*, vol. 1, Boston: Beacon Press.

—— (1987) *Theory of Communicative Action*, vol. 2, Boston: Beacon Press.

Hall, B. M. and Kratochwil, F. V. (1993) "Medieval tales: neorealist 'science' and the abuse of history," *International Organization* 47(3): 479–491.

Hardin, R. (1982) *Collective Action*, Baltimore MD: Johns Hopkins University Press.

Harries, O. (1993) "The collapse of the West," *Foreign Affairs* 72(4): 41–53.

Harrod, J. (1986) *The Unprotected Worker: The Social Relations of Subordination*, New York: Columbia University Press.

Hart, H. L. A. (1961) *The Concept of Law*, Oxford: Clarendon Press.

Harvey, D. (1989) *The Condition of Postmodernity*, Oxford: Basil Blackwell.

Hassan, I. (1971) *The Dismemberment of Orpheus: Toward a Postmodern Literature*, Oxford: Oxford University Press.

—— (1987) *The Postmodern Turn*, Columbus: Ohio State University Press.

Havel, V. (1994) "A call for sacrifice," *Foreign Affairs* 73(2): 2–7.

Hawley, H. (1950) *Human Ecology: A Theory of Community Structure*, New York: Ronald Press.

Hays, D. (1989) *Europe in the Fourteenth and Fifteenth Centuries*, 2nd edn, London: Longman.

Head, J. G. (1962) "Public goods and public policy," *Public Finance* 17(2): 197–219.

Heisbourg, F. (1992) "The future of the Atlantic Alliance: whither NATO, whether NATO?" *Washington Quarterly* 15(2): 127–134.

Helmreich, J. E. (1991) "The United States and the formation of EURATOM," *Diplomatic History* 15(3): 387–410.

Hempel, C. G. (1965) *Aspects of Scientific Explanation*, New York: Free Press.

Henrikson, A. K. (1975) "The map as an 'idea': the role of cartographic imagery during the Second World War," *American Cartographer* 2(1): 19–88.

Herlihy, D. (1974) "Ecological conditions and demographic change," in R. L. de Molen (ed.) *One Thousand Years Western Europe in the Middle Ages*, Boston: Houghton Mifflin.

—— (1985) *Medieval Households*, Cambridge MA: Harvard University Press.

Herman, R. G. (1996) "Identity, norms, and national security: the Soviet foreign policy revolution and the end of the Cold War," in P. J. Katzenstein (ed.) *The Culture of National Security. Norms and Identity in World Politics*, New York: Columbia University Press.

Herz, J. H. (1957) "Rise and demise of the territorial state," *World Politics* 9(4): 473–493.

—— (1968) "The territorial state revisited—reflections on the future of the nation-state," *Polity* 1(1): 11–34.

Hilderbrand, R. C. (1990) *Dumbarton Oaks· The Origins of the United Nations and the Search for Postwar Security*, Chapel Hill: University of North Carolina Press.

Hinsley, F. H. (1963) *Power and the Pursuit of Peace*, Cambridge: Cambridge University Press.

—— (1967) "The concept of sovereignty and the relations between states," *Journal of International Affairs* 21(2): 242–252.

Hirsch, F. (1978) "The ideological underlay of inflation," in F. Hirsch and J. H. Goldthorpe (eds) *The Political Economy of Inflation*, Cambridge MA: Harvard University Press.

Hirschman, A. O. (1977) *The Passions and the Interests: Political Arguments for Capitalism Before its Triumph*, Princeton NJ: Princeton University Press,.

—— (1980) [1945] *National Power and the Structure of Foreign Trade*, Berkeley: University of California Press.

Hoffmann, S. (1970) "International organization and the international system," *International Organization* 24(3): 389–413.

Hogan, M. J. (1984) "Revival and reform: America's twentieth-century search for a new economic order abroad," *Diplomatic History* 8(4): 287–310.

—— (1987) *The Marshall Plan: America, Britain, and the Reconstruction of Europe*, New York: Cambridge University Press.

Hohenberg, P. M. and Lees, L. H. (1985) *The Making of Urban Europe, 1000–1950*, Cambridge MA: Harvard University Press.

Holden, G. (1990) "The end of an alliance: Soviet policy and the Warsaw Pact, 1989–90," *PRIF Reports*, Peace Research Institute, Frankfurt, no. 16: 1–36.

Hollinger, D. A. (1995) *Postethnic America. Beyond Multiculturalism*, New York: Basic Books.

Hollis, M. and Smith, S. (1990) *Explaining and Understanding International Relations*, Oxford: Clarendon Press.

—— (1991) "Beware of gurus: structure and action in international relations," *Review of International Studies* 17(4): 393–410.

Holsti, K. (1991) "Governance without government: modes of coordinating, managing and controlling international politics in nineteenth century Europe," paper presented to annual meeting of International Studies Association, Vancouver, Canada

Holsti, O. R. (1992) "Public opinion and foreign policy: challenges to the Almond–Lippmann consensus," *International Studies Quarterly* 36(4): 439–466.

Holsti, O. R. and Rosenau, J. N. (1979) "The three-headed eagle: the United States and system change," *International Studies Quarterly* 23(3): 339–359.

Holzner, B. (1972) *Reality Construction in Society*, Cambridge MA: Schenkman Press.

Howard, M. (1985) "Introduction," in O. Riste (ed.) *Western Security: The Formative Years*, Oslo: Universitetsforlaget.

Hudson, D. J. (1977) "Vandenberg reconsidered: Senate Resolution 239 and American foreign policy," *Diplomatic History* 1(1): 46–63.

Hudson, G. F. (1968) "Collective security and military alliances," in H. Butterfield and M. Wight (eds) *Diplomatic Investigations*, Cambridge MA: Harvard University Press.

Huntington, S. (1996) *The Clash of Civilizations and the Remaking of World Order*, New York: Simon and Schuster.

Hurwitz, J. and Peffley, M. (1987) "How are foreign policy attitudes structured? A hierarchical model," *American Political Science Review* 81(4): 1100–1120.

Hurwitz, J., Peffley, M., and Seligson, M.A. (1993) "Foreign policy belief systems in comparative perspective: the United States and Costa Rica," *International Studies Quarterly* 37(3): 245–270.

Huyssen, A. (1984) "Mapping the postmodern," *New German Critique* 33: 5–52.

Ikenberry, G. J. (1992) "A world economy restored: expert consensus and the Anglo-American postwar settlement," *International Organization* 46(1): 289–321.

International Studies Quarterly (1986) "Of Rifts and Drifts: a symposium on beliefs, opinions, and American foreign policy," 30(4).

International Telecommunication Union (1965) *From Semaphore to Satellite*, Geneva: ITU.

Jackson, R. (1990), *Quasi-States: Sovereignty, International Relations, and the Third World*, Cambridge: Cambridge University Press.

—— (1993) "The weight of ideas in decolonization: normative change in international relations," in J. Goldstein and R. O. Keohane (eds) *Ideas and Foreign Policy*, Ithaca NY: Cornell University Press.

Jakobson, P. V. (1996) "Use and abuse of military threats in Bosnia-Herzegovina: why compellence and deterrence failed," paper prepared for 37th annual convention, International Studies Association, San Diego CA, 16–20 April 1996.

James, A. (ed.) (1973) *The Bases of International Order*, London: Oxford University Press.

Jameson, F. (1984) "Postmodernism, or the cultural logic of late capitalism," *New Left Review* 146: 53–92.

—— (1989) "Marxism and postmodernism," *New Left Review* 176: 31–45.

Jay, M. (1985) "Habermas and modernism," in R. J. Bernstein (ed.) *Habermas and Modernity*, Cambridge MA: MIT Press.

Jepperson, R. L., Wendt, A., and Katzenstein, P. J. (1996) "Norms, identity, and culture in national security," in P. J. Katzenstein (ed.) *The Culture of National Security: Norms and Identity in World Politics*, New York: Columbia University Press.

Jervis, R. (1970) *The Logic of Images in International Relations*, Princeton: Princeton University Press.

—— (1976) *Perception and Misperception in International Politics*, Princeton: Princeton University Press.

—— (1978) "Cooperation under the security dilemma," *World Politics* 30(2): 167–214.

—— (1980) "The impact of the Korean War on the Cold War," *Journal of Conflict Resolution* 24(4): 563–592.

—— (1983) "Security regimes," in S. D. Krasner (ed.) *International Regimes*, Ithaca NY: Cornell University Press.

—— (1985) "From balance to concert: a study of international security cooperation," *World Politics* 38(1): 58–79.

—— (1989) *The Meaning of the Nuclear Revolution*, Ithaca NY: Cornell University Press

Johnson, D. G. (1984) "World food and agriculture," in I. L. Simon and H. Kahn (eds) *The Resourceful Earth A Response to "Global 2000,"* New York: Basil Blackwell.

Johnson, J. and Percy, W. (1970) *The Age of Recovery. The Fifteenth Century*, Ithaca NY: Cornell University Press.

Johnston, A. I. (1995) *Cultural Realism: Strategic Culture and Grand Strategy in Chinese History*, Princeton: Princeton University Press.

—— (1996) "Cultural realism and strategy in Maoist China," in P. J. Katzenstein (ed.) *The Culture of National Security: Norms and Identity in World Politics*, New York: Columbia University Press.

Jonas, M. (1966) *Isolationism in America*, Ithaca NY: Cornell University Press.

Jones, E. L. (1981) *The European Miracle· Environments, Economics, and Geopolitics in the History of Europe and Asia*, Cambridge: Cambridge University Press.

Kahler, Miles (1993) "Multilateralism with small and large numbers," in J. G. Ruggie (ed.) *Multilateralism Matters· The Theory and Praxis of an Institutional Form*, New York: Columbia University Press..

Kaiser, D. (1990) *Politics and War. European Conflict from Philip II to Hitler*, Cambridge MA: Harvard University Press.

Kaplan, L. S. (1985) "An unequal triad: the United States, Western Union, and NATO," in O. Riste (ed.) *Western Security. The Formative Years*, Oslo: Universitetsforlaget.

—— (1988) *NATO and the United States The Enduring Alliance*, Boston: Twayne Publishers.

Kapstein, E. B. (1991/1992) "We are US: the myth of the multinational," *National Interest* 26: 55–62.

—— (1996) "Workers and the world economy," *Foreign Affairs* 75(3): 16–37.

Katzenstein, P. J. (1996a) *Cultural Norms and National Security*, Ithaca· Cornell University Press.

—— (ed.) (1996b) *The Culture of National Security: Norms and Identity in World Politics*, New York: Columbia University Press.

—— (1996c) "Introduction: alternative conceptions on national security," in P. J. Katzenstein (ed.) *The Culture of National Security· Norms and Identity in World Politics*, New York· Columbia University Press.

Kay, D. A. and Skolnikoff, E. B. (1972) "International institutions and the environmental crisis: a look ahead," *International Organization* 26(2): 469–478.

Keal, P. (1984) *Unspoken Rules and Superpower Dominance*, London: Macmillan.

Keck, O. (1995) "Rationales kommunikatives Handeln in den internationalen Beziehungen: Ist eine Verbindung von Rational-Choice-Theorie und Habermas' Theorie des kommunikativen Handelns möglich?" *Zeitschrift für Internationale Beziehungen* 1: 5–48.

Keeley, J. F. (1990) "Toward a Foucauldian analysis of international regimes," *International Organization* 44(1): 83–105.

Keir, E. (1995) *Imagining War· French and British Military Doctrine Between the Wars*, Princeton: Princeton University Press.

—— (1996) "Culture and French military doctrine before World War II," in P. J. Katzenstein (ed.) *The Culture of National Security: Norms and Identity in World Politics*, New York· Columbia University Press.

Kelley, A. C. and Williamson, I.G. (1984) *What Drives Third World City Growth? A Dynamic General Equilibrium Approach*, Princeton NJ: Princeton University Press.

Kennan, C. (1956) Letter to editor, *Washington Post*, 3 November 1956: A8.

Kennan, G. F. (1967) *Memoirs· 1925–1950*, Boston: Little, Brown.

Kennedy, D. (1984) "Introduction," in P. R. Ehrlich et al. (eds) *The Cold and the Dark The World after Nuclear War*, New York: W. W. Norton.

—— (1987) "The move to institutions," *Cardozo Law Review* 9(1): 841–988.

Keohane, R. O. (1980) "The theory of hegemonic stability and changes in international economic regimes, 1967–1977," in O. R. Holsti, R. M. Siverson, and A. L George (eds) *Change in the International System*, Boulder CO: Westview Press.

—— (1983a) "The demand for international regimes," in S. D. Krasner (ed.) *International Regimes*, Ithaca NY: Cornell University Press.

—— (1983b) "Associative American development, 1776–1860," in J. G. Ruggie (ed.) *The Antinomies of Interdependence. National Welfare and the International Division of Labor*, New York: Columbia University Press.

—— (1984) *After Hegemony*, Princeton: Princeton University Press.

—— (ed.) (1986a) *Neorealism and its Critics*, New York: Columbia University Press.

—— (1986b) "Reciprocity in international relations," *International Organization* 40(1): 1–28.

—— (1988) "International institutions: two approaches," *International Studies Quarterly* 32(4): 379–396.

—— (1990a) "Multilateralism: an agenda for research," *International Journal* 45(4): 731–764.

—— (1990b) "International liberalism reconsidered," in John Dunn (ed.) *The Economic Limits to Modern Politics*, New York: Cambridge University Press.

—— (1993) "Institutional theory and the realist challenge after the Cold War," in D. A. Baldwin (ed.) *Neorealism and Neoliberalism: The Contemporary Debate*, New York: Columbia University Press.

—— (1995) "Hobbes's dilemma and institutional change in world politics: sovereignty in international society," in H. H. Holm and Georg Sorensen (eds) *Whose World Order?* Boulder CO: Westview.

—— (1996) Remarks at Annual Convention, American Political Science Association.

Keohane, R. O. and Nye, J. S. (1971) "Transnational relations and world politics: an introduction," *International Organization* 25(3): 329–350.

—— (eds) (1972) *Transnational Relations and World Politics*, Cambridge MA: Harvard University Press.

—— (1974) "Transgovernmental relations and international organizations," *World Politics* 27(1): 39–62.

—— (1975) "International interdependence and integration," in F. I. Greenstein and N. W. Polsby (eds) *Handbook of Political Science*, vol. 8, Reading MA: Addison-Wesley.

—— (1977) *Power and Interdependence*, Boston: Little, Brown.

Keohane, R. O. and Martin, L. (1995) "The promise of institutionalist theory," *International Security* 20(1): 39–51.

Kimball, W. F. (1991) *The Juggler: Franklin Roosevelt as Wartime Statesman*, Princeton NJ: Princeton University Press.

Kindleberger, C. P. (1973) *The World in Depression, 1929–1939*, Berkeley: University of California Press.

—— (1975) "The rise of free trade in Western Europe, 1820–1875," *Journal of Economic History* 35(1): 20–55.

King, G., Keohane, R., and Verba, S. (1994) *Designing Social Inquiry*, Princeton: Princeton University Press.

Kissinger, H. A. (1964) *A World Restored*, New York: Universal Library.

—— (1993) "Not this partnership," *Washington Post*, 24 November 1993: A17.

—— (1994a) *Diplomacy*, New York: Simon and Schuster.

—— (1994b) "Expand NATO now," *Washington Post*, 19 December 1994: A27.

Kleinman, D. S. (1980) *Human Adaptation and Population Growth*, Montclair NJ: Allanheld, Osmun.

Klotz, A. (1995) *Protesting Prejudice· Apartheid and the Politics of Norms in International Relations*, Ithaca NY: Cornell University Press.

Knock, T. J. (1992) *To End All Wars· Woodrow Wilson and the Quest for a New World Order*, New York: Oxford University Press.

Koselleck, R. (1985) *Futures Past. On the Semantics of Historical Time*, K. Tribe (trans.), Cambridge MA: MIT Press.

Koslowski, R. and Kratochwil, F. V. (1995) "Understanding change in international politics: the Soviet empire's demise and the international system," in R. N. Lebow and T. Risse-Kappen (eds) *International Relations Theory and the End of the Cold War*, New York: Columbia University Press.

Kowert, P. and Legro, J. (1996) "Norms, identity, and their limits," in P. J. Katzenstein (ed.) *The Culture of National Security: Norms and Identity in World Politics*, New York: Columbia University Press.

Krasner, S. D. (1976) "State power and the structure of international trade," *World Politics* 28(2): 317–347.

—— (1978) *Defending the National Interest*, Princeton: Princeton University Press.

—— (1979) "The Tokyo round: particularistic interests and prospects for stability in the global trading system," *International Studies Quarterly* 23(4): 491–531.

—— (ed.) (1983) *International Regimes*, Ithaca NY: Cornell University Press.

—— (1984) "Approaches to the state: alternative conceptions and historical dynamics," *Comparative Politics* 16(2): 223–246.

—— (1985) *Structural Conflict: The Third World Against Global Liberalism*, Berkeley: University of California Press.

—— (1988) "Sovereignty: an institutional perspective," *Comparative Political Studies* 21(1): 66–94.

—— (1991) "Global communications and national power: life on the Pareto frontier," *World Politics* 43(3): 336–366.

—— (1993) "Westphalia and all that," in J. Goldstein and R. O. Keohane (eds) *Ideas and Foreign Policy*, Ithaca NY: Cornell University Press.

—— (1995/96) "Compromising Westphalia," *International Security* 20(3): 115–151.

—— (1997) "Sovereignty and its discontents," Stanford University, unpublished manuscript.

Kratochwil, F. V. (1984) "The force of prescriptions," *International Organization* 38(4): 685–708.

—— (1989) *Rules, Norms and Decisions,* New York: Cambridge University Press.

Krauss, M (1978) *The New Protectionism. The Welfare State in International Trade*, New York: New York University Press.

Kuhn, T. S. (1962) *The Structure of Scientific Revolutions*, Chicago: University of Chicago Press.

Kupchan, C. A. (1996) "Reviving the West," *Foreign Affairs* 75(3): 92–104.

Kupchan, C. A. and Kupchan, C. A. (1991) "Concerts, collective security, and the future of Europe," *International Security* 16(1): 114–161.

Kurzweil, E. (1980) *The Age of Structuralism*, New York: Columbia University Press.

Kuttner, R. (1991) *The End of Laissez-Faire*, New York: Knopf.

—— (1995) "Look who wants to tinker with market forces," *Business Week* 2 October 1995, 444(1): 26.

Ladurie, E. L. R. (1971) *Times of Feast, Times of Famine: A History of Climate Since the Year 1000*, B. Bray (trans), Garden City NY: Doubleday

LaFeber, W. (1989a) *The American Age: United States Foreign Policy at Home and Abroad Since 1750*, New York: Norton.

—— (1989b) "NATO and the Korean War," *Diplomatic History* 13(4): 461–478.

Lakatos, I. (1970) "Falsification and the methodology of scientific research programmes," in I. Lakatos and A. Musgrave (eds) *Criticism and the Growth of Knowledge*, Cambridge: Cambridge University Press.

Langhorne, R. (1986) "Reflections on the significance of the Congress of Vienna," *Review of International Studies* 12(4).

Lapid, Y. and Kratochwil, F. (1997) "Revisiting the 'national': toward an identity agenda in neorealism?" in Lapid and Kratochwil (eds) *The Return of Culture and Identity in International Relations Theory*, Boulder CO: Rienner.

Larrabee, F. S. (1996) "Ukraine's balancing act," *Survival* 38(2): 143–165.

Lattimore, O. (1940) *Inner Asian Frontiers of China*, London: Oxford University Press.

—— (1962) *Studies in Frontier History*, London: Oxford University Press.

Layne, C. (1993) "The unipolar illusion: why new great powers will rise," *International Security* 17(4): 5–51.

Leach, E. (1961) *Rethinking Anthropology*, London: Athlone Press.

Le Goff, J. (1976) "The town as an agent of civilization," in C. M. Cipolla (ed.) *The Middle Ages*, London: Harvester Press.

—— (1980) *Time, Work, and Culture in the Middle Ages*, A. Goldhammer (trans.), Chicago: University of Chicago Press.

—— (1992) *History and Memory*, New York: Columbia University Press,

Leifer, M. (1996) "The ASEAN regional forum takes shape," *Adelphi Paper No. 302*, London: Oxford University Press.

Lentricchia, F. (1983) *Criticism and Social Change*, Chicago: University of Chicago Press.

Lévi-Strauss, C. (1967) *Structural Anthropology*, New York: Doubleday.

Lewis, P. (1992) "UN says Somalis must disarm before peace," *New York Times*, 6 December 1992: 15.

Lincoln, E. (1990) *Japan's Unequal Trade*, Washington DC: Brookings Institution.

Lindberg, L. N. (1970) "Political integration as a multidimensional phenomenon requiring multivariate measurement," *International Organization* 24(4): 649–731.

Linn, J. F. (1983) *Cities in the Developing World*, New York: Oxford University Press.

Lipset, S. M. (1996) *American Exceptionalism A Double-Edged Sword*, New York: Norton.

Litfin, K. (1994) *Ozone Discourses*, New York: Columbia University Press.

Little, R. (1989) "Deconstructing the balance of power," *Review of International Studies* 15(2): 87–100.

—— (1995) "Neorealism and the English School: a methodological, ontological and theoretical reassessment," *European Journal of International Relations* 1(1): 14–27.

Locke, J. (1947) [1690] *Two Treatises of Government*, T. I. Cook (ed.), New York: Hafner.

Lorch, D. (1993) "Italian forces come under fire in tense Somalia," *New York Times*, 17 July 1993: A3.

Luhman, N. (1982) *The Differentiation of Society*, S. Holmes and C. Larmore (trans.), New York: Columbia University Press.

Lumsdaine, D. H. (1993) *Moral Vision in International Politics*, Princeton: Princeton University Press.

Lundestad, G. (1980) *America, Scandinavia, and the Cold War, 1945–1949*, New York: Columbia University Press.

Lyotard, J.-F. (1984) *The Postmodern Condition*, Minneapolis: University of Minnesota Press.

McCullough, D. (1992) *Truman*, New York: Simon and Schuster.

Mackinder, H. J. (1904) "The geographical pivot of history," *Geographical Journal* 23(4): 421–444.

McLuhan, M. (1962) *The Gutenberg Galaxy*, Toronto: University of Toronto Press.

McNeill, W. H. (1982) *The Pursuit of Power*, Chicago: University of Chicago Press.

Macpherson, C. B. (1962) *The Political Theory of Possessive Individualism*, New York: Oxford University Press.

Maier, C. S. (1977) "The politics of productivity: foundations of American international economic policy after World War II," *International Organization* 31(4): 607–634.

Mallinson, A. (n.d.) "Doctrine dilemma has only two horns," unpublished manuscript.

Mann, M. (1988) *States, War, and Capitalism*, New York: Basil Blackwell.

Martin, L. (1992) *Coercive Cooperation. Explaining Multilateral Economic Sanctions*, Princeton: Princeton University Press.

—— (1993) "Interests, power, and multilateralism," in J. G. Ruggie (ed.) *Multilateralism Matters· The Theory and Praxis of an Institutional Form*, New York: Columbia University Press.

Martines, L. (1979) *Power and Imagination: City-States in Renaissance Italy*, New York: Vintage Books.

Mattingly, G. (1964) *Renaissance Diplomacy*, Baltimore MD: Penguin.

Mayers, D. (1988) *George Kennan and the Dilemmas of US Foreign Policy*, New York: Oxford University Press.

Mead, W. R. (1987) *Mortal Splendor*, Boston: Houghton Mifflin.

Mearsheimer, J. J. (1983) *Conventional Deterrence*, Ithaca NY: Cornell University Press.

—— (1990) "Back to the future: instability in Europe after the Cold War," *International Security* 15(1): 5–56.

—— (1994/5) "The false promise of international institutions," *International Security* 19(3): 5–49.

—— (1995) "A realist reply," *International Security* 20(1): 82–93.

Meinecke, F. (1957) [1924] *Machiavellism*, D. Scott (trans.), New Haven CT: Yale University Press.

Mikesell, R. F. (1947) "The role of the international monetary agreements in a world of planned economies," *Journal of Political Economy* 55(6): 497–512.

Milgrom, P. R., North, D. C., and Weingast, B. R. (1990) "The role of institutions in the revival of trade: the law merchant, private judges, and the champagne fairs," *Economics and Politics* 2(1): 1–23.

Milner, H. (1991) "The assumption of anarchy in international relations theory," *Review of International Studies* 17(1): 67–85.

Mitrany, D. (1943) *A Working Peace System*, Chicago: Quadrangle Press.

Moran, T. (1990) "The globalization of America's defense industries: managing the threat of foreign dependence," *International Security* 15(1): 57–99.

Morgan, Henry L. (1963) [1877] *Ancient Society*, reprinted edition, E. Leacock (ed.), Gloucester MA: Peter Smith.

Morgan, P. M. (1993) "Multilateralism and security prospects in Europe," in J. G. Ruggie (ed.) *Multilateralism Matters: The Theory and Praxis of an Institutional Form*, New York: Columbia University Press..

Morgenthau, H. (1946) *Scientific Man vs. Power Politics*, Chicago: University of Chicago Press.

—— (1956) Letter to editor, *New York Times*, 13 November 1956: 36.

—— (1985) [1948] *Politics Among Nations*, 6th edn, revised by Kenneth W. Thompson, New York: Knopf.

Mower, E. C. (1931) *International Government*, Boston: Heath.

Mueller, H. (1994) "Internationale Beziehungen als Kommunikativen Handeln: Zur

Kritik der utilitarischen Handlungstheorien," *Zeitschrift für Internationale Beziehungen* 1(1): 15–44.

—— (1995) "Spielen Hilft Nicht Immer: Die Grenzen des Rational-Choice-Ansatzens under der Platz der Theorie kommunikativen Handelns in der Analyse international Beziehungen," *Zeitschrift für Internationale Beziehungen* 2(2): 371–391.

Nagel, E. (1961) [1942] *The Structure of Science*, New York: Harcourt, Brace, and World.

Nash, R. (1991) "The use of counterfactuals in history: a look at the literature," *Newsletter of the Society for Historians of American Foreign Relations*, no. 22.

NATO (1996) "Final communiqué," ministerial meeting of the North Atlantic Council in Berlin, NATO Press Communiqué 3 June.

Neufield, M. (1993) "Interpretation and the 'science' of international relations," *Review of International Studies* 19(1): 39–61.

Neumann, I. B. (1997) "Conclusion," in I. B. Neumann and O. Wæver (eds) *The Future of International Relations: Masters in the Making?*, London: Routledge.

Neumann, I. B. and Wæver, O. (eds) (1997) *The Future of International Relations Masters in the Making?*, London: Routledge.

Neumann, I. B. and Welsh, J. M. (1991) "The other in European self-definition: an addendum to the literature on international society," *Review of International Studies* 17(4): 327–348.

New York Times (1992) "Excerpts from a resolution on delivering Somalia aid," 4 December 1992: A14.

Niebuhr, R. (1944) *The Children of Light and the Children of Darkness*, New York: Scribners.

—— (1953) *Christian Realism and Political Problems*, Fairfield NJ: A. M. Kelley.

Nincic, M. (1992) *Democracy and Foreign Policy: The Fallacy of Political Realism*, New York: Columbia University Press.

Ninkovich, F. (1994) *Modernity and Power: A History of the Domino Theory in the Twentieth Century*, Chicago: University of Chicago Press.

Nordlinger, E. A. (1995) *Isolationism Reconfigured: American Foreign Policy for a New Century*, Princeton NJ: Princeton University Press.

North, D. C. and Thomas, R. P. (1973) *The Rise of the Western World: A New Economic History*, Cambridge: Cambridge University Press.

North, D. C. and Weingast, B. R. (1989) "Constitutions and commitment: the evolution of institutions governing public choice in seventeenth-century England," *Journal of Economic History* 49(4): 803–832.

Nurkse, Ragnar (1944) *International Currency Exchange: Lessons of the Inter-war Period*, Secretariat, League of Nations, Economic, Financial and Transit Department .

Nye, J. S. (1988) "Neorealism and neoliberalism," *World Politics* 40(2): 235–251.

Onuf, N. (1989) *Worlds of Our Making*, Columbia: University of South Carolina Press.

Osborne, O. (1970) *Oxford Companion to Art*, New York: Oxford University Press.

Oye, K. A. (1985) "The sterling–dollar–franc triangle: monetary diplomacy, 1929–1937," *World Politics* 38(1): 173–199.

—— (ed.) (1986) *Cooperation Under Anarchy*, Princeton NJ: Princeton University Press.

Page, B. I. and Shapiro, R.Y. (1992) *The Rational Public: Fifty Years of Trends in Americans' Policy Preferences*, Chicago: University of Chicago Press.

Palin, R. H. (1995) "Multinational military forces: problems and prospects," *Adelphi Paper no. 294*, London: Oxford University Press.

Palloix, C. (1977) "The self-expansion of capital on a world scale," *Review of Radical Political Economics* 9(2): 1–28.

Pape, R. A., Jr (1992) "Coercion and military strategy: why denial works and punishment doesn't," *Journal of Strategic Studies* 15(4): 423–475.

Peirce, C. S. (1955) *Philosophical Writings*, Justus Buchler (ed.), New York: Dover.

Peterson, V. S. and Runyan, A. S. (1993) *Global Gender Issues*, Boulder CO: Westview.

Pilat, J. F. and Pendley, R. E. (eds) (1990) *Beyond 1995: The Future of the NPT Regime*, New York: Plenum Press.

Pocock, J. G. A. (1975) *The Machiavellian Moment*, Princeton NJ; Princeton University Press.

Poggi, G. (1978) *The Development of the Modern State*, Stanford: Stanford University Press.

Polanyi, K. (1944) *The Great Transformation*, New York: Farrar and Rinehart.

—— (1957) "Aristotle discovers the economy," in K. Polanyi et al. (eds) *Trade and Markets in the Early Empires*, Glencoe IL: Free Press.

Polkinghorne, D. (1988) *Narrative Knowing and the Human Sciences*, Albany NY: State University of New York Press.

Pollard, R. (1985) *Economic Security and the Origins of the Cold War*, New York: Columbia University Press.

Pomfret, J. (1994) "UN to attempt sending convoys without Bosnian factions' permission," *Washington Post*, 28 February 1994: A12.

Popper, K. (1968) *Conjectures and Refutations*, New York: Harper and Row.

Posen, B. (1984) *The Sources of Military Doctrine*, Ithaca NY: Cornell University Press.

—— (1993a) "Nationalism, the mass army, and military power," *International Security* 18(2): 80–124.

—— (1993b) "The security dilemma and ethnic conflict," *Survival* 35(3): 27–47.

Powell, R. (1991) "The problem of absolute and relative gains in international relations theory," *American Political Science Review* 85(4): 1303–1320.

—— (1994) "Anarchy in international relations theory: the neorealist-neoliberal debate," *International Organization* 48(2): 313–334.

President's Materials Policy Commission (1952) *Resources for Freedom: Report of the President's Materials Policy Commission*, Washington DC: US Government Printing Office.

Price, R. (1995) "A genealogy of the chemical weapons taboo," *International Organization* 49(1): 73–103.

Price, R. and Tannenwald, N. (1996) "Norms and deterrence: the nuclear and chemical weapons taboos," in P. J. Katzenstein (ed.) *The Culture of National Security: Norms and Identity in World Politics*, New York: Columbia University Press.

Prigogine, I. (1980) *From Being to Becoming: Time and Complexity in the Physical Sciences*, New York: W. H. Freeman.

Rawls, J. (1955) "Two concepts of justice," *Philosophical Review* 64(1): 3–33.

Reiss, M. (1988) *Without the Bomb: The Politics of Nuclear Nonproliferation*, New York: Columbia University Press.

Repetto, Robert (1986) *The Global Possible: Resources, Development, and the New Century*, New Haven CT: Yale University Press.

Ricoeur, P. (1984) *Time and Narrative*, vol. I, K. McLaughlin and D. Pellauer (trans.) Chicago: University of Chicago Press.

Riding, A. (1991) "Europeans in accord to create vastly extended trading bloc," *New York Times*, 23 October 1991: A1.

Ridker, R. G. (1979) "Resource and environmental consequences of population and economic growth," in P. H. Hauser (ed) *World Population and Development*, Syracuse: Syracuse University Press.

Risse-Kappen, T. (1995) "Reden ist nicht bilig: Zur Debate um Kommunkation und Rationalität," *Zeitschrift für Internationale Beziehungen* 2(1): 171–184.

—— (1996) "Collective identity in a democratic community: the case of NATO," in P. J. Katzenstein (ed.) *The Culture of National Security: Norms and Identity in World Politics*, New York: Columbia University Press.

Ritchie, R. C. (1986) *Captain Kidd and the War Against the Pirates*, Cambridge MA: Harvard University Press.

Rittberger, V. (1983) "Global conference diplomacy and international policy-making," *European Journal of Political Research* 11(2): 167–182.

Rodrik, D. (1997) *Has Globalization Gone Too Far?*, Washington DC: Institute for International Economics.

Rorig, F. (1967) *The Medieval Town*, Berkeley: University of California Press.

Rosenau, P. (1990) "Once again into the fray: international relations confronts the humanities," *Millennium: Journal of International Studies* 19(1): 83–110.

Rosenberg, E. R. (1993) "The Cold War and the discourse of national security," *Diplomatic History* 17(2): 277–284.

Rotberg, R. I. and Raab, T. K. (eds) (1981) *Climate and History: Studies in Interdisciplinary History*, Princeton NJ: Princeton University Press.

Russell, M. (1984) "Energy is an international good," in E. N. Castle and K. A. Price (eds) *US Interests and Global Natural Resources: Energy, Minerals, Food*, Washington DC: Resources for the Future.

Russell, R. W. (1973) "Transgovernmental interaction in the international monetary system, 1960–1972," *International Organization* 27(4): 431–464.

Russett, B. M. (ed.) (1968) *Economic Theories of International Politics*, Chicago: Markham.

—— (1984) "Dimensions of resource dependence: some elements of rigor in concept and policy analysis," *International Organization* 38(3): 481–499.

Russett, B. M. and Sullivan, J. D. (1971) "Collective goods and international organizations," *International Organization* 25(4): 845–865.

—— (1985) "The mysterious case of vanishing hegemony: or, is Mark Twain really dead?" *International Organization* 39(2): 207–232.

Sack, R. D. (1986) *Human Territoriality. Its Theory and History*, New York: Cambridge University Press.

Sagan, C. (1983/4) "Nuclear war and climatic catastrophe: some policy implications," *Foreign Affairs* 62(2): 257–292.

Salter, A. (1939) *Security: Can We Retrieve It?* London: Macmillan.

Sambunaris, G. (1981) "Strategic minerals and the Third World," *Agenda* 4(6): 1116.

Samuelson, P. (1945) "The pure theory of public expenditures," *Review of Economics and Statistics* 36(4): 387–389.

Sandler, T. M., Loehr, W., and Cauley, J. T. (1978) *The Political Economy of Public Goods and International Cooperation*, Denver: University of Denver Monograph Series in World Affairs.

Sassen, S. (1996) *Losing Control? Sovereignty in an Age of Globalization*, New York: Columbia University Press.

Schelling, T. C. (1960) *The Strategy of Conflict*, Cambridge, MA: Harvard University Press.

—— (1966) *Arms and Influence*, New Haven CT: Yale University Press.

Schlesinger, A. M. (1958) "The coming of the new deal," *The Age of Roosevelt*, vol. 2, Boston: Houghton Mifflin.

Schluchter, W. (1989) *Rationalism, Religion, and Domination: A Weberian Perspective*, Berkeley: University of California Press.

Schmalz-Bruns, R. (1995) "Die Theorie kommunikativen Handelns—eine Flaschenpost?" *Zeitschrift für Internationale Beziehungen* 2(2): 347–370.

Schmitter, P. C. (1969) "Three neo-functionalist hypotheses about international integration," *International Organization* 23(1): 161–166.

Schneider, W. (1997) "The new isolationism," in R. J. Lieber (ed.) *Eagle Adrift: American Foreign Policy at the End of the Century*, New York: Longman.

Schroeder, P. (1994) "Historical reality vs. neo-realist theory," *International Security* 19(1): 108–148.

Schweller, R. (1994) "Bandwagoning for profit: bringing the revisionist state back in," *International Security* 19(1): 72–107.

Searle, J. (1984) *Minds, Brains and Science*, Cambridge, MA: Harvard University Press.

—— (1995) *The Construction of Social Reality*, New York: Free Press.

—— (1997) "Consciousness and the philosophers," *New York Review of Books*, 6 March 1997: 43–50.

Sebenius, J. K. (1991) "Crafting a winning coalition: negotiating a regime to control global warming," in R. E. Benedick et al. (eds) *Greenhouse Warming: Negotiating a Global Regime*, Washington DC: World Resources Institute.

Sekerez, U. (1996) "Can Bosnia destroy the UN?," paper prepared for 37th annual convention, International Studies Association, San Diego, CA, 16–20 April 1996.

Sewell, J. P. (1966) *Functionalism and World Politics*, Princeton: Princeton University Press.

Sewell, W. H. (1992) "A theory of structure: duality, agency, and transformation," *American Journal of Sociology* 98(1): 1–29.

Shain, Y. (1994) "Marketing the democratic creed abroad: US diasporas in the era of multiculturalism," *Diaspora* 3(1): 85–111.

—— (1994/5) "Ethnic diasporas and US foreign policy," *Political Science Quarterly* 109(5): 811–841.

Shapiro, R. Y. and Page, B. I. (1994) "Foreign policy and public opinion," in D. A. Deese (ed.) *The New Politics of American Foreign Policy*, New York: St. Martin's Press.

Sikkink, K. (1993) "Human rights, principled issue-networks, and sovereignty in Latin America," *International Organization* 47(3): 411–441.

Sikkink, K. and Keck, M. (forthcoming) *Activists Beyond Borders: Advocacy Networks in International Politics*, Ithaca: Cornell University Press.

Simmons, B. (1994) *Who Adjusts? Domestic Sources of Foreign Economic Policy During the Interwar Years*, Princeton: Princeton University Press.

—— (1996) "Rulers of the game: Central Bank independence during the interwar years," *International Organization* 50(3): 407–443.

Simon, J. L. (1981) *The Ultimate Resource*, Princeton NJ: Princeton University Press.

Simon, J. L. and Kahn, H. (eds) (1984) *The Resourceful Earth: A Response to "Global 2000,"* New York: Basil Blackwell.

Skidelsky, R. J. A. (1976) "Retreat from leadership: the evolution of British economic foreign policy, 1870–1939," in B. M. Rowland (ed.) *Balance of Power or Hegemony: The Interwar Monetary System*, New York: New York University Press.

Skinner, Q. (1985) *The Return of Grand Theory in the Human Sciences*, New York: Cambridge University Press.

Smith, J. E. (1990) *Lucius D. Clay: An American Life*, New York: Henry Holt.

Smith, P. M. (1970) *The Air Force Plans for Peace, 1943–1945*, Baltimore MD: Johns Hopkins University Press.

Smith, T. (1994) *America's Mission: The United States and the Worldwide Struggle for Democracy in the Twentieth Century*, Princeton NJ: Princeton University Press.

Snidal, D (1985) "The limits of hegemonic stability theory," *International Organization* 39(4): 579–614.

—— (1990) "IGOs, regimes, and cooperation: challenges for international relations theory," in M. P. Karns and K. A. Mingst (eds) *The United States and Multilateral Institutions*, Boston: Unwin Hyman.

—— (1991) "Relative gains and the pattern of international cooperation," *American Political Science Review* 85(3): 701–726.

Snyder, J. (1984) *The Ideology of the Offensive*, Ithaca NY: Cornell University Press.

Sorokin, P. A. (1964) *Sociocultural Causality, Space, Time*, New York: Russell and Russell.

Sprout, H. and Sprout, M. (1962) *Foundations of International Politics*, Princeton NJ: Van Nostrand.

Spruyt, H. (1994) *The Sovereign State and Its Competitors: An Analysis of Systems Change*, Princeton NJ: Princeton University Press.

Stairs, D. (1970) "The United States and the politics of the Korean War," *International Journal* 25(2): 302–320.

Stein, A. (1983) "Coordination and collaboration: regimes in an anarchic world," in S. D. Krasner (ed.) *International Regimes*, Ithaca NY: Cornell University Press.

—— (1984) "The hegemon's dilemma: Great Britain, the United States, and the international economic order," *International Organization* 38(2): 355–386.

Stephanson, A. (1989) *Kennan and the Art of Foreign Policy*, Cambridge MA: Harvard University Press.

—— (1995) *Manifest Destiny: American Expansion and the Empire of Right*, New York: Hill and Wang.

Stokes, B. (1990) "Continental shift," *National Journal* 22, 33, 34: 1996–2001.

Stopford, J. M. and Strange, S. (1991) *Rival States, Rival Firms: Competition for World Market Shares*, Cambridge UK: Cambridge University Press.

Strang, D. (1991) "Anomaly and commonplace in European political expansion: realist and institutionalist accounts," *International Organization* 45(2): 143–162.

Strange, S. (1976) *International Monetary Relations*, vol. II of A. Shonfield (ed.) *International Economic Relations of the Western World*, London: Oxford University Press for the Royal Institute of International Affairs.

—— (1982) "Still an extraordinary power: America's role in a global monetary system," in R. E. Lombra and W. E. Witte (eds) *Political Economy of International and Domestic Monetary Relations*, Ames: Iowa State University Press.

—— (1983) "*Cave! Hic dragones*: a critique of regime analysis," in S. D. Krasner (ed.) *International Regimes*, Ithaca NY: Cornell University Press..

Strayer, J. R. (1970) *On the Medieval Origins of the Modern State*, Princeton NJ: Princeton University Press.

Strayer, J. R. and Munro, D. C. (1959) *The Middle Ages*, New York: Appleton-Century-Crofts.

Strong, T. (1974) "Dramaturgical discourse and political enactments: toward an artistic foundation for political space," in S. Lyman and R. Brown (eds) *Structure, Consciousness, and History*, New York: Cambridge University Press.

—— (1980) "Taking the rank with what is ours: American political thought, foreign policy, and questions of rights," in P. R. Newberg (ed.) *The Politics of Human Rights*, New York: New York University Press.

Summers, R. S. (1977) "Naive instrumentalism and the law," in P. S. Hacker and J. Raz (eds) *Law, Morality, and Society*, Oxford: Clarendon Press.

Taft, R. A. (1951) *A Foreign Policy for Americans*, Garden City NY: Doubleday.

Taylor, A. J. P. (1971) *The Struggle for Mastery of Europe, 1848–1918*, New York: Oxford University Press.

Teggart, F. J. (1925) *Theory of History*, New Haven CT: Yale University Press.

Thomson, J. E. (1990) "State practices, international norms, and the decline of mercenarism," *International Studies Quarterly* 34(1): 23–48.

—— (1994) *Mercenaries, Pirates and Sovereigns*, Princeton: Princeton University Press.

Thomson, J. E. and Krasner, S. D. (1989) "Global transactions and the consolidation of sovereignty," in E. O. Czempiel and J. N. Rosenau (eds) *Global Changes and Theoretical Challenges*, Lexington MA: Lexington Books.

Thompson, R. L. (1978) "Water as a source of conflict," *Strategic Review* 6(2): 62–72.

Tillapaugh, J. (1978) "Closed hemisphere and open world? The dispute over regional security at the UN conference, 1945," *Diplomatic History* 2(1): 25–42.

Tilly, C. (1975) "Reflections on the history of European state-making," in C. Tilly (ed.) *The Formation of National States in Western Europe*, Princeton NJ: Princeton University Press.

—— (1985) *Big Structures. Large Processes. Huge Comparisons*, New York: Russell Sage.

—— (1990) *Coercion, Capital, and European States AD 990–1990*, Cambridge MA: Basil Blackwell.

Tilton, J. E. and Landsberg, H. H. (1983) "Non-fuel minerals: the fear of shortages and the search for policies," in E. N. Castle and K.A. Price (eds) *US Interests and Global Natural Resources: Energy, Minerals, Food*, Washington DC: Resources for the Future.

Toulmin, S. (1972) *Human Understanding*, Princeton: Princeton University Press.

Traynor, D. E. (1949) *International Monetary and Financial Conferences in the Interwar Period*, Washington DC: Catholic Universities Press of America.

Triffin, R. (1960) *Gold and the Dollar Crisis*, New Haven: Yale University Press.

—— (1976) "Jamaica: major revision or fiasco," in E. M. Sernscin *et al.* (eds) *Reflections on Jamaica*, Princeton NJ: Princeton Essays in International Finance, 115.

Tuchman, B. (1978) *A Distant Mirror: The Calamitous 14th Century*, New York: Ballantine.

Tucker, Robert C. (1978) *The Marx–Engels Reader*, 2nd edn, New York: Norton.

Tully, J. (1980) *A Discourse on Property: John Locke and His Adversaries*, New York: Cambridge University Press.

Turco, R. P. et al. (1983) "Nuclear winter: global consequences of multiple nuclear explosions," *Science* 222(4630): 1283–1292.

Ullman-Margalit, E. (1977) *The Emergence of Norms*, Oxford: Clarendon Press.

United Nations (1980) *Patterns of Urban and Rural Population Growth*, New York: United Nations.

—— (1992) *An Agenda for Peace*, New York: United Nations.

—— (1994) "Comprehensive review of the whole question of peace-keeping operations in all their aspects: command and control of United Nations peace-keeping operations," Report of the Secretary-General, UN Document A/49/681 (21 November).

—— (1995) "Supplement to an agenda for peace," Report of the Secretary-General, UN Document A/50/60, S/1195/3 (3 January).

United Nations Association of the United States of America (UNA–USA) (1995) "US public support for UN unexpectedly grows, new poll shows," survey conducted by the Wirthlin Group, 7 December 1995.

US Congress (1980) *Nonfuel Minerals Policy Review*, 96th Congress, 2nd Session.

—— (1981a) *A Congressional Handbook on US Materials Import Dependency/Vulnerability*, 97th Congress, 1st Session.

—— (1981b) *The Possibility of a Resource War in Southern Africa*, 97th Congress, 1st Session.

US Department of the Army (1994) *Peace Operations*, Washington DC: Field Manual 30: 100–230.

US Department of Defense (1992) *A Doctrinal Statement of Selected Joint Operational Concepts*, Washington DC: Office of the Joint Chiefs of Staff: 1–22.

Van Dormael, A. (1978) *Bretton Woods: Birth of a Monetary System*, London: Macmillan.

Van Evera, S. (1984) "Causes of war," PhD dissertation, University of California, Berkeley.

—— (1990/1) "Primed for peace: Europe after the Cold War," *International Security* 15(3): 7–57.

Verlinden, O. (1963) "Markets and fairs," in *Cambridge Economic History of Europe*, vol. 3, Cambridge: Cambridge University Press.

Vernon, R. (1971) *Sovereignty at Bay*, New York: Basic Books.

Viner, J. (1947) "Conflicts of principle in drafting a trade charter," *Foreign Affairs* 25(4): 612–628.

—— (1951) "The most-favored-nation clause," *International Economics*, Glencoe IL: Free Press.

Wæver, O. (1995) *The European Security Triangle*, Copenhagen: Centre for Peace and Conflict Research.

—— (1997) "John G. Ruggie: transformation and institutionalization," in I. B. Neumann and O. Wæver (eds) *The Future of International Relations: Masters in the Making?*, London: Routledge.

Walker, R. B. J. (1989) "History and structure in the theory of international studies," *Millennium: Journal of International Studies* 18(2): 163–183.

—— (1993) *Inside/Outside: International Relations as Political Theory*, New York: Cambridge University Press.

Wallender, C., Celeste, A., and Keohane, R. O. (1995) "Toward an institutional theory of alliances," paper presented to Annual Meeting of International Studies Association, Chicago IL, 22–25 February 1995.

Wallerstein, I. (1974) *The Modern World System*, vol. I, New York: Academic Press.

—— (1980) *The Modern World System*, vol. II, New York: Academic Press.

Wallwork, E. (1972) *Durkheim: Morality and Milieu*, Cambridge MA: Harvard University Press.

Walt, S. (1987) *The Origins of Alliances*, Ithaca NY: Cornell University Press.

Walter, B. F. (1996) "Negotiating civil wars: why bargains fail," paper presented to Military Intervention in Civil Wars conference, Columbia University, 17–18 May 1996.

Waltz, K. N. (1959) *Man, the State, and War*, New York: Columbia University Press.

—— (1970) "The myth of national interdependence," in C. P. Kindleberger (ed.) *The International Corporation*, Cambridge, MA: MIT Press.

—— (1975) "Theory of international relations," in F. I. Greenstein (ed.) *Handbook of Political Science*, vol. 8, Reading MA: Addison-Wesley.

—— (1979) *Theory of International Politics*, Reading MA: Addison-Wesley.

—— (1986) "Reflections on *Theory of International Politics*: a response to my critics," in R. O. Keohane (ed.) *Neorealism and its Critics*, New York: Columbia University Press.

—— (1993) "The emerging structure of international politics," *International Security* 18(2): 44–79.

Walzer, M. (1967) "On the role of symbolism in political thought," *Political Science Quarterly* 82(2): 191–204.

Wapner, P. (1995) "Politics beyond the state: environmental activism and world civic politics," *World Politics* 47(3): 311–340.

Watson, A. (1992) *The Evolution of International Society*, London: Routledge.

Weber, M. (1946) "Bureaucracy," in H. Gerth and C. W. Mills (eds) *From Max Weber Essays in Sociology*, New York: Oxford University Press.

—— (1949) *The Methodology of the Social Sciences*, E. Shils and H. A. Finch (trans.), Glencoe IL: Free Press.

—— (1958) *The Protestant Ethic and the Spirit of Capitalism*, Talcott Parsons (trans.), New York: Scribners.

—— (1975) "Marginal utility theory and 'The Fundamental Law of Psychophysics'," *Social Science Quarterly* June: 21–36.

—— (1978) *Economy and Society*, G. Roth and C. Wittich (eds), Berkeley and Los Angeles CA: University of California Press.

Weber, S. (1990) "Realism, detente, and nuclear weapons," *International Organization* 44(1): 55–82.

—— (1993) "Shaping the postwar balance of power: multilaterism in NATO," in J. Ruggie (ed.) *Multilateralism Matters: The Theory and Praxis of an Institutional Form*, New York: Columbia University Press.

—— (1995) "Security after 1989: the future with nuclear weapons," in P. Garrity (ed.) *The Future of Nuclear Weapons*, New York: Plenum Press.

Weiss, T. G. and Jordan, R. S. (1976) "Bureaucratic politics and the world food conference: the international policy process," *World Politics* 28(3): 422–439.

Wellmer, A. (1985) "On the dialectic of modernism and postmodernism," *Praxis International* 4(4): 337–362.

Wendt, A. (1987) "The agent-structure problem in international relations theory," *International Organization* 41(3): 335–350.

—— (1991) "Bridging the theory/meta-theory gap in international relations," *Review of International Studies* 17(4): 383–392.

—— (1994) "Collective identity formation and the international state," *American Political Science Review* 88(2): 384–396.

—— (1995) "Constructing international politics," *International Security* 20(1): 71–81.

—— (1992) *Social Theory and International Politics*, New York: Cambridge University Press.

White, J. (1987) *The Birth and Rebirth of Pictorial Space*, Boston: Faber and Faber.

White, T. H. (1978) *In Search of History: A Personal Adventure*, New York: Harper and Row.

Widenor, W. C. (1982) "American planning for the United Nations: have we been asking the right questions?" *Diplomatic History* 6(3): 245–266.

Wight, M. (1973) "The balance of power and international order," in A. James (ed.) *The Bases of International Order*, London: Oxford University Press.

—— (1977) *Systems of States*, Leicester UK: Leicester University Press.

Williams, R. (1989) "When was modernism?" *New Left Review* 175: 48–52.

Williamson, O. (1975) *Markets and Hierarchies*, New York: Free Press.

Wittkopf, E. R. (1986) "On the foreign policy beliefs of the American people: a critique and some evidence," *International Studies Quarterly* 30(4): 425–445.

Wohlforth, W. C. (1994/5) "Realism and the end of the Cold War," *International Security* 19(3): 91–129.

Wolfers, A. (1962) "Collective defense versus collective security," in A. Wolfers (ed.) *Discord and Collaboration*, Baltimore: Johns Hopkins University Press.

Wolin, S. (1960) *Politics and Vision*, Boston: Little, Brown.

Wood, A. (1994) *North–South Trade, Employment and Equality*, Oxford: Clarendon Press.

Woods, R. B. (1992) "Internationalism stillborn," *Diplomatic History* 16(4): 611–616.

World Bank (1984) *World Development Report, 1984*, New York: Oxford University Press for World Bank.

Wright, Q. (1942) *A Study of War*, Chicago: University of Chicago Press.

Yaeger, L. B. (1976) *International Monetary Relations: Theory, History, and Policy*, New York: Harper and Row.

Yee, A. S. (1996) "The causal effects of ideas on policies," *International Organization* 50(1): 69–108.

Young, O. R. (1979) *Compliance and Public Authority*, Baltimore: Johns Hopkins University Press.

—— (1980) "International regimes: problems of concept formation," *World Politics* 32(3): 331–356.

—— (1983) "Regime dynamics: the rise and fall of international regimes," in S. D. Krasner (ed.) *International Regimes*, Ithaca NY: Cornell University Press.

Zacher, M. W. (1993) "Multilateral organizations and the institution of multilateralism: the development of regimes for the non-terrestrial spaces," in J. G. Ruggie (ed.) *Multilateralism Matters: The Theory and Praxis of an Institutional Form*, New York: Columbia University Press..

Zelikow, P. (1996) "The masque of institutions," *Survival* 38(1): 6–18.

Zerubavel, E. (1982) "The standardization of time: a sociohistorical perspective," *American Journal of Sociology* 88(1): 1–23.

Zimmermann, W. (1995) "The last ambassador: a memoir of the collapse of Yugoslavia," *Foreign Affairs* 74(2): 2–20.

Index

Printed in the United States
204885BV00002B/33/A